FIRST CANADIAN EDITION

The Sentence to Paragraph
WORKPLACE

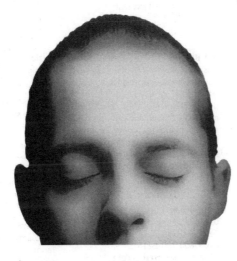

CLIFFORD WERIER Mount Royal College,
Calgary, Alberta

SANDRA SCARRY Recently with the
Office of Academic Affairs,
City University of New York

JOHN SCARRY Hostos Community College,
City University of New York

THOMSON
★ ™
NELSON

Australia   Canada   Mexico   Singapore   Spain   United Kingdom   United States

THOMSON

NELSON

The Sentence to Paragraph Workplace
First Canadian Edition

by Clifford Werier, Sandra Scarry, and
John Scarry

Editorial Director and Publisher:
Evelyn Veitch

Aquisitions Editor:
Anne Williams

Marketing Manager:
Cara Yarzab

Developmental Editor:
Shefali Mehta

Production Editors:
Susan Calvert/Wendy Yano

Copy Editor:
Wayne Herrington

Production Coordinator:
Hedy Sellers

Creative Director:
Angela Cluer

Cover Design:
Ken Phipps

Cover Image:
Mirek Weichsel/First Light

Compositor:
Janet Zanette

Indexer:
Edwin Durbin

Printer:
Victor Graphics

**National Library of Canada
Cataloguing in Publication Data**

Werier, Clifford M. (Clifford
Myles), 1954–
    The sentence to paragraph
workplace

1st Canadian ed.
Includes index.
Based on: The Writer's workplace:
    sentences to paragraphs/Sandra
    Scarry, John Scarry
ISBN 0-7747-3764-6

1. English language—Paragraphs—
Problems, exercises, etc. 2. English
language—Rhetoric—Problems,
exercises, etc. 3. Report writing—
Problems, exercises, etc. I. Scarry,
Sandra, 1946– II. Scarry, John
III. Scarry, Sandra, 1946– . Writer's
workplace. IV. Title.

PE1439.W47 2002   808'.042'076
C2001-904028-8

PREFACE

Overview

The *Writer's Workplace* series of textbooks has been very popular in the United States because it offers a flexible and comprehensive approach to the teaching of basic and introductory composition. As editor of the Canadian versions of *The Writer's Workplace: Sentences to Paragraphs* and *The Writer's Workplace: Essays*, I have kept the structure of the original American texts but have added Canadian examples that make the books more attractive to both instructors and students. It was my intention to enhance the usability of the texts for a Canadian audience by choosing examples and model essays that refer directly to Canadian life and popular culture. I believe that students and instructors will enjoy both the pedagogical design of these Canadian editions and the fresh, contemporary content.

The Sentence to Paragraph Workplace teaches step-by-step mastery of the basic building blocks of any writing course: the sentence and the paragraph. This book offers students thorough preparation for successful sentence construction and paragraph writing through comprehensive explanations, plentiful exercises, and writing practice. This emphasis on exercises and practice is the greatest strength of this text—not only are the principles of good writing examined in clear language, but the teaching is linked to copious exercises that provide an effective link between theory and practice. An answer key to selected exercises at the back of the text helps students to monitor their own progress toward the mastery of each element. In addition, numerous model paragraphs illustrate key points and provide examples of the different rhetorical modes. The readings, many by Canadian authors, demonstrate how paragraphs work together in beautifully constructed essays.

Organization

The Sentence to Paragraph Workplace is divided into four parts called "Steps."

- *Step 1: Looking at the Whole* provides an overview of the entire writing process.

- *Step 2: Creating Effective Sentences* provides a thorough grammar review along with an examination of the relationship between correct usage and the clear expression of ideas at the sentence level.

- *Step 3: Understanding the Power of Words* discusses the implications of diction and may be especially useful for ESL students.

- *Step 4: Creating Effective Paragraphs* teaches developmental patterns in paragraph writing along with a thorough examination of the major rhetorical modes.

The appendices contain an alphabetical listing of irregular verbs, a summary of the parts of speech, and the answer key to selected exercises. The final section contains a good selection of readings (along with discussion and writing questions) that can be used as models of effective writing.

Instructors are certainly not bound by the order of these steps—they are free to choose a path that best suits their own style and syllabus. For example, some instructors may feel more comfortable beginning with the paragraph and then reviewing sentence elements later in the semester. No matter what the organizational choices, instructors should be delighted by the quality and number of exercises. The philosophy of this text is that students master grammatical rules and develop as writers by writing and revising, and I know of no other text that does a better job of providing thoughtful and challenging opportunities for practice.

Acknowledgments

The development and writing of *The Sentence to Paragraph Workplace* was a truly collaborative project that involved a number of talented writers and editors. I would like to thank Anne Williams of Nelson for initiating the project and inspiring me to get involved. I would especially like to acknowledge the contributions of Shefali Mehta, my astute editor at Nelson, who has been a delight to work with at every stage in the development of this book. I tip my hat to Lazaros and Juanita Simeon of George Brown College, gifted writers who translated my unintelligible squiggles on a manuscript into the revised sentences and exercises that comprise this Canadian edition.

On a personal note, I would like to acknowledge the inspiration that I received from my colleagues in the Department of English at Mount Royal College—a group of dedicated and innovative writing teachers. Finally, I would like to thank my family (Sabrina, Cynthia, and Alex) for putting up with the mess of papers on the dining room table and all my grumbling and complaining. I think the result will satisfy even their exacting standards.

BRIEF CONTENTS

CONTENTS

LOOKING AT THE WHOLE

CONTENTS

Discovering the Writing Process

Every time you pick up a pen, you are sharing a very long tradition, one that began thousands of years ago. What people wrote in the past still speaks to us today. Through writing, we connect with our past; we relate to each other in the present; and we build bridges to the future.

Many languages from the past have disappeared. The materials used by writers of ancient languages, from clay tablets to papyrus, are now only in museums. However, the writers' methods have remained unchanged to the present day. Writers everywhere work in surprisingly similar ways. Although many people think writers must be born with a special talent or possess an almost magical creative ability, most writers learn their craft by diligently practising their skills.

Fortunately for all of us who need to improve our writing, the process of transforming ideas into written form is a skill like any other; it *can* be learned. Like other skills—playing the piano or guitar, for instance—writing requires a combination of many separate skills. Learning to read music, learning to count rhythms, and developing finger dexterity are all part of the process of becoming a musician. Writing is not very different. A writer must learn to read well, recognize the standard forms of the language, and strengthen necessary skills through regular practice. In this first chapter, we will examine how writers learn to write. As a developing writer, you will have many opportunities throughout this book to practise skills that will improve your writing.

ACTIVITY 1

Take a few minutes to write about your experiences so far as a writer. How often did you write in the last year you attended school? How many opportunities have you had to practise your writing skills since then? Do you enjoy writing? When you write, where do you prefer to be? Do you use pencil or pen, or do you compose on a computer? What do you consider your strengths and weaknesses?

_____

_____

_____

_____

_____

_____

_____

_____

_____

_____

_____

_____

_____

_____

Writers use commonplace books, diaries, and journals

A widespread practice in William Shakespeare's day was to keep what people called **commonplace books.** These were books of blank pages in which people would collect favourite poems, parts of longer works—anything, in fact, that they thought was especially meaningful to them. Sometimes they would include their own work as well. Most writers today, in one way or another, use this same method. They collect various items that they read and that strike them as particularly relevant to their own lives or even for possible use in their own writing projects. Most bookstores sell these blank books, some very simple and others with lovely fabric covers. They are intended for the many people who now are rediscovering the satisfaction of keeping a personal book, a volume that can be devoted to recording one's thoughts. Today, we do not need to copy by hand the items that interest us; we can easily photocopy and paste them in our books.

WHAT TO PUT INTO A COMMONPLACE BOOK

1. Short sayings, verses, poems, quotations that are meaningful to you

2. Letters and postcards from friends

3. Copies of newspaper and magazine articles, pieces that you want to read again or think about further

4. Favourite song lyrics

5. Cartoons and pictures that strike you as especially artistic or provocative

6. Any writing you find that impresses you

You can gather your own thoughts and ideas between the covers of a different kind of book—the **personal diary.** For some people, it is important to keep a record of the events in their lives, a record very much like an expanded calendar with notes. This record could be made up of lists with dates, places, and people's names, with or without brief comments.

For others, such an abbreviated record is not enough. Some people want to write about their lives in a more detailed way—to explore their feelings and reactions to events around them. For these people, a personal diary contains longer entries.

As a teenager, you may have kept a locked diary in a bedroom drawer, guarding its secret contents from the world (usually a younger sister or brother). It is no coincidence that many teenagers keep diaries because adolescence is often a time of identity crisis. Everyone, at certain times in life, needs the chance for private reflection, and a personal diary can be a useful and meaningful way to express thoughts.

WHAT TO KEEP IN A PERSONAL DIARY

1. Daily record of your activities

2. Reactions to special events in life

3. Your opinions on stories in the news

4. Your thoughts about an event that caught your attention (something a teacher or a friend said, something that angered, pleased, or surprised you)

5. Your thoughts on your day-to-day relationships with people

6. A dialogue with yourself on the challenges you face in your life and how to deal with them

7. Your reflections on whatever comes across your mind as you are writing

For many of today's students, a slightly more public way to express and develop ideas on a particular subject is the **working journal.** Here your *purpose* and *audience* are more defined. Usually the audience is your instructor, who might want to collect the journal once a week to check on your progress. Another possible audience is your class, and occasionally you may be asked to read one of your entries to the class. The purposes of a working journal could be as various as the subjects you are studying. For students who are actively developing writing skills, an instructor will usually suggest the range of subjects for their journals—you may be encouraged to explore your interests, or you may be directed to develop certain reactions to required readings.

WHAT COULD BE INCLUDED IN A WORKING JOURNAL

1. Summaries of required readings or personal reactions to required readings

2. Daily writing entries on subjects designated by the instructor or left up to the individual

3. Record of field work, such as student teaching or work/study experience

ACTIVITY 2

Some people place memorable sayings, verses, or quotes above their desks or on the walls of their rooms for encouragement and inspiration. Work together as a class to gather some of these sayings that seem universally true. These could be the beginning of a collection of materials for your own commonplace book.

_____

_____

_____

_____

_____

_____

ACTIVITY 3

Write an entry for your personal diary for this day. You may want to focus on a conversation you had with someone. You could record your thoughts on something you have read in the newspaper this morning or have heard on the news, or you could describe the classroom you are now in and the people who are sitting around you.

Preparing to write: Gathering ideas

No matter what method writers use as they approach their work, they all have one thing in common: They recognize that the planning stage is a crucial part of producing a formal piece of writing. As a result, they take time to prepare. You, too, will want to use prewriting techniques to gather your ideas before you write.

Writers listen and talk with others

One way to prepare for writing is to listen to what others think about the topic you are planning to develop. You might speak with an instructor for a few minutes or spend a longer time in discussion with some of your classmates. Now you are ready to put down on paper the thoughts that have been forming in your mind. These are still preliminary ideas and they need not be complete.

Writers use brainstorming: Listing or clustering

You can start recording your ideas in two ways. The first method is to make a listing of your ideas. This brainstorming should be done without any concern for the order or the importance of the ideas. At this point, you are making your first explorations on paper; your judgments will come later. For example, imagine you were asked to write about "Challenges Facing First-Year Students." Here is how a brainstorming list might look:

figuring out the system
how to get a library card
how to get my schedule changed
making friends
finding the right major
time management
children need to be more helpful
spouse can care for kids on Saturdays
find a study group
feeling stressed out
how to get money for books
find out about student loans

There is another approach to brainstorming that is often used; this is called clustering. When you cluster, you jot down the same kinds of items you would if you were making up a brainstorming list, except this time you make a visual map of your ideas. First, you take a key idea and write it in a circle that you have drawn in the centre of a blank page. Next, you write down all the words or short phrases that you associate with that original key idea. You then use lines or branches to connect all of your circled words and phrases. By connecting your ideas in this way, you are showing that all of your ideas are related to your central starting point. Here is a brainstorming cluster on the same topic:

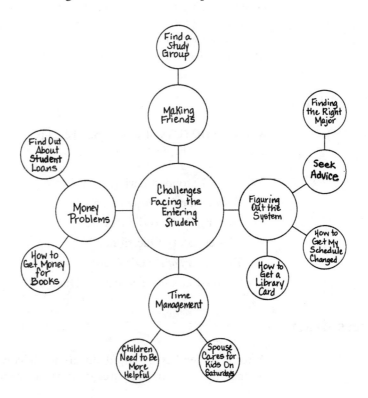

After you have written as many words or phrases as readily come to mind, review your list or cluster. If other ideas come to mind, add them now. If you are using a list, you will find it necessary to put the items in a certain order before you begin to write. You may find that if you use a cluster, you will more quickly see the ways your ideas are related. The activity of listing or clustering often suggests a certain order to your ideas as they emerge. Planning techniques such as these help a writer tap into the mind's many resources.

ACTIVITY 4

Use brainstorming (with a group of classmates if possible) to gather material on one of the following subjects. Use listing or clustering, whichever you prefer.

Dating etiquette

Cleaning the apartment (or house)

Weekend entertainment

Shopping wisely

Now you have become familiar with some of the prewriting techniques writers use. What happens next?

Writers consider purpose and audience

When creating a piece of work, the careful writer always has a clear idea of **purpose:** Why are you writing? Do you intend to give the reader information, to entertain, or to persuade that reader to change an opinion or belief? These three intentions are the most common motives writers have when they work. Depending on the purpose, a writer is able to choose a different approach.

Closely connected to the idea of purpose is the question of the intended **audience** for the writer's work. What do the intended readers most likely already know about the topic? What are their present attitudes toward the topic? These questions help a writer target a message more effectively; every reader benefits when a writer pays close attention to these questions.

ACTIVITY 5

Below are the titles of several published pieces. In each case, point out the intended audience and the writer's purpose.

"Why I Stopped Eating Meat"

Word Processing Step by Step

"Baking Soda to the Rescue"

"Water Safety Questioned"

The Mystery of the Old Clock

"Three Stars for The Peking Duck House"

Writers draft

After a writer has explored different ideas with others, and has brainstormed by making a list or a cluster, and after there has been careful thought about purpose and audience, a first draft is written. Most writers find that writing the first draft is hard work, but prewriting techniques help the work to flow more easily. As you draft, look back on your list or your cluster. Have you included all the points you listed? Have you developed each idea as fully as possible? If you become stuck at any point, use the items from your list as a guide to keep your draft moving forward.

Writers revise for unity and coherence

After preparing a first draft, it is a good idea to leave your writing for a day or so and do something else. Then when you come back to what you have created, you will be able to look at it with some degree of objectivity. Read it aloud to yourself (and someone else if possible). Your major concern as you approach the job of revising is to make sure your ideas are clear and your organization is logical.

As you read your draft, listen for those places where something strikes you as not quite right. For example, does each sentence move logically to the next? Writers call this relation of each part of a piece of writing to each other part **coherence**. Did you stay focused on your topic? A clear sense of focus is called **unity**. Modern technology has made it somewhat easier for a writer to achieve unity: If you are working on a computer, it is easy to move a sentence to a different place, move a paragraph somewhere else, cut out a complete section entirely, or insert a new sentence or paragraph.

Writers edit for errors

Your work in this book will help you in the editing stage of your writing. Throughout the various chapters, you will learn to edit for fragments, run-ons, punctuation, combining ideas with correct conjunctions, and other sentence level skills. If you are able to use a computer, it will help you in the editing process. You will be able to check each page for spelling errors. Learn to run a spell check before you hand in any piece of written work.

Creating a writer's portfolio

At the end of each chapter of this book, a feature called *Working Together* encourages you to investigate a topic along with your classmates and then to write about that topic on your own. Specific types of writing are needed in college and university courses, while other modes of writing will most certainly be required in your future career. Included in the *Working Together* writing assignments are such skills as interviewing for information, summarizing for main ideas, narrating to present a story more effectively, creating examples to make your points stronger, taking a position on an issue, and even writing your own reviews of restaurants, books, or films.

Each piece of writing you will do is a work in progress. As such, each of these writing projects should be preserved; you are very likely to come back to some of them and rework the material into more developed papers. You may want to save some of your other notes as expressions of ideas that matter to you.

Use an expandable folder that will be large enough to keep your growing number of writing projects. Such writings will become documents of your development as a writer. Many colleges and universities now recognize the significance of student portfolios as a way of demonstrating writers' efforts and achievements. As your portfolio increases in size and importance, it will become not only a useful academic resource, but also a very treasured personal possession.

Points to remember

For future writing projects, use the elements of good writing that we have studied in this chapter. You should know the answers to the following questions when you write.

- Do you prepare to write by brainstorming or clustering words, phrases, or thoughts that come to mind as you think about the topic?
- Who is your audience?
- What is your purpose?
- What is the unifying or central theme of your piece?
- Does the writing achieve coherence (each sentence growing out of what has come before)?

Working Together

People who are starting to write have a few things in common with experienced writers. Both know how difficult it can be to find the right inspiration, and both understand how important it is to find the time to write. We recommend you begin by keeping an informal writing journal. This technique can improve your writing skills and help you find inspiration.

In the article below, Vancouver-born writer Evelyn Lau shares some of her experiences about the writing process.

THE ARTIST'S LIFE: EVELYN LAU

Inspiration for me comes largely from my immediate life, what I'm seeing and experiencing as opposed to something that I read about in a newspaper. It could be an actual event, something that triggers something inside of me, but I need to be in some way connected to it....

I work constantly or not at all. When I'm in the throes of writing a book or a poem, everything else falls by the wayside. It can be the middle of the night and I will get up every few hours and continue. I'll stop while walking down the street and take a scrap of paper out of my wallet and write. But then there are periods when I don't write at all. It's not that I'm not working—I'll be taking notes, jotting down lines of conversation, or thinking about work, but I might not have a single word on a page at the end of the day....

I used to try to work through a creative block. I'd sit down and force myself to write when nothing was there. But it was frustrating ... so I realized that if it wasn't happening, I'd do something else—talk on the phone, do errands, go and read. It's not the most efficient way of writing, but it seems to work....

There's little material reward [in the life of a writer]. There are times at the end of the day when you have nothing to show for your work. But then there are moments when it completely envelops you and I feel as if I've never been happier....

Through your writing, you can get a better idea of what you think, believe, and hope for. You can gain some valuable insight about who you are. At the same time, writing is more than a process of self-discovery. Sharing your ideas is also a vital part of the writing process. Throughout this course, you will be encouraged to work together to solve problems and to exchange ideas on different topics.

Break up into small groups to discuss Evelyn Lau's insights on writing. How much of what she describes have you felt? Is writing something that comes naturally to you, or does it hold frustration and anxiety? Discuss what each of you hopes to gain from taking this course.

Step 2

CREATING EFFECTIVE SENTENCES

CONTENTS

Finding Subjects and Verbs in Simple Sentences

Why should we use complete sentences when we write?

We do not always speak in complete sentences. Sometimes we abbreviate a thought into a word or two, knowing that the person to whom we are talking will understand our meaning. We all do this in our casual conversations with friends and family.

For example, if a friend walked up to you around lunch time and said, "Lunch?" you would probably assume that your friend was hoping to have lunch with you. While the word "lunch" is not a complete thought, the situation allowed you to guess the probable meaning.

In writing down thoughts, however, the reader is not likely to be totally familiar with your thoughts or the circumstances surrounding your words. The reader often cannot interpret or fill in the missing parts. Therefore, one characteristic of good writing is that the ideas are expressed in complete sentences.

What is a complete sentence?

> A *complete sentence* contains a subject and a verb, and expresses a complete thought.

In this chapter, we will look at some basic sentences in order to practise finding the subjects and the verbs. These basic sentences are called *simple sentences* because each of them has only one subject and verb group. (Later we will practise with compound and complex sentences in which two or more ideas are combined giving the sentence more than one subject and verb group.)

How do you find the subject of a sentence?

For most simple sentences, you can find the subject by keeping five points in mind:

1. The subject often answers the question, "Who or what is the sentence about?"

2. The subject often comes early in the sentence.

3. The subject is usually a *noun* or a *pronoun.*

4. Noun or pronoun subjects can be modified by *adjectives.*

5. The subject can be *compound.*

Understanding parts of speech: Nouns, pronouns, adjectives

> A *noun* is a word that names persons, places, or things.
> A *noun* can function as a subject, an object, or a possessive in a sentence.
>
> The *Ford* is parked outside.
> We parked the *Ford* outside.
> The *Ford's* hood is dented.

Nouns can be either *common* nouns or *proper* nouns. Most nouns in our writing are common nouns. They are not capitalized. Proper nouns name particular persons, places, or things. They are always capitalized.

NOUNS

Common	*Proper*
cousin	Cousin Bill
province	Manitoba
car	Ford

Another way to categorize nouns is into *concrete* or *abstract* nouns. Concrete nouns are all the things we can see or touch, such as *desk, car,* or *friend*. Abstract nouns are the things we cannot see or touch, such as *justice, honesty,* or *friendship*.

NOUNS

Concrete	*Abstract*
store	commerce
crowd	pleasure
book	knowledge

> A *pronoun* is a word used to take the place of a noun. Just like a noun, a pronoun can be used as the subject, the object, or in some cases to show possession.
>
> *It* is parked outside.
> We parked *it* outside.
> *Its* hood is dented.

Pronouns can also be categorized or divided into groups: personal, indefinite, relative, or demonstrative.

PRONOUNS

Personal Pronouns (refer to people or things)

Personal pronouns have three forms depending on how they are used in a sentence: as a subject, an object, or a possessive.

	Subjective		*Objective*		*Possessive*	
	Singular	**Plural**	**Singular**	**Plural**	**Singular**	**Plural**
1st person	I	we	me	us	my (mine)	our (ours)
2nd person	you	you	you	you	your (yours)	your (yours)
3rd person	he she it	they	him her it	them	his (his) her (hers) its (its)	their (theirs)

Relative Pronouns	*Demonstrative Pronouns*	*Indefinite Pronouns*			
(can introduce noun clauses and adjective clauses)	(can point out the antecedent)	(refer to non-specific persons or things)			
		Singular			
who, whom, whose	this	everyone	someone	anyone	no one
which	that	everybody	somebody	anybody	nobody
that	these	everything	something	anything	nothing
what	those	each	another	either	neither
whoever					
whichever		**Singular** or **Plural** (depending on meaning)			
whatever		all	more	none	
		any	most	some	
		Plural			
		both	few	many	several
					others

Noun or pronoun subjects can be modified by **adjectives.**

> An *adjective* is a word that modifies (describes or limits) a noun or a pronoun.
>
> *young* Robert
> *one* boy

Adjectives usually come directly in front of the nouns they modify, but they can also appear later in the sentence and refer back to the noun.

> The boy is *young.*

The subject can be *compound*.

> A *compound subject* is made up of two or more nouns or pronouns joined by *and, or, either/or,* or *neither/nor.*
>
> *Mark* and his *friend* are old schoolmates.

• PRACTICE

The following seven sentences present the different kinds of subjects you will encounter in this chapter. Examine each of the following sentences and ask yourself who or what each sentence is about. Draw a line under the word (or words) you think is the subject in each sentence. Then on the line to the right, label the word you have underlined as a noun, compound subject, or pronoun.

1. The old man thought.   _____

2. Old Mark thought.   _____

3. He thought.   _____

4. The room grew cold.   _____

5. The wind blew.   _____

6. An idea suddenly struck him.   _____

7. A good dinner and a nap would warm him. _____

Note: Not every noun or pronoun in a sentence is necessarily the subject of a verb. Nouns and pronouns function as subjects and as objects. In the following sentence, which noun is the subject and which noun is the object?

Mark tasted the fish.

For some students, the following exercises will seem easy. However, for many, analyzing the structure of the sentence is unfamiliar. As you practise, get into the habit of referring back to the definitions, charts, and examples. Remind yourself of the five points. You can, with a little practice, learn to identify those words that serve as the subjects of sentences.

EXERCISE 1   Finding the Subject of a Sentence

Underline the subject in each of the following sentences. An example is done for you.

The fall <u>festival</u> brought everyone outdoors.

1. The street lamps and festival lights glowed brightly.

2. People crowded the streets.

3. The musicians tuned their instruments.

4. Anticipation filled the air.

5. The music finally began.

6. The mood was joyous.

7. Many moved their feet rhythmically.

8. The evening grew late.

9. Devoted fans remained attentive.

10. Sleepy children rubbed their eyes.

EXERCISE 2   Finding the Subject of a Sentence

Underline the subject in each of the following sentences. An example is done for you.

The eager <u>hikers</u> brought their equipment.

1. The mountain trail looked dangerously steep.

2. Brent and his friends had travelled many miles.

3. The expedition seemed impossible.

4. A lone eagle flew overhead.

5. The most experienced hiker smiled.

6. This was a good sign.

7. The mountain passes were icy and slick.

8. A durable climbing rope held the group together.

9. Everyone worked as a team.

10. Pride and confidence replaced their fears.

EXERCISE 3   Finding the Subject of a Sentence

Underline the subject in each of the following sentences. An example is done for you.

The lively <u>discussion</u> lasted several hours.

1. The auditorium filled.

2. The presenters studied their notes.

3. The chair introduced the speakers.

4. Gloria Jenkins appeared confident.

5. She was the first speaker.

6. Everyone enjoyed the discussion.

7. The audience applauded.

8. The applause was thunderous.

9. People left the program reluctantly.

10. Mr. George Sanders planned the next presentation.

How do you find the subject in sentences with prepositional phrases?

The sentences in previous exercises were short and basic. If we wrote only such sentences, our writing would sound choppy. Complex ideas would be difficult to express. One way to expand the simple sentence is to add prepositional phrases.

> **Example:** She set the vase on the table.
> *On* is a preposition.
> *Table* is a noun used as the object of the preposition.
> *On the table* is the prepositional phrase.

> A *prepositional phrase* is a group of words containing a preposition and an object of the preposition with its modifiers. Prepositional phrases contain nouns or pronouns, but these nouns or pronouns are never the subject of the sentence.

In sentences with prepositional phrases, the subject may be difficult to spot. What is the subject of the following sentence?

> In the student lounge, the couches have been recovered.

In the sentence above, what is the prepositional phrase? Who or what is the sentence about? To avoid making the mistake of thinking that a noun in the prepositional phrase could be the subject, it is a good practice to cross out the prepositional phrase.

> ~~In the student lounge,~~ the couches have been recovered.

With the prepositional phrase crossed out, it now becomes clear that the subject of the sentence is the noun *couches*.

> When you are looking for the subject of a sentence, do not look for it within the prepositional phrase.

You can easily recognize a prepositional phrase because it always begins with a preposition. Study the following list so that you will be able to quickly recognize all of the common prepositions.

COMMON PREPOSITIONS			
about	below	in	since
above	beneath	inside	through
across	beside	into	to
after	between	like	toward
against	beyond	near	under
along	by	of	until
among	down	off	up
around	during	on	upon
at	except	outside	with
before	for	over	within
behind	from	past	without

In addition to these common prepositions, English has a number of prepositional combinations that also function as prepositions.

COMMON PREPOSITIONAL COMBINATIONS		
ahead of	in addition to	in reference to
at the time of	in between	in regard to
because of	in care of	in search of
by means of	in case of	in spite of
except for	in common with	instead of
for fear of	in contrast to	on account of
for the purpose of	in the course of	similar to
for the sake of	in exchange for	

EXERCISE 1   Creating Sentences with Prepositional Phrases

Use each of the ten prepositions that follow to write a prepositional phrase. Then write a sentence containing that prepositional phrase. An example is done for you.

Preposition: among

Prepositional Phrase: among my friends

Sentence: Among my friends, I am the most flexible.

Notice that when a prepositional phrase begins a sentence, a comma usually follows that prepositional phrase. (Sometimes, if the prepositional phrase is short, the comma is omitted.)

1. Preposition: *off*

   Prepositional Phrase: _____

   Sentence: _____

2. Preposition: *without*

   Prepositional Phrase: _____

   Sentence: _____

3. Preposition: *along*

   Prepositional Phrase: _____

   Sentence: _____

4. Preposition: *on account of*

   Prepositional Phrase: _____

   Sentence: _____

5. Preposition: *in case of*

   Prepositional Phrase: _____

   Sentence: _____

6. Preposition: *to*

   Preposition Phrase: _____

   Sentence: _____

7. Preposition: *until*

   Preposition Phrase: _____

   Sentence: _____

8. Preposition: *past*

   Preposition Phrase: _____

   Sentence: _____

9. Preposition: *beneath*

   Preposition Phrase: _____

   Sentence: _____

10. Preposition: *across*

    Preposition Phrase: _____

    Sentence: _____

EXERCISE 2   Finding Subjects in Sentences with Prepositional Phrases

Remember that you will never find the subject of a sentence within a prepositional phrase. In each of the following sentences, cross out any prepositional phrases. Then underline the subject of each sentence. An example is done for you.

~~During the piano recital,~~ a <u>cell phone</u> started ringing ~~in the audience.~~

1. For many people, cell phones are a way of life.

2. On every street corner, you will find people talking on one.

3. With a cell phone in your pocket or purse, you never have to say goodbye to a friend at the bus stop after school.

4. When they first appeared, they were too big and cumbersome for the average user.

5. Among teenagers, cell phones are considered status symbols.

6. In recent years, the use of cell phones on campuses, in shopping malls, and in cars has created a new series of problems for administrators and legislators.

7. In cinemas, patrons must turn off their cell phones and pagers during movies as a courtesy to others.

8. In fact, many of the teachers I know must remind their students to turn off their cell phones at the beginning of each class.

9. The growing number of car accidents caused by people talking on their cell phones while driving may lead to laws prohibiting their use in those situations.

10. With the increasing popularity of cell phones, a quiet night at a nice restaurant has become a thing of the past.

EXERCISE 3   Finding Subjects in Sentences with Prepositional Phrases

Remember that you will never find the subject of a sentence within a prepositional phrase. In each of the following sentences, cross out any prepositional phrases. Then underline the subject of each sentence. An example is done for you.

> ~~For most people without experience or knowledge about cars,~~
> the <u>purchase</u> ~~of a good used car~~ is difficult.

1. With her end of the year bonus, Maggie looked for a used car.
2. Due to a recent fare increase, the cost of commuting had risen dramatically.
3. With several of her colleagues, she planned a carpool for some extra help with transportation costs.
4. In addition, ownership of a car meant increased recreational opportunities.
5. With a car at her disposal, Maggie could go to the beach at a moment's notice.
6. In the search for a good buy, Maggie sorted through many advertisements.
7. In her opinion, the advertisements were often misleading.
8. In general, sellers often hid their cars' problems.
9. In addition to low mileage, air conditioning, and trunk space, Maggie searched for a sporty late model.
10. Instead of a dream car, Maggie settled for an old Hyundai in good working condition.

What are the other problems in finding subjects?

Sentences with a change in the normal subject position

Some sentences begin with words that indicate that a question is being asked. Such words as *why, where, how,* and *when* give the reader the signal that a question will follow. Such opening words are not the subjects. The subjects will be found later on in these sentences. The following sentences begin with question words:

> *Why* is she staring at me?
> *How* did he answer the questions?

Notice that in each case the subject is not found in the opening part of the sentence. By answering questions or changing the question into a statement, the subject is easier to spot.

> *She* is staring at me . . .
> *He* answered the questions . . .

Using *there* or *here*

Such words as *there* or *here* can never be the subjects of sentences:

> *There* was a ring at the door.
> *Here* comes my daughter now.

Who or what is this first sentence about? This sentence is about a ring. *Ring* is the subject of the first sentence. Who or what is the second sentence about? This sentence is about the daughter. *Daughter* is the subject of the second sentence.

Commands

Sometimes a sentence contains a verb that gives an order:

> *Go* to bed.
> *Get* some rest.

In sentences that give orders, the subject *you* is not written, but it is understood. This is the only case where the subject of a sentence may be left out.

Sentences that contain appositive phrases

> An *appositive phrase* is a group of words in a sentence that gives extra information about a noun in the sentence.
>
> John Russell, *the jazz musician*, played a gig in Montreal.

In this sentence, the words *the jazz musician* make up the appositive phrase because they give extra information about John Russell. Notice that commas separate the appositive phrase from the rest of the sentence. If you leave out the appositive phrase when you read this sentence, the thought will still be complete:

> John Russell played a gig in Montreal.

Now the subject is clear: John Russell

When you are looking for the subject of a sentence, you will not find it within an appositive phrase.

EXERCISE 1   Finding Hidden Subjects

Each of the following sentences contains an example of a special problem in finding the subject of a sentence. First cross out any prepositional phrases or appositive phrases. Then underline the subject of each sentence. An example is done for you.

> ~~In the attic of most houses,~~ <u>boxes</u> ~~of forgotten toys and old clothes~~ could be tossed out.

1. How can you get rid of all those unwanted items in your apartment or home?

2. Hold a garage sale!

3. Bob L. Berko, author of "Holding Garage Sales for Fun and Profit," warns of the difficulties in having your own sale.

4. In addition to the dragging of everything up or down stairs, garage sales require careful planning and skillful dealings with people.

5. Why are some garage sales more successful than others?

6. Here are some tried and true methods for garage sale success.

7. Advertise and carefully price all items ahead of time.

8. Improve the chances of a sale by separating the items into categories.

9. Of course, the best items should go in the most visible spot.

10. There is a treasure for someone in all your junk.

EXERCISE 2   Finding Hidden Subjects

Each of the following sentences contains an example of a special problem in finding the subject of a sentence. First cross out any prepositional phrases or appositive phrases. Then underline the subject of each sentence. An example is done for you.

There is a <u>star</u> visible ~~to the unaided eye in the Northern Hemisphere.~~

1. For the first time, astronomers have established the existence of a planet around another star.

2. Why should this be of interest to us?

3. For one reason, our solar system would no longer be unique.

4. In fact, the likelihood of life in some other planetary system would be increased.

5. Planets of a dead star, however, cannot support life.

6. On October 6, 1995, two Swiss astronomers announced their observations.

7. There was some skepticism about the discovery at first.

8. Then at Lick Observatory near San Jose, California, two American astronomers took a look on four nights and confirmed the discovery.

9. This new planet, half the size of Jupiter, is orbiting the star named 51 Pegasus.

10. Here is its distance from the earth: 40 light years.

EXERCISE 3   Finding Hidden Subjects

Each of the following sentences contains an example of a special problem in finding the subject of a sentence. First cross out any prepositional phrases or appositive phrases. Then underline the subject of each sentence. An example is done for you.

~~Of all the places in Canada,~~ the <u>territory</u> ~~of the North~~ is the most haunting and foreboding.

1. There is a part of Canada that is still virtually unexplored.

2. The territory north of the 60th degree of north latitude, a land of forests, tundra, permafrost, and ice, is Canada's North.

3. Look at a map of Canada for an idea of how much of the country lies "North of 60."

4. Just south of Baker Lake, Nunavut, lies a spot that is the precise geographic centre of Canada.

5. In this vast area, however, lives less than one percent of the country's population.

6. At first glance, the North looks bare, desolate, and inhospitable.

7. How could artists, such as the painter Lawren Harris and pianist Glenn Gould, find inspiration in that harsh environment?

8. For outsiders, the solitude and simplicity of the northern landscape are challenges against which they can measure their own courage and imaginations.

9. Why have so many people from across Canada begun to settle in the North in recent years?

10. The North, once the ultimate symbol of man's powerlessness over nature, may finally succumb to a new wave of explorers searching for hidden wealth in the tundra such as oil, gas, precious gems, and minerals.

["Canada." *Merriam Webster's Geographical Dictionary: Third Edition*. Springfield, MA: 1997.]

How do you find the verb of a sentence?

Every sentence must have a verb. Verbs can be divided into three classes.

Action: An *action verb* tells what the subject is doing.

Martin Short *acted* in that film.

Linking: A *linking verb* indicates a state of being or condition.

The reviewers *seemed* enthusiastic.

Helping: A *helping verb* combines with a main verb to form a verb phrase and gives the main verb a special time or meaning.

His fans *will* rush to the film.

Verbs tell time. Use this fact to test for a verb. If you can put the verb into different tenses in the sentence, that word is a verb.

Present: (Today) he *acts*.
Past: (Yesterday) he *acted*.
Future: (Tomorrow) he *will act*.

Action verbs

Action verbs tell us what the subject is doing and when the subject does the action.

The man *studied* drama.

What was the man doing?   studying
What is the time of the action?   past (*-ed* is the past tense ending)

ACTION VERBS

Most verbs are *action verbs*. Here are a few examples:

arrive	learn	open	watch
leave	forget	write	fly
enjoy	help	speak	catch
despise	make	teach	wait

EXERCISE 1   **Finding Action Verbs**

Each of the following sentences contains an action verb. First underline the subject of the sentence. Then circle the action verb (the word that tells what the subject is doing). Note also the time of the action: past, present, or future. An example is done for you.

The <u>pitcher</u> (threw) a curved ball. (past)

1. Zoe signed up for another season of Little League.

2. Last year she played outfield.

3. Her red jersey carried the name of a local restaurant on the back.

4. The other four girls on the team slowly dropped out or did not show up for practice.

5. The boys generally ignored Zoe.

6. She sat slightly apart from the others on the bench and warmed up alone.

7. Zoe's mom worked as a construction worker.

8. Zoe's mother understood her daughter's feelings.

9. Often the only woman on a job site, she also faced the isolation of crossing gender boundaries.

10. In new or unusual roles, people often pay an unfair price.

EXERCISE 2   **Finding Action Verbs**

Each of the following sentences contains an action verb. First, underline the subject. Then circle the action verb (the word that tells what the subject is doing). Note also the time of the action: past, present, or future. An example is done for you.

<u>Brenda Stubbert</u> (played) the fiddle and piano. (past)

1. Many people love folk music.

2. Folk music enthusiasts travel to festivals around the country.

3. Cape Breton offers traditional Celtic music.

4. Ashley MacIsaac plays a new style of Celtic music.

5. The island of Cape Breton hosts an annual Celtic music festival.

6. Scottish people settled in Cape Breton two hundred years ago.

7. They maintained a very strong musical tradition.

8. Scottish musicians learn the old music styles from their Canadian cousins.

9. Cape Breton attracts music lovers from around the world.

10. Many fiddlers prefer the traditional Celtic music style.

Linking verbs

> A *linking verb* is a verb that links the subject of a sentence to one or more words that describe or identify the subject.

For example:

The building (was) a landmark.

The supervisor (seems) competent.

The tenants (look) happy.

In each of these examples, the verb links the subject to a word that identifies or describes the subject. In the first example, the verb *was* links *building* with *landmark*. The verb *seems* links the noun *supervisor* with *competent*. Finally, in the third example, the verb *look* links the noun *tenants* with *happy*.

COMMON LINKING VERBS

act	grow
appear	look
be (am, is, are, was,	seem
were, have been)	smell
become	sound
feel	taste

EXERCISE 1   Finding Linking Verbs

Each of the following sentences contains a linking verb. Find the linking verb by first underlining the subject of the sentence. Then draw an arrow to the word or words that identify or describe the subject. Finally, circle the linking verb. An example is done for you.

This day (is becoming) better by the moment.

1. My mood has never been worse.

2. I was tired in the morning.

3. I felt as dreary as the rainy weather outside.

4. My apartment seemed messy and cluttered.

5. Even after my shower, my world appeared gloomy.

6. Even my dog looked depressed.

7. The coffee in the local diner tasted burnt.

8. I grew resigned to a bad day.

9. My work day seemed endless.

10. In spite of all this, I feel hopeful about tomorrow.

EXERCISE 2 Finding Linking Verbs

Each of the following sentences contains a linking verb. Find the linking verb by first underlining the subject of the sentence. Then draw an arrow to the word or words that identify or describe the subject. Finally, circle the linking verb. An example is done for you.

The night became magical.

1. Her grad night was fabulous.

2. Monique looked lovely in her prom gown.

3. Her mother had been very helpful.

4. Everything seemed in order.

5. The limousine appeared right on time.

6. The hall was decorated with lights.

7. The food tasted extra special.

8. The band sounded professional.

9. Everyone felt so grown up.

10. Grad night seemed to be a complete success.

Helping verbs (also called auxiliary verbs)

Some verbs can be used to help the main verb express a special time or meaning.

Auxiliary verbs	**Time expressed by auxiliary verbs**
He *is* reading.	right now
He *might* read.	maybe now or in the future
He *should* read.	ought to, now, or in the future
He *could have been* reading.	maybe in the past

COMMON HELPING VERBS

can, could

may, might, must

shall, should

will, would

forms of the irregular verbs *be, do,* and *have.*

Remember that *be, do,* and *have* are also used as the main verbs of sentences. In such cases, *be* is a linking verb while *do* and *have* are action verbs. All the other helping verbs are usually used only as helping verbs.

> *Adverbs* are words that can modify verbs, adjectives, or other adverbs.

Watch out for *adverbs* that may come in between the helping verb and the main verb. In the following sentence, the word *often* is an adverb coming between the verb phrase *can change*. For a list of adverbs, see Appendix B: Parts of Speech (pp. 413–419).

A book can often change one's life.

EXERCISE 1   Finding Helping Verbs

Each of the following sentences contains a helping verb. In each sentence, first underline the subject. Then circle the entire verb phrase. An example is done for you.

Tofu could become the most popular food of the future.

1. The country of Argentina can claim the highest consumption of beef in the world.

2. Argentina's four billion dollar beef industry has always been an important national symbol.

3. Argentina's grass-fed cattle are considered leaner and lower in cholesterol than North American grain-fed cattle.

4. Even so, concerns about health and an economic recession may be changing the country's diet.

5. Many Argentines have begun to eat lighter and cheaper.

6. Necessity will force even the most dedicated meat-eaters to try new kinds of foods.

7. Clearly, some do not wish to alter their eating habits.

8. Not surprisingly, however, many Argentines have found they actually like tofu and pasta salads.

9. Argentina will not let its national symbol of beef fade away without a fight.

10. Beef producers must sell more beef abroad due to decreased local consumption.

EXERCISE 2   Finding Helping Verbs

Each of the following sentences contains a helping verb in addition to the main verb. In each sentence, first underline the subject. Then circle the entire verb phrase. An example is done for you.

Many people would consider their dreams a very important part of their lives.

1. You should record your dreams in a journal.

2. Your dreams will reveal your innermost concerns.

3. Elderly people can often recall events from twenty-five years ago.

4. Dreams could be put to good use.

5. Imagination might be developed through dreams.

6. Dreams are usually forgotten shortly after waking.

7. Children may not know the difference between dreams and reality.

8. They may create imaginary friends.

9. Dreams have brought contentment to many people's lives.

10. A dream book could be your most valuable possession.

Parts of speech

In this chapter, you have learned how most of the words in the English language function. These categories for words are called *parts of speech.* You have learned to recognize and understand the functioning of *nouns, pronouns, adjectives, verbs, adverbs,* and *prepositions.* (In later chapters you will learn how the *conjunction* functions.) You can review your understanding of these parts of speech as you practise identifying them in the exercises provided here. You may also refer to Appendix B (at the back of the book) for a quick summary whenever you want to refresh your memory.

EXERCISE 1   Identifying Parts of Speech

In the sentences below, identify the part of speech for each underlined word. Choose from the following list:

a. noun   d. verb
b. pronoun   e. adverb
c. adjective   f. preposition

_____ 1. The hospital volunteer <u>delivered</u> the newspapers.

_____ 2. Regrettably, he delivered them to the wrong <u>patients</u>.

_____ 3. He misplaced his <u>delivery</u> list.

_____ 4. A nurse <u>quickly</u> corrected his mistake.

_____ 5. She redelivered the papers <u>inconspicuously</u>.

_____ 6. Walking quickly, the <u>volunteer</u> continued on his rounds.

_____ 7. <u>Everyone</u> in the hospital thought he was charming.

_____ 8. <u>Between</u> you and me, I think he has a future in a people-oriented field.

_____ 9. The duty nurse always watched out <u>for</u> the hospital volunteer.

_____ 10. The volunteer appreciated the nurse's <u>helpfulness</u>.

EXERCISE 2   Identifying Parts of Speech

In the sentences below, identify the part of speech for each underlined word. Choose from the following list:

a. noun   d. verb
b. pronoun   e. adverb
c. adjective   f. preposition

_____   The people of the <u>country</u> of Mali, in Africa,

_____   built a mosque out of <u>mud</u> bricks. The Great

_____   Mosque <u>in</u> the town of Djenne was built

_____   by the Mali people sometime <u>between</u> A.D. 1100–1300.

_____   <u>Most</u> of the leaders of Mali at that time

_____   were <u>Muslims</u>. Djenne became a centre of Islamic

_____   learning. When the leader Konboro <u>converted</u> to

_____   Islam he <u>asked</u> a holy man, "How may I please God?"

_____   The holy man said, "<u>Build</u> a mosque. The people

_____   will bless your <u>name</u> for centuries."

EXERCISE 3   Identifying Parts of Speech

In the following sentences, identify the part of speech for each underlined word. Choose from the following list:

a. noun   d. verb
b. pronoun   e. adverb
c. adjective   f. preposition

_____ 1. The little girl received a <u>remarkable</u> toy.

_____ 2. Her grandmother was watching for the <u>reaction</u> of her granddaughter.

_____ 3. The child <u>smiled</u> as she tore open the gift wrap.

_____ 4. A <u>feeling</u> of satisfaction came over the grandmother.

_____ 5. <u>For</u> her safety, the child played on the floor not the couch.

_____ 6. The girl's parents <u>appreciated</u> the grandmother's efforts.

_____ 7. The parents <u>beamed</u> as they watched their daughter play.

_____ 8. Their daughter was totally captivated <u>by</u> the new toy.

_____ 9. The entire <u>family</u> is cooperating for the good of the child.

_____ 10. <u>Without</u> hesitation, the little girl embraced her parents and grandmother.

Mastery and editing tests

TEST 1

Finding Subjects and Verbs in Simple Sentences

Using all you have learned in this chapter, underline the subject and circle the verb in each of the following sentences.

1. Jacques Cartier, the French explorer, learned of the medicinal properties of common North American herbs and plants.

2. In the winter of 1535, scurvy killed many of the men on his expedition to Canada.

3. Scurvy, a disease caused by a deficiency in vitamin C, leads to a swelling of the gums and improper healing of wounds.

4. The Hurons, a native peoples who lived nearby, saved Cartier's men by giving them herbal tea made from the foliage of white cedar.

5. The natives of North America have helped Europeans by showing them how to use local herbs and plants to cure a variety of illnesses.

6. Fevers, stomach ailments, and rheumatism are everyday sicknesses that can be cured with the right herbs and plants.

7. Echinacea, commonly known as the purple coneflower, is one such herb.

8. It had been used by natives to cure snakebites, sore throats, and toothaches for thousands of years prior to Europeans settling in North America.

9. How do the medicinal properties of this herb work?

10. There are new studies that suggest echinacea may stimulate the immune system to help fight some viral and bacterial infections.

[D. Gillmor and P. Turgeon. *Canada: A People's History, Volume One.* Toronto: McClelland and Stewart Ltd., 2000, p. 64.]

TEST 2

Finding Subjects and Verbs in Simple Sentences

Using all you have learned in this chapter, underline the subject and circle the verb in each of the following sentences.

1. A certain amount of stress can be a good thing.

2. In many cases, stress motivates us.

3. When does stress become distress?

4. Your own self-awareness is the best place to start.

5. Have there been changes in your sleep or appetite?

6. Are you using alcohol or drugs too much?

7. Anxious people feel trapped by pressure and disappointment.

8. There is usually help from your family and friends.

9. Many can offer you their observations and advice.

10. Clinical depression, a more serious condition, usually responds well to the right combination of psychotherapy and the right medicine.

TEST 3

Finding Subjects and Verbs in Simple Sentences

Using all you have learned in this chapter, underline the subject and circle the verb in each of the following sentences.

1. The X-ray can be used to illuminate and cure illness.

2. It can also bring some risk from misuse.

3. Consumers should stay vigilant about unnecessary X-rays.

4. Both the benefits and the risks must be balanced.

5. Modern imaging techniques can spare patients unnecessary surgery.

6. In the 1970s, for example, bad stomach pain triggered exploratory surgery for appendicitis.

7. Intense doses of radiation can also kill cells.

8. When is the use of intense doses of radiation a benefit?

9. In cancer treatments, radiation therapy is often beneficial.

10. With massive exposure, however, chromosomes or bone marrow could be damaged.

TEST 4

Finding Subjects and Verbs in Simple Sentences

Using all you have learned in this chapter, underline the subject and circle the verb in each of the following sentences.

1. Most people, at one time or another, suffer from fatigue.

2. There could be many reasons for fatigue.

3. It is the body's way of warning us.

4. How can a person figure out the reason?

5. Sensations of sleepiness or feelings of physical weakness are separate symptoms with different causes.

6. Too much work and not enough sleep can cause fatigue.

7. Anemia, a condition of too little hemoglobin in the blood, can be diagnosed with a blood test.

8. Has anyone heard of obstructive sleep apnea or snoring sickness?

9. Infections such as mononucleosis, hepatitis, and Lyme disease are notorious for their exhausting effects.

10. After a tragedy such as the death of a spouse, profound fatigue is natural.

TEST 5   Finding Subjects and Verbs in Simple Sentences

In each of the following sentences, cross out any prepositional phrases or appositive phrases. Then underline the subject and circle the complete verb.

1. For some, chronic lateness may be considered a serious problem.

2. Students with this bad habit will often fail their classes.

3. Teachers must warn these students of the serious consequences of their tardiness.

4. Those same students often show up late to their after-school jobs as well.

5. Their social lives can be negatively affected at an important time of their lives.

6. Friends can become angry at waiting for these latecomers.

7. Why does anyone put up with these kinds of friends?

8. Parents and counsellors at schools search for solutions for these people, often without success.

9. Constant reminders may only annoy these people or even slow them down.

10. In truth, the individual must suffer the consequences of these actions.

Working Together

CROSSWORD PUZZLE: REVIEWING THE TERMS
FOR SENTENCE PARTS

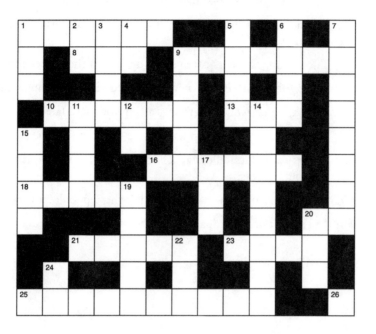

ACROSS

1. *Ecuador, Queen Victoria,* and *Reebok* are all examples of this type of noun.
8. Choose the action verb in the sentence below.
   The dog was fed before ten o'clock.
9. *Seem, appear,* and *feel* are all examples of this kind of verb.
10. Which of the following is a proper noun and should be capitalized?
    street   boston   bridge   poster
13. Which word is used as an adjective in the sentence below?
    The art bin is filled with supplies that can be used.
16. Which word in the sentence below is a helping verb?
    You should try not to become angry so easily.
18. What is the subject in the following sentence?
    In that shop, there is an outstanding array of sweaters from which to choose.
20. A common preposition
21. In the following sentence, which word is an adjective?
    The young girls played sports in the afternoon.
23. Which word in the sentence below is a helping verb?
    Will you please bill me for this belt?
25. In the following sentence, what is the name for the underlined phrase?
    Dander, <u>my roommate's cat</u>, often causes my sneezing fits.
26. A personal pronoun

DOWN

1. Which of the following is an action verb?
   pie   may   was   pry   can
2. A common preposition

3. Which one of the three underlined words is a concrete noun?
   He <u>pats</u> his <u>pets</u> before he <u>puts</u> them to bed.
4. In the following sentence, locate the proper noun.
   He gave a warm welcome to his niece and her new husband Ed.
5. Which one of the following words is a proper noun and should be capitalized?
   inch   inca   aunt   only
6. Which one of the following words is an example of an action verb?
   gift   wilt   will   seem
7. Which word in the following sentence is an adjective?
   The engineer asked an ignorant question of the judge.
9. Which of the following words is not an abstract noun?
   truth   lunch   faith   sense
11. A common preposition
12. Which word in the following sentence is a preposition?
    Here is an answer to our letter.
14. The following pronouns are examples of which group of pronouns?
    who   which   what   whose
15. Which of the following words is a demonstrative pronoun?
    mine   many   whom   that
17. A common pronoun
19. Which of the following words is an example of a personal pronoun?
    these   yours   whose   every
20. Which word is the indefinite pronoun in the sentence below?
    Who here thinks they can eat all of this ice cream?
22. Which of the following words is an action verb?
    get   can   may   yet
24. A common preposition

Chapter 3

Making Subjects and Verbs Agree

Now that we understand why a complete sentence must have a subject for its verb, we must turn our attention to a related problem: making sure the subject and verb agree in the sentence.

What is subject-verb agreement?

> A verb must agree with its subject in number (singular or plural).
>
> When the subject is a singular noun, the verb takes an *s* in the present tense.
>
> > The student studies.
>
> When the subject is a plural noun, the verb does not take an *s* in the present tense.
>
> > The students study.

Notice that when you add *s* or *es* to an ordinary noun, you form the plural of that noun. However, when you add an *s* to a verb, and you want the verb to be in the present tense, you are writing a singular verb. This rule causes a lot of confusion for student writers, especially those whose first language is not English. It may also be confusing to students who already speak and write English, but whose local manner of speaking does not follow this rule. While there is no one way of speaking that is correct or incorrect, society does recognize a standard form that is agreed upon as acceptable in the worlds of school and business. Since we must all master this standard form, the material contained in this chapter is of the greatest importance to your success.

Pronouns can also present problems for subject-verb agreement

The following chart shows personal pronouns used with the verb *study*. After you have studied the chart, what can you tell about the ending of a verb when the subject of that verb is a personal pronoun?

PERSONAL PRONOUNS	
Singular	**Plural**
I study	we study
you study	you study
he, she, it studies	they study

PRACTICE

Underline the correct verb in the following sentences.

1. The child (laughs, laugh).

2. The joke (amuses, amuse) him.

3. His friends (likes, like) to hear jokes.

4. He (memorizes, memorize) several of the jokes from his new book every day.

5. His parents (enjoys, enjoy) these jokes, too.

Pay special attention to the verbs *do* and *be*

It is common to hear phrases such as *it don't matter* or *we was working*. These expressions are not considered standard English.

THE VERB *TO DO*

Singular		Plural	
I	do	we	
you	do	you	do
he		they	
she	does		
it			

never *he don't, she don't,* or *it don't*

THE VERB *TO BE*

Present Tense				*Past Tense*			
Singular		Plural		Singular		Plural	
I	am	we		I	was	we	
you	are	you	are	you	were	you	were
he		they		he		they	
she	is			she	was		
it				it			

never *we was, you was,* or *they was*

PRACTICE

Underline the verb that agrees with the subject.

1. She (doesn't, don't) go to that coffee shop anymore.

2. We (was, were) disappointed with the food there too often.

3. The coffee (doesn't, don't) ever taste fresh.

4. (Was, Were) you there this morning?

5. Janna (doesn't, don't) know any other place where we can meet.

EXERCISE 1   Making the Subject and Verb Agree

In the blanks next to each sentence, write the subject of the sentence and the correct form of the verb.

	Subject	Verb
1. Tandy (loves, love) the theatre.		
2. Her brother Michael (is, are, be) an actor.		
3. Dress rehearsals (begins, begin) this week.		
4. The actors all (worries, worry) about memorizing their lines.		
5. Tandy often (calls, call) Michael in order to encourage him.		
6. She (is, are, be) very supportive of his career.		
7. On Friday, we (plans, plan) to see the show.		
8. Michael (doesn't, don't) know we are coming.		
9. We (hopes, hope) to surprise him with roses.		
10. I (is, am, be, are) sure the audience will love the show.		

EXERCISE 2   Making the Subject and Verb Agree

In the blanks next to each sentence, write the subject of the sentence and the correct form of the verb.

	Subject	Verb
1. Exercise (is, are) good for you.		
2. It (provides, provide) health and entertainment benefits.		
3. There (is, are) many forms of exercise.		
4. You (has, have) circuit training and aerobics.		
5. Circuit training (strengthens, strengthen) and tones muscles.		
6. Aerobic exercise (burns, burn) fat.		
7. Swimming (offers, offer) another excellent form of exercise.		
8. Exercise (does, do) wonders for both body and mind.		

	Subject	Verb
9. Motivational music (makes, make) your workout more fun.	_____	_____
10. Regular exercise (has, have) many benefits.	_____	_____

EXERCISE 3   Making the Subject and Verb Agree

In the blanks next to each sentence, write the subject of the sentence and the correct form of the verb.

	Subject	Verb
1. Television (offers, offer) the opportunity to be informed and entertained.	_____	_____
2. For some however, television (is, are) a form of addiction.	_____	_____
3. Sesame Street (teaches, teach) children how to read and count.	_____	_____
4. Jeopardy (expands, expand) your base of knowledge.	_____	_____
5. Other shows (caters, cater) to a taste for violence.	_____	_____
6. Instructional television (provides, provide) access to a wide range of subjects.	_____	_____
7. You (learns, learn) how to cook, sew, build houses, or repair cars.	_____	_____
8. Some television programs merely (makes, make) you laugh.	_____	_____
9. Television news shows (informs, inform) us about local, national, and international matters.	_____	_____
10. Television (brings, bring) the world into your home.	_____	_____

Subject-verb agreement with hard to find subjects

As we learned in Chapter 2, a verb does not always immediately follow the subject. Other words or groups of words such as prepositional phrases or appositive phrases can come between the subject and verb. Furthermore, subjects and verbs can be inverted as they are in questions or sentences beginning with *there* or *here*.

Now let us look for subject-verb agreement in sentences where the subjects are more difficult to find. Keep in mind two points:

- Subjects are not found in prepositional phrases or appositive phrases.
- Subjects can be found after the verb in sentences that are questions and in sentences that begin with *there* or *here*.

EXERCISE 1   Agreement with Hidden Subjects

Underline the subject of each sentence, and then circle the correct form of the verb.

1. Here (are, is) a story about school uniforms.

2. Interest in requiring uniforms (is, are) growing throughout the country.

3. A few provinces, among them Alberta and British Columbia, (are, is) considering laws to allow schools to have uniforms if they wish.

4. The government of Ontario (has, have) passed a law allowing the majority of parents in a school district to set the student dress code.

5. Why (do, does) some people, including parents, object to these new laws?

6. Some parents (believe, believes) that the behaviour of children cannot be changed by changing the clothes they wear.

7. Others feel that school dress codes (encourages, encourage) respect and unity among students.

8. School uniforms (are, is) often based on the colours of a particular school.

9. My little sister (hopes, hope) that she does not have to wear a school uniform.

10. The colours of her school (are, is) brown and yellow.

EXERCISE 2   Agreement with Hidden Subjects

Underline the subject of each sentence, and then circle the correct form of the verb.

1. Knowledge of household safety measures (is, are) important.

2. Where (is, are) the closest escape route?

3. Parents should, as early as possible, (teaches, teach) their children about safety.

4. Children as well as adults in a house (needs, need) to practise safety procedures.

5. What (is, are) some common safety tips everyone should know?

6. Batteries in the smoke detector (warns, warn) you about a smoky situation.

7. "Stop, drop, and roll" (is, are) steps to follow when there is a fire.

8. Always (knows, know) how to gain access to the fire escape.

9. Every family member, especially young children, (is, are) expected to memorize the home telephone number and house address.

10. In the home, there (is, are) safety procedures to reduce the chances of a disaster.

EXERCISE 3   Agreement with Hidden Subjects

Find the subject of each sentence by first crossing out prepositional or appositive phrases. In the blank next to each sentence, write the subject of the sentence and the correct form of the verb.

	Subject	Verb

1. There (is, are) some topics that concern everyone.

2. One of those topics (is, are) the weather.

3. What (does, do) the meteorologist say about the weather today?

4. Adults all across the nation (wants, want) to know what tomorrow's weather will be.

5. Farmers in particular (needs, need) to know the rainfall predictions for planting.

6. Pilots (relies, rely) on air traffic controllers when taking off and landing airplanes.

7. The number of days without rain (tends, tend) to be a favourite statistic.

8. Each region of British Columbia (has, have) its own distinct climate.

9. Here (is, are) the weather predictions for the week.

10. For the next few days, your umbrellas (is, are) needed.

Special problems with subject-verb agreement

1. Subject-verb agreement with group nouns

Look at the list of group nouns given below. Do you think a group noun should be considered singular or plural? In English, the answer to that question depends on whether the group acts as a single unit, or if the individuals in the group are acting separately.

- A group noun takes a singular verb if the noun acts as a unit. To test this, substitute the pronoun *it* for the noun.

   The French club is holding a fall bake sale.
   Test: *It* is holding a fall bake sale.

- A group noun takes a plural verb if the members of the group act as individuals. To test this, substitute the pronoun *they* for the noun.

   The French club are preparing their baked goods for this event.
   Test: *They* are preparing their baked goods for this event.

COMMON GROUP NOUNS			
audience	committee	family	orchestra
assembly	council	group	public
board	crowd	jury	team
class	faculty	number	

EXERCISE 1   Subject-Verb Agreement with Group Nouns

Circle the correct verb in each sentence below.

1. The crowd (was, were) eagerly awaiting the start of the meeting.
2. Tonight, the committee (makes, make) a full report on the search for a new manager.
3. The audience (was, were) in place at exactly seven o'clock.
4. The panel (sits, sit) behind a long table, reports in hand.
5. A group of parents (lines, line) up behind a microphone, waiting to speak.
6. A number of guards (stands, stand) waiting by the door, in case there would be any trouble.
7. Finally, the board at the long table (gestures, gesture) for silence.
8. When the name is announced, a number of people in the audience (gasps, gasp) in amazement.
9. The staff of the local newspaper (runs, run) to the phone.
10. The entire assembly (prepares, prepare) for a confrontation.

EXERCISE 2   Subject-Verb Agreement with Group Nouns

Circle the correct verb in each sentence below.

1. Every year the graduating class (decides, decide) if it should have a concert.
2. The band (takes, take) several weeks to prepare.
3. The faculty (shows, show) complete understanding by not giving any tests during this time.
4. The rest of the staff (is, are) very cooperative also.
5. Each club in the school (demonstrates, demonstrate) support in more than one way.
6. The football team (cooperates, cooperate) by holding the big game on a separate day.
7. The cast of the school play (sells, sell) tickets for the event.
8. Even the congregation of the local church (gets, get) together to buy a block of tickets.
9. On the day of the concert, the full assembly (is, are) wonderful to see.
10. Naturally, the family of each member of the graduating class (comes, come) to the event without fail.

EXERCISE 3   Subject-Verb Agreement with Group Nouns

Circle the correct verb in each sentence below.

1. The jury (decides, decide) the fate of a defendant.
2. Our class (plans, plan) to visit a trial in session.
3. The planning committee (expects, expect) to visit several courts before a decision is made.
4. A number of cases (is, are) being considered.
5. One group of students (wants, want) to sit in on a murder trial.
6. Some groups (prefers, prefer) a less sensational trial experience.
7. A hundred students (is, are) the maximum permitted in the courtroom.
8. A panel of ten teachers and students (makes, make) the final decision.
9. A team of students (has, have) agreed to write about their jury experience.
10. The legal club (gets, get) credit for coming up with this terrific idea.

2. Subject-verb agreement with indefinite pronouns

Care should be taken to learn which indefinite pronouns are singular and which are plural.

INDEFINITE PRONOUNS

Indefinite Pronouns Taking a Singular Verb:

everyone	someone	anyone	no one
everybody	somebody	anybody	nobody
everything	something	anything	nothing
each	another	either	neither

Everyone *is* expecting a miracle.

Indefinite Pronouns Taking a Plural Verb:

both	few	many	several

The talks between the two countries failed.

Both *were* to blame.

Indefinite Pronouns Taking a Singular or Plural Verb Depending on the Meaning in the Sentence:

any	all	more	most
none	some		

The books are gone. All were very popular.
The sugar is gone. All of it was spilled.

EXERCISE 1 Subject-Verb Agreement with Indefinite Pronouns

Circle the correct verb in each sentence.

1. Nobody (knows, know) how many drugs are contained in plants that grow in the rainforest.
2. Some (argues, argue) that wonderful drugs could be derived from many plants.
3. Most of the pharmaceutical experts (remains, remain) skeptical.
4. All of the research (is, are) expensive and often (proves, prove) fruitless.
5. Everybody (agrees, agree) the tropical forest is a source of medicine.
6. One of the dangers (is, are) that if we wait, the tropical forest may disappear.
7. One of two drug companies in Costa Rica (is, are) aggressively pursuing medicinal herbs.
8. Each of the companies (is, are) paying for the right to search the rainforest.
9. Among scientists, some (recommends, recommend) that governments subsidize drug research.
10. Vincristine and vinblastine are two medicines found in the rainforest; both (is, are) used for cancer treatment.

EXERCISE 2 Subject-Verb Agreement with Indefinite Pronouns

Circle the correct verb in each sentence below.

1. Everyone (wants, want) to breathe clean air.
2. Many (complains, complain) about the amount of pollution.
3. Some of the businesses around my town (is, are) committing themselves to a cleaner environment.
4. (Doesn't, Don't) everyone deserve a healthy environment?
5. Most of us (takes, take) clean air and water for granted, but we should not.
6. Some (has, have) recommended conservation as a way to limit pollution.
7. Another form of pollution (is, are) chemical pollution.
8. All of the research (tells, tell) us that we must protect the environment from pollution.
9. Each person (has, have) a duty to reduce pollution.
10. Several of the new technologies developed to resolve environmental problems (is, are) not cost effective.

EXERCISE 3   Subject-Verb Agreement with Indefinite Pronouns

Circle the correct verb in each sentence below.

1. Anybody (is, are) capable of learning to use a computer.

2. Some (thinks, think) computers are the enemy.

3. Most of our children, without fear of any kind, (finds, find) computers fun.

4. Nobody (knows, know) how many computers are in homes, schools, and businesses.

5. Somebody (is, are) using all those machines.

6. Nearly everybody today (has, have) discovered the usefulness of the computer.

7. Most of the banks (depends, depend) entirely on computers for record keeping.

8. One of the most popular software packages (is, are) MS-Word.

9. Each of the computer companies (tries, try) to make its software easy to use.

10. One of the major concerns for consumers (is, are) the cost of computers for personal use.

3. Subject-verb agreement with compound subjects

- If the conjunction used to connect the compound subjects is *and*, the verb is usually plural.

  Mary and Steve *are* my good friends.

  The exception to this is if the two subjects together are thought of as a single unit.

  Peanut butter and jelly *is* my favourite sandwich.

- If the conjunction used to connect the compound subjects is *or, nor, either, either/or, neither, neither/nor, not only/but also,* you need to be particularly careful.

- The verb is singular if both subjects are singular.

  Mary or Steve *is* going to help me.

  The verb is plural if both subjects are plural.

  My friends or my two brothers *are* going to help me.

  The verb agrees with the subject closest to the verb if one subject is singular and one subject is plural.

  My friends or my brother *is* going to help me.

EXERCISE 1   Subject-Verb Agreement with Compound Subjects

Circle the correct verb in each sentence below.

1. Our teenager and his friends (consumes, consume) massive amounts of food.
2. Bacon and eggs (is, are) their favourite breakfast.
3. Neither my husband nor his relatives (eats, eat) the way these kids do.
4. Perhaps their football practice along with their bicycling to and from school (increases, increase) their appetite.
5. Not only the refrigerator but the freezer (is, are) raided every afternoon.
6. Juice and snacks (disappears, disappear) within a day.
7. Either the friends or Jeffrey (feels, feel) hungry less than an hour after dinner.
8. However, neither my husband nor I (wants, want) the job of cooking again.
9. The family budget or our patience (is, are) sometimes stretched to the limit.
10. Parents and children (needs, need) to be considerate of each other.

EXERCISE 2   Subject-Verb Agreement with Compound Subjects

Circle the correct verb in each sentence below.

1. Opera and theatre (is, are) my favourite forms of entertainment.
2. This form of entertainment or others like it (attracts, attract) millions of supporters.
3. Either transportation costs or ticket prices (discourages, discourage) many from going to the opera or the theatre.
4. Neither the difficulties of parking nor the cost of an opera ticket (keeps, keep) me from enjoying a favourite activity.
5. My brother and sisters (has, have) gone to the Canadian Opera Company with me.
6. Wine and cheese (is, are) served at intermission.
7. Yvonne or Rita (is, are) generally bored.
8. My sisters and brother, on the other hand, (enjoys, enjoy) movies.
9. My sisters Yvonne and Rita (prefers, prefer) action-adventure movies.
10. Neither the prices of admission tickets nor the cost of "goodies" (upsets, upset) them.

EXERCISE 3   Subject-Verb Agreement with Compound Subjects

Circle the correct verb in each sentence below.

1. Chicken and fish (is, are) part of a healthy diet.
2. These foods and others like them (contains, contain) less fat.
3. Grains and vegetables (provides, provide) fibre as part of a balanced diet.

4. Shopping and buying habits (changes, change) as we learn more about good nutrition.

5. Neither hypertension nor high cholesterol (needs, need) to be a major concern if we eat properly.

6. Either a salad or a piece of fruit (is, are) a better choice than a hamburger with fries.

7. Excess fat, salt, and sugar (leads, lead) to potential health problems.

8. Too many eggs or dairy products (increases, increase) the cholesterol level.

9. Neither alcohol nor tobacco (promotes, promote) good health.

10. Diet and exercise (contributes, contribute) to a healthy and happier life.

4. Subject-verb agreement with unusual nouns

Don't assume that every noun ending in *s* is plural, or that all nouns that do not end in *s* are singular. There are some exceptions. Here are a few of the most common.

Some nouns are always singular but end in *s:*

mathematics	diabetes	United States
economics	measles	Northwest Territories

Some nouns have an irregular plural form that does not end in *s* or *es:*

people	feet	men	data
children	mice	women	alumni (masculine) or alumnae (feminine)

Some nouns are always plural:

clothes	scissors	fireworks
eyeglasses	tweezers	pants

EXERCISE 1   Subject-Verb Agreement with Unusual Nouns

Circle the correct verb in each sentence below.

1. People (come, comes) from many different nations to live and work in Canada.

2. On Canada Day, one of the best places to be (is, are) Ottawa.

3. Spectacular fireworks (lights, light) up the night sky around the Parliament Buildings.

4. Like Canada, the United States (is, are) a diverse country.

5. Economics (is, are) a major factor in children's quality of life.

6. Measles (has, have) been one of the most serious childhood diseases.

7. His pants (is, are) in need of ironing.

8. The eyeglasses (allows, allow) him to avoid walking into doors.

9. Diabetes (affects, affect) children and adults.

10. Data (shows, show) the benefits of insulin in the treatment of diabetes.

EXERCISE 2 Subject-Verb Agreement with Unusual Nouns

Circle the correct verb in each sentence below.

1. Physics (requires, require) a knowledge of math.

2. Mathematics (reveals, reveal) your ability to use logic.

3. The United States (wants, want) to train more people in the fields of math and science.

4. Mice (lives, live) in dark, warm spaces.

5. People, especially females, (fears, fear) rodents such as mice.

6. Children, on the other hand, (treats, treat) mice like household pets.

7. Moose (sheds, shed) their antlers annually.

8. The scissors (seems, seem) to be lost again.

9. Another name for the Netherlands (is, are) Holland.

10. The alumnae of my college (is, are) having a reunion.

Mastery and editing tests

TEST 1   Making the Subject and Verb Agree

In the blanks next to each sentence, write the subject of the sentence and the correct form of the verb.

	Subject	Verb
1. A recent study of thousands of smokers (reveals, reveal) that nicotine in tobacco is addictive.	_____	_____
2. People who (has, have) smoked for a prolonged period make perfect subjects for research studies.	_____	_____
3. Both the sense of taste and breath control (is, are) affected.	_____	_____
4. A large group of researchers (believes, believe) that second-hand smoke is as deadly as inhaling.	_____	_____
5. One of the findings (is, are) that smokers lose their sense of smell.	_____	_____
6. Children who (smokes, smoke) cigarettes risk serious lung problems as they grow older.	_____	_____

	Subject	Verb
7. Filtered cigarettes (is, are) not the answer to reduce the negative effects of tobacco.	_____	_____
8. Tobacco companies (gives, give) away their products to encourage people to smoke.	_____	_____
9. Addictions to tobacco (is, are) difficult to break.	_____	_____
10. Concern over the effects of tobacco (is, are) growing.	_____	_____

TEST 2   Making the Subject and Verb Agree

In the blanks next to each sentence, write the subject of the sentence and the correct form of the verb.

	Subject	Verb
1. Canada (want, wants) to protect its culture and traditions.	_____	_____
2. One of the ways to accomplish this (is, are) to increase funding to the arts and historical societies.	_____	_____
3. Everybody (feel, feels) strongly about preserving Canada's traditions.	_____	_____
4. Both politicians and artists (hopes, hope) to revitalize Canadian culture.	_____	_____
5. Economics (affect, affects) Canadian culture.	_____	_____
6. The offices of more than one major film studio (are, is) located in the United States.	_____	_____
7. Canadians' desire for American films (has, have) grown steadily over the years.	_____	_____
8. People (worry, worries) about the survival of Canada's institutions and traditions.	_____	_____
9. Teachers of young people (strive, strives) to introduce students to the uniqueness of Canada's culture.	_____	_____
10. Solutions to this problem (have, has) become more difficult to realize.	_____	_____

TEST 3   Making the Subject and Verb Agree

In the blanks next to each sentence, write the subject of the sentence and the correct form of the verb. An example follows:

	Subject	Verb
The eleven proposals for the development of a new building on Portage Avenue (has, have) been submitted to the city.	*proposals*	*have*

1. The price of airline tickets to England (has, have) remained fairly reasonable. _____ _____

2. His decision (requires, require) a lot of thought. _____ _____

3. She (doesn't, don't) know the answers to any of the test questions. _____ _____

4. Either the elevator operator or the security guard (see, sees) every visitor. _____ _____

5. The committee (agree, agrees) to the fund-raising projects for this year. _____ _____

6. Potato chips and pop (makes up, make up) most of her diet. _____ _____

7. One of the people in the audience (is, are) my brother. _____ _____

8. There (was, were) two raccoons sleeping in the barn last night. _____ _____

9. Posted on the bulletin board (was, were) the assignments for the week. _____ _____

10. Everyone (takes, take) the test on Monday. _____ _____

TEST 4   Making the Subject and Verb Agree

Complete each of the following sentences, being sure that the verb in each sentence agrees with the subject of that sentence. Use verbs in the present tense.

1. Mathematics _____

_____

_____

2. One of the courses _____

_____

_____

3. Either the dean or the professors _____

_____

_____

4. Everyone _____

_____

_____

5. There _____

_____

_____

6. Where _____

_____

_____

7. The United States _____

_____

_____

8. The alumni _____

_____

_____

9. My work for two semesters _____

_____

_____

10. The complaint about the problems with parking tickets _____

_____

_____

TEST 5   Making the Subject and Verb Agree

Complete each of the following sentences, being sure that the verb in each sentence agrees with the subject of that sentence. Use verbs in the present tense.

1. The committee _____

_____

_____

2. One of the members _____

_____

_____

3. The report on the hospitals _____

_____

_____

4. The results of the test _____

_____

_____

5. Neither the visitors nor the mayor _____

    _____

    _____

6. Why _____

    _____

    _____

7. In the entire room, there _____

    _____

    _____

8. Each of the _____

    _____

    _____

9. My sister and best friend (refering to the same person) _____

    _____

    _____

10. Nobody in the crowd _____

    _____

    _____

Working Together

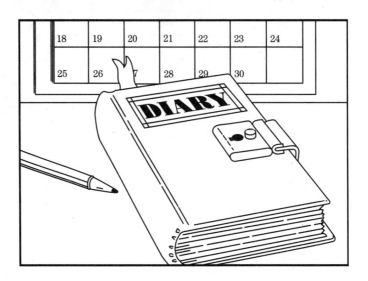

The excerpt below was written by a woman who lived under difficult circumstances in Brazil. Her words express the basic and universal truth that often the most beautiful things we experience in life do not cost anything.

> The sky is beautiful, worthy of contemplation because the drifting clouds are forming dazzling landscapes. Soft breezes pass by carrying the perfume of flowers, and the sun is always punctual at rising and setting. The birds travel in space, showing off in their happiness. The night brings up the sparkling stars to adorn the blue sky. There are so many beautiful things in the world that are impossible to describe. Only one thing saddens us: the prices when we go shopping. They overshadow all the beauty that exists.

> —*Child of the Dark:*
> *The Diary of Carolina Maria de Jesus*

Divide into groups. Each group should brainstorm in order to make up a list of many of the good things that do not cost anything. With this list in mind, each student should write an individual journal entry. You might use the above journal entry as well as the class brainstorming list as a resource for your own entry. Then finish the entry in the same way that the diarist did. Find one aspect of life that saddens you.

Chapter 4

Correcting the Fragment in Simple Sentences

The *fragment* is a major problem for many student writers. A thought may be clear in your mind, but on paper this same idea may turn out to be incomplete because it does not include a subject, a verb, or express a complete thought. In this chapter, you will improve your ability to spot incomplete sentences or fragments, and you will learn how to correct them. This practice will help you to avoid fragments in your writing. Here, for example, is a typical conversation between two people. It is composed entirely of fragments, but the two people who are speaking have no trouble understanding each other:

Dad: Going out?
Sam: Just to the store.
Dad: What for?
Sam: A notebook for school.

If we use complete sentences to rewrite this brief conversation, the result might be the following:

Dad: Are you going out?
Sam: I'm just going to the store.
Dad: What do you need?
Sam: I need a notebook for school.

In the first conversation, misunderstanding is unlikely since the two speakers stand face-to-face, see each other's gestures, and hear the intonations of each other's voice to help understand the meaning. These short phrases may be enough for communication since the speakers are using more than just words to convey their thoughts. They understand each other because the person spoken to is able to complete the thoughts that are in the speaking person's mind.

In writing, however, readers cannot be present at the scene to observe the situation for themselves. They cannot be expected to read the author's mind. Only the words grouped into sentences and the sentences grouped into paragraphs provide the clues to the meaning. Since writing often involves thoughts that are abstract and even complex, fragments cause great difficulty and sometimes total confusion for the reader.

PRACTICE   Putting a Conversation into Complete Sentences

The following conversation is one that a couple of workers might have had at the start of their work day. Rewrite the conversation in complete sentences. Remember the definition of a sentence:

> A *complete sentence* has a subject and a verb and expresses a complete thought.

Li: You again!
         Late as usual.
Sarah: Had an emergency.
Li: What now?
Sarah: My car.
Li: More bad luck, huh?
Sarah: Yep, a flat tire this time.
Li: What next?

1. _____

2. _____

3. _____

4. _____

5. _____

6. _____

7. _____

8. _____

Remember, when you write in complete sentences, this writing may be somewhat different from the way you would express the same idea in everyday conversation with a friend.

Although you will occasionally spot incomplete sentences in professional writing, you may be sure the writer is using these fragments intentionally. In such cases, the fragment may capture the way a person thinks or speaks, or it may create a special effect. A student developing his or her writing skills should be sure to use only standard sentence form so that thoughts will be communicated effectively. Nearly all the writing you will do in your life—letters to friends, business correspondence, papers in school, or reports in your job—will demand standard sentence form. Fragments will be looked upon as a sign of ignorance rather than creative style!

What is a fragment?

> A *fragment* is a piece of a sentence.

A fragment is not a sentence for one of the following reasons:

a. The subject is missing:

recorded the totals in the notebook

b. The verb is missing:

The accountant in the notebook

c. Both the subject and verb are missing:

in the notebook

d. The subject and verb are present, but the words do not express a complete thought:

The accountant recorded

EXERCISE 1   Understanding Fragments

Each of the ten examples is a fragment. In the blank to the right of each fragment, identify what part of the sentence is missing and needs to be added to make the fragment into a sentence. Choose from the following possibilities:

a. needs a subject
b. needs a verb
c. needs a subject and a verb
d. the subject and verb are present, but the sentence needs to express a complete thought

Group of Words   **What Is Needed?**

Example: into my soup   c. needs a subject and a verb

1. came to dinner for the first time   _____

2. the author at the conference   _____

3. barked all night   _____

4. above the twentieth floor   _____

5. the salesperson considered   _____

6. called her mother every week   _____

7. sweetly the songbird   _____

8. on our dormitory floor   _____

9. inspired me to paint   _____

10. the taxicab driver deposited   _____

EXERCISE 2   Understanding Fragments

Each of the following groups of words is a fragment. In the blank to the right of each fragment, identify what part of the sentence is missing and needs to be added to make the fragment into a sentence. Choose from the following possibilities:

a. needs a subject

b. needs a verb

c. needs a subject and a verb

d. the subject and verb are present, but the sentence needs to express a complete thought

An example is done for you.

Fragment   **What Is Needed?**

   Example: The dancers   b. verb

1. arrived at the scene   _____

2. a crowd out of control   _____

3. between the dance floor and the exit _____

4. thick smoke in the stairway   _____

5. in the middle of the night   _____

6. gasping for breath   _____

7. only one exit from the rave   _____

8. the danger of trampling each other   _____

9. more careful in the future about dancing at crowded raves   _____

10. who inspected   _____

EXERCISE 3   Understanding Fragments

Each of the following groups of words is a fragment. In the blank to the right of each fragment, identify what part of the sentence is missing and needs to be added to make the fragment into a sentence. Choose from the following possibilities:

a. needs a subject

b. needs a verb

c. needs a subject and a verb

d. the subject and verb are present, but the sentence needs to express a complete thought

An example is done for you.

Fragment   **What Is Needed?**

   Example: on the road   c. subject and a verb

1. the bicycle race   _____

2. athletes from all over   _____

3. across France   _____

4. five straight days   _____

5. the incredible energy   _____

6. lined up to watch   _____

7. the publicity of the race   _____

8. crowding to catch a glimpse   _____

9. who put   _____

10. handed water to tired racers   _____

How do you correct a fragment?

1. Add the missing part or parts.

Example: Fragment: across the lake
 Add: subject and verb
 Sentence: I swam across the lake.

Note: The prepositional phrase *across the lake* is a fragment because a prepositional phrase cannot function as the subject or the verb in a sentence. Furthermore, the words do not express a complete thought.

2. Join the fragment to the sentence that precedes it or to the sentence that follows it, depending on where it belongs.

Often the complete thought is already present in the text where the fragment occurs. The writer did not recognize that the fragment belonged to the sentence coming before or the sentence following. Study the example below:

Wrong: In the middle of the night I swam. Across the lake.
The camp counsellor was waiting at the other side.

Correct: In the middle of the night, I swam across the lake.
The camp counsellor was waiting at the other side.

Why is this error so prevalent? One reason could be carelessness. Usually, however, the reason is that the writer does not fully understand the necessary parts of a sentence. In addition, when some writers do not have a clear idea of what they are trying to say, fragments and other errors are more likely to occur. Sometimes further thought or another try at expressing the same idea may produce a better result.

In the following exercises, practise correcting both kinds of fragments.

EXERCISE 1   Changing Fragments into Sentences

Change each of the fragments below into complete sentences by adding the missing part or parts that you have already identified in the previous set of exercises. An example is done for you.

Fragment: into my soup

Add: subject and verb

Complete sentence: A spider fell into my soup.

1. came to dinner for the first time

   _____

2. the author at the conference

   _____

3. barked all night

   _____

4. above the twentieth floor

   _____

5. the salesperson considered

   _____

6. called her mother every week

   _____

7. sweetly the songbird

   _____

8. on our dormitory floor

   _____

9. inspired me to paint

   _____

10. the taxicab driver deposited

   _____

EXERCISE 2   Changing Fragments into Sentences

Create a complete sentence for each of the fragments given. Add the missing part or parts that you have already identified for these fragments in the previous set of exercises. An example is done for you.

Fragment:	The dancers
Add:	the verb
Complete sentence:	The dancers smiled.

1. arrived at the scene

   _____

2. a crowd out of control

   _____

3. between the dance floor and the exit

   _____

4. thick smoke in the stairway

   _____

5. in the middle of the night

   _____

6. gasping for breath

   _____

7. only one exit from the rave

   _____

8. the danger of trampling each other

   _____

9. more careful in the future about dancing at crowded raves

   _____

10. who inspected

   _____

EXERCISE 3   Changing Fragments into Sentences

Create a complete sentence for each of the fragments given. Add the missing part or parts that you have already identified for these fragments in the previous set of exercises. An example is done for you.

Fragment: on the road
Add: subject and verb
Complete sentence: The judges drew the line on the road.

1. the bicycle race

   _____

2. athletes from all over

   _____

3. across France

   _____

4. five straight days

   _____

5. the incredible energy

   _____

6. lined up to watch

   _____

7. the publicity of the race

   _____

8. crowding to catch a glimpse

   _____

9. who put

   _____

10. handed water to tired racers

   _____

EXERCISE 1 Finding Fragments That Belong to Other Sentences

Each of the following passages contains a fragment or two. First, read each passage. Then locate each fragment. Circle the fragment and draw an arrow to the sentence to which it should be connected. An example is done for you.

Peter helped comb the children's hair. (Before each portrait was taken.)
The photographer took three poses of each child.

Passage 1

Snow was very dangerous for airplane pilots. Until the invention of radar. The distance from an airplane to a snowfield below was almost impossible to judge. Sometimes a "whiteout" seemed to be a mile beneath a plane when actually it was only fifty feet. Some pilots have seen snow come up to their cockpit. Before they know it. They are at a complete stop with their engines still running.

Passage 2

The dandelion is the enemy of every gardener, but it is also a powerful herb. With wonderful medicinal properties. Perhaps it received its name from the French words *dent de lion,* or *lion's tooth.* The leaves of the plant have jagged edges. Like the lion's teeth. Others disagree. They say the plant's yellow flower is like the colour of a lion.

Passage 3

Pictures from everyday life are among the most impressive objects to survive from ancient Egypt. We see farmers labouring in the fields. And craftsmen working in their studios. Sometimes the colours are as fresh as ever. The pictures show a deep love for life and for the things of the earth.

EXERCISE 2 Finding Fragments That Belong to Other Sentences

Each of the following passages contains a fragment or two. First, read each passage. Then locate each fragment. Next, circle the fragment and draw an arrow to the sentence to which it should be connected.

Passage 1

Mr. Howell loves gardening. He devotes long hours to working in his garden. Behind the garage in the back yard. His garden is the pride of the neighbourhood. Sometimes he enters garden competitions. He usually comes home happy. With a first place trophy.

Passage 2

Photography can be a wonderful hobby. The only equipment required is a camera. And a good pair of eyes to view the world around you. This hobby can lead to a career. Along with the possibility of good earnings. Consider photography for either pleasure or profit.

Passage 3

Demasduwit, or Mary March as she was named in English, was a Beothuk. In March 1819 a group of armed settlers from Notre Dame Bay encountered a small party of Beothuk at Red Indian Lake. A fight ensued, in which the settlers captured Demasduwit. She was renamed Mary March. Her second name referring to the month of her capture. The settlers took her in the hope that she could be taught to speak English and might become an agent of contact with her people. When the time came for her to return to the Beothuk, Demasduwit discovered she had tuberculosis. Instead of taking her back alive, a military expedition returned her body. Which they left in early February at the deserted Beothuk camp where she had been captured the previous year.

EXERCISE 3   Finding Fragments That Belong to Other Sentences

Each of the following passages contains a fragment or two. First, read each passage. Then locate the fragment in each passage. Circle the fragment and draw an arrow to the sentence to which it should be connected.

Passage 1

During the War of 1812, invading American armies met some of their fiercest opposition from the French in Quebec. Then called Lower Canada. Charles-Michel de Salaberry, commander of the resistance against the American invaders, was from an old French-Canadian family. De Salaberry chose to confront the Americans on the banks of the Châteauguay River. His three hundred volunteers faced an army of three thousand. The Americans fired the first volley, but the Canadians held their ground. They returned fire. From their entrenched positions. The Americans fell back across the border. The French Canadians repelled another American attack a few weeks later. At a place called Crysler's Farm, a small force of French defeated a much larger American army. This ended American plans to conquer Lower Canada.

Passage 2

The construction of the Canadian Pacific Railway in the 1880s played an important part in Canadian history. It connected the country from coast to coast. However, the contribution of Chinese labourers in its construction is often overlooked. In total, some 15,700 Chinese were recruited to work on the railroad. They did some of the hardest and most dangerous work. Including digging tunnels and handling explosives. They were also treated unfairly. These workers were paid $1.00 a day and had to pay for their own camping gear. In contrast, white labourers were paid $1.50 to $2.50 a day and did not have to pay for their gear. Many Chinese workers often died from exhaustion due to the hard work. Some perished in explosions. Or were buried in collapsed tunnels. The Chinese labourers helped to link Canada from coast to coast.

What is a phrase?

A *phrase* is a group of words that go together but that lack one or more of the elements necessary to be classified as a sentence.

Fragments are usually made up of phrases. These phrases are often mistaken for sentences because they are words that go together as a group. However, they do not fit the definition of a sentence. *Do not confuse a phrase with a sentence.*

How many kinds of phrases are there?

The English language has six phrases (three of which you have already studied in Chapter 2). Learn to recognize each of these phrases. Remember that a phrase is *never* a sentence.

1. **Noun phrase:** a noun plus its modifiers

    large square bricks

2. **Prepositional phrase:** a preposition plus its object and modifiers

    around our neighbourhood

3. **Verb phrase:** the main verb plus its helping verbs

    is walking
    could have walked
    should have been walking

The three remaining phrases are formed from *verbs.* However, these phrases do not function as verbs in the sentence. Study carefully how to use them.

4. **Participial phrase:**

    How is the participial phrase formed?

    a. the present form of a verb ending in *-ing* and any other words necessary to complete the phrase:

      running home
      looking very unhappy

    b. the past form of a verb usually ending in *-ed* and any other words necessary to complete the phrase:

      greatly disappointed
      told tearfully

How does the participial phrase function? Participial phrases function as **adjectives** in a sentence. Study how the above phrases could be made into complete sentences. These phrases will function as adjectives for the noun or pronoun that follows.

Running home, the worker lost her wallet.
Looking very unhappy, she retraced her steps.
Greatly disappointed, she could not find it.
Told tearfully, her story saddened her friends.

> Students often make the mistake of confusing a participle with a verb. When a participle is used as a verb, there *must* be a helping verb with it.
>
> **Incorrect:** I running in the marathon
>
> **Correct:**   I *am* running in the marathon.

5. **Gerund phrase:** the present form of a verb ending in *-ing*, and any other words necessary to complete the phrase

   The gerund phrase functions as a noun.
   a. subject of the sentence:

   > *Running in a marathon* is strenuous exercise.

   b. direct object of the sentence:

   > I like *running in a marathon*.

6. **Infinitive phrase:** *to* plus the verb and any other words necessary to complete the phrase

   > *to run* the race

   Note: The word *to* can also function as a preposition. I ran *to school*.

EXERCISE 1   Identifying Phrases

Identify each of the phrases.

1. in grade six   _____
2. the graduation ceremony   _____
3. to celebrate   _____
4. that slender, dark-haired, olive-skinned girl   _____
5. would push   _____
6. during lunch hour   _____
7. on their faces   _____
8. would have been playing   _____
9. spoke sympathetically and firmly   _____
10. to think carefully   _____

EXERCISE 2   Identifying Phrases

Identify each of the phrases.

1. the rescue team   _____
2. among the toughest jobs   _____
3. would be yelling   _____
4. were finding   _____
5. to use   _____
6. in a short time   _____
7. rescue dogs   _____
8. have now located   _____
9. in the middle of winter   _____
10. the grateful crowd   _____

EXERCISE 3   Identifying Phrases

Identify each of the underlined phrases in the following sentences.

1. An unusual combination of weather systems stalled over parts of Eastern Canada, coating the area in ice.

  1. _____
  2. _____
  3. _____

2. The ice was over 10 centimetres thick in some places.

  4. _____

3. Broken power lines would lead to power failures in Montreal.

  5. _____

4. The ice-coated landscape would have been beautiful to look at for many people.

  6. _____
  7. _____

5. The military was called in to bring stability to the chaos.

  8. _____

6. For almost two million people, conducting everyday tasks became difficult.

  9. _____

7. The ice storm of January 1998 will be remembered as the most expensive natural disaster in Canadian history.

  10. _____

Understanding the uses of the present participle

The present participle causes a good deal of confusion for students working with the fragment. Because the participle can be used sometimes as a verb, sometimes as an adjective, and sometimes as a noun, you will want to be aware of which of these uses you intend.

EXERCISE 1   Using the Participle in a Verb Phrase

Below are five present participles. Use each of them as part of a verb phrase in a sentence. An example has been done for you.

> **Present participle:** jumping
>
> **Verb phrase:** was jumping
>
> **Sentence:** The boy was jumping on the couch.

1. singing _____
2. buying _____
3. climbing _____
4. forgetting _____
5. fixing _____

EXERCISE 2   Using the Participial Phrase as an Adjective

Each of the underlined words below is a present participle. Use the word along with the phrase provided to compose sentences in which the phrase functions as an adjective. An example has been done for you.

> **Present participle:** jumping
>
> **Participial phrase:** jumping on the couch
>
> **Participial phrase used as an adjective phrase in the sentence:** Jumping on the couch, the boy laughed with glee.

1. Singing in the shower

   _____

   _____

2. Buying the tickets

   _____

   _____

3. Climbing the steps

   _____

   _____

4. Forgetting the address

   _____

   _____

5. <u>Fixing</u> the window

_____

_____

EXERCISE 3   Using the Participial Phrase as a Noun (Gerund)

Each of the underlined words below is a present participle. Use the word along with the phrase provided as a noun phrase in a sentence. An example has been done for you.

Present participle: jumping

Participial phrase: jumping on the couch

Participial phrase used as a noun phrase in a sentence: <u>Jumping on the couch</u> was fun.

1. <u>Singing</u> in the shower

_____

_____

2. <u>Buying</u> the tickets

_____

_____

3. <u>Climbing</u> the steps

_____

_____

4. <u>Forgetting</u> the address

_____

_____

5. <u>Fixing</u> the window

_____

_____

How do you make a complete sentence from a fragment that contains a participle?

Fragment: Our neighbour <u>walking his dog</u>.

1. Add a helping verb to the participle:

   Our neighbour <u>is walking</u> his dog.

2. Change the participle to a different form of the verb:

   Our neighbour <u>walks</u> his dog every morning.

3. Use the participle as an adjective, being sure to provide a subject and verb for the sentence:

>   <u>Walking his dog</u>, our neighbour often stops to chat.

4. Use the participle as a noun (gerund):

>   <u>Walking the dog</u> can be good exercise.

EXERCISE 1   Correcting the Fragment That Contains a Participle

Make four complete sentences from each of the following fragments. Use the following example as your model.

>   **Fragment:** <u>carrying</u> the porcelain vase

a. Add a helping verb to form a verb phrase.

>   She <u>is carrying</u> the porcelain vase.

b. Change the participle to a different verb form.

>   She <u>carried</u> the porcelain vase.

c. Use the participial phrase as an adjective phrase.

>   <u>Carrying the porcelain vase</u>, she stepped carefully on the ice.

d. Use the participial phrase as a gerund phrase.

>   <u>Carrying the porcelain vase</u> on the ice was tricky.

1. presenting the weather report

   a. _____

   b. _____

   c. _____

   d. _____

2. driving the taxi

   a. _____

   b. _____

   c. _____

   d. _____

3. bending over the sink

   a. _____

   b. _____

   c. _____

   d. _____

4. waiting for the bus

   a. _____

   b. _____

   c. _____

   d. _____

5. reviewing the material

   a. _____

   b. _____

   c. _____

   d. _____

EXERCISE 2   Correcting the Fragment That Contains a Participle

Make four complete sentences from each of the following fragments. Use the following example as your model.

Fragment: <u>working</u> in an insurance office

a. Add a helping verb to the verb phrase.

   We <u>are working</u> in an insurance office.

b. Change the participle to a different form of the verb.

   We <u>work</u> in an insurance office.

c. Use the participle to form an adjective phrase.

   <u>Working in an insurance office</u>, we learn how to read documents carefully.

d. Use the participle to form a gerund phrase.

   <u>Working in an insurance office</u> can be interesting.

1. living in a large city

   a. _____

   b. _____

   c. _____

   d. _____

2. studying for exams

   a. _____

   b. _____

   c. _____

   d. _____

3. buying on credit

   a. _____

   b. _____

   c. _____

   d. _____

4. travelling during the summer

   a. _____

   b. _____

   c. _____

   d. _____

5. investing in the stock market

   a. _____

   b. _____

   c. _____

   d. _____

EXERCISE 3   Correcting the Fragment That Contains a Participle

Make four complete sentences from each of the following fragments. Use the following example as your model.

Fragment: <u>calling</u> the doctor's office

a. Add a helping verb to the verb phrase.

   She <u>is calling</u> the doctor's office.

b. Change the participle to a different verb form.

   She <u>called</u> the doctor's office.

c. Use the participial phrase as an adjective phrase.

   <u>Calling the doctor's office</u>, she quickly made an appointment.

d. Use the participial phrase as a gerund phrase.

   <u>Calling the doctor's office</u> can be time consuming.

1. marking the chart

   a. _____

   b. _____

   c. _____

   d. _____

2. talking about late night television

   a. _____

   b. _____

   c. _____

   d. _____

3. chewing gum

   a. _____

   b. _____

   c. _____

   d. _____

4. making an appointment

   a. _____

   b. _____

   c. _____

   d. _____

5. checking the time

   a. _____

   b. _____

   c. _____

   d. _____

Mastery and editing tests

TEST 1   Correcting Fragments

Rewrite each fragment so that it is a complete sentence.

1. waking up before the sun rises

   _____

2. to plan the day's schedule

   _____

3. is always quiet and peaceful

   _____

4. slowly appears over the horizon

   _____

5. the only sight the street lights blinking off

   _____

6. sitting and waiting for the water to boil

   _____

7. savouring a hot cup of tea

_____

8. the day's chores

_____

9. myself for the day's events

_____

10. my special time of the day

_____

TEST 2   Correcting Fragments

Each of the following groups of words is a phrase. First, name each phrase. Second, make each phrase into a complete sentence.

1. at the top of the hill

   Name of phrase: _____

   Sentence: _____

2. running around in circles

   Name of phrase: _____

   Sentence: _____

3. to believe in Santa Claus

   Name of phrase: _____

   Sentence: _____

4. with his goals clearly in mind

   Name of phrase: _____

   Sentence: _____

5. on the outside of the building along the corners

   Name of phrase: _____

   Sentence: _____

6. to decide on a profession

   Name of phrase: _____

   Sentence: _____

7. mowing the lawn for hours

   Name of phrase: _____

   Sentence: _____

8. lifting the squealing baby high into the air

   Name of phrase: _____

   Sentence: _____

9. to purchase a home

   Name of phrase: _____

   Sentence: _____

10. from one day to the next

    Name of phrase: _____

    Sentence: _____

TEST 3   Recognizing and Correcting the Fragment

Each of the following passages contains a fragment. Rewrite the passage so that it is composed of complete sentences.

1. The moon rose high in the sky. All of us worked quickly to pitch the tent. Then making a fire.

   Revised passage: _____

   _____

   _____

2. Raising the drinking age to twenty-one saves the lives of all drivers. The drinkers and the nondrinkers. Every province should raise the drinking age to twenty-one.

   Revised passage: _____

   _____

   _____

3. Companies do a lot of research before they name a new product. Based on the results of a market research team. The company makes its final selection.

   Revised passage: _____

   _____

   _____

4. The day of my eighteenth birthday, reservations made at a fine restaurant. My father came home early from work.

   Revised passage: _____

   _____

   _____

5. Francie loved to see her mother grind the coffee. Her mother would sit in the kitchen with the coffee mill clutched between her knees. Grinding away with a furious turn of her left wrist. The room filled up with the rich odour of freshly ground coffee.

   Revised passage: _____

   _____

   _____

TEST 4   Recognizing and Correcting the Fragment

The following paragraph contains fragments. Read the paragraph and underline each fragment. Then rewrite the paragraph being careful to use only complete sentences.

HINT: 6 fragments

We called it our house. It was only one room. With about as much space as a tent. Painted in a pastel colour with a red tiled roof. The front window reaching nearly from the sidewalk to the roof. We could look up and down the street. Sitting indoors on the window seat. Our kitchen was a small narrow area. With the brick stove and two benches to serve as shelves. Three steel bars and a short piece of lead pipe from a scrap heap to make a grate.

_____

_____

_____

_____

_____

_____

_____

_____

_____

_____

_____

_____

_____

_____

TEST 5   Recognizing and Correcting the Fragment

The following paragraph contains fragments. Read the paragraph and underline each fragment. Then rewrite the paragraph being careful to use only complete sentences.

HINT: 5 fragments

The snow came down all night long. And well into the next day. By the time. The snowstorm ended. My mother woke me up. Saying that it was time for me to get up and shovel the driveway. When I ran out of the kitchen door. I saw that the car had been snowed in. I then realized that my job was going to be harder than ever. Somewhere underneath all that snow. There lay the snow shovel.

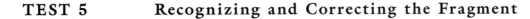

_____

_____

_____

_____

_____

_____

_____

_____

_____

_____

_____

_____

_____

_____

_____

_____

Working Together

Read the advertisement. Like many advertisements, the style is short and crisp and sometimes uses phrases rather than sentences. This is done to attract readers and hold their interest. Study the advertisement carefully. How many of the sentences are really fragments? Consult with a partner or a group to make your decisions. Then revise the fragments you have found so that each one is a complete sentence.

At their house, it's rare if both cars are ever in the driveway. Step into their home and you'll be going a hundred different directions. Piano lessons. Hockey. Work. Birthday parties. But remarkably, this family finds time to be together. Like every Sunday, for example, when they watch Disney on CBC Television. That's family time. And for these few precious years, that's not likely to change.

CBC Television

UNIQUE TELEVISION. ESSENTIAL AUDIENCE.

Chapter 5

Combining Sentences Using the Three Methods of Coordination

So far you have worked with the simple sentence. If you go back and read a group of these sentences, such as the practice sentences on page 56, you will see that writing only simple sentences results in a choppy style and also makes it difficult to express more complicated ideas. You will need to learn the three ways of combining simple sentences:

- Use a comma plus a coordinating conjunction.
- Use a semicolon, an adverbial conjunction, and a comma.
- Use only a semicolon.

In this chapter, you will practise the skill of combining sentences using **coordination.**

What is coordination?

> *Coordination* is the combining of two simple sentences (which we will now refer to as Independent Clauses) that are related and contain ideas of equal importance. The result is a compound sentence.

Note: Don't be confused by the term "independent clause." A *clause* is a group of words having a subject and a verb. An *independent clause* (IC) is a clause that could stand alone as a simple sentence. You may think of these terms in the following way:

Simple sentence = One independent clause
Compound sentence = Two independent clauses joined by coordination

First method: Use a comma plus a coordinating conjunction

> The most common way to form a compound sentence is to combine independent clauses using a comma plus a coordinating conjunction.

IC	, *coordinating conjunction*	IC
She wrote passionately	, and	her readers were totally engrossed

Since there are only seven common coordinating conjunctions and three pairs of coordinating conjunctions, a little time should be invested now in memorizing the list. By doing this, you will avoid confusion when you are using a different set of conjunctions to combine clauses.

CONNECTORS: COORDINATING CONJUNCTIONS	
and	*Used in Pairs*
but	either . . . or
or, nor	neither . . . nor
for (meaning *because*)	not only . . . but also
yet	
so	

• PRACTICE

In each of the following compound sentences, draw a single line under the subject and draw two lines under the verb for each independent clause. Then draw a circle around the coordinating conjunction and the comma. The following example has been done for you.

The <u>driver</u> <u><u>stepped</u></u> on the brake, (and) the <u>truck</u> <u><u>came</u></u> to a stop.

1. The streets were slippery, yet the trucker drove fast.

2. The night was cold and damp, and the rain froze in patches on the roads.

3. Either he had an emergency, or he was careless and irresponsible.

4. The light ahead was red, but the driver didn't slow down.

Did you find a subject and verb for both independent clauses in each sentence?

Now that you understand the structure of a compound sentence, you need to think about the meanings of the different coordinating conjunctions and how they can be used to show the relationship between two ideas, each idea being given equal importance.

MEANINGS OF COORDINATING CONJUNCTIONS	
to add an idea:	and
to add an idea when the first clause is in the negative:	nor
to contrast two opposing ideas:	but, yet
to introduce a reason:	for
to show a choice:	or
to introduce a result:	so

EXERCISE 1   **Combining Sentences Using Coordinating Conjunctions**

Each of the following examples contains two simple sentences that could be related with a coordinating conjunction. Decide what relationship the second sentence has to the first, and then select the conjunction that will make sense. Write the two simple sentences as a single sentence joined with the appropriate coordinating conjunction. An example is done for you.

> The chef was trained at the Culinary Institute.
> Everyone anticipated an impressive banquet.

Relationship of second sentence to first: result
The conjunction that introduces this meaning: so
New compound sentence:

> The chef was trained at the Culinary Institute, so everyone anticipated an impressive banquet.

1. Alicia and Greg thought about breaking up.

   They could not agree on many things.

   Relationship of second sentence to first: _____

   Conjunction that introduces this meaning: _____

   Combined sentences: _____

   _____

   _____

2. Alicia thought Greg was too possessive.

   Greg thought Alicia did not care enough.

   Relationship of second sentence to first: _____

   Conjunction that introduces this meaning: _____

   Combined sentences: _____

   _____

   _____

3. Alicia's mother wanted her to date other boys.

   Greg was completely against that idea.

   Relationship of second sentence to first: _____

   Conjunction that introduces this meaning: _____

   Combined sentences: _____

   _____

   _____

4. Alicia and Greg argued frequently.

   They both had strong personalities.

   Relationship of second sentence to first: _____

   Conjunction that introduces this meaning: _____

   Combined sentences: _____

   _____

   _____

5. Greg did not like many of Alicia's friends.

   Alicia did not care for Greg's friends.

   Relationship of second sentence to first: _____

   Conjunction that introduces this meaning: _____

   Combined sentences: _____

   _____

   _____

6. Alicia wanted to go away to college.

   Greg wanted her to stay home for college.

   Relationship of second sentence to first: _____

   Conjunction that introduces this meaning: _____

   Combined sentences: _____

   _____

   _____

7. They could try to talk with other couples.

   They could seek professional counselling.

   Relationship of second sentence to first: _____

   Conjunction that introduces this meaning: _____

   Combined sentences: _____

   _____

   _____

8. The couple did not get along well together.

   They did not really want to separate.

   Relationship of second sentence to first: _____

   Conjunction that introduces this meaning: _____

   Combined sentences: _____

   _____

   _____

9. Dating can be stressful.

    It has its rewards.

    Relationship of second sentence to first: _____

    Conjunction that introduces this meaning: _____

    Combined sentences: _____

    _____

    _____

10. Deciding to date is easy.

    Deciding to break up is more difficult.

    Relationship of second sentence to first: _____

    Conjunction that introduces this meaning: _____

    Combined sentences: _____

    _____

    _____

EXERCISE 2   Combining Sentences Using Coordinating Conjunctions

For each example, add a second independent clause using the given coordinating conjunction. Be certain that your new sentence makes sense.

1. (but)   The two detectives carefully checked the scene for fingerprints _____

    _____

2. (and)   The safe was open _____

    _____

3. (so)   There was no sign of forced entry _____

    _____

4. (nor)   The restaurant owner could not be found _____

    _____

5. (for)   Suddenly they became interested in one of the tables _____

    _____

6. (so)   The missing tablecloth could be significant _____

    _____

7. (and)   One detective looked in the closets _____

    _____

8. (or)   They might find another clue _____

    _____

9. (yet)   There were no witnesses _____

    _____

10. (or) Either they get a break in this case _____

_____

EXERCISE 3 Combining Sentences Using Coordinating Conjunctions

Compose ten of your own compound sentences using the coordinating conjunction indicated.

1. and _____

_____

2. but _____

_____

3. or _____

_____

4. for (meaning *because*) _____

_____

5. yet _____

_____

6. so _____

_____

7. nor _____

_____

8. neither/nor _____

_____

9. not only/but also _____

_____

10. either/or _____

_____

Second method: Use a semicolon, an adverbial conjunction, and a comma

A second way to form a compound sentence is to combine independent clauses by using a semicolon, an adverbial conjunction, and a comma.

IC	; *adverbial conjunction,*	IC
I had worked hard	; therefore,	I expected results.

Conjunctions in this category are called **adverbial conjunctions** (or conjunctive adverbs). These conjunctions have meanings similar to the common coordinating conjunctions, but they sound slightly more formal than the shorter conjunctions such as *and* or *but*. These connecting words give a compound sentence more emphasis.

CONNECTORS: FREQUENTLY USED ADVERBIAL CONJUNCTIONS		
Addition (and)	**Alternative (or)**	**Result (so)**
in addition	instead	accordingly
also	otherwise	consequently
besides		hence
furthermore		therefore
likewise		thus
moreover		
Contrast (but)	**Emphasis**	**To Show Time**
however	indeed	meanwhile
nevertheless	in fact	
nonetheless		

PRACTICE

In each of the following compound sentences, draw a single line under the subject and draw two lines under the verb for both independent clauses. Then circle the semicolon, adverbial conjunction, and comma. For example:

The airport <u>bus</u> <u><u>was</u></u> the most dependable way to get there; (moreover,) <u>it</u> <u><u>was</u></u> the most comfortable.

1. Jennifer was too tired during the week to meet me; consequently, I met her for lunch on Saturday.

2. I suggested roller blading; otherwise, I proposed we see a movie.

3. We didn't own roller blades; however, we could have rented them.

4. We spent at least an hour trying to decide what to do; meanwhile, the time was passing.

5. Jennifer didn't want to spend any money; therefore, we ended up taking a walk through the park just like every other Saturday afternoon.

EXERCISE 1   Combining Sentences Using Adverbial Conjunctions

Combine each pair of sentences below to make a compound sentence. Use a semicolon, an adverbial conjunction, and a comma. Be sure the conjunction you choose makes sense in the sentence. For example:

Two simple sentences: The trip was fantastic.
We decided to stay another day.

Compound sentence: The trip was fantastic; consequently, we decided to stay another day.

1. Iceland is often thought to be covered by ice.

   It is gloriously green.

   _____

   _____

2. The country is small.

   It is 31,000 square kilometres larger than New Brunswick.

   _____

   _____

3. The population numbers about a quarter million.

   It is the most sparsely populated country in Europe.

   _____

   _____

4. Miles of rich tundra cover the landscape.

   Deep lakes, bubbling hot springs, and tumbling waterfalls await the traveller.

   _____

   _____

5. Iceland has more lava than any place on earth.

   Some of it is in furious eruption.

   _____

   _____

6. Iceland is closer to Toronto than Vancouver.

   Canadians are surprisingly ignorant of the place.

   _____

   _____

7. The history of Iceland goes back 11,000 years.

   Nearly every Icelandic citizen is steeped in this history.

   _____

   _____

8. The Icelandic language has remained virtually unchanged for over 1,000 years.

   Children and adults delight in reading the ancient legends of the country with their real life heroes, trolls, and witches.

   _____

   _____

9. The whole of Iceland lies close to the Arctic Circle.

   The Gulf Stream warms its shores and softens its climate.

   _____

   _____

10. Iceland uses its underground hot springs to heat its many greenhouses.

    Icelanders can enjoy fresh tropical fruit all year long.

    _____

    _____

EXERCISE 2   Combining Sentences Using Adverbial Conjunctions

For each example, add the suggested adverbial conjunction and another independent clause that will make sense. Remember to punctuate correctly.

1. (nevertheless)   The beach goers were warned about swimming in the ocean

   _____

   _____

2. (consequently)   The student did not adequately prepare for his driving test

   _____

   _____

3. (otherwise)   He went to the only community college that accepted him

   _____

   _____

4. (indeed)   The computer was not too expensive _____

   _____

   _____

5. (moreover)   The skater broke her ankle _____

   _____

   _____

6. (in fact)   The newspaper apologized for the error _____

   _____

   _____

7. (therefore)   The heat wave continued for several days _____

   _____

   _____

8. (meanwhile)   I studied all night for the exam _____

   _____

   _____

9. (however)   The new doctor was quite nervous

_____

_____

10. (in addition)   A vacation is one way to relax and renew your spirit

_____

_____

EXERCISE 3   Combining Sentences Using Adverbial Conjunctions

Using each of the adverbial conjunctions, compose your own compound sentences.

1. (meanwhile) _____

_____

2. (instead) _____

_____

3. (besides) _____

_____

4. (nonetheless) _____

_____

5. (indeed) _____

_____

6. (in addition) _____

_____

7. (however) _____

_____

8. (accordingly) _____

_____

9. (likewise) _____

_____

10. (moreover) _____

_____

Third method: Use a semicolon

The third and less commonly used way to form a compound sentence is to combine two independent clauses by using only a semicolon.

IC	;	IC
He arrived at ten	;	he left at midnight.

Two independent clauses: Last year I read Alice Munro's *Lives of Girls and Women*.

Tonight I saw the television version of her book.

Compound sentence: Last year I read Alice Munro's *Lives of Girls and Women;* tonight I saw the television version of her book.

The semicolon was used in this example to show that the content of both sentences is closely related and therefore could be combined into one sentence.

When sentences are combined by using a semicolon, the grammatical structure of each sentence is often similar:

Leonard Cohen wrote the song; Patricia O'Callaghan sang it.

EXERCISE 1   Combining Sentences Using a Semicolon

For each of the independent clauses, add your own independent clause that has a similar grammatical structure or is a closely related idea.

1. I hope to do some travelling next year.

2. I tried contacting her.

3. The concert hall was packed with people.

4. The school bell rang.

5. Music was blaring from the street corner.

EXERCISE 2   Combining Sentences Using a Semicolon

For each of the independent clauses, add your own independent clause that has a similar grammatical structure or is a closely related idea.

1. My car needs a lot of repair.

   _____

   _____

2. The countryside was peaceful.

   _____

   _____

3. The interview went well.

   _____

   _____

4. Saturday mornings at our house are always busy.

   _____

   _____

5. It was lunchtime at the auto factory.

   _____

   _____

EXERCISE 3   Combining Sentences Using a Semicolon

For each of the independent clauses, add your own independent clause that is a related idea with a similar grammatical structure. Join the two clauses with a semicolon.

1. The beach house was spacious and airy.

   _____

   _____

2. Customers rushed to the Going Out of Business Sale.

   _____

   _____

3. I want to travel to France and Spain.

   _____

   _____

4. He thought of me.

   _____

   _____

5. Heavy metal is a popular form of music for young people.

_____

_____

Mastery and editing tests

TEST 1   **Combining Sentences Using Coordination**

Each of the following examples contains two sentences that could be combined using one of three methods of coordination. First, decide what relationship the second sentence has to the first, and then combine each pair using one of the methods studied.

1. The Guess Who was playing at the Air Canada Centre.

   My friend Eddie said he could get tickets.

   _____

   _____

2. My anticipation began to grow.

   My stereo played all their albums that day.

   _____

   _____

3. Most old rock stars lose their appeal as they age.

   Their music loses its excitement.

   _____

   _____

4. The Guess Who has been playing for thirty years.

   I didn't know what to expect.

   _____

   _____

5. We went to Toronto by train.

   We would have been stuck in traffic.

   _____

   _____

6. The concert didn't start on time.

   It began one hour late.

   _____

   _____

7. The first band was really loud.

   The Guess Who was more subdued.

   _____

   _____

8. I'd only seen them in pictures.

I was shocked at how chubby they were.

_____

_____

9. They weren't just good musicians.

Musical stories were spun before my eyes.

_____

_____

10. I didn't know if I'd enjoy their music.

I now have a new appreciation for subtlety.

_____

_____

TEST 2   Combining Sentences Using Coordination

Each of the following examples contains two sentences that could be combined using one of three methods of coordination. First, decide what relationship the second sentence has to the first, and then combine each pair using one of the methods studied.

1. The Stampeders and Lions played a football game for the Western Conference final last week.

I knew it would be an exciting game.

_____

_____

2. As champions, the winner would represent the West in the Grey Cup.

As a result, the loser would have to wait until next year to try again.

_____

_____

3. I couldn't wait for the contest to start.

All my friends planned a party for game time.

_____

_____

4. The Stampeders had a tough, gritty, and angry team.

They wore down their foes.

_____

_____

5. The Lions' offence showed balance and flair.

   They were able to move the ball and score points.

   _____

   _____

6. In a monumental clash, both teams played well.

   The momentum swung to each side like a pendulum.

   _____

   _____

7. The Lions outplayed the Stampeders.

   They couldn't put the Stampeders away.

   _____

   _____

8. The Stampeders converted only three out of ten second downs into first downs.

   They converted all four third downs that they attempted.

   _____

   _____

9. Mistakes by the Lions proved to be too costly.

   The Stampeders won by the slimmest of margins.

   _____

   _____

10. The loss ensured that the Lions wouldn't advance to the Grey Cup.

    They would have to wait until next year.

    _____

    _____

TEST 3   Combining Sentences Using Coordination

Combine each pair of sentences to make a compound sentence. Choose from the three methods you have studied in this chapter. Be sure that the conjunctions you choose clearly show the relationships between the ideas.

1. There is a hole in the ozone layer.

   The environment is in danger of global warming.

   _____

   _____

2. Plant life is being negatively affected around the world.

   An increase of a few degrees in average temperatures can have serious effects.

   _____

   _____

3. Many nations are concerned about the effects of global warming.

   They are making the scientific study of global warming a priority.

   _____

   _____

4. World farming is negatively affected by global warming.

   Nations continue to pollute the environment.

   _____

   _____

5. A continual change in temperature patterns can affect our seasons.

   We may no longer have four distinct seasons.

   _____

   _____

6. Canadians are used to reasonably priced fresh produce.

   They cannot imagine paying high prices for imported foods on a daily basis.

   _____

   _____

7. Wetlands contain a wide variety of plant and animal life.

   Their disappearance could seriously upset the ecological balance of nature.

   _____

   _____

8. A hole in the ozone layer allows dangerous ultraviolet rays to penetrate our atmosphere.

   People still flock to the beaches in search of the perfect suntan.

   _____

   _____

9. Changes in world temperatures will change the ways we live.

   We continue to pollute our environment and do further damage.

   _____

   _____

10. We all live on this planet called Earth.

    We all have a responsibility to protect it.

    _____

    _____

TEST 4   Combining Sentences Using Coordination

The following paragraph needs punctuation. Sentences have been joined together using coordination, but the punctuation has been omitted.

Susan was asked to create an advertisement for the violin concert so she designed a flyer. She figured she needed 100 copies to post around town therefore she went to the print shop. Susan presented the flyer to the man behind the counter he determined it was suitable for reproduction. It could be reproduced on a copier or it could be reproduced on a printing press. The printing press would generate higher quality the copier however would be quicker. Both time and quality were factors thus she had a decision to make. Susan decided to let cost be the determining factor so she inquired about the difference in price. Copies were five cents each yet the cost of using the press wasn't fixed. As more copies were made, the cost per copy decreased therefore at some point using the press would become more cost effective. The cost effective point, she was told, was 150 so Susan chose to use the copier.

TEST 5   Combining Sentences Using Coordination

The following paragraph needs punctuation. Sentences have been joined together using coordination, but the punctuation has been omitted.

Two hours after dinner, Jeanne and John were still hungry so they asked Dad for a pizza. Dad had had a long day furthermore no pizza shops were delivering at that late hour. His first answer was no however the persistence of a six-year-old and nine-year-old can be very persuasive. Reluctantly, Dad agreed to make the trip besides he was getting hungry himself. The car had trouble starting meanwhile Dad was beginning to have an increasing sense of doom about the trip. The children were hyperactive in the car moreover they expected Dad to determine who was responsible for their backseat fight. At the pizza shop, their bickering continued accordingly on their way home they fought over who could hold the pizza. Dad advised them to take turns. John held the pizza for awhile but the heat on his bare legs became too much for him. Suddenly he yanked the pizza box off his scorched lap. The pizza flew out of the box and landed cheese down on top of Jeanne nonetheless their anticipation of pizza proved greater than their dismay. At home both children enjoyed eating the now cheeseless pizza.

Working Together

Both reporters on a newspaper and the secretaries who record the minutes of meetings must give accurate summaries of information. They must also be careful not to include misleading or irrelevant information. Also, there must be every attempt to be fair, and all personal prejudices must be avoided. Good reporters always recognize the difference between their own ideas and the ideas of others.

For this Working Together activity, you will write a report on a presentation and its follow-up discussion in your classroom. To begin this activity, the instructor or a member of the class will make an informal five-minute presentation on an important issue on your campus. Take notes and record some of the statements, taking down a few direct quotations. After the presentation, class members may ask questions and present any information or personal opinions that they have on this issue. (One person should be asked to listen carefully and warn the class if the discussion is getting off the track.) Keep the discussion period to no longer than fifteen minutes.

Following the discussion, each student should write at least ten sentences to summarize the main ideas from the presentation and discussion. This report tests your ability to hear what other people are saying. Do not include your own comments or thoughts on the subject.

Your instructor may read several reports out loud to see if there is general agreement on what were the main ideas from the presentation and discussion. What accounts for the differences in what people report as the main ideas?

In order to practise sentence skills learned in this chapter, each student should find one sentence of coordination in his or her report and put this sentence on the board for the class to edit. This will provide an opportunity for the class to review sentences of coordination.

As part of the editing process, ask the following questions:

1. In each case, has the writer combined two independent clauses?

2. In each sentence, does the coordinating conjunction carry the correct meaning for the sentence?

3. In each sentence, is the punctuation correct?

Chapter 6

Combining Sentences Using Subordination

In the last chapter, when you used coordination to combine sentences, the idea in each clause of the new compound sentence carried equal weight. However, a writer often wants to combine ideas that are not equally important. This chapter will focus on *subordination*. Here you will combine clauses that are not equally important. One idea will be dependent on the other.

Recognizing independent and dependent clauses.

Using subordinating conjunctions.

Using relative pronouns.

What is subordination?

> *Subordination* is the combining of two clauses containing ideas that are not equally important. The more important idea is called the *independent clause* and the less important idea is called the *dependent clause*. The result is a *complex sentence.*

In coordination, you used certain connecting words called coordinating conjunctions or adverbial conjunctions to combine ideas. In subordination, you use two different sets of connecting words: *subordinating conjunctions* or *relative pronouns*.

What is the difference between an independent and dependent clause?

An independent clause stands alone as a complete thought; it could be a simple sentence.

Independent clause: We ordered lunch.

A dependent clause begins with a connecting word, and although the thought has a subject and a verb, it does not stand alone as a complete thought. The idea needs to be completed.

Dependent clause: when we ordered lunch. . . .

Before you write your own complex sentences, practise the following exercises to be sure you understand the difference between an independent clause and a dependent clause.

EXERCISE 1   Recognizing Dependent and Independent Clauses

In the blank to the left of each group of words, write the letters IC if the group is an independent clause (a complete thought) or DC if the group of words is a dependent clause (not a complete thought even though it contains a subject and a verb):

_____ 1. when they arrived at the restaurant

_____ 2. there were no tables available

_____ 3. even though we lived near each other

_____ 4. we rarely saw or talked to one another

_____ 5. I was delighted by her call

_____ 6. unless you intend to spend the night

_____ 7. after the baby arrived

_____ 8. our lives changed dramatically

_____ 9. whether you like it or not

_____ 10. you must follow the doctor's orders

EXERCISE 2   Recognizing Dependent and Independent Clauses

In the blank to the left of each group of words, write the letters IC if the group is an independent clause (a complete thought) or DC if the group of words is a dependent clause (not a complete thought even though it contains a subject and a verb):

_____ 1. although university is different from high school

_____ 2. you are required to study and take exams

_____ 3. because he had no fear of the computer

_____ 4. he learned to use a computer in no time at all

_____ 5. she lived at home with her parents

_____ 6. until she entered university

_____ 7. she graduated with honours

_____ 8. because she studied hard

_____ 9. he stared at the movie screen

_____ 10. as if he were glued to the seat

EXERCISE 3   Recognizing Dependent and Independent Clauses

In the blank to the left of each group of words, write the letters IC if the group is an independent clause (a complete thought) or DC if the group of words is a dependent clause (not a complete thought, even though it contains a subject and a verb):

_____ 1. Mike Myers is an amazing actor

_____ 2. since he was born in Toronto

_____ 3. though he became popular playing in comedies

_____ 4. he is also a devoted hockey fan

_____ 5. after he portrayed the leading role in the movie *Wayne's World*

_____ 6. stardom was assured

_____ 7. where the film *Austin Powers* was playing

_____ 8. when he starred as Dr. Evil

_____ 9. he played ice hockey in high school

_____ 10. even though he has yet to win a major award

Using subordinating conjunctions

Following is a list of subordinating conjunctions. The use of one of these connecting words signals the beginning of a dependent clause. It is a good idea to memorize them just as you did the coordinating conjunctions. Remember these different groups of connecting words have different principles for punctuation, so you really need to memorize them in these groups.

CONNECTORS: COMMON SUBORDINATING CONJUNCTIONS		
after	if, even if	unless
although	in order that	until
as, as if	provided that	when, whenever
as long as, as though	rather than	where, wherever
because	since	whether
before	so that	while
even though	though	

The subordinating conjunctions are grouped by their meanings in the following chart. When you use these conjunctions, you need to be absolutely sure that the connection one of these conjunctions makes between the independent and dependent clause is the meaning you intend.

FUNCTION OF SUBORDINATING CONJUNCTIONS

To introduce a *condition:*   if, even if, as long as,

provided that,

unless (after a negative independent clause)

I will go *as long as* you go with me.
I won't go *unless* you go with me.

To introduce a *contrast:*   although, even though, though

I will go *even though* you won't go with me.

To show *cause:*   because, since

I will go *because* the meeting is very important.

To show *time:*   after, before, when, whenever,

while, until (independent clause is negative)

I will go *whenever* you say.
I won't go *until* you say it is time.

To show *place:*   where, wherever

I will go *wherever* you send me.

To show *purpose:*   in order that, so that

I will go *so that* I can hear the candidate for myself.

You have two choices of how to write a complex sentence. You can begin with the independent clause, or you can begin with the dependent clause.

First way:	*IC*	*DC*
Example:	We can finish our homework	if Barbara leaves.

Second way:	*DC*	,	*IC*
Example:	If Barbara leaves	,	we can finish our homework.

Notice that only the second version uses a comma; this is because the second version begins with the dependent clause. When a sentence begins with the independent clause, no comma is used. Your ear may help you with this punctuation. Read a sentence that begins with a dependent clause. Do you notice that there is a tendency to pause at the end of that dependent clause? This is a natural place to put a comma.

EXERCISE 1   **Using Subordinating Conjunctions**

Use a subordinating conjunction to combine each of the following pairs of sentences. Remember, the independent clause will be the more important of the two ideas in the sentence.

1. Use the subordinating conjunction *after*.

    Monica left the game.

    She watched the halftime show.

    a. Begin with the independent clause:

    _____

    b. Begin with the dependent clause:

    _____

2. Use the subordinating conjunction *when*.

    My husband returned to university this fall.

    I was very pleased.

    a. Begin with the independent clause:

    _____

    b. Begin with the dependent clause:

    _____

EXERCISE 2   **Using Subordinating Conjunctions**

Use each of the following subordinating conjunctions to compose a complex sentence. An example has been done for you.

Subordinating conjunction: after

Complex sentence: *After* the experiment was completed, the lab assistants had a coffee break.

Note: *After* could also be used as a preposition.

After the experiment, the lab assistants had a coffee break.

Keep in mind that a complex sentence has one independent clause and at least one dependent clause. Every clause must have a subject and a verb. Check your sentences by underlining the subject and verb in each clause.

1. until

    _____

    _____

2. since

    _____

    _____

3. even if

_____

_____

4. because (Begin with the independent clause. Traditional English grammar teaches that a sentence should not begin with *because*. However, since you will see many sentences in print that do begin with *because*, ask your instructor for his or her opinion.)

_____

_____

5. as though

_____

_____

EXERCISE 3   Using Subordinating Conjunctions

Use each of the following subordinating conjunctions to compose a complex sentence:

1. although _____

_____

2. while _____

_____

3. unless _____

_____

4. whenever _____

_____

5. whether _____

_____

EXERCISE 1   Combining Sentences Using Subordination

Combine each pair of sentences using subordination. Look back at the list of subordinating conjunctions if you need to. An example has been done for you.

two sentences:

I'll wait for you.

You'll be ready by eight.

combined by subordination:

I'll wait for you if you'll be ready by eight.

1. She decided to move.

   The traffic became too noisy.

   _____

   _____

2. I fixed dinner.

   Andrea did her homework.

   _____

   _____

3. You do your chores.

   I'll give you your allowance.

   _____

   _____

4. I felt sleepy.

   I decided to watch the late movie anyway.

   _____

   _____

5. You should not eat ice cream.

   You wish to gain weight.

   _____

   _____

EXERCISE 2   Combining Sentences Using Subordination

Combine each pair of sentences using subordination. Look back at the list of subordinating conjunctions if you need to.

1. He was eating breakfast.

   The results of the election came over the radio.

   _____

   _____

2. The town council voted against the plan.

   They believed the project was too expensive.

   _____

   _____

3. I will see Margaret Atwood tonight.

   She is speaking at the university.

   _____

   _____

4. The worker hoped for a promotion.

   Not one person in the department had received a promotion last year.

   _____

   _____

5. The worker hoped for a promotion.

   He made sure all his work was done accurately and on time.

   _____

   _____

EXERCISE 3   Combining Sentences Using Subordination

Here are five pairs of sentences. Combine each pair by using a subordinating conjunction. Write the sentence two different ways. First, begin the sentence with the dependent clause and use a comma. Second, begin the sentence with the independent clause and do not use any comma.

1. (Use *since*)   The computer was on sale.

   The businessperson decided to purchase it.

   a. _____

   _____

   b. _____

   _____

2. (Use *after*)   The play ended at 10 p.m.

   The couple went out for dessert.

   a. _____

   _____

   b. _____

   _____

3. (Use *when*)   The new school term begins in September.

   You can expect larger class sizes.

   a. _____

   _____

   b. _____

   _____

4. (Use *while*)   He recovered from a broken leg.

   He read more than twenty novels.

   a. _____

   _____

   b. _____

   _____

5. (Use *before*)   The family decided on a ski vacation.

They considered several alternatives.

a. _____

_____

b. _____

_____

Using a relative pronoun to create a complex sentence

Often sentences can be combined with a relative pronoun.

COMMON RELATIVE PRONOUNS	
who	
whose	refers to people
whom	
which	refers to things
that	refers to people and/or things

Two simple sentences:	The engineer solved a problem. She was designing a complicated machine.
Combined sentences **(using a relative clause):**	The engineer, *who was designing a complicated* *machine*, solved a problem.
A third idea added **(using a relative clause):**	The engineer, who was designing a complicated machine, solved a problem *that had been delaying* *production*.

> *Remember:* A clause beginning with a relative pronoun must be placed directly after the word it relates to.

How do you punctuate a clause with a relative pronoun?

Punctuating relative clauses can be tricky because there are two types of relative clauses:

1. Those relative clauses that are basic to the meaning of the sentence:

Never eat meat *that isn't cooked thoroughly.*

The basic meaning of the sentence is not *never eat meat.* The relative clause is necessary to restrict the meaning. This clause is called a ***restrictive clause*** and does not use commas to set off the clause. *Note:* The pronoun *that* is usual in such a case.

2. Those relative clauses that are not basic to the meaning of the sentence:

> Mother's meat loaf, which consisted of beef, veal, and pork, was delicious.

In this sentence, the relative clause is not basic to the main idea. In fact, if the clause were omitted, the main idea would not be changed. This clause is called a *nonrestrictive clause*. Commas are required to indicate the information is nonessential. *Note:* The pronoun *which* is usual in such a case.

• PRACTICE   Identifying Essential and Nonessential Clauses

Choose whether or not to insert commas in the following sentences. Use the following examples as your models.

> The woman who is standing beside my brother is my mother-in-law.

In this sentence, the woman can only be identified by the clause *who is standing beside my brother*. Therefore, the relative clause *who is standing beside my brother* is essential to the meaning. No commas are necessary.

> Alice, who is my mother-in-law, can fix a flat tire in record time.

The main idea in this sentence is that Alice can fix a flat tire. The relative clause *who is my mother-in-law* is not essential to the meaning. Therefore, commas are needed to set off this nonessential information.

1. My cousin's Bar Mitzvah reception which was held at a lake resort lasted late into the night.

2. The band that my uncle hired for the night played a variety of music.

3. Everyone who came to the event danced until dawn.

4. Even the folks who didn't like rock music enjoyed themselves on the dance floor.

5. The caterer whose food was delicious joined in the train of dancers parading around the room.

• PRACTICE   Combining Sentences Using a Relative Pronoun

Examine the following five pairs of sentences. Combine each pair of sentences into one complex sentence by using a relative pronoun. An example has been done for you.

    Two simple sentences: The woman is my daughter's kindergarten teacher.
                                           She is wearing the green blouse.

    Combined by subordination: The woman who is wearing the green blouse is my daughter's kindergarten teacher.

1. The shoes are very expensive.

   I bought the shoes last week.

   Combined: (use *that*) _____

   _____

2. The exercise equipment at the local YWCA is very effective.

   I use it every day.

   Combined: (use *that*) _____

   _____

3. The librarian is busy at the moment.

   He is sitting at the reference table.

   Combined: _____

   _____

4. Here is the new atlas.

   I told you about it.

   Combined: _____

   _____

5. Mrs. Faigle is your adviser.

   She is the older woman on the stage.

   Combined: _____

   _____

Now you are ready to practise joining your own sentences with relative pronouns, being sure to punctuate carefully. The following exercises ask you to insert a variety of relative clauses into simple sentences.

EXERCISE 1   Combining Sentences Using Relative Pronouns

Add a relative clause to each of the following ten sentences. Use each of the possibilities at least once: *who, whose, whom, which, that.* An example has been done for you.

    Simple sentence: The report has three sections.
    Complex sentence: The report, which is due next week, has three sections.

1. The computer specialist _____
   asked her colleagues for assistance.

2. Her coworkers _____
   agreed to meet with her.

3. The problem _____
   concerned developing the right program for their needs.

4. The team _____
   got right down to work.

5. The plans _____
   were very complicated.

6. The meeting _____
   lasted until closing time.

7. Each comment _____
   was taken seriously.

8. The solutions _____
   slowly began to emerge.

9. Everyone _____
   was surprised how well the meeting went.

10. Finally the group _____
    finalized their decisions and left work feeling satisfied.

EXERCISE 2   Combining Sentences Using Relative Pronouns

Add a relative clause to each of the following ten sentences. Use each of the possibilities at least once: *who, whose, whom, which, that.* Be sure to punctuate correctly.

1. The senior executive _____
   asked his office managers for input.

2. The office managers _____
   agreed to a weekend meeting.

3. The future of the company _____
   was in jeopardy.

4. Many of the stockholders _____
   were visibly upset.

5. The reorganization plan _____
   was both reasonable and impressive.

6. The emergency meeting _____
   lasted well into the night.

7. Every proposal _____
   was given serious attention.

8. Charts _____
   showed the major areas of weakness.

9. Two office managers _____
   were vocally opposed to the reorganization.

10. The senior executive and the office managers agreed on a plan _____
    _____

EXERCISE 3   Combining Sentences Using Relative Pronouns

Combine the following pairs of sentences using a relative pronoun.

1. Chris Hadfield was the first Canadian to go on a space walk.

   He was born in Sarnia, Ontario.

   _____

   _____

2. Hadfield's mission was to install the Canadarm2 on the International Space Station.

   The Canadarm2 was designed by Canadian engineers.

   _____

   _____

3. The Canadarm2 is a robot claw installed on the space station to help in its construction.

   The Canadarm2 weighs 1.5 tonnes and spans over 17 metres.

   _____

   _____

4. Getting the Canadarm2 installed and working was critical to the construction schedule.

   Construction is expected to continue until 2006.

   _____

   _____

5. The crew had to test the effectiveness of the Canadarm2.

   The crew was made up of people from four different countries.

   _____

   _____

6. Hadfield commanded the original Canadarm.

   The original Canadarm is attached to the space shuttle.

   _____

   _____

7. Canadarm2 lifted a pallet over the cargo bay of the space shuttle.

   The Canadarm2 was commanded from inside the space station.

   _____

   _____

8. Hadfield then manoeuvred the shuttle's arm to reach over and grasp the pallet.

   Hadfield is an experienced pilot and skilled technician.

   _____

   _____

9. This "handshake" was the highlight of the mission.

   The "handshake" took place between the two robot Canadarms.

   _____

   _____

10. The space shuttle crew returned to earth safely.

    The crew was made up of many talented people.

    _____

    _____

Mastery and editing tests

TEST 1   **Combining Sentences Using a Subordinating Conjunction
              or a Relative Pronoun**

Combine each of the following pairs of sentences using either a subordinating conjunction or a relative pronoun.

1. The elderly woman lives alone with three cats.

   They sleep on the floor beside her bed.

   _____

   _____

2. The crowd was asked to move back.

   The paramedics needed more space.

   _____

   _____

3. The dancer walked across the room in tap shoes.

   They made a distinct clicking sound.

   _____

   _____

4. My sister is extremely generous with her time.

   Her name is Eileen.

   _____

   _____

5. His talent was evident.

   His costume was tattered and dirty.

   _____

   _____

6. The bank manager would not smile.

   He realized our common interests.

   _____

   _____

7. I begin a new job tomorrow.

   I stayed awake reading a novel.

   _____

   _____

8. The baseball player tripped and sprained his ankle.

   He was trying to catch a fly ball.

   _____

   _____

9. Immediately, his face screwed up with pain.

   His face generally showed no emotion at all.

   _____

   _____

10. I was reading a book.

    The cat jumped into my lap.

    _____

    _____

TEST 2 — Combining Sentences Using a Subordinating Conjunction or a Relative Pronoun

Combine each of the following pairs of sentences using either a subordinating conjunction or a relative pronoun.

1. Ahmed chose to play the saxophone.

   He likes jazz music the best.

   _____

   _____

2. The sun finally emerged from behind the clouds.

   All the puddles dried up.

   _____

   _____

3. The monks sat down to lunch.

   They dined in silence.

   _____

   _____

4. The books were arranged in alphabetical order.

   They were put on the shelf.

   _____

   _____

5. The computer is brand new.

   Something is wrong with the disk drive.

   _____

   _____

6. The tea is brewing.

   I will make a sandwich.

   _____

   _____

7. I can't go with you to the gym tonight.

   I have a math test.

   _____

   _____

8. Daniel Lanois is a famous Canadian producer.

   He has produced CDs for U2.

   _____

   _____

9. The clock read twelve o'clock.

   The cuckoo popped out.

   _____

   _____

10. The children's clothes are dirty.

    Yesterday they played soccer.

    _____

    _____

TEST 3   Combining Sentences Using a Subordinating Conjunction or a Relative Pronoun

Combine each of the following pairs of sentences using either a subordinating conjunction or a relative pronoun.

1. Our best friend lives far away.

   His name is Muneer.

   _____

   _____

2. We don't see each other very often.

   We write many letters.

   _____

   _____

3. He likes to collect stamps.

   They are very colourful.

   _____

   _____

4. Betty came to visit us.

   She lives in Halifax.

   _____

   _____

5. Her parents usually arrive on time.

   Today they were late.

   _____

   _____

6. You cannot go out.

   You must clean your room.

   _____

   _____

7. Marco is studying weaving.

   Not many people study weaving.

   _____

   _____

8. Fall is my favourite season.

   I would like to travel in the fall.

   _____

   _____

9. Ballet demands great discipline.

   Ballet is very beautiful to watch.

   _____

   _____

10. Ballerinas are very graceful.

    They practise for many hours every day.

    _____

    _____

TEST 4   Combining Sentences Using a Subordinating Conjunction or a Relative Pronoun

Combine each of the following pairs of sentences using either a subordinating conjunction or a relative pronoun.

1. The CN Tower has an observation deck.

   The observation deck is closed for repair.

   _____

   _____

2. The ferryboat is making a comeback.

   The ferryboat has not been popular for a long time.

   _____

   _____

3. Earth is the third planet from the sun.

   Earth lies between Venus and Mars.

   _____

   _____

4. My favourite shirt has a rip in the sleeve.

   My girlfriend made it for me.

   _____

   _____

5. I wanted an invitation to the poetry reading.

   The poet was one of my favourites.

   _____

   _____

6. I bought a cup of coffee.

   The coffee smelled better than it tasted.

   _____

   _____

7. Banff National Park contains pristine wilderness.

   Parts of Banff are experiencing urban problems.

   _____

   _____

8. I share an apartment with my sister.

   I have my own room.

   _____

   _____

9. The airline lost my suitcase.

   I flew to Nunavut to visit my sister.

   _____

   _____

10. Wheat is grown in Saskatchewan.

Tobacco is grown in Ontario.

_____

_____

TEST 5   Combining Sentences Using Coordination and Subordination

Below is a paragraph composed of mostly simple sentences. Rewrite the paragraph combining sentences wherever you think the combining would improve the meaning or style. Don't be afraid to change the wording slightly to accommodate the changes you want to make. Combine clauses using coordination and subordination.

Al Waxman was one of Canada's most talented actors. He was born in Toronto to Jewish immigrants. His parents owned and operated a small restaurant. They worked hard. They wanted their son to become a doctor or lawyer. Al knew what he wanted to do with his life. He fell in love with acting when he saw the film *The Al Jolson Story*. By the time he turned 17 he was performing live radio drama on the CBC. Al knew that he needed formal training as an actor. He went to New York City. He went to London, England, in 1961. It was in London that Al landed his first role in a movie. He is best known for his role in the Canadian sitcom *The King of Kensington*. That series ended after many years. He had a major part in another hit TV series, *Cagney and Lacey*. Waxman worked hard to perfect his talent. His hard work paid off. He received numerous acting awards and nominations. He was made a member of the Order of Canada in 1997. He was preparing to star in a play at the Stratford Festival. He died in January 2001. Al Waxman's life was a success in more ways than one. He led the way for generations of young Canadian actors to find their places on the international stage.

_____

_____

_____

_____

_____

_____

_____

_____

_____

_____

_____

_____

_____

_____

_____

_____

_____

_____

_____

_____

_____

_____

_____

_____

_____

_____

_____

Working Together

1. A good news report should answer the questions of who, what, when, where, why, and how:

   Who was involved in the event?

   What exactly happened?

   When did the event take place?

   Where did the event take place?

   Why did the event take place?

   How did the event take place?

   The newspaper account at right reports what happened to one Toronto woman who was arrested for allegedly disturbing the shooting of a feature film. Use a highlighter to mark the part of the account that answers each of the above questions and write the question answered—who, what, when, where, why, or how—in the margin. Is any part missing? Write a complete sentence to answer each of the questions. Your sentences will make a good summary of the news event.

   When _____

   Where _____

   _____

   Who _____

   _____

   What _____

   _____

   _____

   How _____

   _____

   Why _____

   _____

   What additional information would you like to have known?

   _____

   _____

   _____

   _____

   _____

When She Whistled While They Worked

TORONTO, Apr. 20 (CP)—The life of Mary Fish, 52-year-old den mother to 20 children, grandchildren and foster kids, would make a great movie.

Just don't ask to shoot it in her neighbourhood.

The amiable artist ... says her health and peace of mind have been shattered by an incident last fall involving a "rude and belligerent" movie crew and some overzealous police officers they hired to keep order around the set.

"I bet my family crosses that intersection a hundred times a day," Ms. Fish says, pointing to the street corner flanked by vegetable stands and cafés [in Toronto's Kensington Market] where she was wrestled into a police car, handcuffed and forced to sit scrunched up in the back seat for 45 minutes last Oct. 16. The offence the severely arthritic woman allegedly committed was to disturb the shooting of feature film *Claire's Hat* by whistling as she strolled down the street.

When the director shouted "Silence!" she didn't notice him pointing at her, and moments later was apprehended by two police officers....

Although she begged the officers to loosen the handcuffs and let her straighten her body because of the pain she was in due to her osteoarthritis, she was handled roughly and her pleas were ignored, she said. She was held in the cruiser until on-duty officers could come and bring her to a police station, where she was strip-searched, held overnight and charged with causing a disturbance....

Yesterday, she went to Old City Hall for her sixth mandatory court appearance on the charges.

"I have to go to court every month for whistling," she said softly, a bemused smile spreading across her placid face. "I could end up with a criminal record."

During her first court appearances she had to wait for hours in the chaotic, hard-benched courtroom where accused offenders have to show up regularly to receive their next court dates.

Now she has legal aid and a lawyer who helps speed her through the system. Ms. Fish also has a civil lawyer who filed a $500,000 lawsuit against the movie company, the police officers and the Toronto Police Services Board....

"[Mayor] Mel Lastman and city council are promoting Toronto as Hollywood North. You can't go for a drive anywhere in Toronto without seeing the pylons and the movie trucks," [Barry Swadron, the lawyer handling the civil suit] said. "It is a real question of what rights the movie companies acquire when they get a permit from the city."

It is clear filmmakers can purchase the right to park where others are not allowed, but not that they can prevent people talking loudly or whistling as they walk down the street, he said.

"When a movie company somehow assumes a role as boss of the police, there's bound to be friction. The rules have to be publicized so people understand them and don't wind up on the wrong side of the law."

—*The Globe and Mail*, April 20, 2001

The information on page 117 answers the objective facts of the event. The job of a journalist is to report these facts. Everyone also has opinions about events. Write a few sentences about your opinion on this issue. Did this reporter let his or her opinions show? Where in a newspaper do you read people's opinions about news events?

_____

_____

_____

_____

_____

_____

_____

_____

_____

_____

_____

2. Write your own account of a news event that has occurred within the last month. As you write your account (with at least ten sentences), be sure to answer all the traditional questions given on the previous page. Exchange your paper with another student. In the paper you read, place a check next to each sentence that is an example of subordination. Has the sentence been punctuated correctly?

Chapter 7

Correcting the Run-On

In conversation, when we relate an event that involves a series of connected actions, we may string together our thoughts as if they were all one long thought. This does not mean the written form should be one long sentence! When you put this same spoken narrative into written form, there are many ways for separating the parts or combining the parts into acceptable sentences. Writing ideas down into acceptable sentences calls for careful understanding of the clause and how clauses are punctuated when they are combined. This chapter is about learning how to recognize and avoid run-on sentences in your own writing.

The following is a narrative that was first spoken. When the writer tried to put it into written form, it ended up as one long string of events in a run-on sentence. How could the writer have divided the parts into sentences, or how could the clauses have been combined correctly?

> We started on our road trip from Calgary to Edmonton by then we found ourselves completely lost on a little road so we decided to see where it led to and after a few hours of breathtaking scenery we found ourselves in the town of Drumheller, Alberta, it was an old coal mining town and the area around it contains some of the largest finds of dinosaur fossils in the world a lot of which are on display in the Royal Tyrrell Museum located there and we would never have found it if we hadn't gotten lost.

What is a run-on?

> *Run-on sentences* are independent clauses that have been combined incorrectly.
>
> *Remember: Independent clauses cannot be combined without some kind of punctuation.*

How many kinds of run-ons are there?

Some writers have run-on sentences because they are not sure when their ideas are complete, or they are not sure how to connect those ideas. Certain punctuation must signal the spot where two clauses join, or end punctuation must signal the end of a thought. Generally, writers make one of the three following mistakes:

1. *The fused run-on:* Two or more independent clauses that run together without any punctuation

   Incorrect: We brought the lunch they brought the music.

2. *The comma splice:* Two or more independent clauses that run together with only a comma

Incorrect: We brought the lunch, they brought the music.

3. *The "and" run-on:* Two or more independent clauses that are connected with a coordinating conjunction, but there is no punctuation

Incorrect: We brought the lunch and they brought the music.

How do you make a complete sentence from a run-on?

1. Make two sentences with end punctuation.

Correct: We brought the lunch. They brought the music.

2. Make a compound sentence using one of the three methods of coordination.

Correct: We brought the lunch, and they brought the music.
We brought the lunch; moreover, they brought the music.
We brought the lunch; they brought the music.

3. Make a complex sentence using subordination.

Correct: Since we brought the lunch, they brought the music.
They brought the music since we brought the lunch.

EXERCISE 1   Recognizing and Editing Run-Ons

The following story is written as one sentence. Rewrite the story, making sure to correct the run-on sentences. Put a period at the end of each complete thought. You may have to omit some of the words that loosely connect the ideas, or you may want to use coordination and subordination. Remember to make each new sentence begin with a capital letter.

We started on our road trip from Calgary to Edmonton by then we found ourselves completely lost on a little road so we decided to see where it led to and after a few hours of breathtaking scenery we found ourselves in the town of Drumheller, Alberta, it was an old coal mining town and the area around it contains some of the largest finds of dinosaur fossils in the world a lot of which are on display in the Royal Tyrrell Museum located there and we would never have found it if we hadn't gotten lost.

_____

_____

_____

_____

_____

_____

_____

_____

_____

_____

_____

_____

_____

EXERCISE 2   Recognizing and Editing Run-Ons

The following story is written as one sentence. Rewrite the story, making sure to correct the run-on sentences. Put a period at the end of each complete thought. You may have to omit some of the words that loosely connect the ideas, or you may want to use coordination and subordination. Remember to make each new sentence begin with a capital letter.

The mail came and it contained a pile of bills, catalogues, and an ominous envelope with the logo of my insurance company, what now I wondered, they must be sending me another rejection letter and sure enough when I opened it they had returned the cheque I gave them for last month with a form letter stating they had "no record of contract" but every month the same thing happens I write to them, I take off a day's work and go down to the central office to tell them of my problem, I call them on the phone and whomever I speak to they say they will look into it but meanwhile if something happens to me I wonder if I will have auto insurance, maybe I'll have a stroke over this bureaucratic nightmare.

EXERCISE 3   Recognizing and Editing Run-Ons

The following story is written as one sentence. Rewrite the story, making sure to correct the run-on sentences. Put a period at the end of each complete thought. You may have to omit some of the words that loosely connect the ideas, or you may want to use coordination and subordination. Remember to make each new sentence begin with a capital letter.

> Today, I have so many things to do and I don't have enough time for all of them I have to buy groceries for dinner tonight and I have to return books to the library and then I have to pick up the children from separate day camps and when I finish that I have to meet my husband at the train station because his car is not working and to top it off after dinner tonight I must help my youngest with a camp project.

_____

_____

_____

_____

_____

_____

_____

_____

_____

_____

_____

EXERCISE 1   Revising Run-Ons

Each of the following examples is a run-on sentence. Supply four possible ways to revise each run-on. Use the guide on page 120 if you need help.

1. I read Margaret Atwood's *Alias Grace* again it's one of my favourite books.

   Two simple sentences:

   _____

   _____

   _____

   Two kinds of compound sentences:

   a. _____

   _____

   b. _____

   _____

Complex sentence:

_____

_____

_____

2. She has written over a dozen books, most of her novels deal with the lives of women.

   Two simple sentences:

   _____

   _____

   _____

   Two kinds of compound sentences:

   a. _____

   _____

   b. _____

   _____

   Complex sentence:

   _____

   _____

   _____

3. Margaret Atwood has written books on many topics, she has won numerous awards for her writing.

   Two simple sentences:

   _____

   _____

   _____

   Two kinds of compound sentences:

   a. _____

   _____

   b. _____

   _____

   Complex sentence:

   _____

   _____

   _____

EXERCISE 2   Revising Run-Ons

Each of the following examples is a run-on sentence. Supply four possible ways to revise each run-on. Use the guide on page 120 if you need help.

1. Pier 21 in Halifax, Nova Scotia, was recently renovated it was restored as a museum.

   Two simple sentences:

   _____

   _____

   _____

   Two kinds of compound sentences:

   a. _____

   _____

   b. _____

   _____

   Complex sentence:

   _____

   _____

   _____

2. The new museum at Pier 21 is wonderful it brings to life the experiences of so many past immigrants to Canada.

   Two simple sentences:

   _____

   _____

   _____

   Two kinds of compound sentences:

   a. _____

   _____

   b. _____

   _____

   Complex sentence:

   _____

   _____

   _____

3. For many, Pier 21 was the gateway to a new life in Canada many who landed there went on to make a positive impact in their new country.

Two simple sentences:

_____

_____

_____

Two kinds of compound sentences:

a. _____

_____

b. _____

_____

Complex sentence:

_____

_____

_____

EXERCISE 3   Revising Run-Ons

Each of the following examples is a run-on sentence. Supply four possible ways to revise each run-on. Use the guide on page 120 if you need help.

1. Examinations are one way to measure knowledge they are not always the best method.

Two simple sentences:

_____

_____

_____

Two kinds of compound sentences:

a. _____

_____

b. _____

_____

Complex sentence:

_____

_____

_____

2. Alcohol and tobacco are dangerous to health they should be avoided.

   Two simple sentences:

   _____

   _____

   _____

   Two kinds of compound sentences:

   a. _____

   _____

   b. _____

   _____

   Complex sentence:

   _____

   _____

   _____

3. Reading broadens your mind you should read every day.

   Two simple sentences:

   _____

   _____

   _____

   Two kinds of compound sentences:

   a. _____

   _____

   b. _____

   _____

   Complex sentence:

   _____

   _____

   _____

Mastery and editing tests

TEST 1   Editing for Run-Ons

Edit the following paragraph, correcting all three kinds of run-on sentences.

The human body was not designed to go through the day without a brief period of rest. Many siesta cultures, which honour the body's need for rest, exist throughout the world and businesses shut down in the early afternoon while workers take time to relax or nap. Canada, however, is not so sleep-friendly and workers are encouraged to drink coffee or eat candy in order to stay awake and be productive although naps are not normally acceptable in the workplace, they are much more effective and healthy than the previous methods and employers should recognize the value of such naps. Short naps, known as powernaps, need not take away hours of the workday and powernaps as short as 5 or 10 minutes can leave a person refreshed and energized and ready to concentrate on work. In light of recent research, employers should not feel disdain for napping but should consider it a valuable way to ensure a safe workplace. Martin Moore, author of the *Twenty-four Hour Society,* warns that the worldwide financial cost of accidents caused by human fatigue is $80 billion per year most of us remember the *Exxon Valdez* oil spill caused not only by an inebriated captain, but by sleepy navigators with this in mind, we should all honour our natural needs for sleep and forgo the afternoon coffee or candy break for a refreshing powernap.

TEST 2 — Editing for Run-Ons

Edit the following paragraph, correcting all three kinds of run-on sentences.

Most people today find it difficult to believe at the beginning of the twentieth century women in Canada were not considered to be persons under the Constitution. The Famous Five changed this they were all strong believers in the rights of women and they demanded that the Government of Canada declare women to be "persons" under the Constitution. Emily Murphy, Louise McKinney, Nellie McClung, Henrietta Muir Edwards, and Irene Parlby all lived in Alberta in the 1920s and at the time only men were allowed to participate in public office and affairs of state the Constitution stated that women were not persons. In 1928, the five women petitioned the Supreme Court of Canada to clarify the status of women under the Constitution and they asked, "Does the 'persons' in Section 24 of the British North America Act, 1867, include female persons?" Amazingly, the Supreme Court of Canada responded that, no, women were not persons. The women received the support of the Prime Minister and they appealed this judgment to the Judicial Committee of the Privy Council of England this was Canada's highest court of appeal at the time. Finally, the women were successful from that point on women were considered persons under Canadian law and could fully participate in public office. To honour the efforts of these women, a monument was recently unveiled in Calgary, Alberta, to celebrate the 70th anniversary of the "Persons" Case it depicts the Famous Five as they are now known. The large bronze statues were sculpted by Edmonton artist Barbara Paterson and the monument is a tribute to the women who changed the face of Canadian history by changing the definition of the word "persons" to include both men and women. A replica of this monument was later unveiled in Ottawa this was the first sculpture of Canadian women to grace Parliament Hill.

TEST 3 — Editing for Run-Ons

Edit these ten run-on sentences by writing them as complete sentences and in the form of a complete paragraph.

1. There are health benefits from soy protein, a study finds soy protein a potent weapon in lowering cholesterol.

2. Researchers report that soy protein lowers cholesterol levels in people with moderately high to high cholesterol and the addition of soy protein to the ordinary Canadian diet appears to be beneficial in lowering cholesterol.

3. Elevated cholesterol levels sharply increase the risk of heart attacks and strokes but soy protein may prove a safe, painless, even tasty weapon in the battle against cardiovascular disease.

4. People are already familiar with soy protein in products such as tofu and soy milk, now researchers are determining how much soy protein one would have to eat to bring down elevated cholesterol levels.

5. According to scientists, the higher a person's cholesterol level, the greater is the power of soy protein to reduce it they determined that a diet of 47 grams of soy protein a day cuts cholesterol levels in a month by an average of 9.3 percent.

6. Soy protein specifically cuts the type of cholesterol one wants to minimize: low-density lipoprotein but high-density lipoprotein, the good cholesterol, is not affected by the soy protein.

7. Another approach to reducing cholesterol is a low-fat diet and anti-cholesterol medications have the undesirable effect of decreasing HDL as well as LDL concentrations.

8. A 10 percent to 15 percent reduction in blood cholesterol levels results in a 20 to 30 percent reduction in the risk of coronary heart disease this has the potential of making a huge impact on Canadian public health.

9. Doctors generally recommend that people do what they can to keep cholesterol levels below 200 milligrams per decilitre, and under 180 when possible, it is great news that something as simple as soy protein is effective in lowering serum cholesterol.

10. Beyond its beneficial effects on cholesterol, soy beans have shown potential in studies for helping to prevent cancer, osteoporosis, and other chronic illnesses so soy protein is pretty potent stuff.

TEST 4   Editing for Run-Ons

Edit the following paragraph, correcting all three kinds of run-on sentences.

In 1895, Joshua Slocum was the first solo sailor he sailed around the world without radar. He was the first to circle the world alone and he did it without any of the technological aids that help protect sailors today. He told time with a tin clock that lost its minute hand halfway through the journey, he had the humility to acknowledge that his adventures were tame compared with the writing of earlier explorers. Born in Nova Scotia, Slocum had been around the world five times on tall ships before his solo voyage and he had commanded a ship by the age of 30. He was out of work in 1892 when a captain offered to give him a sailboat, the boat needed some repairs. Really, the boat needed rebuilding, which Slocum proceeded to do and three years later he sailed from Boston, headed east. He planned to sail through the Mediterranean but he reversed his course, crossed back toward South America and continued west. He entered the Strait of Magellan in February 1896. It took him two months to pass through he was set back by winds so heavy that his mainsail was torn to rags. Slocum's journey took three years, with stops at various island ports he raised money by giving talks and enjoyed the local hospitality. His story is a tale of the intelligence, skill, and fortitude that drove a master navigator.

TEST 5

Editing for Run-Ons

Edit these ten run-on sentences.

1. Many parents worry that their children are not reading others worry about what they are reading.

2. Most children are not reading anything at all, the home is filled with the sounds from stereos and television sets.

3. Children should have library cards and parents should accompany them regularly to the library to pick out books.

4. Children need to see their parents reading magazines, books, and newspapers reflect the tastes and interests of the adults in a home.

5. Books can be bonds between children and their parents so parents should read aloud to their children as often as possible.

6. What do you think of parents who are not involved in the school they are usually quick to go to make a complaint about a teacher.

7. Maps are wonderful geography lessons and they remind children they are not at the centre of the world.

8. Some parents think their child is gifted, it is a mistake to let your child think this.

9. Memorizing poetry should be encouraged we learn the rhythms of our language and strengthen our speech and writing.

10. A child who doesn't read will be at the mercy of other people reading encourages children to think through many issues that they might not normally experience themselves.

Working Together

DINING OUT

The newspaper review of a neighbourhood restaurant contains complete information about the eatery, including the location, the days and hours of operation, and the menu.

Write a review of a dining spot in your neighbourhood. Give all the information needed for the reader to decide whether or not this restaurant is worth patronizing. You may want to include the personality of the owner, the friendliness of the staff, or the quality of the atmosphere. Use the review as a guide for what information could be included.

If you appreciate authentic Chinese food, you should go for lunch or dinner to the Golden Fortune Restaurant, located at 99 Elm Avenue in Ormsby. It is just above the South Side Plaza, walking distance from the centre of town. The Golden Fortune Restaurant is the kind of restaurant you will want to visit more than once. The food is expertly prepared, the prices are very moderate, and the service is always friendly. We particularly liked the warm and relaxed atmosphere, partly the result of soft classical music playing in the background.

Many of the lunch and dinner selections at the Golden Fortune are traditional, with a few surprises. All of the vegetables used are fresh, and there is a choice of white or brown rice. The appetizers are large enough to serve two people. On our first visit, we were delighted with the combination platter. It is the most popular appetizer on the menu because it allows diners to sample a half dozen of the house specialties.

One unique touch at this restaurant is the choice of 24 different teas. Instead of the ordinary pot of green tea that is placed in front of you in most Chinese restaurants, at the Golden Fortune you have a wide variety to choose from. These include green tea with passion fruit, peach tea, or even milk tea with oatmeal. Customers enjoy trying new combinations each time they visit. Our favourite is the black tea with plum.

Some of the most popular main courses are beef with garlic sauce, crispy honey chicken on a bed of rice and vegetables, and a variety of delicious stir-fry dishes. If you choose a stir-fry at the Golden Fortune, you may select a favourite sauce and type of noodle along with a meat or fish, and the kitchen will make up the dish you want.

The Golden Fortune is open for lunch from noon to 4 p.m. and for dinner from 5 p.m. until 11 p.m. every day of the week. No reservations are needed. For takeout orders, call 548-4407 after 11 a.m.

Making Sentence Parts Work Together

In Chapter 3, you focused on one major way that sentence parts must work together, namely, verbs must agree with their subjects. In this chapter, you will look at other elements in the sentence that must agree or be in balance. These other parts include:

Pronouns and case
   a. comparisons
   b. compound constructions
   c. who/whom constructions
Pronoun-antecedent agreement
Parallel structure
Misplaced or dangling modifiers

With practice, you can learn to recognize these structures in your own writing.

Pronouns and case

Many personal pronouns change in form depending on how they are used in the sentence; that is, they can be used as subjects, objects, possessives, or reflexives.

I taught *her their* rules *myself*.
She taught *me their* rules *herself*.

The following chart may be useful as a reference.

PRONOUNS AND CASE				
	Pronouns used as subjects	*Pronouns used as objects*	*Pronouns used as possessives*	*Pronouns used as reflexives*
Singular	I	me	my, mine	myself
	you	you	your, yours	yourself
	he	him	his	himself
	she	her	hers/her	herself
	it	it	its	itself
Plural	we	us	our, ours	ourselves
	you	you	your, yours	yourselves
	they	them	their, theirs	themselves
Singular or Plural	who	whom	whose	

- There are no such forms as *hisself* or *theirselves*.
- Do not confuse *whose* with *who's* or *its* with *it's*. (Who's means *who is*, and *it's* means *it is*.)

In general, most of us use pronouns in the correct case without thinking. Three constructions, however, require some special attention: comparisons, compound constructions, and the use of *who/whom*.

Comparisons

In a comparison, picking the correct pronoun is easier if you complete the comparison.

That gymnast is more flexible than (he, him, his).

That gymnast is more flexible than (he, him, his) is.

The second sentence shows that *he* is the correct form because the pronoun is used as the subject for the clause *he is*.

PRACTICE

1. My children did not enjoy the meal as much as (I, me).

   try: as much as (I, me) did

2. The pool in the backyard impressed the children more than (I, me).

   try: more than it impressed (I, me)

EXERCISE 1   Choosing the Correct Pronoun in Comparisons

Circle the correct pronoun in each of the sentences.

1. I am as deeply involved in this report as (they, them).
2. Karen's research has been more extensive than (we, us, our, ours).
3. She studied the final report less than (I, me).
4. Unfortunately, the competing report was just as attractive as (we, us, our, ours).
5. Their company had acquired fewer clients than (we, us).
6. Our policies are much better than (them, theirs).
7. The contract was awarded to us rather than to (they, them).
8. The results will matter more to the client than to (she, her).
9. I will celebrate much longer tonight than (she, her).
10. An immediate vacation is more important for me than for (he, him).

Compound constructions

When you have a compound subject or a compound object, picking the correct pronoun is easier if you test your choice by leaving out the other subject or object.

My daughter and (I, me) went skating.

(I, me) went skating.

• PRACTICE

1. Melinda and (I, me) made the dessert.

   try: (I, me) made the dessert.

2. They invited both Sara and (I, me).

   try: They invited (I, me).

EXERCISE 2   Choosing the Correct Pronoun in Compound Constructions

Circle the correct pronoun in each of the sentences.

1. Sara called from St. John's to speak with Leslie and (I, me).
2. Both Damon and (I, me) keep a daily journal.
3. Today we received the letters from you and (she, her).
4. Among Sasha, Jerry, and (I, me), Sasha is the best writer.
5. Karen and (she, her) are hoping for good grades this term.
6. Because Martin and (she, her) decided to go, the group could no longer fit into one car.
7. (He, Him) and (I, me) handed our journals in to the professor.
8. When we were sick, my aunt ran lots of errands for Kathleen and (I, me).
9. Jim and (he, him) wrote an essay together.
10. The professor returned the papers to my friend and (I, me).

Who/whom constructions

The use of these two pronouns is at times confusing to most of us. When in doubt, you need to consider if the pronoun is used in a subject position or in an object position.

Subject Position: *Who* is the director of that film?

Object Position: *Whom* did the director choose for the lead?
To *whom* did the director give the lead role?

If there is more than one clause in the sentence, you will find it helpful to cross out all other clauses so you can see how *who/whom* functions in its clause.

• PRACTICE

1. ~~She is the friend~~ (who, whom) I treasured.

   look at: (who, whom) I treasured

2. ~~She is the friend~~ (who, whom) ~~I knew~~ could be trusted.

   look at: (who, whom) could be trusted

3. I don't know (who, whom) should do the work.

4. That is the girl (who, whom) I saw last night.

EXERCISE 3   Choosing the Correct Pronoun Using Who/Whom

Circle the correct pronoun in each of the sentences.

1. (Who, Whom) is singing at the choral concert tonight?

2. (Whoever, Whomever) sold us the tickets gave us the best seats in the house.

3. From (who, whom) can we obtain a program?

4. (Who, Whom) of these singers can you tell needs more practice?

5. The director gave the solo parts to (whoever, whomever) was qualified.

6. I haven't decided yet (who, whom) is better.

7. (Who's, Whose) solo do you think was performed with the most musicality?

8. (Whoever, Whomever) played the piano accompaniment did a wonderful job.

9. Just between the two of us, (who, whom) do you believe is the more musically inclined?

10. (Who's, Whose) music was left on the piano?

EXERCISE 1   Choosing Correct Pronoun Forms

Circle the correct pronoun in each of the sentences.

1. (He, Him) is delivering the keynote address.

2. This evening after the keynote address, you and (they, them) have to lead the discussion.

3. The box office gave (they, them) the best seats as a reward for their tireless efforts in organizing the presentation.

4. At the end of the address, the star can perform with (whoever, whomever) he pleases.

5. His career choice in music is more lucrative than (her, hers, she).

6. (Who, Whose, Whom) muddy shoes were left in the auditorium lobby?

7. (They, Them) are making a mess of the lobby carpet.

8. Next week, he and (I, me) need to finalize our business travel plans for the next presentation.

9. (Whoever, Whomever) wants to go on the trip with us should sign up now.

10. Your last minute travel options are riskier than (they, them, theirs).

EXERCISE 2   Choosing Correct Pronoun Forms

Circle the correct pronoun in each of the sentences.

1. Claudia and (he, him) prepared the presentation together.

2. According to both you and (I, me), it was spectacular.

3. Their explanations will benefit (whoever, whomever) will use the data after them.

4. Claudia is a better presenter than (he, him).

5. (Whoever, Whomever) listened to them agreed with us about the quality of their presentation.

6. (Who, Whom) do you think was the most persuasive?

7. I only hope I will be as well prepared as (they, them).

8. Their data was better researched than (me, my, mine).

9. The audience gave both Claudia and (he, him) standing ovations.

10. My team and (I, me) have our work cut out for us.

EXERCISE 3   Choosing Correct Pronoun Forms

In each sentence, fill in the blank with a pronoun form that correctly completes the meaning.

When my sister and _____ decided to buy a house together, some of our relatives objected to the plan. My parents said we could not manage all the demands of a house, and _____ and our grandparents tried to discourage us. To _____ could we turn in an emergency? Our parents, _____ were our loudest critics, obviously wanted us to stay at home. My father kept saying that the purchase of a house might be all right if my sister or _____ were mechanically inclined. I pointed out that our brother was handy, and he could help when it became too much for _____ or _____ . My mother, _____ was quiet when she heard this, could tell how important this purchase was to _____ . It was pretty clear that we would always be more confident than _____ about our ability to manage a house.

Pronoun-antecedent agreement

When we use a pronoun in our writing, that pronoun must refer to a word used previously in the text. This word is called the ***antecedent.***

An ***antecedent*** is the word (or words) that a pronoun replaces.

The pool was crowded. It was a popular place on a hot summer day.

In this example, the pronoun *It* replaces the word *pool. Pool,* in this case, is referred to as the *antecedent* to the pronoun *it.*

The following three rules for antecedents are important for even the most experienced writers to keep in mind when they write. Study each of these rules and work with the exercises that follow.

1. A pronoun must agree in number (singular or plural) with any other word to which it refers. The following sentence contains a pronoun-antecedent disagreement in *number:*

Lacks agreement: *Everyone* practised *their* speech.

The problem in this sentence is that *everyone* is a singular word, but *their* is a plural pronoun. You may have heard people use the plural pronoun *their* to refer to a singular subject. In fact, the above sentence may sound correct, but it is considered a mistake in formal writing. Here are two approaches a writer might take to correct this sentence:

Sexist: Everyone practised *his* speech.

Although you may encounter this approach in current writing, it is unpopular because it is widely considered a sexist construction.

Awkward: Everyone practised *his* or *her* speech.

This form is technically correct, but if it is used several times in the same paragraph, it sounds awkward and repetitious.

The best solution may be to revise such a construction so that the antecedent is plural:

All the students practised their speeches.

Another problem with pronoun-antecedent agreement in number occurs when a demonstrative pronoun (*this, that, these, those*) is used with a noun. That pronoun must agree with the noun it modifies:

Singular: *this kind, that type*

Incorrect: *These kind* of pens don't last.

Correct: *This kind* of pen doesn't last.

Plural: *these kinds, those types*

Incorrect: *Those type* of apples make good pies.

Correct: *Those types* of apples make good pies.

• PRACTICE 1

Rewrite each of the following sentences so that the pronoun agrees with its antecedent in number.

1. Everyone should bring their recommendations for the conference to the meeting.

   _____

2. This types of envelopes are required by the Post Office.

   _____

3. No one cared what they were eating.

   _____

4. If the angler hoped to catch anything, one must rise early.

   _____

5. These group of plants appears to be poisonous.

   _____

2. Pronouns must also agree with their antecedents in person. The following sentence contains a pronoun-antecedent disagreement in person:

   When performing surgery, *one* must maintain *your* concentration at all times.

   When you construct a piece of writing, you choose a *person* to whom you direct your words. Some teachers ask students not to choose the first person (*I*) because they believe such writing sounds too personal. Other teachers warn students not to use *you* because it is too casual. Whatever guidelines your teacher gives you, the important point is to be consistent in person.
   Here are some of the correct possibilities for the sentence:

   When performing surgery, *you* must maintain *your* concentration at all times.

   When performing surgery, *I* must maintain *my* concentration at all times.

   When performing surgery, *we* must maintain *our* concentration at all times.

PRACTICE 2

Correct each of the following sentences so that the pronoun agrees with its antecedent in person.

1. We love quiz shows because you can demonstrate what you know.

2. As I studied science, we found that self-examination helped prepare us for quiz show questions.

3. Game show contestants need to rehearse your responses in order to remember them.

4. Quiz shows can be enjoyable for one if you have a sense of curiosity.

5. When preparing for a quiz show, you must remember that we must practise, practise, practise.

3. The antecedent of a pronoun should not be missing, ambiguous, or repetitious.

   a. **Missing antecedent:**

   In Victoria, *they* have many beautifully developed retirement areas.

   Possible revision: Victoria has many beautifully developed retirement areas.

   Explanation: In the first sentence, who is *they?* If the context has not told us that *they* refers to the government or to the developers, then the antecedent is missing. The sentence should be rewritten in order to avoid *they*.

   b. **Ambiguous antecedent:**

   Ken told his son that *he* needed to find a job.

   Possible revision: Ken said that his son needed to find a job.

   Explanation: In this first example, *he* could refer to either Ken or the son. The sentence should be revised in a way that will avoid this confusion.

   c. **Repetitious pronoun and antecedent:**

   The magazine article, *it* said that whole grain breads are a key to good health.

   Possible revision: The magazine article said that whole grain breads are a key to good health.

   Explanation: The subject should be either *article*, or if there is already an antecedent, *it*. Using both the noun and the pronoun results in needless repetition.

PRACTICE 3

Rewrite the following sentences so that the antecedents are not missing, ambiguous, or repetitious.

1. The tenant asked the superintendent to bring back his receipt.

   _____

   _____

2. At the pharmacy, they said the prescription could not be refilled.

   _____

   _____

3. The venetian blind dropped onto the air conditioner, and it was damaged.

   _____

   _____

4. In the newspaper, it says the heat wave will continue for at least another week.

   _____

   _____

5. We don't enjoy the daily newspaper anymore because they have become too sensational.

   _____

   _____

EXERCISE 1   Making Pronouns and Antecedents Agree

Each of the following sentences contains an error with pronouns. Revise each sentence so that pronouns agree with their antecedents and there are no missing, ambiguous, or repetitious antecedents.

1. Her dance instructor mailed her her dance recital video.

   _____

   _____

2. Everyone wants their salary increased.

   _____

   _____

3. When a business does not computerize its functions, they pay a price in lost business.

   _____

   _____

4. The female graduate has more job options available to them than in the past.

   _____

   _____

5. Everybody wants their own dreams fulfilled.

   _____

   _____

6. The nurse said that those kind of inoculations are given here.

   _____

   _____

7. If the hikers expect to sleep tonight, each one should put up their tent.

   _____

   _____

8. These style of dresses look terrific on you.

   _____

   _____

9. In the magazine, it says you must return the entry form before the end of the month.

   _____

   _____

10. Each of the students looks forward to their summer break.

    _____

    _____

EXERCISE 2   Making Pronouns and Antecedents Agree

Each of the following sentences contains an error with pronouns. Revise each sentence so that pronouns agree with their antecedents and there are no missing, ambiguous, or repetitious antecedents.

1. Every student must have their I.D. card to use the library.

   _____

   _____

2. If one wants to get a seat, you have to be there early.

   _____

   _____

3. When a child flies alone, they usually get special attention from the flight attendant.

   _____

   _____

4. Those sort of movies depress me.

   _____

   _____

5. That nurse is in danger of having their job eliminated.

_____

_____

6. These helium balloons will float away if you don't hold onto it.

_____

_____

7. These type of fabric tends to run in the wash.

_____

_____

8. They have a new cereal out now that I like.

_____

_____

9. Everyone was given a corsage for their dress.

_____

_____

10. The teacher gave the girl her special pen.

_____

_____

EXERCISE 3   Making Pronouns and Antecedents Agree

Each of the following sentences contains an error with pronouns. Revise each sentence so that pronouns agree with their antecedents and there are no missing, ambiguous, or repetitious antecedents.

1. One should try rock climbing if you like adventure.

_____

_____

2. Her friend forwarded her her blue sweater.

_____

_____

3. The iron scorched the shirt, so it had to be thrown away.

_____

_____

4. In the article, it said that nicotine is a carcinogen.

_____

_____

5. It also said pregnant women shouldn't expose her baby to smoke.

_____

_____

6. I usually do well on this kind of tests.

_____

_____

7. Girls must bring your gym clothes on Tuesdays and Thursdays.

_____

_____

8. Jack created a copy of his demo for Carlos.

_____

_____

9. They ought to do something about the national debt.

_____

_____

10. Sue told Sarah that she had won the lottery.

_____

_____

Parallel structure: Making a series of words, phrases, or clauses balanced within the sentence

Which one of the following sentences achieves a better balanced structure?

His favourite hobbies are playing the trumpet, listening to jazz, and to go to concerts.

His favourite hobbies are playing the trumpet, listening to jazz, and going to concerts.

If you selected the second sentence, you made the better choice. The second sentence uses parallel structure to balance the three phrases in the series (*playing, listening,* and *going*). By matching each of the items in the series with the same *-ing* structure, the sentence becomes easier to understand and more pleasant to read. You can make words, phrases, and even sentences in a series parallel:

1. Words in a series should be the same parts of speech.

   Lacks balance: The town was small, quiet, and the atmosphere was peaceful. (The series is composed of two adjectives and one clause.)

   Balanced: The town was small, quiet, and peaceful. (*Small, quiet,* and *peaceful* are adjectives.)

2. Phrases in a series should be the same kinds of phrases (infinitive phrases, prepositional phrases, verb phrases, noun phrases, participial phrases).

   Lacks balance: Her lost assignment is in her closet, on the floor, and a pile of clothes is hiding it. (two prepositional phrases and one clause)

Balanced: Her lost assignment is in her closet, on the floor, and under a pile of clothes.
(three prepositional phrases beginning with *in, on,* and *under*)

3. Clauses in a series should be parallel.

Lacks balance: One clerk polished the antique spoons; they were placed into the display case by the other clerk.

Balanced: One clerk polished the antique spoons; the other clerk placed them in the display case.

PRACTICE

Each of the following sentences has an underlined word, phrase, or clause that is not parallel. Make the underlined section parallel.

1. My favourite sweater is misshapen, worn, and <u>has stains everywhere</u>.

   _____

2. They love travelling overseas, visiting the sites, and <u>also to eat in fine restaurants</u>.

   _____

3. He admires doctors who donate their medical skills to the needy and <u>willingly encouraging new research</u>.

   _____

EXERCISE 1   Revising Sentences for Parallel Structure

Each of the following sentences lacks parallel structure. Underline the word, phrase, or clause that is not parallel and revise it so that its structure will balance with the other items in the pair or series.

1. The Barbara Gowdy book was exciting, startling, and made me horrified.

   _____

   _____

2. Clothes were thrown on the chairs, across the sofa, and the floor was covered.

   _____

   _____

3. Reading, decorating, and to paint with water colours are three hobbies she enjoys.

   _____

   _____

4. He appeared drained, worn, and longed to sleep after the long search for his dog.

   _____

   _____

5. The house was empty and without any sign of life.

_____

_____

6. Aruba is always breezy and has sunny weather.

_____

_____

7. The table was solid oak, carved with beautiful details, and I'm thinking the price is right.

_____

_____

8. The collector enjoys buying the stamps, studying their history, and likes to put them in albums.

_____

_____

9. The old book is torn, water-stained, and has mould spots.

_____

_____

10. The people of the community are not only pleased but they are also feeling a lot of pride.

_____

_____

EXERCISE 2   Revising Sentences for Parallel Structure

Each of the following sentences lacks parallel structure. Underline the word, phrase, or clause that is not parallel and revise it so that its structure will balance with the other items in the pair or series.

1. The editor told her the writing was interesting, accurate, but she was not concise.

_____

_____

2. The journalist researched the story, wrote a first draft, and taking it to the editor for changes.

_____

_____

3. She was undecided about continuing in her present job, quitting to look for a new job, or she could ask her supervisor for some changes.

_____

_____

4. William is not only a gifted painter, but he is also working with teaching children very well.

_____

_____

5. The child's demeanour, his actions, and whenever he talked amused me.

_____

_____

6. Employers should look for people who are competent, honest, and cooperation is a quality they possess.

_____

_____

7. The gambler must either stop going to the casinos or to risk the ruination of her entire family.

_____

_____

8. The young lawyer would rather work seven days a week than spending one day with his mother-in-law.

_____

_____

9. The kitchen faced a brick wall, you couldn't get any fresh air, and was painted an ugly dark colour.

_____

_____

10. I would rather visit the East Coast than to go to Alberta this year.

_____

_____

EXERCISE 3   Revising Sentences for Parallel Structure

Each of the following sentences lacks parallel structure. Underline the word, phrase, or clause that is not parallel and revise it so that its structure will balance with the other items in the pair or series.

1. She's a good singer, a fine dancer, and acts also.

_____

_____

2. I would rather watch television than doing homework.

_____

_____

3. On each table were a vase of flowers, a bowl of fruit, and ice which had been put into a bucket.

_____

_____

4. The composition displayed the student's imagination and having a great wit.

_____

_____

5. On my trip to Winnipeg, I plan to visit relatives, do some sightseeing, and to eat at a fine restaurant.

_____

_____

6. Gardening, golfing, and to sew curtains are three of my grandmother's favourite hobbies.

_____

_____

7. She seemed exhausted, ill, and needed to eat after the journey.

_____

_____

8. He cleaned the cellar, washed the windows, and painting the back door.

_____

_____

9. The movie was expensive, too long, and I was bored.

_____

_____

10. The counsellor makes everyone feel comfortable, speaks in a gentle voice, and she is getting everyone to participate.

_____

_____

Misplaced and dangling modifiers

Notice how the meaning changes in each of the following sentences, depending on where the modifier *only* is placed:

Only Charlene telephoned my brother yesterday.
Charlene *only* telephoned my brother yesterday.
Charlene telephoned *only* my brother yesterday.
Charlene telephoned my *only* brother yesterday.
Charlene telephoned my brother *only* yesterday.

> *Modifiers* are words or groups of words that function as adjectives or adverbs.
>
> Examples: my *only* brother
>   the server *who is my brother*
>   *only* yesterday
>
> A modifier must be placed close to the word, phrase, or clause that it modifies in order to be understood by the reader.

Be especially careful in your own writing when you use the words in the following list. They are often misplaced.

OFTEN MISPLACED MODIFIERS				
almost	exactly	just	nearly	scarcely
even	hardly	merely	only	simply

Examples follow of some special problems that can happen when modifiers are not used correctly. Study how the sentences have been revised, so you will be able to correct any misplaced or dangling modifiers in your own writing.

1. Misplaced Modifiers

> A *misplaced modifier* is a modifier that has been placed in a wrong, awkward, or ambiguous position.

a. The modifier is in the wrong place.

> **Wrong:** The salesperson sold the used car to the customer that needed extensive body work.
>
> Who or what needed body work—the customer or the car?
>
> **Revised:** The salesperson sold the customer the used car that needed extensive body work.

b. The modifier is positioned awkwardly, interrupting the flow of the sentence, as in the following split infinitive.

> **Awkward:** Alex planned to exactly arrive on time.
>
> The infinitive *to arrive* should not be split.
>
> **Revised:** Alex planned to arrive exactly on time.

c. The modifier is in an ambiguous position; that is, it could describe the word or words on either side of it (sometimes called a "squinting modifier").

> **Squinting:** Ms. Douglass having arranged other parties secretly planned the surprise party for her friend.

Did she secretly arrange parties or secretly plan the surprise party? From the wording above, you cannot tell which is the correct interpretation.

Revised: Having arranged other parties, Ms. Douglass secretly planned the surprise party for her friend.

2. Dangling Modifiers

> A *dangling modifier* is a modifier without a word, phrase, or clause that the modifier can describe.

Dangling: Working on the car's engine, the dog barked all afternoon.

Who is working on the engine? Was it the dog?

Revised: Working on the car's engine, I heard the dog barking all afternoon.

or

The dog barked all afternoon while I was working on the car's engine.

EXERCISE 1   Revising Misplaced or Dangling Modifiers

Revise each sentence so there is no misplaced or dangling modifier. An example is done for you.

Incorrect: While typing at the computer, my foot went to sleep.

Correct: My foot went to sleep while I was typing at the computer.

1. Maurice fed the baby holding his bowling ball in one hand.

   _____

   _____

2. Reading the newspaper, the chipmunk scurried across the patio.

   _____

   _____

3. Walking up the steps of the cathedral, the organ music could be faintly heard.

   _____

   _____

4. Leaving for work this morning, the children reminded me of our plan to play baseball when I got home.

   _____

   _____

5. Being quite blind, the darkness posed no unusual problem for him.

   _____

   _____

6. After painting the house all day, the dip in the pool was refreshing.

   _____

   _____

7. When cooking spaghetti, a strainer helps.

   _____

   _____

8. Found in the park, the police returned the purse to the owner.

   _____

   _____

9. Crossing the railroad tracks, great caution is recommended.

   _____

   _____

10. A tick was found in my leg that had to be pulled out.

    _____

    _____

EXERCISE 2   Revising Misplaced or Dangling Modifiers

Revise each sentence so there is no misplaced or dangling modifier. An example is done for you.

Incorrect: Born on Halloween, my daughter's birthday party is usually a Halloween party as well.

Correct: Since my daughter was born on Halloween, her birthday party is usually a Halloween party as well.

1. Wagging his tail, I pet the little spaniel pup.

   _____

   _____

2. Stuck in the stroller, I called the police to help me get the baby out.

   _____

   _____

3. Hiking on the trail, his sadness vanished.

   _____

   _____

4. Working late at night, the coffeepot is often perking.

   _____

   _____

5. Disappointed and discouraged, a good brisk walk helped to cheer him up.

   _____

   _____

6. After being polished, I was surprised how the car looked.

   _____

   _____

7. Encouraged by the teacher's help, the student's paper would be easier to organize.

   _____

   _____

8. Moved by his words, tears came to my eyes.

   _____

   _____

9. Taking the math test, my answers were done in ink rather than pencil.

   _____

   _____

10. An overdue book was found in my closet that needed to be returned to the library.

   _____

   _____

EXERCISE 3   Revising Misplaced or Dangling Modifiers

Revise each sentence so there is no misplaced or dangling modifier.

Incorrect: While waiting for my paycheque, my phone service was cut off.

Correct: My phone service was cut off while I was waiting for my paycheque.

1. Dolores fed the bird wearing her evening gown.

   _____

   _____

2. Visiting Drumheller, Alberta, the Tyrrell Museum was my destination.

   _____

   _____

3. Expecting to hear the weather report, the radio was turned on by 6 a.m.

   _____

   _____

4. A variety of plant life was discovered in the Amazon that had been thought extinct.

   _____

   _____

5. Walking outside in our neighbourhood, the six o'clock whistle can be heard.

   _____

   _____

6. While cleaning my binocular lens, the rare bird disappeared.

   _____

   _____

7. Dangling from the playground monkey bars, my mother caught sight of her three children.

   _____

   _____

8. Meowing all night, I heard the cat next door.

   _____

   _____

9. After cleaning my apartment, my dog scratched the door to go out.

   _____

   _____

10. The marathon caused a traffic slowdown, which promised all proceeds would go to charity.

    _____

    _____

Mastery and editing tests

TEST 1   Making Sentence Parts Work Together

Each sentence has a part that does not work with the rest of the sentence. Find the error and correct it.

1. Him and me enjoyed our camping trip.

   _____

   _____

2. If you are afraid of heights, one mustn't look down.

   _____

   _____

3. My duties at work include making telephone calls, working on the computer, and to pick up the mail.

   _____

   _____

4. When we went shopping today, we saw the man whom is always singing.

   _____

   _____

5. They went biking in Italy, hiking in England, and to pick grapes in France.

   _____

   _____

6. These kind of trips seem to be getting popular.

_____

_____

7. Jean and me called for more information.

_____

_____

8. In France, they have many beautiful castles to visit.

_____

_____

9. Did anyone bother to finish their assignment?

_____

_____

10. Wouldn't you prefer to eat a peanut butter sandwich than drinking that vegetable juice?

_____

_____

TEST 2   Making Sentence Parts Work Together

Each sentence has a part that does not work with the rest of the sentence. Find the error and correct it.

1. Jonathan created his art project quicker than me.

_____

_____

2. Amy told Nancy she didn't like her shoes.

_____

_____

3. I love to go to the theatre and spending time at a museum.

_____

_____

4. They love going to Kelly's class because you can always get up and sing.

_____

_____

5. To who should I address this letter?

_____

_____

6. Our cats like eating, sleeping, and they stretch when they wake up.

   _____

   _____

7. My mom asked my brother and I if we wanted to go to the museum today.

   _____

   _____

8. They say *Mamma Mia!* at the Royal Alexandra Theatre is a great success.

   _____

   _____

9. My daily chores are making my bed and to wash the dishes.

   _____

   _____

10. My daughter's favourite teddy bear has a yellow hat, a blue coat, and he is wearing red shoes.

    _____

    _____

TEST 3   Making Sentence Parts Work Together

The paragraph below needs to be rewritten, keeping in mind all you have learned in this chapter about making sentence parts work together. Look for problems with pronouns and case, pronouns and antecedents, parallel structure, and dangling modifiers.

My adviser and me met to discuss my career options. Later, the Career Centre turned out to be a better source of guidance than him. These kind of choices are complicated. According to the centre, the first year of college, it should be a chance to explore a variety of possible careers. The centre suggested that I take advantage of computer training, internship programs, and when experts come to visit the campus. Since the new generation of students is likely to change careers several times, versatility, they said, will be one key to success. I found out what was necessary to get a job in several fields in which I am interested. Internships open doors. It can lead to a job opportunity. When hiring new employees, they always demand job experience. I was told to constantly explore the job market. We also need to keep abreast of developments in our field even after we have a job. Walking back to my dorm after this discussion, my future career seemed more promising.

_____

_____

_____

_____

_____

_____

TEST 4   Making Sentence Parts Work Together

Each example contains a problem with pronouns and case, pronouns and antecedents, parallel structure, or misplaced or dangling modifiers. Edit each example so that it is correct.

1. Jeremy finally decided to change jobs. He told hisself that the move was a good one.

2. His wife is not as convinced as him. The new company is smaller than the one he is leaving.

3. The offer was given to whoever could qualify. Jeremy told Ron that he needed to review before he took the test.

4. Those kind of tests can be tricky. People can freeze and not be able to do their best.

5. Everyone worked on their exam carefully. All those taking the test wanted to get the job.

6. After taking the exam, the results were calculated. The applicants were told a letter would be sent to them shortly.

7. The letter, it said Jeremy had received the highest score. The job was his if he wanted it.

8. The new job would mean moving the family to a new location, leaving all their friends, and a big pay raise.

9. The job will be a challenge which is in North Bay, Ontario. Everyone says they will like the city.

10. Moving is a big adjustment. Jeremy hopes his wife and him will be happy.

TEST 5   Making Sentence Parts Work Together

Each example contains a problem with pronouns and case, pronouns and antecedents, parallel structure, or misplaced or dangling modifiers. Edit each example so that it is correct.

1. Some parts of the world cannot take water for granted; it has to be grateful for what water there is.

2. The Middle East is an example of these kind of situations. Water there is usually a problem.

3. Looking at a map of Saudi Arabia, most of the land is not suitable for farming.

4. Oil production, it can be controlled, but not water.

5. In the dry lands of the Middle East, a short river called a wadis can be dry all year and suddenly they fill up with water.

6. The oasis is a more dependable water source which is all over the Middle East.

7. Water needs have led governments to hire engineers, build dams, and planning for the future.

8. Taking salt water from the sea, fresh water can be produced by a special process.

9. For the nomadic people in these areas, who have a herd only of animals, the search for water makes life hard.

10. We are surprised how many cities grew up in these areas; however, the reason, you remember, is because their locations made them important centres for trade.

Working Together

The photograph shows a family recording a special event. What is the earliest picture you have of members of your own family? What documents (such as birth certificates) do you have that give you some information about these relatives? What stories have you been told about them? What do you believe you can tell about them from looking at their photographs? Use the next twenty minutes to write on this subject. When you have finished your work, exchange your paper with another student. Look for sentences that contain the kinds of errors you have studied so far: subject-verb agreement, pronoun-antecedent agreement, parallel structure, and misplaced or dangling modifiers. Mark sentences that need revision by using the correction symbols listed inside the back cover of this book.

Chapter 9

Practising More with Verbs

In Chapter 2, you learned how to recognize the verb in a sentence. In Chapter 3, you learned that verbs must agree with their subjects. Chapter 4 discussed how to form participles, gerunds, and infinitives from the verb. This chapter will continue your study of verbs with the focus on the following:

- Principal parts of irregular verbs
- How to use the present perfect and past perfect tenses
- Sequence of tenses
- How to avoid unnecessary shifts in verb tense
- The difference between active or passive voice
- The subjunctive mode
- Confusions with *should* and *would*

What are the principal parts of the irregular verbs?

The English language has more than one hundred verbs that do not form the past tense or past participle with the usual *-ed* ending. Their forms are irregular. When you listen to children aged four or five, you often hear them utter expressions such as "Yesterday I *cutted* myself." Later on, they will hear that the verb "cut" is unusual, and they will change to the irregular form, "Yesterday I *cut* myself." The best way to learn these verbs is to listen to how they sound. You will find an extensive list of these verbs in the appendix of this book. Pronounce them out loud over and over until you have learned them. If you find that you don't know a particular verb's meaning, or you cannot pronounce a verb and its forms, ask your instructor for help. Most irregular verbs are very common words that you will be using often in your writing and speaking. You will want to know them well.

Practising 50 irregular verbs

THE THREE PRINCIPAL PARTS OF IRREGULAR VERBS		
Simple Form	*Past Form*	*Past Participle*
(also called Infinitive Form)		(used with perfect tenses after, "has," "have," or "will have" or with passive voice after the verb "to be.")
ride	rode	ridden

EIGHT VERBS THAT DO NOT CHANGE THEIR FORMS (NOTICE THEY ALL END IN -T OR -D)		
Simple Form	*Past Form*	*Past Participle*
bet	bet	bet
cost	cost	cost
cut	cut	cut
fit	fit	fit
hit	hit	hit
hurt	hurt	hurt
quit	quit	quit
spread	spread	spread

TWO VERBS THAT HAVE THE SAME SIMPLE PRESENT FORM AND THE PAST PARTICIPLE		
Simple Form	*Past Form*	*Past Participle*
come	came	come
become	became	become

PRACTICE 1

Fill in the correct form of the verb in the following sentences.

1. Last year I noticed that the price of men's clothing had _____ an all
   (hit)
   time high.

2. I took my old suits to the tailor, hoping he could _____ what I already
   (fit)
   had.

3. He took one suit and _____ it on the table.
   (spread)

4. The tailor _____ the price for me since I was a good customer.
   (cut)

5. Even so, the cost of alterations has _____ to be extremely expensive.
   (come)

TWENTY VERBS THAT HAVE THE SAME SIMPLE PAST FORM AND PAST PARTICIPLE		
Simple Form	*Past Form*	*Past Participle*
bend	bent	bent
lend	lent	lent
send	sent	sent
spend	spent	spent
creep	crept	crept
keep	kept	kept
sleep	slept	slept
sweep	swept	swept
weep	wept	wept
teach	taught	taught
catch	caught	caught
bleed	bled	bled
feed	fed	fed
lead	led	led
speed	sped	sped
bring	brought	brought
buy	bought	bought
fight	fought	fought
think	thought	thought
seek	sought	sought

• PRACTICE 2

In the following paragraph, five verbs are incorrect. Cross out each incorrect word, and write the correct form of the verb below.

The boy was responsible for all the sheep, and already he had brung most of them back to the ranch. He had catched two of the slowest ones wandering off. When he lead the most cooperative ones to the enclosure, he fighted with the latch on the gate in order to get it open. Then he returned to the meadow where he creeped up on the last stray just before dark.

1. _____

2. _____

3. _____

4. _____

5. _____

TWENTY VERBS THAT HAVE ALL DIFFERENT FORMS		
Simple Form	*Past Form*	*Past Participle*
blow	blew	blown
fly	flew	flown
grow	grew	grown
know	knew	known
throw	threw	thrown
begin	began	begun
drink	drank	drunk
ring	rang	rung
shrink	shrank	shrunk
sink	sank	sunk
sing	sang	sung
spring	sprang	sprung
swim	swam	swum
bite	bit	bitten (or bit)
hide	hid	hidden (or hid)
drive	drove	driven
ride	rode	ridden
stride	strode	stridden
rise	rose	risen
write	wrote	written

PRACTICE 3

Fill in the correct form of the verb in the following sentences.

1. One weekend, I decided to write my essay assignment in the park, so before dawn I _____ from my bed.
   (spring)

2. By the time I packed a lunch and searched for my sunglasses, I noticed the sun had _____ .
   (rise)

3. After I had _____ to the park, I realized I had forgotten my notes
   (drive)
   from the class.

4. When I sat down on a bench to work, I was immediately _____ by
   (bite)
   an insect.

5. Finally, I decided to go back to my desk; I had not _____ a word that
   (write)
   I had planned.

EXERCISE 1   Irregular Verbs

Supply the past form or the past participle for each verb in parentheses.

1. The cat has _____ the milk from the saucer on the steps.
   (drink)

2. She _____ from behind the garage.
   (come)

3. We _____ most of our winter in doors.
   (spend)

4. The wind _____ the snow in under the door.
   (blow)

5. She _____ her head down on the table.
   (bend)

6. She _____ in great relief.
   (weep)

7. The cheque _____ just in time.
   (come)

8. We had _____ the price of the loan.
   (know)

9. The interest rate had been _____ very high.
   (set)

10. The truth of our situation _____ in slowly.
    (sink)

EXERCISE 2   Irregular Verbs

Supply the past form or the past participle for each verb in parentheses.

1. The teenager _____ his father's car.
   (drive)

2. He was _____ by a mosquito.
   (bite)

3. His record of absences _____ his chances for the job.
   (hurt)

4. Have you ever _____ a letter to your legislator?
   (send)

5. The ideas _____ from a book she had read last year.
   (spring)

6. The women have _____ smoking.
   (quit)

7. Jasmine _____ sixty laps before taking a break.
   (swim)

8. She has _____ her talent from us.
   (hide)

9. We had _____ that she could win the scholarship.
   (bet)

10. The good news of the results _____ fast.
    (spread)

EXERCISE 3   Irregular Verbs

Supply the past form or the past participle for each verb in parentheses.

Ever since people _____ to fly, they have _____ to every
        (begin)   (fly)

corner of the earth. Few people _____ that the aerospace industry
                                        (think)

would grow so dramatically. Travel writers now have _____ about
                                                              (write)

every country in the known world. The aerospace industry _____
                                                                  (rise)

out of the imaginations of curious people. The very idea of air

travel _____ them occupied for years. They _____ the
         (keep)   (feel)

possibilities for air travel were limitless. It is amazing how air travel

has _____ the world. The aerospace industry has _____
       (shrink)   (grow)

into a major economic force.

Appendix A at the back of this book gives an alphabetical listing of most English
irregular verbs. Use that list to supply the correct form for each verb in the following exercises.

EXERCISE 1   More Practice with Irregular Verbs

Choose the correct past form or past participle for each of the examples below. If
necessary, consult Appendix A.

1. The argument _____ over which candidate to choose.
                    (arise)

2. The chairperson _____ the responsibility for the decision.
                        (bear)

3. She had _____ with many decisions like this before.
                (deal)

4. They finally _____ the one they thought was best qualified.
                    (choose)

5. Not everyone _____ the same about the decision.
                    (feel)

6. The discussion had _____ nearly out of hand.
                          (get)

7. The committee had _____ so many promising candidates.
                          (see)

8. They had _____ to several interesting individuals.
                (speak)

9. One candidate _____ out from all the others.
                      (stick)

10. Hopefully, the right person has been _____ .
                                              (find)

EXERCISE 2   More Practice with Irregular Verbs

Read the paragraph. Several irregular verbs are incorrect. First circle each incorrect irregular verb form you find. Then write the correct form on the lines below. If necessary, consult Appendix A.

> I seen a deer in my backyard this morning. He come out of the woods behind the barn. I set and watched him for some time. I drunk my coffee and ate my toast before I leaved for work. I have went to those woods to hunt plenty of times, but I never got a deer. I freezed my fingers once, but no deer. I guess I quitted too soon.

_____   _____

_____   _____

_____   _____

_____   _____

EXERCISE 3   More Practice with Irregular Verbs

Choose the correct past form or past participle in each of the sentences below. If necessary, consult Appendix A.

The volumes were _____ in a beautiful leather. The shopper _____
                (bind)   (buy)

the books for a gift. She _____ into her purse for the credit card.
                         (dig)

She then found a shawl that had been _____ by hand. A bell
                                    (weave)

suddenly _____ in her mind. She had _____ into an old
        (ring)   (fall)

pattern. The shopper _____ she would not spend another penny.
                 (swear)

She _____ a quick glance at her husband. He had _____ the
    (steal)   (take)

time to be with her tonight. She quietly _____ the credit card out
                                  (slide)

of her purse. She and her husband would be _____ with the bill for
                                      (stick)

a long time to come.

How many verb tenses are there in English?

Not all languages have exactly the same verb tenses to express ideas of time. If English is your second language, learning how to use the tenses correctly may be one of your major tasks in becoming fluent in English. For almost all students, the perfect tenses need special attention since these tenses are generally not well understood nor used consistently in the accepted way. Watch out for unnecessary shifts in verb tense.

ENGLISH VERB TENSES

present	I sing
present continuous	I am singing
present perfect	I have sung
present perfect continuous	I have been singing
past	I sang
past continuous	I was singing
past perfect	I had sung
past perfect continuous	I had been singing
future	I will sing
future continuous	I will be singing
future perfect	I will have sung
future perfect continuous	I will have been singing

How do you use the present perfect and the past perfect tenses?

Forming the perfect tenses

Present perfect tense: *has* or *have* + past participle of the
main verb
   has lived
   have lived

Past perfect tense: *had* + past participle of the main verb
   had lived

What do these tenses mean?

> The *present perfect tense* describes an action that started in the past and continues to the present time.

Sheila *has lived* at this address for ten years.

This sentence indicates that Sheila began to live at this address ten years ago and is still living there now.

Examine the following time line. What does it tell you about the present perfect tense?

```
                        present
                   (moment of speaking)
   past               |          |                        future
                      x x x x x x x x x x
   ───────────────────┼──────────┼──────────────────────────────▶
                      10 years   still  living
                      ago              now
```

Other example sentences of the present perfect tense:

> She *has played* softball since 1990.
>
> She *has* always *enjoyed* the game.

> The ***present perfect tense*** can also describe an action that has just taken place, or an action where the exact time in the past is indefinite.

> *Has* Sheila *applied* to college yet?
>
> Sheila *has* (just) *applied* to Mount Royal College.
>
> *Have* you ever *been* to Calgary?
>
> Yes, I *have been* there twice.

If the time were definite, you would use the simple past:

> Sheila *applied* to Mount Royal College last week.
>
> Yes, I *was* there twice last year.

> The ***past perfect tense*** describes an action that occurred in the past before another activity or another point of time in the past.

> Sheila *had studied* at a community college for two semesters before she moved away.

In this sentence, there are two past actions: Sheila *studied*, and Sheila *moved*. The action that took place first is in the past perfect (*had studied*). The action that took place later, and was also completed in the past, is in the simple past (*moved*).

	present (moment of speaking)	
past		future
first action in the past x	second action in the past x	
had studied	moved	

Other example sentences using the past perfect tense:

> I *had* just *started* when the telephone *rang*.
>
> Chris *claimed* that Mark *had warned* us of the faulty brakes.
>
> He *had told* us *long before* the accident.

PRACTICE

Complete each of the following sentences by filling in each blank with either the present perfect tense or past perfect tense of the verb given.

William _____ as a nurse at Sick Kids Hospital since last May.
(work)

William told us that he _____ of visiting Red Deer before he began
(dream)

this full-time job last year. Unfortunately he was not able to save enough

money at that time. Red Deer always _____ William because his
(interest)

parents were born there. Now the idea of a trip to Red Deer is even more

important to him because his grandmother _____ a family reunion
(plan)

for next year. Over the last decade, the grandchildren _____ out
(spread)

over several provinces even though the entire family always _____
(live)

in the West until the 1980s. Today, the idea of returning to the family

farm to meet his many aunts and uncles _____ a wonderful way for
(become)

William to understand his past.

What is the sequence of tenses?

> The term *sequence of tenses* refers to the proper use of verb tenses in complex sentences (sentences that have an independent clause and a dependent clause).

The following guide shows the relationship between the verb in the independent clause (IC) and the verb in the dependent clause (DC).

SEQUENCE OF TENSES

Independent Clause	Dependent Clause	Time of the DC in Relation to the IC

If the tense of the independent clause is in the present (He *knows*), here are the possibilities for the dependent clause:

	that she *is* right.	same time
He knows	that she *was* right.	earlier
	that she *will be* right.	later

If the tense of the independent clause is in the past (He *knew*), here are the possibilities for the dependent clause:

	that she *was* right.	same time
He knew	that she *had been* right.	earlier
	that she *would be* right.	later

If the independent clause is in the future (He *will tell*), here are the possibilities for the dependent clause:

	if she *goes.*	same time
He will tell us	if she *has gone.*	earlier
	if she *will go.*	later

• PRACTICE   Sequence of Tenses

In each of the following sentences, choose the correct verb tense for the verb in the dependent clause.

1. The examination <u>will continue</u> after the noise _____.
   (to stop)

2. The students <u>did not understand</u> the importance that silence _____ on their performance.
   (to have)

3. The teacher <u>will tell</u> us tomorrow if she _____ the old exam or give us another exam.
   (to give)

4. Some students <u>passed</u> the exam because they _____ very diligent in their preparations.
   (to be)

5. I only <u>studied</u> for teachers that I _____ .
   (to like)

6. My teacher <u>thinks</u> it is likely that I _____ concerned about my grades when I get my tests back.
   (to be)

7. I <u>realize</u> that education _____ important if I want to succeed in life.
   (to be)

8. The other students <u>thought</u> that I _____ more than I really did.
   (to study)

9. The students walked into class the next day. They <u>hoped</u> that the exam results _____ out to be positive.
   (to turn)

10. The teacher entered the classroom. She <u>said</u> that the exam _____ well.
    (to go)

Avoid unnecessary shift in verb tense

Do not shift verb tenses as you write unless you intend to change the time of the action.

Shifted tense: The customer *asked* (past tense) for the prescription, but the pharmacist *says* (present tense) that the ingredients *are being ordered* (present continuous passive voice).

Revised: The customer *asked* (past tense) for the prescription, but the pharmacist *said* (past tense) that the ingredients *were being ordered* (past continuous passive voice).

Note: An exception to this occurs when the subject is a book (or other work) created in the past but still enjoyed today. In such a case, the present tense is used. For example, we say *Hamlet* is a great play, even though Shakespeare wrote it four centuries ago.

EXERCISE 1   Correcting Unnecessary Shift in Verb Tense

In each sentence, the writer unnecessarily shifted the verb tense. Revise the second underlined verb in each example below so that the tense remains consistent with the first verb that is underlined. An example is done for you.

Unnecessary shift in verb tense:

The student <u>was doing</u> his assignments carefully when suddenly a friend <u>comes</u> along and <u>takes</u> his mind away from his work.

Consistent verb tenses:

The student <u>was doing</u> his assignments carefully when suddenly a friend <u>came</u> along and <u>took</u> his mind away from his work.

1. Once I <u>finish</u> this book, I <u>returned</u> it to the library.   _____

2. From the start she <u>liked</u> the course; by the end she <u>is feeling</u> that she learned a lot.   _____

3. The booklet <u>provides</u> detailed instructions, but there <u>were</u> no diagrams.   _____

4. Stacy <u>finished</u> her report and <u>asks</u> me to look it over.   _____

5. Alida <u>waited</u> on the train station platform. She <u>is shivering</u> from the cold.   _____

6. While she <u>waited</u>, she <u>notices</u> a small child.   _____

7. My friend <u>told</u> me to be at her house at 5:30 and that she <u>is driving</u> us to the concert.   _____

8. This <u>is</u> a fascinating article, but it <u>didn't</u> have
enough examples to convince me.   _____

9. My daughter <u>leaves</u> in a rush and <u>worried</u> that she
will miss the train.   _____

10. I understand the doctor <u>is</u> very busy, but she
<u>provided</u> me with a service that I pay for. _____

EXERCISE 2   Correcting Unnecessary Shift in Verb Tense

Each sentence has an unnecessary shift in verb tense. Revise each sentence so that
the tense remains consistent.

1. In the beginning of the play, the characters' motives were clear; by the end, I
am as confused as the rest of the audience.

_____

_____

2. The actors meet with the audience after the play, but they didn't explain what
motivates their characters.

_____

_____

3. While discussing the play with the actors, the director loses his notes and
spoke from memory.

_____

_____

4. One actor talked about preparing for his role while another talks about his
techniques for memorizing.

_____

_____

5. I think the play is wonderful because the actors were so authentic in their
portrayals.

_____

_____

6. While viewing the production, the woman seated next to me dropped her
purse and asks me for help.

_____

_____

7. She asked me to check under my seat, but I say nothing was there.

_____

_____

8. After I leave the theatre, I took a taxicab home.

_____

_____

9. The play finished before 11 p.m., and I am stranded without a ride.

_____

_____

10. Overall, the evening is a success, and I decided to visit the theatre again.

_____

_____

EXERCISE 3   Correcting Unnecessary Shift in Verb Tense

The following paragraph contains unnecessary shifts in verb tense. Find these unnecessary shifts and revise them so that the tense remains consistent.

The writer Alistair MacLeod was born in North Battleford, Saskatchewan, in 1936. He lived on the Prairies until the age of ten when his parents move back to the family farm on Cape Breton Island in Nova Scotia. He completes his studies in the United States at Notre Dame University and becomes deeply interested in the art of writing. He began to gather international acclaim for his short stories while spending most of his energy teaching and raising a family of seven children. He lectures at the University of Windsor until his retirement a few years ago. His only novel, *No Great Mischief*, takes him ten years to complete and wins him a major international literary award.

What is the difference between passive and active voice?

PASSIVE AND ACTIVE VOICE

In the *active voice*, the subject does the acting:

Our team won the game.

Choose the active voice generally in order to achieve direct, economical, and forceful writing. Most writing, therefore, should be in the active voice.

In the *passive voice*, the subject is acted upon:

The game was won by our team.
or
The game was won.

Notice in these passive sentences, the actor is not only de-emphasized by moving out of the subject place but may be omitted entirely from the sentence.

Choose the passive voice to de-emphasize the actor or to avoid naming the actor altogether.

Study the three sentences that follow. All three state the fact of George Brown's assassination. Discuss with your classmates and instructor what reasons might lead a writer to prefer one of the sentences to express the same basic fact.

1. George Bennett shot George Brown on March 25, 1880.

2. George Brown was shot by George Bennett on March 25, 1880.

3. George Brown was shot on March 25, 1880.

How do you form the passive voice?

Subject Acted Upon	+ Verb "To Be"	+ Past Participle	+ "by" Phrase (Optional)
The race	was	won	(by the runner)
The fish	was	cooked	(by the chef)
The books	are	illustrated	(by the artists)

•PRACTICE

Fill in the chart by showing how the sentences in the active voice could be put into passive voice and how the sentences in the passive voice could be put into the active voice. Then discuss with your classmates and instructor the circumstances under which you would choose active or passive voice to express these ideas.

Active Voice

1. The rain pounded against the roof of the car.

2. _____
   _____
   _____

3. The Prime Minister announced his decision in the Commons.

4. _____
   _____

5. _____
   _____

Passive Voice

1. _____
   _____

2. In the 1700s, powdered wigs were worn by fashionable men and women.

3. _____
   _____

4. Edmonton was hit with a hugh tornado last year.

5. Many new ideas were proposed (by various people) over the years.

What is the subjunctive?

The *subjunctive* is an as yet unrealized situation.

Study the three instances that require the subjunctive and note the form of the verb used in each case.

1. Unreal conditions using *if* or *wish* (use *were*)

   If <u>she were</u> the nurse, I would feel more confident.
   I *wish* <u>she were</u> the nurse.

2. Clauses starting with *that* after verbs such as *ask, request, demand, suggest, order, insist,* or *command* (use infinitive form of verb)

> I *asked* that <u>he be</u> quiet.
>
> The conductor *insisted* that <u>each person remain</u> seated.

3. Clauses starting with *that* after adjectives expressing urgency, as in *it is necessary, it is imperative, it is urgent, it is important,* and *it is essential* (use infinitive form of verb)

> *It is necessary* that <u>he be</u> accurate.
>
> *It is urgent* that <u>Tania answer</u> the letter.

In each of these three instances, notice that the verb following the italicized word or phrase does not agree with its subject.

• PRACTICE

In each of the following sentences, underline the word or phrase that determines the subjunctive. Then circle the subjunctive (the subject and verb that does not agree). An example has been done for you.

> She <u>ordered that</u> the (books be) sent immediately.

1. The writing required that Alice first define several words.

2. It was necessary that she go to the library for help.

3. If she were focused, she would finish the work quickly.

4. The librarian suggested that Alice consult a particularly good medical encyclopedia in the reference section.

5. Alice wishes that this librarian were always available for advice.

Confusions with *should* and *would*

Do not use more than one modal auxiliary (*can, may, might, must, should, ought*) with the main verb.

> **Incorrect:** Julius *shouldn't ought* to interfere.
>
> **Correct:**   Julius *ought not* interfere.
>
>   or
>
> Julius *shouldn't* interfere.

Do not use *should of, would of,* or *could of* to mean *should have, would have,* or *could have.*

> **Incorrect:** Claudia *would of* come if she *could of.*
>
> **Correct:**   Claudia *would have* come if she *could have.*

Mastery and editing tests

TEST 1   **Editing for Correct Verbs**

Edit the following paragraph to correct all errors with verbs.

I would be so happy if Carlos was given a promotion. He worked in this company since 1985. He has brung out the best in people no matter in which department he works. I requested he is considered for the promotion. The supervisor said today that she already made up her mind last week. I hope to change her mind. The work is always done accurately and fast by Carlos [change this sentence to active voice]. Furthermore, when a colleague of his become ill last year, Carlos done all of the colleague's work in addition to his own without one complaint. Just now I have wrote a formal letter on his behalf.

TEST 2   **Editing for Correct Verbs**

Edit the following paragraph to correct all errors with verbs.

We hurried toward the gate at Toronto's Skydome because we would of been late for the start of the baseball game. I was not knowing this at the time, but we passed beneath the artwork of one of Canada's most famous artists, Michael Snow. The 14 large shiny figures of sports fans make up a single sculpture known as "The Audience" and are locating at the northeast and northwest corners of the Skydome. Other examples of Michael Snow's art can be finded in some of the most famous galleries and museums in the world. You can also be viewing some of his art if you walk around downtown Toronto. For example, the fibreglass replicas of Canada geese that hanged from the ceiling of the Eaton Centre were also being created by Michael Snow. Since the 1950s, he is one of Canada's best known artists. As we approached the Skydome that day, I would never of thought that I would be looking at famous art. I was only wanting to see a baseball game.

TEST 3   **Editing for Correct Verbs**

Edit the following paragraph to correct all errors with verbs.

The leader is announcing that the presentation will resume after the lunch period will finish. She says that we shouldn't ought to miss the two o'clock lecture. It will be presented by the Director of Consumer Affairs [change to active voice]. Although we had invited her many times before, she had never spoke to our group until now. She is in her position since 1990 and can speak with a great deal of experience. The video equipment, which has laid in the storage area all week, will be set up. I asked that the director speaks about several issues that are of concern to us. The announcer reminded us that the director's work last year has a great effect on the safety of children's car seats. I remember that after the lecture last year, the audience ask many questions. My friend and I prepared several questions that we want to ask, but on the way to lunch we lose our notes and have to go back to the auditorium to look for them.

TEST 4   Editing for Correct Verbs

Edit the following paragraph to correct all errors with verbs.

Maxine should of went to camp last summer; instead, she stood at home, looking for things to do. I seen her walking to the candy store every day, sometimes alone, sometimes with a friend. Her mother wishes she had gone and she tells her so, but Maxine don't listen. Maybe her judgment will improve after the summer ends. Her father told her that if she wanted to go to camp next year, he will pay for it. Since 1990, he had been sending his children to camp, and he sees no reason why Maxine should miss out on it. Camp was a benefit for the rest of the children; now the youngest child had to make up her mind to get that benefit.

TEST 5   Editing for Correct Verbs

Edit the following paragraph to correct all errors with verbs.

In the fifth century, people built Venice on low mud islands between the mouths of two rivers [change to passive]. The city, half on land and half in the water, is called "The Bride of the Adriatic" since the sixteenth century. The setting of this city is unique. One hundred and seventy canals make up the streets and avenues. Gondolas are rode by tourists the same way taxicabs serve as transportation in other cities. This Italian city is rich in tradition, a tradition that dated back well over a thousand years. Venetian architects builded magnificent palaces and churches. They are filled with priceless treasures that hadn't ought to be lost. Students by the thousands have spend time in Venice studying the beautiful sculpture and paintings. Venetian libraries also hold priceless relics and manuscripts. The city may be a rich museum, but it is also a city with modern problems. Erosion, pollution, and tides are taking a toll on the structures. There are churches that are world famous, but their paintings and statues suffered from the toxic fumes of the motor boats that constantly make waves in the city's canals. I wish we was able to publicize all of the problems of this famous place so something could be done. We don't want to read in the newspaper someday that Venice has sank into the sea. I suggest the best prize for our newspaper's annual essay contest is a romantic two week trip to Venice for two.

Many single people want to meet new people and develop significant relationships. However, they often feel that there is nobody out there to meet, or that there is no place to go where they can socialize with other eligible single people. Today, how does a single person meet others?

An important part of the writing process is to brainstorm before you actually write. If you can brainstorm with several other people, you are in an even better position to gather a variety of ideas. You do not need to use every idea that comes up during the brainstorming process.

The class should divide into groups to discuss the topic in some detail. One member of the group may be chosen to keep notes on the points being made. After discussing the issue for twenty minutes or so, the group should develop a list of pointers that could be given to a single person seeking new friendships. Once this list is as complete as possible, put it into an order that you can now use to write a summary of the ideas generated during class discussion.

Your instructor may encourage you to provide an actual outline form with your summary. In an outline, you may have major headings and items under the major headings, called subheadings.

Using Correct Capitalization and Punctuation

Ten basic rules for capitalization

Many students are often confused or careless about the use of capital letters. Sometimes these students capitalize words without thinking, or they capitalize *important* words without really understanding what makes them important enough to deserve a capital letter. The question of when to capitalize words becomes easier to answer when you study the following rules and carefully apply them to your own writing.

1. Capitalize the first word of every sentence.
2. Capitalize the names of specific things and places.

   Specific buildings:

   > We visited the Calgary Tower.
   >> *but*
   >
   > We visited the tower.

   Specific streets, cities, provinces, countries:

   > He lives outside Moncton.
   >> *but*
   >
   > He lives outside the city.

   Specific organizations:

   > Judd belongs to the Lions Club.
   >> *but*
   >
   > Judd belongs to several clubs.

   Specific institutions:

   > The librarian is from the University of Manitoba.
   >> *but*
   >
   > The librarian is from a university in Manitoba.

Specific bodies of water:

> They live along the Grand River.
>
> *but*
>
> They live along the river.

3. Capitalize days of the week, months of the year, and holidays. Do not capitalize the names of seasons.

> The first Monday in September is Labour Day.
>
> *but*
>
> My favourite season is autumn.

4. Capitalize the names of all languages, nationalities, races, religions, deities, and sacred terms.

> My Colombian friend speaks Spanish.
>
> The Torah is the sacred book of Judaism.

5. Capitalize the first word and every important word in a title. Do not capitalize articles, prepositions, or short connecting words in the title.

> *In the Skin of a Lion* was written by Michael Ondaatje.

6. Capitalize the first word of a direct quotation.

> The child said, "Take me home right now."
>
> *but*
>
> "Take me home," the child cried, "right now."

Note: *right* is not capitalized because it is not the beginning of the sentence in quotation marks.

7. Capitalize historical events, eras, and documents.

> The Quiet Revolution
>
> The Great Depression
>
> Confederation

8. Capitalize the words north, south, east, and west when they are used as places rather than as directions.

> The conference was held in the Far East.
>
> *but*
>
> Brandon is southwest of Winnipeg.

9. Capitalize people's names.

Proper names:

> Carole Chin

Professional titles when they are used with the person's proper name:

| Dean Wiley | *but* | a dean |
| Doctor Perez | *but* | a doctor |

Term for a relative (such as mother, sister, nephew, uncle) when it is used in the place of the proper name:

I spoke with Father yesterday.

Note: terms for relatives are not capitalized if a pronoun, article, or adjective is used with the name.

I spoke with my father yesterday.

10. Capitalize brand names.

| Twinings Earl Grey Tea | *but* | tea |
| Skippy Peanut Butter | *but* | peanut butter |

EXERCISE 1   Capitalization

Capitalize wherever necessary.

1. When my family visited sweden, we stayed near stockholm in a little town called tumba.

2. The town is situated in the southeast part of the country.

3. I was very glad to be there on june 24 to participate in their spring holiday called midsummer day.

4. The weather was beautiful, and a cool breeze came from the baltic sea.

5. My cousin asked me, "have you ever been sailing?"

6. I had only watched people sailing on lake ontario.

7. we decided to explore some of the 24,000 islands that attract tourists every year.

8. Not only was cousin lars an outstanding engineer, he was also an experienced sailor.

9. My parents, who were less adventurous, enjoyed taking the steamboat called the cinderella to visit the island where the king and queen live.

10. Before we left, I visited uppsala university, the country's oldest and largest university, founded in 1477.

EXERCISE 2   Capitalization

Read the paragraph and capitalize wherever necessary.

Michael Ondaatje was born in sri lanka in 1943. In 1954, he moved to london, england, with his mother. After relocating to canada in 1962, he studied at the university of toronto and at queen's university in kingston, ontario. He is best known for his novel *the english patient*, which was the first novel by a canadian author to win the prestigious booker prize. The book was set in italy during the final months of the second world war. Later, the book was adapted for screen, and it won nine academy awards in 1996. Although most of us know him as a novelist, ondaatje began his writing career with four books of poetry. Ondaatje currently resides in toronto with his wife, linda spalding. Together they edit the literary journal *brick*.

EXERCISE 3   Capitalization

Read the paragraph and capitalize wherever necessary.

The 18th century is sometimes called the golden age of piracy. When the war of the spanish succession ended, unemployed sailors in france and england were tempted to support themselves by robbing the treasures off the ships of the spanish fleet, the ships that brought treasures from the spanish colonies in the west indies back to spain. One of the "gentleman pirates" was major stede bonnet, a wealthy landowner from barbados, who became a pirate simply for adventure. He counted among his friends a man by the name of edward teach, better known to us today as blackbeard. Bonnet equipped a sloop called the revenge, and in 1717, he began to raid ships in the atlantic ocean near the coast of virginia. He was hanged for piracy in november 1718. The only female pirates known to history were mary read and anne bonny, captured on calico jack's ship in 1720 and brought to trial at st. jago de la vega, jamaica. Contrary to popular belief, pirates seldom killed their victims, and there is no record that pirates ever forced people to walk the plank.

Eight basic uses of the comma

Many students feel uncertain about when to use the comma. The starting point is to concentrate on a few basic rules. These rules will cover most of your needs.

The tendency now in English is to use fewer commas than in the past. There is no one perfect, complete set of rules on which everyone agrees. However, if you learn these basic eight, your common sense will help you figure out what to do in other cases. Remember that a comma usually signifies a pause in a sentence. As you read a sentence out loud, listen to where you pause within the sentence. Where you pause is often your clue that a comma is needed. Notice that in each of the examples for the following eight uses, you can pause where the comma is placed.

1. **Use a comma to separate items in a series. (A series means more than two items.)**

   The coach was angry, tense, and argumentative.

   Her job required hauling heavy equipment, keeping track of shipments, and mediating disputes between workers.

   - Some writers omit the comma before the *and* that introduces the last item.

   The coach was angry, tense and argumentative.

- When an address or date occurs in a sentence, each part is treated like an item in a series. A comma is put after each item, including the last:

He lived at 569 Gladstone Avenue, Ottawa, Ontario, for most of his life.

The interview was televised on October 3, 1995, from Toronto.

- A group of adjectives may be regarded as a series if the adjectives equally modify the noun. You can usually test this by putting *and* between the adjectives to see if the idea is still clear.

Use commas: The huge, welcoming crowd awaited the dignitary.
                         (*Test:* The phrase *huge and welcoming crowd* makes sense.)

Do not use commas: She packed the charcoal grey sweater.
                         (*Test: charcoal and grey sweater* does not make sense. The adjectives *charcoal grey* belong together.)

• PRACTICE 1

In each of the following sentences, insert commas wherever they are needed.

1. Anyone who listens to the radio watches television and reads books newspapers and magazines cannot help but be aware of statistics.

2. Statistics appear in the claims of advertisers in predictions of election results and opinion polls in cost-of-living indexes and in reports of business trends and cycles.

3. On the basis of statistics, important decisions are made in the fields of government industry and education.

4. Statistical data are usually collected by consulting existing source material by setting up a survey and collecting data at firsthand from individuals or organizations and by conducting scientific experiments that measure or count under controlled conditions.

5. The results of statistical investigation may be stated in a simple sentence presented in the form of a numerical table or shown in the form of a graph or chart.

2. **Use a comma along with a coordinating conjunction to combine two simple sentences (also called independent clauses) into a single compound sentence. Remember the seven coordinating conjunctions you learned in Chapter 5: *and, but, or, nor, for, yet, so.***

The situation was tense, but the pilot and co-pilot
were determined to do their best.

Be careful that you use the comma with the conjunction only when you are combining sentences. If you are combining only words or phrases, no comma is used.

I was tired but elated.

My friends and family congratulated me.

PRACTICE 2

In each of the following sentences, insert commas wherever they are needed.

1. The satirical news show *This Hour Has 22 Minutes* is one of my favourite programs but I especially like one segment on it called "Talking to Americans."

2. Rick Mercer plays a TV reporter who travels through the United States and he asks average Americans questions that are designed to test their knowledge of Canada.

3. Some Americans do not want to admit their ignorance about Canada nor do they want to pass up a chance to be on TV.

4. The degree of American ignorance about Canada is remarkable for some people actually think that the Canadian government operates out of a giant igloo.

5. The show illustrates the fact that Canadians may know a lot about the United States yet Americans know almost nothing about their neighbours to the north.

3. **Use a comma to follow introductory words, expressions, phrases, or clauses.**

   A. Introductory words (such as *yes, no, oh, well*)

      Yes, you are correct.

   B. Introductory expressions (transitions such as *as a matter of fact, finally, secondly, furthermore, consequently*)

      Finally, the work is complete.

   C. Introductory phrases

Long prepositional phrase:	During the first few years, the business made little profit.
Participle phrase:	Looking carefully, I recognized the background.
Infinitive phrase:	To illustrate, let us imagine a small family grocery store.

   D. Introductory dependent clauses beginning with a subordinating conjunction (see Chapter 6).

      If he arrives late, he won't get the job.

PRACTICE 3

In each of the following sentences, insert commas wherever they are needed.

1. Before World War II people with disabilities had little chance to find employment in industry.

2. With the severe labour shortage at that time employers took a second look at the remaining population.

3. Recognizing many physically challenged people were well trained and capable industrial leaders began to hire these people.

4. As a matter of fact the physically disabled men and women turned out to be a significant asset rather than a liability.

5. Yes statistics show that physically challenged workers are more enthusiastic about their jobs have fewer absences have fewer accidents on the job and are less likely to shift from one job to another than the general population of workers.

4. Use commas surrounding a word, phrase, or clause when the word or group of words interrupts the main idea.

   A. Interrupting word

       The choice, however, is up to you.

   B. Interrupting phrase

Prepositional phrase:	They may, in fact, take the trip.
Appositive phrase:	Donna, the woman in the black knit dress, is my childhood friend.

   C. Interrupting clause:

       The train will, I am sure, depart on time.

       Donna, who is wearing the black knit dress, is my childhood friend.

Note: Sometimes the same word, phrase, or clause can be used in more than one way. Often this changes the rule for punctuation.

Example: the word *however*

Use commas if the word interrupts in the middle of a clause:

       The facts, however, are not encouraging.

Use a semicolon and a comma if the word connects two independent clauses:

       The public is enthusiastic; however, the facts are not encouraging.

Example: the relative clause *who is wearing the black knit dress*

Use commas if the clause interrupts and is not essential to the main idea:

       Donna, who is wearing the black knit dress, is my childhood friend.

Do not use commas if the clause is part of the identity, necessary to the main idea:

       The woman who is wearing the black knit dress is my childhood friend Donna.

The clause *who is wearing the black knit dress* is necessary for identifying which woman is being referred to as the childhood friend.

PRACTICE 4

In each of the following sentences, insert commas wherever they are needed.

1. The McMichael Art Gallery which is located in Kleinburg Ontario is home to many beautiful paintings.

2. It has among other works paintings by my favourite artist Lawren Harris.

3. The gallery a large wooden house overlooking the East Humber River Valley was first built by Robert and Signe McMichael in 1951.

4. Robert McMichael a wealthy businessman collected art by Canadian artists.

5. Now of course McMichael's collection has become a national treasure.

5. Use a comma around nouns in direct address. (A noun in direct address is the name or title used in speaking to someone.)

I wondered, Peter, if you should leave soon.

PRACTICE 5

In each of the following sentences, insert commas wherever they are needed.

1. I think Denise your paper was very well written.

2. Helen when does your flight arrive?

3. I insist Mr. Senator on your putting more thought into this matter.

4. Honey why don't we eat out tonight?

5. Dad could I borrow the car on Friday?

6. When following the imperial rather than metric system of measurement, use a comma or commas in numbers of one thousand or larger.

4,567

2,345,678,910

PRACTICE 6

In each of the following numbers, insert commas wherever they are needed.

1. 3640722

2. 41555

3. 298066400

4. 987

5. 6432

7. Use a comma to set off exact words spoken in dialogue.

"I expect," he shouted, "absolute obedience."

- The comma as well as the period is always placed inside the quotation marks.

• PRACTICE 7

In each of the following sentences, insert commas wherever they are necessary.

1. "I hope" she pleaded "you'll agree to our terms."
2. "Perhaps" I answered "but we will need time to study the document."
3. "You won't" she added "get a better offer."
4. I responded "We never make a hasty decision."
5. "Well then" she concluded "I'll hope to hear from you soon."

8. Use a comma where it is necessary to prevent a misunderstanding.

After eating, the guest returned to his room.

• PRACTICE 8

In each of the following sentences, insert commas wherever they are needed to prevent a misunderstanding.

1. Waking the woman felt the sun on her face.
2. If you will swallow your ears will clear.
3. Whoever this is is certainly making a mistake.
4. For Melinda Timothy Findley is her favourite writer.
5. Studying in groups often helps teachers say.

EXERCISE 1   Using the Comma Correctly

Edit the following paragraph by inserting commas wherever needed.

In Peru a country known for its different landscapes Lake Titicaca has the special distinction of being the highest navigable lake in the world. It is 12500 feet above sea level. It is also South America's largest lake and is about half the size of Lake Ontario. In early June before the tourists arrive the weather is cold but beautiful. To tell the truth that is the best time to visit. The lake which is a famous tourist attraction seems more breathtaking when only the indigenous people are to be seen. In the early morning you might ride a boat illuminated by candles out to the islands of the Uros Indians or you might visit the hilly island of Taquile. There you would see the men dressed in traditional sandals black trousers ruffled-sleeved white shirts, short black and white vests a pin striped white wrap around the waist and red and white caps flopped to one side.

EXERCISE 2   Using the Comma Correctly

Edit the following paragraph by inserting commas wherever needed.

At the time of Confederation many Canadians considered lacrosse Canada's national sport. The National Lacrosse Association founded in 1867 and its slogan *Our Country and Our Game* certainly clamed that status. Lacrosse was also closely associated with the game of baggataway which was played by several First Nations. On the very day of Canada's creation Kahnawake took the Dominion lacrosse title which was considered a world championship at the time by defeating the Montreal Lacrosse Club. The First Nations in eastern North America originated the sport but non-Natives had altered the game by drawing up new "rules." Even so the Kahnawake team defeated the Montreal team while playing under the non-Native rules. Lacrosse had a sporadic history before 1914. After an enthusiastic beginning in the 1860s it ebbed in the early 1870s as a result they say of the presence of "rowdy" or undesirable elements at many of the matches. The game revived in the 1880s but also changed from amateur to professional. Around the same time lacrosse also became a national sport although the sport didn't boast a national association until 1912.

EXERCISE 3   Using the Comma Correctly

In the paragraph that follows, insert commas wherever they are needed.

Dedication and perseverance mark the career of African-Canadian jazz pianist Oscar Peterson. Born in Montreal on August 15 1925 Peterson was the fourth in a family of five children. Peterson's father a porter with the Canadian Pacific Railway learned to play piano on his own. He also encouraged his children to become proficient musicians. Oscar's long and distinguished career really began to take off when Norman Ganz the legendary jazz producer discovered Oscar playing at a club in Montreal. Oscar then impressed those who came to see him at New York's Carnegie Hall. Since the 1950s he has been considered the best jazz pianist in the world and has toured throughout North America Europe and Asia. In 1993 Oscar suffered a serious stroke. He could not play for two years; however he overcame this setback and is still touring recording and composing today. He has since received a Grammy Award for Lifetime Achievement and an International Jazz Hall of Fame Award proof that Oscar Peterson is still regarded as one of the greatest jazz musicians ever to play.

Three uses for the apostrophe

1. To form the possessive.

   A. Add *'s* to singular nouns:

the uniform of the nurse	= the nurse*'s* uniform
the muffler of the bus	= the bus*'s* muffler
the pension of the worker	= the worker*'s* pension

Watch out that you choose the right noun to make possessive. Always ask yourself who or what possesses something. In the sentences above, the nurse possesses the uniform, the muffler belongs to the bus, and the pension belongs to the worker.

Note these unusual possessives:

Hyphenated words: brother-in-law*'s* job

Joint possession: Edwin and Mary*'s* daughter

Individual possession: Victor*'s* and Victoria*'s* secrets

B. Add *'s* to irregular plural nouns that do not end in *-s*.

the dresses of the women = the women*'s* dresses

the revenge of the mice = the mice*'s* revenge

C. Add *'s* to indefinite pronouns:

anybody*'s* guess

someone*'s* idea

SOME INDEFINITE PRONOUNS

anyone	everyone	no one	someone
anybody	everybody	nobody	somebody
anything	everything	nothing	something

Possessive pronouns in English (his, hers, its, ours, yours, theirs, whose) do *not* use an apostrophe.

Whose books are these?

These books are *hers*.

Those books are *ours*.

D. Add only an apostrophe to regular plural nouns ending in *-s*.

the hutch of the rabbits   = the rabbits' hutch

the victories of the soccer players = the soccer players' victories

- A few singular nouns ending in the *s* or *z* sound are awkward-sounding if another *s* sound is added. You may in these cases drop the final *s*. Let your ear help you make the decision.

Charles Dickens' novels *not* Charles Dickens's novels

2. To form certain plurals in order to prevent confusion, use *'s.*

    A. Numbers: 200's

    B. Letters: *c*'s and *d*'s

    C. Years: 1900's or 1900s

    D. Abbreviations: M.D.'s

    E. Words referred to in a text: She uses too many *like's* in her conversation.

       • Be sure *not* to use the apostrophe to form a plural in any case other than these.

3. To show where letters have been omitted in contractions, use an apostrophe.

cannot   = can't

should not = shouldn't

will not   = won't (the only contraction that changes its spelling)

I am   = I'm

she will   = she'll

EXERCISE 1   Using the Apostrophe

Fill in each of the blanks using the rules you have just studied for uses of the apostrophe.

  1. the flow of the water   the _____ flow

  2. the office of the president   the _____ office

  3. the hopes of the people   the _____ hopes

  4. the nursery for children   the _____ nursery

  5. The briefcase belongs to you.   the briefcase is _____

  6. the work of everybody   _____ work

  7. They will not open today.   They _____ open today.

  8. in the century of 1900   the _____

  9. the personalities of Jennifer and Michelle   _____

     (individual possession)   _____ personalities

10. the reviews of the critics   the _____ reviews

EXERCISE 2   Using the Apostrophe

Rewrite each of the following sentences using an apostrophe to make a contraction or to show possession. An example is done for you.

    The brakes of your car are faulty.

    Your car's brakes are faulty.

  1. The playground of the school is empty.

    _____

2. <u>The marketplace of the town</u> was crowded.

_____

3. <u>The fees of the lawyers</u> seemed excessive.

_____

4. <u>We have</u> tried to convince him without success.

_____

5. <u>What is</u> for dinner?

_____

6. <u>Who is</u> responsible for this mess?

_____

7. <u>The advice from my sister-in-law</u> is generally good.

_____

8. You will find those sweaters in the <u>department for men.</u>

_____

9. <u>The test scores of Watson and Dana</u> were the highest in the class.

_____

10. <u>The home of my aunt and uncle</u> is warm and inviting.

_____

EXERCISE 3   Using the Apostrophe

Insert apostrophes wherever necessary.

Everybodys talking about Jims new car. Its design is based on an old Italian model first built in the 1930s. Its strange to observe a model youve only seen in old movies. I dont think there are too many of his friends who wont be thrilled to accept an invitation for a ride. All his friends cars are either American or Japanese—Hondas, Chevys, and Fords. His parents generosity allowed him to buy the car, but now Jim realizes the upkeep will cost half his weeks pay. Now hell ask his supervisor about his chances for a small raise.

Other marks of punctuation

Four uses for quotation marks

1. For a direct quotation:

"Thank you," she answered, "but I do not need it."

Not for an indirect quotation:

She answered that she did not need it.

2. For material copied word for word from a source:

According to *Maclean's* magazine, "Government spending on health care has dropped over the past 10 years."

According to *Canadian Geographic* magazine, "Adult male grizzly bears weigh 135 to 390 kilograms; adult females weigh 95 to 275 kilograms. The largest bears live on the west coast of British Columbia and Alaska, where adult males may weigh more than 300 kilograms and adult females weigh more than 200 kilograms."

3. For titles of shorter works such as short stories, one-act plays, poems, articles in magazines and newspapers, songs, essays, and chapters of books:

"Suzanne" is a famous poem by Leonard Cohen.

"The Gold Bug," a short story by Edgar Allen Poe, is a masterpiece of detection.

4. For words used in a special way:

"Smashing" is a term used by the British, the way we would use the word "wonderful."

Underlining

> Underlining is used in handwriting or typing to indicate a title of a long work such as a book, full-length play, magazine, or newspaper. (In print or on many word processors, such titles are put in italics.)

In print: George James is a journalist with *The New York Times.*

In type or handwriting: George James is a journalist with <u>The New York Times</u>.

•PRACTICE 1

In each of the following sentences, insert quotation marks or underlining wherever they are needed.

1. After the Race is a short story included in the book Dubliners by James Joyce.

2. In an address to the Press Club in Washington, D.C., Pierre Trudeau said, Living next to you is like sleeping with an elephant.

3. The director told his actors that they would have to learn their parts in twenty-four hours.

4. The word night should never be spelled nite.

5. He saw the article Digging Near the Nile in last month's issue of Archeology.

Three uses for the semicolon

1. To join two independent clauses whose ideas and/or sentence structure are related:

> The dog sat by the fence all day; the cat refused to jump down.

2. To combine two sentences using an adverbial conjunction:

> The dog sat by the fence all day; consequently, the cat refused to jump down.

3. To separate items in a series when the items themselves contain commas:

> She worked with Vermell, her colleague; Lisa, her daughter; and John, her best friend.

If the writer had used only commas to separate items in the last example, the reader might think six people were listed as helpers.

• PRACTICE 2

In each of the following sentences, insert a semicolon wherever needed.

1. A good way to understand a play is to read it a better way is to see the play produced.
2. The old pipes in the street must be replaced otherwise the water main will burst.
3. The interviewer spoke with Millicent Silver, a musician James O'Leary, a journalist and Charles Bedford, an architect.
4. The bank teller was very polite however he would not release the cheque.
5. Boats are increasingly being made of fiberglass perhaps wooden boats will become obsolete.

Four uses for the colon

1. After a completed independent clause (often using the expressions *the following* or *as follows*) when the material that follows is a list, an illustration, or an explanation

   • A list

   > Be sure to bring the following items: old shoes, a flashlight, and an empty coffee can.

   Notice colons are not used in the middle of clauses in which such expressions as *consists of, including, like,* or *such as* introduce a list:

We like to catch fish such as striped bass, trout, or catfish.

- An explanation or illustration

   She was a remarkable woman: by the age of nineteen she was already a well-known poet.

2. For the salutation of a business letter

   Dear Sir:

   Your Honour:

3. In telling time

   The play begins at 8:00 p.m.

4. Between the title and subtitle of a book

   A Mouthful of Rivets: Women at Work in World War II

PRACTICE 3

In each of the following sentences, insert colons where they are needed.

1. Three tennis players were on television that afternoon Monica Seles, Martina Hingis, and Anna Kournikova.
2. The actress has what every actress needs vanity.
3. The fruit store has several varieties of lettuce such as iceberg and romaine.
4. The institute will prepare you in three important areas office skills, personal grooming, and interview techniques.
5. The clock went off at 610 this morning, but I continued to sleep.

The dash and parentheses

The comma, dash, and parentheses can all be used to show an interruption of the main idea. The particular form you choose depends on the degree of interruption.

Use the dash for a less formal and more emphatic interruption of the main idea.

She was—I really believe this—telling the truth.

He departed—and I can prove this—on the seven thirty flight.

Use the parentheses to insert extra information that some of your readers might want to know but that is not at all essential for the main idea. Such information is not emphasized.

Prime Minister Pierre Trudeau (1919–2000) was well liked by the vast majority of Canadians.

These plummeting figures (see Chart 3) indicate an imminent recession.

PRACTICE 4

Insert dashes or parentheses wherever needed.

1. Scientists announced recently *Nature*, February 2001 that there are 30,000 genes that make up the human genetic code.

2. Scientists have also identified genetic defects more than 3,200 that are linked to various diseases.

3. No technique at least not in my lifetime seems to offer more promise than gene replacement therapy.

4. In Muscular Dystrophy, muscle cells without the protein called dystrophin see photo above waste away.

5. Unfortunately and this has been a big blow to genetic researchers nobody has yet been cured by the experiments with this therapy.

EXERCISE 1   Using All Punctuation Marks Correctly

In each of the following sentences, insert commas, apostrophes, quotation marks, underlining, semicolons, colons, the dash, or parentheses wherever they are needed.

1. The Spanish word for goodbye is adios.

2. I spoke to the man in French he spoke back to me in Greek.

3. My professor could speak the following languages Russian German and Chinese.

4. All foreign words are explained see the glossary at the back of the book.

5. Have you read Judy Rebick's essay Kick'em Again?

6. Please I begged let me visit Ecuador.

7. The man spoke with a distinct accent however I could not guess his first language.

8. Most children in Canada and I think this is a mistake do not take the study of Canadian history seriously.

9. We were hoping to visit cities such as Lima Bogota and Quito.

10. The train departs at 540 therefore we must leave for the station as soon as possible.

EXERCISE 2   Using All Punctuation Marks Correctly

In each of the following sentences, insert commas, apostrophes, quotation marks, underlining, semicolons, colons, the dash, or parentheses wherever they are needed.

1. Emily Carr 1871–1945 was unusual for her time.

2. Women in the nineteenth century learned painting to be refined ladies were never encouraged to be serious artists.

3. Emily went off to San Francisco London and Paris to study painting seriously in fact she emerged as one of Canadas prominent painters.

4. She wrestled with the artists dilemma should she paint in the traditional style of the day or should she experiment with creative styles?

5. I recently bought a calendar that has many of Carrs works reproduced Totem Poles completed in 1912 Blue Sky completed in 1934 Mountain Forest completed in 1936 and Rushing Sea of Undergrowth painted in 1936.

6. Many of her paintings depicted the wilderness and islands of coastal British Columbia native village sites were also favourite subjects for her to paint.

7. The lack of interest in her work made Carr give up painting in 1916 however other Canadian painters some of whom were members of the famous Group of Seven saw her work and encouraged her to continue painting.

8. At the age of 70 when advised for health reasons to slow down Carr turned seriously to writing she received the Governor Generals award for her book Klee Wyck.

9. Painting was an act of self-discovery for Carr she wrote in her journal I always feel when looking at a painting straight in the eye I could have put more into it.

10. She is and I'm serious my favourite artist.

EXERCISE 3   Using All Punctuation Marks Correctly

In each of the following sentences, insert commas, apostrophes, quotation marks, underlining, semicolons, colons, the dash, or parentheses wherever they are needed.

1. Helen plays the saxophone her brother plays the trumpet.

2. Ill take the following items five legal pads a box of paper clips and a box of number two pencils.

3. She never spoke to her neighbours in fact she seldom went out of her house.

4. Winning the prizes were Mr. Hovan chemistry professor Ms. Lopez sociologist and Dr. Madison research scientist at the lab.

5. I found out Peter said that your father was Greek.

6. There is nothing I can do for you today however if you come back tomorrow Ill see what I can do.

7. Women did not act on the stage in Shakespeares time young boys usually played the female roles.

8. Fewer Canadians now live on farms see chart on page 546.

9. He called collect believe it or not just to tell me a joke.

10. I read George Grants well-known book Lament for a Nation.

Mastery and editing tests

TEST 1   **Editing for Correct Capitalization and Punctuation**

In the following sentences, insert correct punctuation and capitalization wherever needed.

1. The plural form for the word mouse is mice.

2. According to his birth certificate he was born in charlottetown, PEI on june 20 1965.

3. The train leaves at 830 and nobodys ready.

4. Moira who is my best friend will meet us at the theatre.

5. If it rains and we pray it doesnt the program will be cancelled.

6. Ladies and gentlemen I am honoured to present the mayor of our great city.

7. My uncle read the newspaper my aunt cooked dinner.

8. My dear said the father kindly you are soon going to feel better.

9. When she returned to work her office coworkers welcomed her back.

10. He grew up west of the rocky mountains but he now lives in halifax.

TEST 2   **Editing for Correct Capitalization and Punctuation**

In the following sentences, insert correct punctuation and capitalization wherever needed.

1. After the guests went home the dirty dishes remained.

2. The word and is a conjunction.

3. She wrote the article for canadian geographic magazine while she was still director of the museum of natural history.

4. While still a baptist minister Tommy Douglas became premier of saskatchewan.

5. The term paper was handed in on time and the quality of the thinking and writing was outstanding.

6. Harold agreed to work late because he wanted to finish the report before the weekend.

7. The Johnsons moved to the west last spring.

8. I called dr. Rosen however I was only able to speak to the nurse.

9. Before eating the dog showed us his tricks.

10. Nancy opened the envelope read the letter and shouted for joy.

TEST 3   Editing for Correct Capitalization and Punctuation

In the following sentences, insert correct punctuation and capitalization wherever needed.

1. Mr. Franklin has retired Eileen Smith will take over his job.
2. I told grandmother to expect me by 700.
3. The score is ten to nothing said the announcer.
4. The woman who is sitting at the desk is the one to ask.
5. Even though she loves to paint Freida is majoring in business.
6. Willy the tall fellow on the right drives up to whistler british columbia nearly every weekend to go skiing.
7. In history class we are studying the french revolution.
8. An interest in expensive clothing nights out and pretty girls caused his bank balance to drop dangerously low.
9. The painting by Titian sold for several million dollars and the museum that purchased it felt it was a bargain.
10. The norwegian student speaks german as well as english.

TEST 4   Editing for Correct Capitalization and Punctuation

Read the following paragraph and insert the correct marks of punctuation and capitalization wherever they are needed.

On february 19 1927 edward samuel rogers called ted rogers made history with the launch of his new radio station. As a child Ted was fascinated with amateur radio. In fact several rooms of his house were filled with equipment and bulky storage batteries. at the time radios operated on batteries which were a real nuisance because they were large unreliable and often leaked dangerous sulphuric acid. Working long hours in his small lab on chestnut street rogers perfected a new way of building radios without batteries. the new batteryless radio gave a reception that was clearer and better than ever before possible. The station started by rogers which is still in existence was known as CFRB. The initials stood for "Canadas First Rogers' Batteryless."

[M. Filey. "Radio Station Celebrates Broadcasting Miracle." *Toronto Sketches 3: The Way We Were*. Toronto: Dundurn, 1994, pp. 59–60.]

TEST 5   Editing for Correct Capitalization and Punctuation

In the following paragraph, insert correct punctuation and capitalization wherever needed.

Without a doubt prime minister trudeaus most controversial decision was to use the war measures act. In the october crisis of 1970 a group of radical separatists in quebec known as the flq kidnapped pierre laporte a prominent quebec politician and james cross a british diplomat. Trudeau then called upon his government to use the war measures act. the act gave the police and the army the powers to do the following detain people indefinitely without a trial search houses without warrants and tap phone lines. Many felt that Trudeau had acted rashly indeed this kind of police action seemed unnecessarily severe. It can be argued that the roots of Quebeckers current mistrust of the canadian government can be traced back to the October Crisis.

Working Together

1. The class should divide into two or more groups. Each group will create an exam that covers the material on capitalization and punctuation in this chapter. Each group must first decide on a plan. You could divide the chapter into sections and choose who will develop the questions for each section. Tests can be made up of multiple choice, fill in the blank, true/false, or sentences or paragraphs to edit. Which kind of test question does your group prefer? Don't forget to decide how many points each question is worth. (The final score should add up to 100% unless you include an extra credit question.) Once your test items are completed, the group will need to read over all the test items for final approval and decide who should set it up on the computer.

   Perhaps your instructor will make copies so that the tests written by the two groups can be exchanged. Each group could then try to take the test written by the other group.

   This exercise will help each member of the class review the material in a way that is fun and productive. After the experience, your class may want to discuss the tests. In what ways are the tests different from each other? What questions or sections are particularly effective? Which sections are most difficult? Finally, are the directions clearly written?

2. Discuss with your group what can be done to help students who feel under pressure at exam time. What should students do to help themselves? What can teachers do to help students reduce their level of anxiety? What can the college or university itself do to help those students who may be unusually tense? Write several paragraphs in which you summarize the advice gathered in your group discussion.

Chapter 11

Review: Using All You Have Learned

Revising more fragments and run-ons

By now, you have learned to recognize the basic fragment or run-on error in your writing. You have worked with revising fairly uncomplicated sentences so that they are correct.

This chapter presents some sentences that are more complicated. Even though a sentence may have more than one dependent clause and several phrases, you must always remember that the sentence must have an independent clause with a subject and verb. For example:

> When my friends and I went to the ballpark, which had been soggy with rain for a week, we never believed that the other team would be there with their equipment.

Cross out all dependent clauses and phrases. Can you find the independent clause? What is the subject? What is the verb? *We never believed* is the independent clause. All other parts of the sentence are dependent clauses that include many prepositional phrases.

The following exercises require mastery of all the skills you have learned in this unit on the sentence. See if you can now revise these more complicated sentences to rid them of fragments and run-ons.

EXERCISE 1   Revising Fragments and Run-Ons

Read each example. Mark each example as a fragment (F), run-on (R), or complete sentence (C). Revise each sentence so it is correct. Use methods you have learned for coordination and subordination.

_____   1. Ten years ago, Niagara Falls, Ontario, was not a lively city it needed a new direction.

_____

_____

_____   2. Trouble began for the city when the economy began to do poorly, this discouraged a much-needed improvement of its infrastructure.

_____

_____

_____   3. The downtown with its casino, new nightclubs, restaurants and even more attractions than ever before.

_____

_____

_____   4. Whenever you walk downtown, you can still hear the roar of the Falls, it echoes throughout the streets of that city.

_____

_____

_____   5. And the large casino is expanding all the time.

_____

_____

_____   6. However, when some people complain that the casino is an unethical way for the city to make money.

_____

_____

_____   7. The wax museum, where people can see replicas of once-popular movie stars and entertainers such as Michael Jackson and Ann-Margret.

_____

_____

_____   8. The atmosphere on Niagara Falls' Clifton Hill, unlike anywhere else in Canada.

_____

_____

_____   9. Upscale establishments such as the Rainforest Café are thriving, and it's harder to find cheesy attractions such as the serpent museum.

_____

_____

_____   10. Stars still shimmering in the night skies through the mists of the Falls.

_____

_____

EXERCISE 2   Revising Fragments and Run-Ons

Read each example. Mark each example as a fragment (F), run-on (R), or complete sentence (C). Revise each sentence so it is correct. Use methods you have learned for coordination and subordination.

_____   1. Because scientists have now confirmed there is a planet like ours with a sun like ours elsewhere in the universe.

_____

_____

_____ 2. The planet which is only forty light years away from earth.

_____

_____

_____ 3. A light year is the distance light travels in a year, it covers six trillion miles in that time.

_____

_____

_____ 4. Some scientists, thinking that it could not be possible to find such a planet so similar to our own earth.

_____

_____

_____ 5. You should go to an observatory and watch how astronomers prove their findings by using the latest equipment.

_____

_____

_____ 6. The new planet has a temperature of 1,800 degrees consequently, it could not have life on its surface.

_____

_____

_____ 7. Planets at these distances are not easy to see you need the most sophisticated equipment.

_____

_____

_____ 8. Astronomers do not have an easy job schedule, they must work through the night.

_____

_____

_____ 9. Although the same question remains about life on other planets.

_____

_____

_____ 10. Meanwhile scientists predict that other such planets in other solar systems in the near future.

_____

_____

EXERCISE 3   Revising Fragments and Run-Ons

Edit the following paragraph to correct all fragments and run-ons.

Joy Kogawa is known for her novels, poetry, and essays, she is also known for her activism. She was born in Vancouver in 1935. As a second-generation Japanese-Canadian. Writing about the stories of Japanese-Canadians. Seeking redress from the Canadian government for its actions against the Japanese-Canadians during the Second World War. Canada was at war with Japan in 1942, the government committed a great injustice. Forcing those Canadians of Japanese descent into special internment camps. As a young girl. Kogawa was one of 20,000 Japanese. Placed in internment camps in British Columbia. The Japanese-Canadians were released after the war but they had nothing when they went home, the Canadian government had taken away their property and their possessions. Kogawa's novel *Obasan* is about her experiences in an internment camp.

EXERCISE 4   Revising Fragments and Run-Ons

Edit the following paragraph to correct all fragments and run-ons.

In a recent issue of *Nature* magazine, scientists have reported the find of new dinosaur fossils. Maybe the biggest meat-eating dinosaur known. Bigger than the Tyrannosaurus Rex. Seventy percent of the skeleton has been recovered consequently scientists can only estimate the creature's size. These fossils were first discovered in Argentina by Ruben Carolini. An automobile mechanic who hunts for dinosaur bones in his spare time. In honour of the discoverer, the dinosaur has been named Giganotosaurus Carolini. This dinosaur resembles Tyrannosaurus Rex but it is thought to have been somewhat longer and three tons heavier. The two dinosaurs lived in completely different times and places, the newly discovered G. Carolini lived 30 million years before T. Rex. Scientists are interested to know if this new dinosaur was a hunter. Or a scavenger.

EXERCISE 5   Revising Fragments and Run-Ons

Edit the following paragraph to correct all fragments and run-ons.

Last spring a talk show host presented a daytime show on laser peels and viewers watched a procedure that took less than two minutes. In front of the television cameras and the live audience. The host had the wrinkles zapped away from around his eyes. These high-energy laser beams are said to be quick, painless, safe, and without scarring. Add this new technology to face-lifts, dermabrasion, collagen injections, and chemical peels! More than 30,000 laser peels have been performed since 1992. Lasers were first used by dermatologists to remove port-wine stains in the 1970s. For many people, this means they can now look as young as they feel but the healing process can be painful and messy. Most physicians believe this is a much more precise method of rejuvenating the skin. Because it's so much more accurate, so much more predictable, and so much safer than other methods. One note of caution. Any physician can buy the equipment with little or no training therefore you should always check out the doctor's experience. A practitioner without experience could zap too deep and cause tissue damage. Following a laser zap, you must scrupulously avoid the sun for several months, afterwards always wear a sunscreen. One bad point. Laser technology is expensive a full-face laser peel costs from $2,000 to $6,000. Sorry, no long-term scientific studies to prove their safety.

Mastery and editing tests

TEST 1   **Editing Sentences for Errors**

The following paragraph contains ten or more sentence errors. Read the paragraph and edit for all errors that you can find.

In a victorian farmhouse on the Eastern shore of Georgian Bay John Watson walks down to the dock and pulls in the nets with the days catch of perch the local specialty. Here John and his wife has one goal to live simply. After working for many years in city jobs this retired couple spend their time tasting the good local fish, creating their own vegetable garden, and the visit of friends from time to time. Mrs. Watson is well versed in the art of preparing gourmet fare but today she favours simple foods. Why make the difficult meals when a simple meal is bound to please she says. Meals are served out on the porch facing the bay. Mrs. Watson does all the cooking herself. No fast food meals. When the boats are in harbour its only a short walk from the house to find out what the fishing is like.

TEST 2   **Editing Sentences for Errors**

The following paragraphs contain ten or more sentence errors. Read the paragraphs and edit for all errors that you can find.

Virtually all societies have maintained some beliefs about witchcraft or sorcery. Before the witch craze European beliefs were similar to those found on other continents witches and sorcerers were sometimes feared sometimes persecuted but often respected and recognized as people who served a useful role in the social order. For instance they provided charms and amulets to protect people from harm or sickness. They would act as oracles to decide the innocence or guilt of accused people. Magic directed against political leaders, however, was regarded as treason.

Belief in witches were a continuing preoccupation of villagers. But not an obsession. The penalties for unauthorized or malicious practice of witchcraft were commensurate with those enforced for other kinds of assault on individuals or their property.

Before C.E. 1000, the church's *Canon Episcopi* law tended to hold that it was both un-christian and illegal to believe in the reality of withes. Witchcraft was not treated as part of the conspiracy theory of the demonic versus God. Except for the *Canon*'s claim that women who believed themselves able to use love incantations or to fly at night with the pagan goddess Diana were suffering from delusions planed by the devil. The *Canon* asserted that the folkloric practice associated with such beliefs would disappear as all people became christian.

Between C.E. 1000 and 1480, witches and sorcerers along with other manifestations of supernatural beings were redefined. Rather than harmless and misunderstood relics of pagan life, they became agents of the devil. In fact many of the accusations made against witches in this period incest, infanticide, and cannibalism were the same as those that had been levelled against the early Christians by pagans. The process whereby folklore witchcraft beliefs ritual magic and devil worship became one overall conspiracy were neither smooth nor gradual it was contested in some areas and embraced in others.

TEST 3   Editing Sentences for Errors

The following paragraph contains ten or more sentence errors. Read the paragraph and edit for all errors that you can find.

Some books describe the common bedbug as harmless but that only means that it causes no pain. And produces no more than a mild reaction on the skin. While this may be true people have been trying to get rid of bedbugs for many centuries. The ancient greeks recommended hanging the feet of a deer at the foot of the bed. A better remedy was to place each leg of the bed in a bowl of water, this prevented bugs from invading the bed although it did not get rid of the bedbugs that were already living in the mattress. Some people trying to figure out the behaviour patterns of bedbugs have watch them leave a bed climb up the wall walk across the ceiling and drop down on the waiting victim. Nearly a century ago it was estimated that four million people in london were plagued with bedbugs and in germany alone seven hundred exterminators were busy all the time trying to get rid of them. No matter what kind of sprays was used including the formulas of such specialists as Southall and Tiffin bedbugs promptly reinvaded rooms where victory had been declared.

TEST 4   Editing Sentences for Errors

The following paragraph contains ten or more sentence errors. Read the paragraph and edit for all errors that you can find.

Recently, a debate has started in Canada on the legalization of marijuana for medical purposes. Marijuana it is claimed relieves symptoms related to the following illnesses epilepsy glaucoma multiple sclerosis and chronic pain. People suffering from the nausea and vomiting associated with some cancer and AIDS therapies. Have found that smoking marijuana brings relief from these side effects. In one case, a man suffering from AIDS has been given the right to cultivate and possess marijuana. To treat his health condition. The ministry of health and welfare has agreed to develop a plan that would include tests on medical marijuana however the recreational use of the drug will still be considered illegal. Although the vast majority of Canadians polled recently favour legalizing marijuana for medical purposes. The government of canada is quick to point out that the drug has not being approved as a therapeutic product in any country.

TEST 5   Editing Sentences for Errors

The following paragraph contains ten or more sentence errors. Read the paragraph and edit for all errors that you can find.

The 1976 Olympic Summer Games was held in Montreal Quebec. They were the first Olympic Games to be held in Canada and will be remembered for among other things their their planning errors labour unrest and construction delays. Most importantly however the Montreal Games ended up costing 10 times more than originally estimated. At the time, the mayor of montreal jean drapeau said that the price would not exceed $124 million. A special lottery Olympic stamps and a series of commemorative coins would help raise the necessary cash to pay for the construction of new facilities. The final cost for the 1976 olympics, however, were about $1.5 billion, a tab that won't be paid off until 2005. In addition, the giant stadium built for the occasion was poorly designed. Although it is impressive to look at. It is an uncomfortable venue for audiences going to see concerts or sporting events. The stadium continues to be a financial burden. A few years ago, a large piece of concrete fell off the exterior of the stadium however nobody was hurt in the incident. The lessons learned during the 1976 Olympics helped the organizers of the 1988 Winter Olympics, which were held in Calgary Alberta. The 1988 Winter Games were on time and on budget and the world-class facilities constructed for the Games are still used to train athletes.

[K. Palmer. "The Montreal Example: How Not to Run Games." *The Toronto Star*, May 19, 2001, pp. B1, B4–B5.]

Working Together

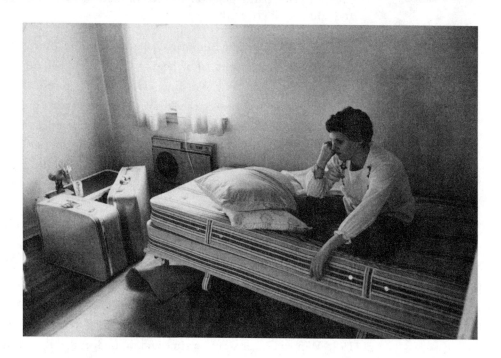

The photograph shows a young woman from Orillia, Ontario, who moved to a large city to begin a career as an actor. The class should divide into two groups. One group should compose five sentences that describe the posture and body language of the woman. The other group should write five sentences that describe the contents and the atmosphere of the room. Each group should put their sentences on the board. Using the material from these group ideas, each student should then write an imaginary diary entry that this young woman might write on her first night in her new surroundings.

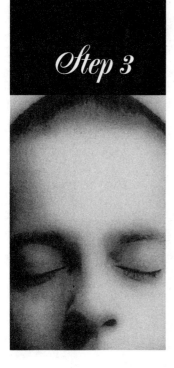

Step 3

UNDERSTANDING THE POWER OF WORDS

CONTENTS

Choosing Words That Work

Using words rich in meaning

Writing is a constant search to find the right word to express thoughts and feelings as accurately as possible. When a writer wants to be precise or wants to give a flavour to a piece of writing, the creative possibilities are almost endless for word choice and sentence construction. The creative writer looks for words that have rich and appropriate meanings and associations.

For instance, if you were describing a young person under five years of age, you might choose one of these words:

imp	brat	youngster
toddler	tot	child
preschooler	rugrat	

Some words have no associations beyond their strict dictionary meaning. These words are said to be neutral. Which word in the list is the most neutral, with the least negative or positive emotional associations?* The person who is writing a brochure for a nursery school would probably choose the word *preschooler* because it identifies the age of the child. A person talking about a child who has just learned to walk would possibly use the word *toddler* because it carries the association of a small child who is toddling along a bit unsteadily. What informal and unkind word might an angry older sibling shout when a younger brother or sister has just coloured all over a favourite book?†

EXERCISE 1   Using Words Rich in Meaning

The following five words all have the same basic meaning as *talk*. For each word, however, an additional meaning makes the word richer and more specific. Match each word in Column A with the letter of the definition from Column B that best fits the meaning of the word.

Column A	Column B
_____ 1. chatter	a. to express ideas in words
_____ 2. gab	b. to exchange thoughts and ideas
_____ 3. blab	c. to reveal secret matters by careless talk
_____ 4. speak	d. to talk rapidly and without stopping
_____ 5. converse	e. to talk idly, often on trivial subjects

---

* Your answer should be *child*.
† Your answer to the second question should be *brat*.

Most languages are rich with words that describe smell. Here are a few English words about *smell*. Match each word in Column A with the letter of the definition from Column B that best fits the meaning of the word.

Column A

_____ 1. odour

_____ 2. scent

_____ 3. stench

_____ 4. fragrance

_____ 5. aroma

Column B

a. a delightful, appealing smell

b. a pleasant smell, often associated with food

c. an odour left by an animal

d. a penetrating objectionable odour

e. a strong smell

EXERCISE 2   Using Words Rich in Meaning

The words *old, car, weak,* or *like* are common neutral words. Listed under each neutral term are four words, each one having its own more precise meaning than the neutral word. In each case, give a definition for the word.

old

1. ancient   _____

2. obsolete   _____

3. antique   _____

4. archaic   _____

car

1. vehicle   _____

2. clunker   _____

3. automobile   _____

4. jalopy   _____

weak

1. feeble   _____

2. frail   _____

3. infirm   _____

4. debilitated   _____

like

1. enjoy   _____

2. relish   _____

3. dote   _____

4. admire   _____

EXERCISE 3   Using Words Rich in Meaning

The words or phrases *careful with money, coarse, plan,* or *firm* are neutral. Listed under each neutral term are four words, each one having its own more precise meaning than the neutral word or phrase. In each case, give a definition for the word.

careful with money

1. stingy   _____

2. thrifty   _____

3. frugal   _____

4. cheap   _____

coarse

1. indelicate _____

2. vulgar   _____

3. obscene   _____

4. crude   _____

plan

1. plot   _____

2. devise   _____

3. conspire   _____

4. scheme   _____

firm

1. harsh   _____

2. stern   _____

3. solid   _____

4. rigid   _____

Understanding loaded words: Denotation/connotation

The careful writer must consider more than the dictionary meaning of a word. Some words have different meanings for different people.

> The *denotation* of a word is its strict dictionary meaning.
> The *connotation* of a word is the meaning (apart from the dictionary meaning) that a person attaches to a word because of the person's personal experience with the word.
>
> *Word:*   liberal
>
> *Denotation:*   to favour nonrevolutionary progress or reform
>
> *Possible connotations:* socially active, free thinking, too generous, far left, favouring many costly government programs

Politicians are usually experts in understanding the connotations of a word. They know, for instance, that if they want to get votes in a conservative area, they should not refer to their views as liberal. The strict dictionary meaning of liberal is "to favour nonrevolutionary progress or reform," certainly an idea that most people would support. However, when most people hear the words *liberal* or *conservative*, they bring to the words many political biases and experiences from their past: their parents' attitudes, the political and social history of the area in which they live, and many other factors that may correctly or incorrectly colour their understanding of a word.

Choosing words that are not neutral but that have more exact or appropriate meanings is a powerful skill for your writing, one that will help your reader better understand the ideas you want to communicate. As your vocabulary grows, your writing will become richer and deeper. Your work will reflect your understanding of all the shades of meanings that words can have.

EXERCISE 1   Denotation/Connotation

In this exercise, you have the opportunity to think of words that are richer in associations than the neutral words that are underlined in the sentences. Write your own word choice in the space to the right of each sentence. Discuss with others in your class the associations you make with the words you have chosen.

1. Peggy's Cove is a unique <u>place</u> located on the coast of Nova Scotia.   _____

2. A highway <u>goes</u> along the coastline and through some small towns.   _____

3. Near the ocean sits a <u>special</u> lighthouse.   _____

4. In the summers, the bagpipe <u>sounds</u> throughout the town and beyond.   _____

5. Tourists often <u>drive</u> for miles to visit the town.   _____

6. I closed my eyes during my visit and listened to the <u>nice</u> sounds of the ocean against the rocks.   _____

7. After our visit, many of us <u>wanted</u> fresh fish and chips.   _____

8. Children <u>were</u> around the wharves in the small harbour.   _____

9. We could hear the fish <u>cooking</u> in the kitchen of the diner.   _____

10. The weather was cool, and the fish and chips tasted <u>good</u>.   _____

EXERCISE 2   Denotation/Connotation

Several sentences follow that contain words that may have positive or negative associations for the reader. Read the sentences and circle the words that carry "emotional" meanings not necessarily contained in the dictionary meaning. Below each sentence, write the emotional meaning the word you have circled has for you. Discuss your answers with your classmates.

1. The top of the mobile home was jammed under the bridge.

   _____

2. The meter maid gave advice to the driver.

   _____

3. Baby clothing from the mobile home was strewn all over the roadway.

   _____

4. Several local merchants stood by watching.

   _____

5. The sirens wailed as the police cruisers drove up.

   _____

EXERCISE 3   Denotation/Connotation

Several sentences follow that contain words that may have positive or negative associations for the reader. Read the sentences and circle the words that carry "emotional" meanings not necessarily contained in the dictionary meaning. Below each sentence, write the emotional meaning the word you have circled has for you. Discuss your answers with your classmates.

1. Be careful if you go into business with someone else because there are some slippery people out there.

   _____

2. Some of them promise to deal fairly, but what they really want is to hog most of the profits.

   _____

3. You have to be businesslike and not too chummy.

   _____

4. One of my friends audited his partner's books and found some glaring errors.

   _____

5. He had swallowed what he had been told and he regretted it.

   _____

Wordiness: In writing, less can be more!

In *The Elements of Style*, essayist E.B. White quotes his old teacher William Strunk, Jr. who said that a sentence "should contain no unnecessary words" and a paragraph "no unnecessary sentences." Strunk's philosophy of writing could be summed up by the commandment he gave many times in his class at Cornell University, "Omit needless words!" It was a lesson that E.B. White took to heart, with wonderful results that we see in his own writing. Often, less is more.

A summary follows of the most important ways you should cut the actual number of words in order to strengthen the power of your ideas. As you read each example of wordiness, notice how the revision has cut out unnecessary words.

Wordy Expressions	**Revision**
1. Avoid redundancy.	
now currently	currently
circle around	circle
blue in colour	blue
2. Avoid wordy phrases.	
due to the fact that	because
for the stated reason that	because
in this day and age	today
at this point in time	now
3. Avoid overuse of the verb *to be*.	
The man is in need of help.	The man needs help.
4. Avoid repeating the same word too many times.	
The book is on the table. The book is my favourite. I have read the book five times.	The book on the table is my favourite. I have read it five times.
5. Avoid beginning a sentence with *there is* or *it is* whenever possible.	
There are two major disadvantages to the new proposal.	The new proposal has two major disadvantages.
6. Avoid flowery or pretentious language.	
It is delightful to contemplate the culinary experience we will enjoy after the termination of this cinematic event.	I can't wait until we have pizza after the movie.
7. Avoid apologetic, tentative expressions.	
in my opinion	
In my opinion, the grading policy for this course should be changed.	The grading policy for this course should be changed.
it seems to me	
Right now, it seems to me that finding a job in my field is very difficult.	Right now, finding a job in my field is very difficult.
I will try to explain	
In this paper, I will try to explain my views on censorship of the campus newspaper.	Censoring the campus newspaper is a mistake.

EXERCISE 1   **Revising Wordy Sentences**

For each of the following sentences, underline the part that is unnecessarily wordy, and on the line below the sentence provide the revision.

1. A large percentage of the people in the waiting room are becoming impatient.

    _____

2. With respect to the matter before the board, I wish to appeal the decision.

    _____

3. Her field of work afforded her many advantages.

    _____

4. The circumstances are such that I do not think we will go there again.

    _____

5. I think he would be happy to have a job along the lines of television writing.

    _____

6. Regarding the doctor's fee, I think I should protest at least part of it.

    _____

7. There are several reasons I have for not wanting to go with her: the first is that I have no time; the second is that I have already seen the movie.

    _____

8. I spoke to him concerning the matter of my future plans.

    _____

9. It is necessary that each member of the team registers for participation in the race.

    _____

10. In terms of the refund, I would expect the full refund as soon as possible.

    _____

EXERCISE 2   **Revising Wordy Sentences**

For each of the following sentences, underline the part that is unnecessarily wordy, and on the line below the sentence provide the revision.

1. Dating practices continue on and obey their own laws no matter how much adults try to regulate them.

    _____

2. There are enormous differences between dating a century ago and dating now.

    _____

3. Back then, the chances for young people to be alone were few in number.

    _____

4. The basic fundamentals of dating were that you had to inform the parents and you had to put up with a chaperone.

   _____

5. A chaperone was a person, usually an aunt or grandmother, who would chaperone a dating situation, to make sure that the situation was in control.

   _____

6. Now all of those restrictions have disappeared from view.

   _____

7. They started to go when the automobile began to be used throughout the whole country.

   _____

8. When World War II came, it appears that the rules for dating changed even more, as society tried to adapt to a stressful time.

   _____

9. After the war, the women's liberation movement was an advance forward in the relations between the sexes.

   _____

10. Today, the basic important essentials of dating seem to be: ask out whoever you want whenever you want.

    _____

EXERCISE 3   Revising Wordy Sentences

For each of the following sentences, underline the part that is unnecessarily wordy, and on the line below the sentence provide the revision.

1. In the scientific century, the twentieth century, we have seen the birth and development of the modern computer.

   _____

2. Computers, it seems to me, are not the only mechanical marvels of our age.

   _____

3. The phonograph, also known as the gramophone, has been with us throughout the century, having come into general use about 1905 or so.

   _____

4. The movies also came into vogue about that time, bringing with them an enthralling new means of entertainment for vast numbers of people.

   _____

5. There is another major invention, of course, which is the automobile.

   _____

6. However, we are using computer-related inventions with more and more frequency in recent years.

   _____

7. The fact is that the washing machines we operate, the radios we play, the remote controls we use for our television sets, all, it turns out, are operated by some sort of computer.

_____

8. In my opinion, if you are not into the use of computers, you are not in the twenty-first century.

_____

9. This is a topic about a current subject that interests nearly everyone.

_____

10. In this day and age, we have to wonder how many of today's jobs will be taken over by computers in the future.

_____

Recognizing appropriate language for formal writing

In speaking or writing to our family and friends, an informal style is always appropriate because it is relaxed and conversational. On the other hand, writing and speaking in school or at work requires a more formal style, one that is less personal and more detached in tone. In formal writing situations, slang is not appropriate and any use of language that is seen as sexist or disrespectful to any individual or groups of individuals is not at all acceptable.

> *Slang* is a term that refers to a special word or expression that a particular group of people use, often with the intention of keeping the meaning to themselves. A characteristic of a slang word or expression is that it is often used only for a limited period of time and then is forgotten. For example:
>
> The party was *grand*. (1940s)
>
> The party was *awesome*. (1990s)

Examples of Slang or Informal Words	Acceptable
bucks	dollars
kids	children
cops	police
a bummer	a bad experience
off the wall	crazy
yummy	delicious

Examples of Clipped Language	
doc	doctor
pro	professional
t.v.	television

Examples of Sexist Language

mailman	letter carrier
common man	average person
The teacher is an important man. He can influence the lives of many children in the community.	Teachers are important people. They can influence the lives of many children in a community.

Notice that in the last example, one way to revise sentences that contain the male references *he, him,* or *his,* is to put each singular reference into the plural. Therefore, *man* becomes *people,* and *he* becomes *they.*

EXERCISE 1   Recognizing Inappropriate Language for Formal Writing

The following sentences contain words that are informal, slang, or sexist. Circle the word in each sentence that is inappropriate for formal writing, and on the line to the right of each sentence, provide a more formal word or expression to replace the informal word.

1. He got special treatment because he's a VIP.   _____

2. He must do it, even though he has no stomach for the job.   _____

3. She is crazy about him and we don't know why.   _____

4. We must hire the best man for the job.   _____

5. That is an awesome car.   _____

6. When they got him in court, he shut up.   _____

7. I kept telling her to remember that no man is an island.   _____

8. I told him to stay with the project, but he dropped the ball.   _____

9. You'd better listen up if you want to pass the course.   _____

10. It is well known that all men are created equal.   _____

EXERCISE 2   Recognizing Inappropriate Language for Formal Writing

The following sentences contain words that are informal, slang, or sexist. Circle the word in each sentence that is inappropriate for formal writing, and on the line to the right of each sentence, provide a more formal word or expression to replace the informal word.

1. He got bad vibes from his boss during the meeting.   _____

2. He has a lot of guts to say that in public.   _____

3. We should turn on the television and listen to the weatherman's report.   _____

4. He swore it was true but I still say it is bull.   _____

5. He had a lot of loony ideas that people thought
    were very strange.   _____

6. Every fireman in town was at the scene.   _____

7. You're the bomb, eh?   _____

8. He is completely off the wall.   _____

9. After the fight with his girlfriend, he tipped and
    was not seen again.   _____

10. Write a letter and ask for an appointment with
    the chairman.   _____

EXERCISE 3   Recognizing Inappropriate Language for Formal Writing

The following sentences contain words that are informal, slang, or sexist. Circle the word in each sentence that is inappropriate for formal writing, and on the line to the right of each sentence, provide a more formal word or expression to replace the informal word.

1. The troubled young man decided to see a shrink.   _____

2. For years he had been having spooky dreams.   _____

3. He felt wired all the time.   _____

4. The lady psychiatrist gave him an appointment.   _____

5. He told her he was going nuts.   _____

6. He wanted some straight talk from her.   _____

7. She told him that some of his fears were nothing
    more than old wives' tales.   _____

8. He thought this doc was good for him.   _____

9. She did charge a pretty penny.   _____

10. Now even though he was broke, he would be O.K.   _____

Mastery and editing tests

TEST 1   Editing for Better Word Choices

The following paragraph contains at least ten examples of words or phrases that need to be revised for more concise written expression. Rewrite the entire paragraph paying particular attention to each underlined segment.

Mary Pickford, born Gladys Louise Smith, was a <u>famous Canadian-born actress who achieved fame</u> by playing in a number of movies during the early years of Hollywood. <u>It was</u> in Toronto that she was born in 1892. At that time, the city was a <u>hick town</u> made up of small brick houses. Her father died after a prolonged illness, leaving his family <u>poor and destitute.</u> Mary had always loved to play-act with her siblings, <u>so it is my opinion that it was no surprise</u> that Mary made her first stage appearance <u>at the age of eight years old</u>. After that, Mary and her family found some success taking roles <u>as actors in theatrical groups</u> that toured throughout Canada and the United States. Still, it was a tough existence, and in many instances Mary would have to live <u>alone and separated from the rest of her family</u>. This would mark Mary for the rest of her life, and she would always have a great empathy for those <u>underprivileged who were less fortunate</u>. Mary eventually became a successful Broadway performer and <u>wowed</u> audiences who came to see her. In 1909, she left a legitimate stage career to play in the movies, which were then in their infancy. She became a <u>really big</u> movie star whose <u>international appeal reached across the globe</u>. She married the famous actor Douglas Fairbanks in 1920, and the two were <u>treated like some really important people</u>. When she died in 1979, <u>she was 87 years old</u>. Mary Pickford was a pioneering film performer and one of the few to make a successful transition from silent to sound pictures.

TEST 2   Editing for Better Word Choices

The following paragraph contains at least ten examples of words or phrases that need to be revised for more concise written expression. Rewrite the entire paragraph paying particular attention to each underlined segment.

<u>The writer Judith Viorst has written about</u> the different kinds of friends we can have in our lives. She divides friendships into a number of types, beginning with what she calls "convenience friends." <u>These are folks we know because it is handy to know them.</u> They are in our carpool, or we meet them in the neighbourhood. These people will take care of our pets when we are away, or take us <u>in their car to the local garage when our car is being fixed.</u> Another type is a "special-interest friend," which means that we share a particular interest with that person but probably not much more. A third type is what the writer calls "historical friends," people who have known us <u>since we were kids back to the earliest parts of our childhood.</u> Some of these friends are people who have gone out of our lives. Viorst calls them "crossroads friends," but <u>we see them annually once a year</u> and stay in touch that way. Slightly different are <u>the friends we know that are parts of couples we know; we would probably not know them if we did not know the other part of that couple.</u> Viorst points out that there are "medium friends, and pretty good friends, and very good friends indeed," and that each kind of friend is defined by the level of intimacy <u>we achieve with him.</u> <u>In my humble opinion,</u> this essay is a good classification of the different friends most people make throughout their lives.

_____

_____

_____

_____

_____

_____

_____

_____

_____

_____

_____

_____

_____

_____

_____

_____

_____

_____

_____

_____

_____

_____

_____

_____

TEST 3   **Editing for Better Word Choices**

The following paragraph contains at least ten examples of words or phrases that need to be revised for more concise written expression. Rewrite the entire paragraph paying particular attention to each underlined segment.

The story of Frederick Philip Grove <u>has got to be one of the most crazy stories</u> in Canadian literary history. When Frederick Philip Grove moved to Manitoba in 1912, he claimed to be from an aristocratic Swedish background. He taught German <u>eight hours a day on a full-time basis</u> in the small rural towns surrounding Winnipeg. The bushland country in Manitoba became the setting of his finest novels. <u>It was</u> in Ontario that he finally settled down. A year before his death in 1948, Grove won the Governor General's Award for non-fiction for his autobiography entitled *In Search of Myself*. <u>Years and years</u> after his death, researchers began <u>investigating and looking into</u> Grove's life. They discovered that he had lied about his identity <u>of who he really was.</u> He was, in fact, a German writer named Felix Paul Greve. <u>I am of the opinion</u> that he fled Europe with his wife, Else, and created this false identity because he had committed fraud and was badly in debt. <u>At that point in time</u> he probably also wanted to hide the fact that he had <u>ditched</u> Else on a farm in Kentucky. <u>It turns out that</u> Grove had lived a fiction for most of his life. <u>No wonder</u> he was so good at writing it.

_____

_____

_____

_____

_____

_____

_____

_____

_____

_____
_____
_____
_____
_____
_____
_____
_____
_____
_____
_____
_____
_____

TEST 4   Editing for Better Word Choices

Each underlined word or phrase could be revised and made richer in meaning. Rewrite the entire passage making each indicated word or phrase more specific.

> I know a <u>spot</u> that is <u>different</u>. <u>Going</u> across the <u>land</u>, we follow <u>a way</u> that leads up to <u>it</u>. The <u>noises</u> of the evening are <u>nice</u>. The <u>people</u> who are with me are ready for our <u>meal</u>. We will <u>make</u> our <u>food</u> over a wood fire. We might be tired, but we will <u>feel good</u> to spend the night <u>here</u>.

_____
_____
_____
_____
_____
_____
_____
_____
_____
_____
_____
_____

TEST 5

Editing for Better Word Choices

Each underlined word or phrase could be revised and made richer in meaning. Rewrite the entire passage making each indicated word or phrase more specific.

It was a great day. The air was good. The athletes were all there. No one talked. Dan was dressed differently. The others all wore the typical clothes. Another thing surprised me as I looked. Dan was in his bare feet. How would he be able to do anything? The event began with the bell.

_____

_____

_____

_____

_____

_____

_____

_____

_____

_____

_____

_____

Working Together

1. Words are charged with meanings that can be encouraging and supportive or hurtful and wounding. Although clerks and other workers in government buildings and public places are there to help the public, they often are so overwhelmed or overworked that they do not always respond in a positive way. Below are seven comments that might be heard in an office where a person has gone to get help. In each case, revise the language so that the comment is more encouraging.

   a. I don't have any idea what you're talking about.

   _____

   _____

   b. Why don't you learn to write so people can read it?

   _____

   _____

   c. We don't accept sloppy applications.

   _____

   d. How old are you anyway?

   _____

   e. Can't you read directions?

   _____

   f. What's the matter with you? Why can't you understand this simple procedure?

   _____

   g. I don't have time today for people like you!

   _____

2. As a class, discuss individual experiences that have involved incidents where the use of language made the person involved feel hurt or encouraged. Class members may have recent examples of experiences at campus offices, local banks, or grocery stores. Perhaps their parents or siblings have had recent experiences. Looking back on these incidents, how could a change of language have made the situations different? Following the discussion, students should summarize these examples given by class members. What advice can you give to a person who is treated unkindly?

3. Write about your ideas of how employers could train workers better so that they would be careful to be polite with customers or clients.

4. If you have worked with the public, you may want to write about the other perspective: how difficult it is to remain polite when so many customers are rude. Do you have examples of some of these experiences? How did you deal with the situation?

Chapter 13

Paying Attention to Look-Alikes and Sound-Alikes

This chapter presents approximately 50 pairs of words that are confusing because they either sound alike or look alike, but they are spelled differently and have different meanings. Master the words in each group before proceeding to the next group.

Group I: Words that sound alike

1. aural/oral

aural	related to hearing
	aural nerve damage
oral	related to the mouth
	an *oral* report

2. buy/by

buy (verb)	to purchase
	buy a car
by (prep.)	near; past; not later than
	to meet *by* the clock
	to walk *by*
	by six o'clock

3. close/clothes

close	to shut
	close the door
clothes	garments
	clothes from the Gap

Note: *Cloth* is a piece of fabric, not to be confused with *clothes*, which is always plural.

4. coarse/course

coarse (adj.)	rough; common or of inferior quality
	a *coarse* joke
	a *coarse* fabric
course (noun)	direction; part of a meal; a unit of study
	the *course* of the spaceship
	the main *course* of the meal
	a required *course*

5. complement/compliment

complement (noun)	something that completes
(verb)	to complete
	The library has a full *complement* of books.
	Her shoes *complement* the outfit.
compliment (noun)	an expression of praise
	The chef received a *compliment*.
(verb)	to praise
	He *complimented* the chef.

6. imminent/eminent

imminent (adj.)	impending; about to happen
	The arrival of the train was *imminent*.
eminent (adj.)	distinguished; notable
	The Queen of England is an *eminent* person.
	There were many *eminent* people at the Gemini Awards ceremony.

7. forward/foreword

forward	to send on to another address; moving toward the front or the future; bold
	Please *forward* my mail.
	He took one step *forward*.
	She is very *forward* when she speaks.
foreword	introduction to a book
	Read the *foreword* first.

8. passed/past

passed (verb)	moved ahead; completed successfully
	She *passed* the test.
past (noun)	time before the present
	Don't live in the *past*.
(prep.)	beyond
	He walked *past* the house.
(adj.)	no longer current
	the *past* year

9. **plain/plane**

plain (adj.)	ordinary; clear
	plain clothing
	plain directions
(noun)	flat land without trees
	across the *plain* by covered wagon
plane	an aircraft; a flat, level surface; a carpenter's tool for levelling wood; a level of development
	passengers on the *plane*
	the *planes* of a crystal
	the carpenter's *plane* and saw
	to think on a different *plane*

10. **presence/presents**

presence	the state of being present; a person's manner
	His *presence* is needed.
	She has a wonderful *presence*.
presents	gifts
	The child's birthday *presents* were many.

EXERCISE 1   Group I Words

Fill in the blanks in each of the following sentences by choosing the correct word to complete that sentence.

1. Even though the child likes the taste of the _____ medicine,
   (aural, oral)

   the _____ medicine that is applied directly into the ear is more
   (aural, oral)

   effective.

2. I'll _____ you lunch if you meet me _____ the escalator at
   (buy, by)   (buy, by)

   12:30 tomorrow afternoon.

3. The reporters and photographers who gathered at the movie star's wedding

   reception said that the arrival of many _____ _____
                                           (imminent, eminent)

   people was _____ .
              (imminent, eminent)

4. As I ran up the street, I could see the tailor _____ the door; I
                                                  (clothes, close, cloth)

   was too late to pick up my _____ .
                              (clothes, close, cloth)

5. I enjoyed the sailing _____ , but I could never manage to keep my
                         (coarse, course)

   boat on _____ .
           (coarse, course)

6. Her jewellery always _____ her outfit, and she is genuinely
   (complements, compliments)

   pleased to get a _____ .
   (complement, compliment)

7. The _____ was written by one of my favourite authors, so I
   (forward, foreword)

   looked _____ to getting the book out of the library.
   (forward, foreword)

8. She _____ her time by the ocean, thinking about the recent
   (passed, past)

   _____ .
   (passed, past)

9. The stewards in the _____ looked in vain for a _____ yogurt
   (plain, plane)   (plain, plane)

   for a passenger.

10. The queen's _____ was a festive occasion; the crowds cheered when
    (presence, presents)

    she held up the _____ she had brought.
    (presence, presents)

EXERCISE 2   Group I Words

Edit the following paragraph for word confusions. Circle the errors and write the correct words on the lines below the paragraph.

Arranging the visit of a foreign head of state or other imminent person to our nation's capital is not something that can be done buy one person. There are scores of people involved in the plans. There are personnel in charge of wardrobe to plan what cloths will be needed. Then too, a certain number of presence must be chosen to present to the leader of the host country. Most importantly, the authorities of the city must be informed so they can begin to make security arrangements. For instance, what plain the dignitary will be taking is secret information that only airport security should know. In the passed as well as today, the protocol will be another concern. Complements are paid to each other and aural presentations are made that are gracious and in good humour. Any course remarks are strictly out of place. Photographers will be on hand to record the event. For the population of the city, a state visit is not always something to look foreword to. For the public, the visit means major traffic jams.

_____   _____

_____   _____

_____   _____

_____   _____

_____   _____

Group II: Words that sound alike

1. principal/principle

principal (adj.)	most important; main
	principal dancer
	principal reason
(noun)	the head of a school; a sum of money
	the *principal* of the school
	the *principal* and interest on the loan
principle (noun)	a rule or standard
	He is a man of *principle*.

2. rain/reign/rein

rain	water falling to earth in drops
	singing in the *rain*
reign	a period of rule for a king or queen
	the *reign* of Henry the Eighth
rein	a strap attached to a bridle, used to control a horse
	the pony's frayed *rein*

3. sight/site/cite

sight	the ability to see; a view
	His *sight* is bad.
	Niagara Falls is an awesome *sight*!
site	the plot of land where something is located; the place for an event
	the *site* for the new courthouse
cite	to quote as an authority or example
	Please *cite* the correct law.

4. stationary/stationery

stationary (adj.)	standing still
	He hit a *stationary* object.
stationery (noun)	writing paper and envelopes
	She wrote the letter on her *stationery*.

5. to/too/two

to (prep.)	in a direction toward
	We walked *to* the movies.
too (adv.)	also; very
	We walked home *too*.
	The tickets were *too* expensive.
two	number
	two children

6. vain/vane/vein

vain	conceited; unsuccessful
	to be *vain*
	a *vain* attempt

vane	an ornament that turns in the wind (often in the shape of a rooster and seen on tops of barns)
	The weather *vane* pointed southwest.
vein	a blood vessel; the branching framework of a leaf; an area in the earth where a mineral such as gold or silver is found; a passing attitude
	The *veins* bring blood to the heart.
	The miner found a *vein* of silver.
	She spoke in a humorous *vein*.

7. waist/waste

waist	the middle portion of a body or garment
	His *waist* was 36 inches around.
waste (verb)	to use carelessly
	He *wasted* too much time watching television.
waste (noun)	discarded objects
	The *waste* was put in the garbage.

8. weather/whether

weather (noun)	atmospheric conditions
	The *weather* in Hawaii is gorgeous.
whether (conj.)	if it is the case that
	I'll go *whether* or not I'm finished.

9. whole/hole

whole	complete
	He ate the *whole* apple.
hole	an opening
	I found a *hole* in the sock.

10. write/right/rite

write	to form letters and words; to compose
	I will *write* a poem for your birthday.
right	correct
	What is the *right* answer?
	to conform to justice, law, or morality
	Trial by jury is a *right* under the law.
	toward a conservative point of view
	The politician's position is to the *right*.
rite	a traditional, often religious ceremony
	rites of passage

EXERCISE 1   Group II Words

Fill in the blanks in each of the following sentences by choosing the correct word to complete that sentence.

1. After he paid the interest and part of the _____ , he decided,
   (principal, principle)

on _____ , never to take out a loan again.
   (principal, principle)

2. The horse's bridle and _____ (rain, reign, rein) were ruined after being left out in

   the _____ (rain, reign, rein) .

3. The archaeological _____ (sight, site, cite) of the newly discovered city was, for the

   archaeologist, a beautiful _____ (sight, site, cite) .

4. Please do not remain _____ (stationary, stationery) at your desk all day—go and buy

   the _____ (stationary, stationery) you need to finish your letters.

5. I want the _____ (to, too, two) of you _____ (to, too, two) have a good time, so please

   go out _____ (to, too, two) a restaurant tonight.

6. The artist was very _____ (vain, vane, vein) about his work, and was especially proud

   of his painted metal weather _____ (vain, vane, vein) in the shape of a rooster.

7. It is a _____ (waist, waste) of money for him to buy clothes now, since his

   _____ (waist, waste) is expanding so rapidly.

8. _____ (Weather, Whether) or not it is raining, we will go; the _____ (weather, whether) will

   not change our plans.

9. The detective felt there was a _____ (whole, hole) in his story, so they waited for

   the _____ (whole, hole) truth to come out.

10. The society felt they had the _____ (right, write, rite) to hold their secret

    _____ (right, write, rite) at the same time every year.

EXERCISE 2   Group II Words

Below is a paragraph using the words from group two. Read the paragraph and choose the words that correctly fit the meaning in the paragraph.

The archaeologist spent an entire summer digging at a newly discovered

_____ (sight, cite, site) in Southern Italy. He was looking for the tomb of a queen whose

_____ (rain, reign, rein) dated to the earliest days of the Roman Empire. It was a very bad

summer for digging: the _____ (whether, weather) was terrible, and for many days the

scientist was up to his _____ (waist, waste) in water. There was so much water, in fact,

that it was difficult to keep some of the equipment _____ . After

(stationary, stationery)

finding inscriptions that proved this had been the queen's _____

(principal, principle)

residence, the archaeologist began to _____ up the first reports of his

(write, right, rite)

investigation; his _____ report would be completed later in more detail. It

(hole, whole)

was _____ much to hope for, but the summer's work had not been

(to, too, two)

in _____ .

(vain, vane, vein)

Group III: Words that sound alike

1. it's/its

it's	contraction of *it is*
	It's late.
its	possessive pronoun
	The dog chased *its* tail.

2. they're/their/there

they're	contraction of they are
	They're working.
their	possessive pronoun
	Their children love popcorn.
there	at that place
	The lifeguard is over *there*.

3. we're/were/where

we're	contraction of *we are*
	We're going out.
were	past tense of *are*
	They *were* certain.
where	at or in what place
	Where are you going?

4. who's/whose

who's	contraction of *who is*
	Who's coming to dinner?
whose	possessive pronoun
	Whose mail is on the table?

5. you're/your

you're	contraction of *you are*
	You're talking too loudly.
your	possessive pronoun
	Your friend just called.

EXERCISE 1 Group III Words

Fill in the blanks in each of the following sentences by choosing the correct word to complete that sentence.

1. _____ going out to dinner tonight, and _____ car should we
   (Who's, Whose)   (who's, whose)
   drive?

2. _____ insurance cheque arrived today, so _____ covered until
   (You're, Your)   (you're, your)
   May.

3. _____ deciding to move to Regina since both _____
   (They're, Their, There)   (they're, their, there)
   families live _____ .
                 (they're, their, there)

4. After work _____ going to the baseball diamond _____
                (we're, were, where)   (we're, were, where)
   the professional teams train.

5. Ever since the toy was left in the rain, _____ wheels have become so
                                              (it's, its)
   wobbly that _____ now unsafe.
                (it's, its)

6. Are you planning _____ weekend so that _____ free for a
                     (you're, your)   (you're, your)
   movie on Sunday?

7. _____ hoping to find the road _____ we
   (We're, Were, Where)   (we're, were, where)
   _____ travelling before we took that detour.
   (we're, were, where)

8. _____ piano is going out of tune, so the chord _____ playing
   (You're, Your)   (you're, your)
   doesn't sound correct.

9. _____ parents beat them in a game of stickball right
   (They're, Their, There)
   _____ in front of _____ friends!
   (they're, their, there)   (they're, their, there)

10. When _____ travelling, _____ top priority should be safety.
              (you're, your)   (you're, your)

EXERCISE 2 Group III Words

Read the following paragraph. Fifteen words are underlined that may have been used correctly or incorrectly. Below the paragraph, write the correct word choice for each of the fifteen examples.

Some people try to learn to play the piano by themselves. [1]There convinced [2]their must be an easy quick trick. [3]Whose method book should they follow? Music with all [4]its theory can seem overwhelming at first. [5]Whose going to really know what will work best for them? Most music teachers can give good advice. [6]There experience is valuable, and [7]there usually happy to explain how a student should practise. Unfortunately, [8]<u>were</u> sometimes reluctant to follow [9]<u>there</u> sound advice because it usually involves slow thoughtful practice. [10]<u>Its</u> going to take time but in order to learn the piano, [11]<u>its</u> necessary to practise slowly rather than trying to play something as fast as possible. Children are impatient. [12]<u>There</u> always wanting to play fast. However, [13]<u>its</u> never too late to learn better practice habits. [14]<u>Your</u> reward for slow and thoughtful practice is an evenness and accuracy in your playing that [15]<u>your</u> sure to appreciate.

1. _____
2. _____
3. _____
4. _____
5. _____
6. _____
7. _____
8. _____

9. _____
10. _____
11. _____
12. _____
13. _____
14. _____
15. _____

Group IV: Words that sound or look almost alike

1. accept/except

accept (verb)   to receive; to admit; to regard as true or right
                 I *accept* with pleasure.
                 I *accept* responsibility.
                 I *accept* your apology.

except (prep.)   other than, but
                 everyone *except* me

2. advice/advise

advice (noun)   opinion as to what should be done about a problem
                 I need good *advice*.

advise (verb)   to suggest; to counsel
                 He *advised* me to take a different course.

3. affect/effect

affect (verb)   to influence; to change
                 Smoking will *affect* your health.

effect (noun)   result
                 the *effect* of the hurricane

effect (verb)   to bring about a result
                 The hurricane *effected* a devastating change in the community.

4. breath/breathe

breath (noun)   air that is inhaled or exhaled
                 out of *breath*

breathe (verb)   to inhale or exhale
                 Don't *breathe* in these fumes.

5. choose/chose

choose (present tense)	select
	Today I *choose* the purple shirt.
chose (past tense)	selected
	Yesterday I *chose* the red one.

6. conscience/conscious/conscientious

conscience	recognition of right and wrong
	His *conscience* bothered him.
conscious	awake; aware of one's own existence
	The patient was *conscious.*
conscientious	careful; thorough
	The student was *conscientious* about doing her homework.

7. costume/custom

costume	a special style of dress for a particular occasion
	The child wore a clown *costume* for Halloween.
custom	a common tradition
	One *custom* at Thanksgiving is to serve turkey.

8. council/counsel/consul

council (noun)	a group that governs
	The student *council*
counsel (verb)	to give advice
	Please *counsel* the arguing couple.
counsel (noun)	advice; a lawyer
	The couple needs *counsel.*
	The prisoner has requested *counsel.*
consul	a government official in the foreign service
	He was appointed a *consul* by the Minister.

9. desert/dessert

desert (verb)	to abandon
	Don't *desert* me now.
desert (noun)	barren land
	The cactus flowers on the *desert* are beautiful.
dessert	last part of a meal, often sweet
	We had apple pie for *dessert.*

10. diner/dinner

diner	a person eating dinner; a restaurant with a long counter and booths
	The *diner* waited for her bill.
	I prefer a booth at the *diner.*
dinner	main meal of the day
	What is for *dinner?*

EXERCISE 1   Group IV Words

Fill in the blank in each of the following sentences by choosing the correct word to complete that sentence.

1. Many families no longer have the _____ of eating meals together.
   (costume, custom)

2. Everyone is in a hurry at breakfast time, and nobody is home to fix _____ in the evening.
   (diner, dinner)

3. Some children eat foods for their evening meals that could be considered _____ .
   (deserts, desserts)

4. Some youth _____ are concerned about the lack of communication
   (counsels, councils)
   between children and parents.

5. They _____ parents to spend more time with their teenagers.
   (advice, advise)

6. _____ parents should always know where their children are.
   (Conscientious, Conscious)

7. How can a parent control who a child will _____ for a friend?
   (choose, chose)

8. The _____ of peer pressure is enormous.
   (affect, effect)

9. Many parents cannot _____ easily on weekends.
   (breath, breathe)

10. Better _____ on parenting teenagers is needed.
    (advice, advise)

EXERCISE 2   Group IV Words

Edit the following paragraph for word confusions. Circle the errors and write the correct words on the lines below the paragraph.

Everyone arrived at the meeting except the lawyer. The group needed advise from someone, so they chose from the crowd a person who claimed to have experience. This person did not have a conscious because he was really quite ignorant of the laws governing the procedure. He was, however, happy to except the payment for his services. While chomping on a desert from his dinner, the young man advised the group to make the payment of a large sum of money, claiming it was a common costume in this particular country. What a pity the group did not have adequate legal council! By the time the Canadian consul arrived, the young man had desserted them. The affects were devastating to those who lost substantial amounts of money.

_____   _____

_____   _____

_____   _____

_____   _____

_____   _____

Group V: Words that sound or look almost alike

1. emigrate/emigrant; immigrate/immigrant

emigrate	to leave a country
	Thousands *emigrated* after the earthquake.
emigrant	a person who leaves one country to settle in another
	Each *emigrant* had hopes of a better life.
immigrate	to come into a country
	Many people *immigrated* to Canada in the early twentieth century.
immigrant	a person who comes into a country to settle there
	The Pier 21 Museum displays photographs of our country's *immigrants*.

2. farther/further

farther	greater distance (physically)
	The river lies *farther* west.
further	greater distance (mentally); to help advance a person or a cause
	She asked for a *further* explanation.
	I am hoping to *further* my career.

3. loose/lose

loose	not tightly fitted
	Your shoelace is *loose*.
lose	unable to keep or find; to fail to win
	I always seem to *lose* my purse.
	I think our team might *lose* the game.

4. personal/personnel

personal	relating to an individual; private
	Don't forget your *personal* belongings.
personnel	people employed by an organization
	This meeting is just for *personnel*.

5. quiet/quit/quite

quiet	free from noise; calm
	He has always been a *quiet* person.
quit	to give up; to stop
	I *quit* my night job.
quite	to a certain extent; completely
	I was *quite* tired after the hike.
	He's not *quite* finished.

6. receipt/recipe

receipt   a bill marked paid

                                     I saved the *receipt* in case the dress didn't fit.

recipe   a formula to prepare a mixture, especially in
                                     cooking

                                     The *recipe* asked for a pinch of salt.

7. special/especially

special (adj.)   not ordinary

                                     Her birthday is a *special* event.

especially (adv.)   particularly

                                     I baked this cake *especially* for you.

8. than/then

than   used to make a comparison

                                     His hair is longer *than* mine.

then   at that time; in that case

                                     She took a nap; *then* she felt better.

9. thorough/though/thought/through/threw

thorough (adj.)   accurate and complete

                                     A good historian is always *thorough*.

though (adv. conj.)   however, despite the fact

                                     I slept even *though* the music blared.

thought (verb)   past tense of to think

                                     I *thought* carefully before I voted.

through (prep.)   to enter one side and exit from the other side

                                     We walked *through* the entire museum.

Note: *thru* is not considered standard spelling.

threw (verb)   past tense of to throw

                                     I *threw* my rough draft into the recycling bin.

10. use/used to

use   to bring or put into service, to make use of

                                     Present: Now I *use* a computer.

                                     Past: Yesterday, I *used* one of the university
                                     computers.

used to   an expression that indicates an activity that is no
                                     longer done in the present

                                     We *used to* play Frisbee on Sundays.

                                     accustomed to or familiar with

                                     I am not *used to* eating this much.

EXERCISE 1 Group V Words

Fill in the blank in each of the following sentences by choosing the correct word to complete that sentence.

1. I _____ to read the paper every morning.
   (use, used)

2. Now I live _____ away from the local newsstand.
   (farther, further)

3. _____ it's not a long walk, I never seem to buy the paper
   (Thorough, Though, Through)
   anymore.

4. I am beginning to _____ touch with current events.
   (loose, lose)

5. I'm sure I am less interesting to talk to _____ before.
   (than, then)

6. I used to be _____ knowledgeable about the news.
   (quiet, quit, quite)

7. Now I rely on the _____ at the office to keep me informed.
   (personal, personnel)

8. Luckily, the people at work are _____ in bringing me up to
   (thorough, though, through)
   date.

9. One worker is always giving me his _____ opinion about sports.
   (personal, personnel)

10. The woman who sits next to me is _____ interested in financial news.
    (special, especially)

EXERCISE 2 Group V Words

Edit the following paragraph for word confusions. Circle the errors and write the correct words on the lines below the paragraph.

  I always carry a lot of lose change in my pocket for the subway. Through I live in the city, I often dream of the countryside. Sometimes on the train I loose track of time. I imagine I am in a quite place. I think special about my grandmother's house. I use to visit her when I was young, and I still remember all that home cooked food. Just the though of her tourtière gets me thorough a hard day's work. Perhaps someday when I retire I will have time to try out all of my grandmother's delicious receipts.

_____ _____

_____ _____

_____ _____

_____ _____

_____ _____

Group VI: Lie/lay; rise/raise; sit/set

These six verbs are perhaps the most troublesome verbs in the English language. First, one must learn the principal parts because they are irregular and easily confused with each other. Secondly, one set is reflexive and cannot take an object while the other set always takes a direct object.

PRINCIPAL PARTS OF REFLEXIVE VERBS LIE—RISE—SIT				
Verb Meaning	Present	Present Participle	Past	Past Participle
to recline	lie	lying	lay	has or have lain
to stand up or move upward	rise	rising	rose	has or have risen
to take a sitting position	sit	sitting	sat	has or have sat

Reflexive verbs **never** take an object:

I lie down.	The cat is lying on the rug.
I rise up.	The sun rose in the East.
I sit down.	The woman sat on the sofa.

Remember that when these verbs are used, the subject is doing the action without any help. No other person or object is needed to accomplish the action.

• PRACTICE

Fill in each blank with the correct form of one of the reflexive verbs given in the box.

1. The sun is _____ at about 6 a.m. this week.

2. He _____ at 7 o'clock every morning.

3. He is _____ at the breakfast table by 7:30.

4. He will not _____ down again until after midnight.

5. His cat is always _____ on the rug.

6. Yesterday he _____ there for seven hours without moving.

PRINCIPAL PARTS OF THE VERBS LAY—RAISE—SET				
Verb Meaning	Present	Present Participle	Past	Past Participle
to put something	lay	laying	laid	has or have laid
to move something up	raise	raising	raised	has or have raised
to place something	set	setting	set	has or have set

These verbs **always** take a direct object.

I *lay the book* down.

I *raise the flag.*

I *set the table.*

• PRACTICE

Fill in the blanks with the correct form of the verb and its direct object.

1. The letter carrier _____ the _____ in the mailbox.

2. He has _____ our _____ under the doormat.

3. The father _____ his _____ to be a sensitive individual.

4. He has _____ our hopes for a successful season.

5. We _____ the _____ in the correct place.

6. Are you _____ a good example for your younger brothers?

EXERCISE 1   Group VI Words

Fill in each blank with the correct form of the verb.

1. Don't forget to _____ your uniform out for school.

2. I had such a headache last night, that I had to _____ down for an hour.

3. On Thanksgiving, we always _____ the table with our best china.

4. The widowed mother is _____ three children on her own.

5. Every day I like to _____ in the same seat in class.

6. Yesterday, my father _____ the carpet in my bedroom.

7. I _____ yesterday in time to have breakfast with my father.

8. I have _____ down to rest for a few minutes, so please don't bother me.

9. _____ the dolls in the corner where they won't get stepped on.

10. They had _____ from bed by the time the telephone rang.

EXERCISE 2   Group VI Words

Fill in each blank with the correct form of the verb.

1. I saw your jacket _____ on the floor.

2. Please _____ from your seats for the singing of the National Anthem.

3. The laundry is _____ in the basket by the door.

4. Where did you _____ the tools?

5. Last year the test scores _____ five percent.

6. The students _____ their test scores by studying harder.

7. Where has the teacher _____ her lesson plans?

8. We have _____ early in order to attend swim practice.

9. The poor woman has _____ in bed ever since last April.

10. I have _____ down now to read the paper.

Mastery and editing tests

TEST 1   Editing for Words Commonly Confused

Edit the following paragraph for ten errors with word confusions. Circle the mistakes you find and write the correct form on the lines provided after the paragraph.

She preferred having a roommate rather then living alone. She wanted a quite person who would not keep her awake at night. She wanted someone who's personal habits would be somewhat like her own. The farther she though about it, the more she was determined to have someone who did not smoke. Her friends advised her to contact a roommate referral service. Before another day past, she went and filled out one of there applications. One question they asked was weather or not she had a pet. Another question was if she had any allergies. Now she looks foreword to seeing who will call her. A person who choses to room with her will know a lot about her in advance.

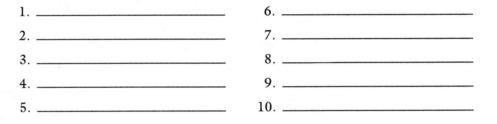

1. _____   6. _____
2. _____   7. _____
3. _____   8. _____
4. _____   9. _____
5. _____   10. _____

TEST 2   Editing for Words Commonly Confused

Edit the following paragraph for ten errors with word confusions. Circle the mistakes you find and write the correct form on the lines provided after the paragraph.

The best way to shop is not at your local mall; it's shopping on-line. All you do is set down at your computer, look thorough the web sight your interested in, and click on the items you want. If you are very busy and cannot get your shopping done on the weekends, it's quiet easy to get your shopping done with a click of the button. For example, every year I by a pair of expensive pants for my uncle. It's a special order because of his very large size. (He has a 56 inch waste.) Yet I am always able to find them on-line with no difficulty and with a great selection. Although I sometimes buy my children's cloths at a local store, I have ordered Halloween costumes for my kids through the Internet, and the outfits were very especial. It is plane to see that the Internet is the answer for anyone's shopping needs.

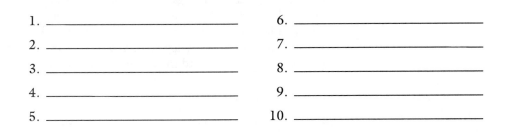

1. _____ 6. _____
2. _____ 7. _____
3. _____ 8. _____
4. _____ 9. _____
5. _____ 10. _____

TEST 3   Editing for Words Commonly Confused

Edit the following paragraph for ten errors with word confusions. Circle the mistakes you find and write the correct form on the lines provided after the paragraph.

     Choose your pharmacist with great care. Thought pharmacists are not doctors, they can answer many of your medical questions. A pharmacist is a good compliment to a doctor for a source of up-to-date information about prescription and nonprescription medication. Its a good idea to find a pharmacist who is not to busy to talk to you. He or she can offer you advise on money-saving generic brands. When you do get a prescription filled, you need to be conscience of any possible side affects of the medication or of any interactions the medicine could have with other medications you might be taking for other unrelated problems. The pharmacist may give you a choice between an oral medication or a topical ointment. He or she will give you information about the importance of taking the hole prescription if you need an antibiotic. Pharmacists wish people would learn to take more responsibility for understanding the medications they take. Patients should not always lay the blame on the medical profession when a medication is wrong. Some responsibility lays with the patient. If you do your research, you can breath easy knowing you are making the best choice given the options that are available to you.

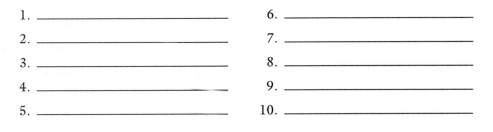

1. _____ 6. _____
2. _____ 7. _____
3. _____ 8. _____
4. _____ 9. _____
5. _____ 10. _____

TEST 4   Editing for Words Commonly Confused

Edit the following paragraph for ten errors with word confusions. Circle the mistakes you find and write the correct form on the lines provided after the paragraph.

     The principle reason people immigrate from their home countries is to improve their lives. Of coarse, this has been the experience of every generation in our country's history, but no nation's population can remain stationery; one country looses people while another country gains. The raise of industrialism in the nineteenth century led to a great demand for workers in this country, so its no surprise that Canada encouraged immigration at that time. Today, thousands of people still want to come to Canada, but many of them wait in vane for the right conditions that will allow them to settle here. Now, it seems, a more through screening process by the government will discourage some who will find the process to difficult.

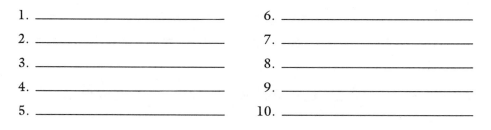

1. _____   6. _____

2. _____   7. _____

3. _____   8. _____

4. _____   9. _____

5. _____   10. _____

TEST 5   **Editing for Words Commonly Confused**

Edit the following paragraph for ten errors with word confusions. Circle the mistakes you find and write the correct form on the lines provided after the paragraph.

When you visit a city such as Ottawa, Ontario, you feel the presents of famous people and important events. First of all, since its the capital city, all around you are the government offices and embassies were national and international decisions are maid. On some streets there are buildings for counsels from many different countries. You can see the personal from the different embassies coming and going all day long. Every citizen should see the sites in Ottawa at least once. When I use to go there in my youth, my favourite places were the Parliament Buildings and the National Gallery. The passed always seemed to come alive when I stood inside these beautiful and moving structures. Last month I visited the recently opened Museum of Civilization. Another wonderful museum now lays in the heart of our nation's capital.

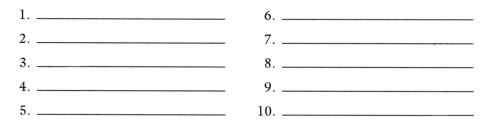

1. _____   6. _____

2. _____   7. _____

3. _____   8. _____

4. _____   9. _____

5. _____   10. _____

Working Together

- Fat consumption is still an average of 35 percent of energy, a long way from the recommended 30 percent. About eight out of ten adults surveyed are eating too much fat. A lot of younger men are well above the goal.
- In Ontario, nine out of ten adolescents consume a diet that is too high in fat.
- Energy intake is low for many women, putting them at risk for a less than adequate intake of certain nutrients. Many women have a marginal intake of iron and calcium.
- Canadians seem to be reluctant to put more carbohydrates and fibre on their plates. Only one in five Ontarians is meeting the carbohydrates goal of 55 percent of energy.

—National Institute of Nutrition

The above statistics were part of the findings of a recent study conducted by the National Institute of Nutrition. Divide into groups and discuss the significance of these results. Why are these findings important? After the discussion, make an individual list of your typical day's complete diet. (Be sure to include any snacks you would normally eat.) Does your diet reflect the findings by the National Institute of Nutrition?

Using the statistics, group discussion, and your own list of foods you eat, write about the whole question of diet and what an individual's approach to a proper diet should be. In your writing, include your thoughts on the typical Canadian diet and your own diet in particular.

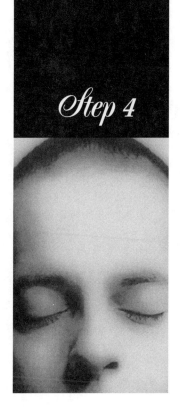

Step 4

CREATING EFFECTIVE PARAGRAPHS

CONTENTS

Chapter 14

Working with Paragraphs: Topic Sentences and Controlling Ideas

What is a paragraph?

> A *paragraph* is a group of sentences that develops one main idea. A paragraph may stand by itself as a complete piece of writing, or it may be a section of a longer piece of writing, such as an essay.

No single rule will tell you how long a paragraph should be, but if a paragraph is too short, the reader will feel that basic information is missing. If the paragraph is too long, the reader will be bored or confused. An effective paragraph is always long enough to develop the main idea that is being presented. A healthy paragraph usually consists of at least six sentences and no more than ten or twelve sentences. You have undoubtedly read paragraphs in newspapers that are only one sentence long, but in fully developed writing one sentence is usually not an acceptable paragraph.

What does a paragraph look like?

Some students are unaccustomed to using margins, indentation, and complete sentences, which are essential parts of paragraph form. Study the following paragraph to observe the standard form.

First word indented. Consistent margin of at least one inch (2.5 cm) on each side. Blank space after the final word.

    I got the job. I worked in a bank's city collection department. For weeks I was like a mouse in a maze: my feet scurried. Every seventh day I received a cheque for fifty dollars. It wasn't much. But, standing beside the pneumatic tube, unloading the bundles of mail that pelted down and distributing them according to their texture, size, and colour to my superiors at their desks, I felt humble and useful.

EXERCISE 1 Standard Paragraph Form

Write the following six sentences in standard paragraph form. As you write, use margins, indentation, and complete sentences. Each sentence must begin with a capital letter and end with a period, question mark, or exclamation point.

1. In the large basement of the school, thirty families huddled in little groups of four or five.

2. Volunteer workers were busy carrying in boxes of clothing and blankets.

3. Two Red Cross women stood at a long table sorting through boxes to find sweaters and blankets for the shivering flood victims.

4. One heavyset man in a red woollen hunting jacket stirred a huge pot of soup.

5. Men and women with tired faces sipped their steaming coffee and wondered if they would ever see their homes again.

6. Outside the downpour continued.

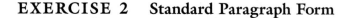

_____

_____

_____

_____

_____

_____

_____

_____

_____

_____

_____

_____

_____

_____

EXERCISE 2   Standard Paragraph Form

Write the following seven sentences in standard paragraph form. As you write, use margins, indentation, and complete sentences. Each sentence must begin with a capital letter and end with a period, question mark, or exclamation point.

1. Friday afternoon I was desperate to get my English homework finished before I left the campus.

2. The assignment was due on Monday, but I really wanted my weekend free.

3. As I sat at the table in the library, I could see dictionaries and other reference books on the nearby shelves.

4. I felt in a good mood because I knew that if I had to find information for my assignment, it would be available to me.

5. The only worry I had was whether or not I would be interrupted by my friends who might stop by, wanting to chat.

6. Luckily, I worked along with no interruptions and was able to finish my work by five o'clock.

7. My weekend was saved!

_____

_____

_____

_____

_____

_____

_____

_____

_____

_____

_____

_____

_____

What is a topic sentence?

> A *topic sentence* states the main idea of a paragraph. It is the most general sentence of the paragraph. All the other sentences serve to explain, describe, extend, or support this main-idea sentence.

Most paragraphs you read will begin with the topic sentence. However, some topic sentences come in the middle of the paragraph; others come at the end. Some paragraphs have no stated topic sentence at all; in those cases, the main idea is implied. Students are usually advised to use topic sentences in all their work in order to be certain that the writing has a focus and develops a single idea at a time. Whether you are taking an essay exam in a history course, doing a research paper for a sociology course, or writing an essay in a composition course, thoughtful use of the topic sentence will always bring better results. Good topic sentences help both the writer and the reader to think clearly about the main points.

On page 254 are two paragraphs. Each paragraph makes a separate point, which is stated in its topic sentence. In both of these paragraphs, the topic sentence happens to be first. Read the paragraphs and notice how the topic sentence is the most general sentence; it is the main idea of each paragraph. The other sentences explain, describe, extend, or support the topic sentence.

MODEL PARAGRAPH 1

I went through a difficult period after my father died. I was moody and sullen at home. I spent most of the time in my bedroom listening to music on the radio, which made me feel even worse. I stopped playing soccer after school with my friends. My grades in school went down. I lost my appetite and seemed to get into arguments with everybody. My mom began to look worried, but I couldn't bring myself to participate in an activity with any spirit. It seemed life had lost its joy for me.

MODEL PARAGRAPH 2

Fortunately, something happened that spring that brought me out of my depression. My uncle, who had been disabled in a car accident, came to live with us. I learned many years later that my mother had asked him to come and live with us in the hope that he could bring me out of myself. I, on the other hand, was told that it was my responsibility to help my uncle feel at home. My mother's plan worked. My uncle and I were both lonely people. A friendship began that was to change both our lives for the better.

EXERCISE 1　Finding the Topic Sentence of a Paragraph

Each of the following five paragraphs contains a topic sentence that states the main idea of the paragraph. Find which sentence best states the main idea and underline it. The topic sentence will not always be the first sentence of the paragraph.

1. Mountains of disposable diapers are thrown into garbage cans every day. Tons of yogurt containers, soda cans, and other plastic items are discarded without so much as a stomp to flatten them out. If the old Chevy is not worth fixing, tow it off to sit with thousands of others on acres of fenced-in junkyards. Radios, televisions, and toasters get the same treatment because it is easier and often less expensive to buy a new product than to fix the old one. Who wants a comfortable old sweater if a new one can be bought on sale? No thought is given that the new one will soon look like the old one after two or three washings. We are the great "Let's junk it" society!

2. Anyone who has been in the hospital with a serious illness can tell you that the sight of a good nurse is the most beautiful sight in the world. Today, the hospital nurse has one of the hardest jobs of all. Although a doctor may direct the care and treatment of a patient, it is the nurse who must see to it that this care and treatment is carried out. A nurse must pay attention to everything, from the condition of the hospital bed to the scheduling of medication throughout the day and night. In addition to following a doctor's orders for the day, the nurse must respond to whatever the patient might need at any given moment. A sudden emergency requires the nurse to make an immediate judgment: Can the situation be handled with or without the doctor being called in? More recently, nurses have become increasingly burdened by paperwork and other administrative duties. Many people worry that the increasing demands on nurses will take them away from what they do best, namely, taking care of people on a one-to-one basis.

3. Anything can happen at an agricultural fair. It is the perfect human occasion, the harvest of the fields and of the emotions. To the fair come the man and his cow, the boy and his girl, the wife and her green tomato pickle, each anticipating victory and the excitement of being separated from his money by familiar devices. It is at a fair that man can be drunk forever on liquor, love, or fights; at a fair that your front pocket can be picked by a trotting horse looking for sugar, and your hind pocket by a thief looking for his fortune.

4. It was one of the most uncomfortable experiences of my life. The 747 from Hong Kong to Vancouver was packed. I barely had room for my overhead luggage and had to keep one of my bags under the seat in front of me. While I could hardly wait to see my little sister, I began to regret buying her that doll in Thailand because it took up all my leg room. My economy class seat was more than a little snug. It also seemed that nobody spoke English. When I asked him where he was headed, the blond haired gentleman next to me nodded politely and said, "Yes, yes." The airplane food was worse than usual, so I refused to eat any of it. For a long, long time I sat in the plane hungry, squished, and staring at the ceiling.

5. On hot summer days, the only room of the house that was cool was the sunporch. My mother brought out all her books and papers and stacked them up on the card table. There she would sit for hours at a stretch with one hand on her forehead trying to concentrate. Baby Kathleen would often sit in her playpen, throwing all her toys out of the pen or screeching with such a piercing high pitch that someone would have to come and rescue mom by giving the baby a cracker. Father would frequently bring in cups of tea for everyone and make mother laugh with his Irish sense of humour. It was there I would love to curl up on the wicker sofa (which was too short for my long legs even at twelve) and read one of the forty or fifty books I had bought for ten cents each at a local book fair. The sounds of neighbourhood activities—muted voices, a back door slamming, a dog barking—all these were a background that was friendly yet distant. During those summer days, the sunporch was the centre of our lives.

EXERCISE 2   Finding the Topic Sentence of a Paragraph

Each of the following five paragraphs contains a topic sentence that states the main idea of the paragraph. Find which sentence best states the main idea and underline it. The topic sentence will not always be the first sentence of the paragraph.

1. Last evening at a party, a complete stranger asked me, "Are you a Libra?" Astrology is enjoying increasing popularity all across Canada. My wife hurries every morning to read her horoscope in the paper. At the local stores, cards, books, T-shirts, and other useless astrological products bring fat profits to those who have manufactured them. Even some public officials, like the British royal family, are known to consider the "science" of astrology before scheduling an important event.

2. Travellers to Canada have usually heard about the wonders of Niagara Falls and the Rocky Mountains. These same tourists are not always so aware that an impressive variety of other sights awaits them in this country. The spectacular beauty of Alberta's Badlands and the wide majesty of the St. Lawrence River are sure to please the tourist. The impressive coastline of the East Coast is a contrast to the purple plains and dramatic skies of the West. The rugged terrain of the Canadian Shield is becoming increasingly popular. Even the area of the North has begun to attract boaters, anglers, and hikers throughout the summer months.

3. When you remember something, your brain uses more than one method to store the information. You have short-term memory, which helps you recall recent events; you have long-term memory, which brings back items that are further in the past; and you have deep retrieval, which gives you access to long-buried information that is sometimes difficult to recall. Whether these processes are chemical or electrical, we do not yet know, and much research remains to be done before we can say with any certainty. The brain is one of the most remarkable organs, a part of the body that we have only begun to investigate. It will be years before we even begin to understand all its complex processes.

4. Some of the homes were small with whitewashed walls and thatched roofs. We were eager to see how they were furnished. The living rooms were simple, often with only a plain wooden table and some chairs. The tiny bedrooms usually had room for only a single bed and a small table. Occasionally, a bedroom would be large enough to have a stove made of richly decorated tiles. Visiting these houses was an experience that would always stay in our memory. All of the windows held boxes for flowers so that even in the dark of winter there was the promise of a blaze of colours in the spring.

5. Advertisements that claim you can lose five pounds overnight are not to be trusted. Nor are claims that your luck will change if you send money to a certain post office box in a distant state or province. You should also avoid chain letters you receive in the mail that promise you large amounts of money if you will cooperate and keep the chain going. Many people are suspicious of the well-publicized million-dollar giveaway promotions that seem to offer enormous cash prizes, even if you do not try the company's product. We should always be suspicious of offers that promise us something for little or no effort or money.

EXERCISE 3   Finding the Topic Sentence of a Paragraph

The topic sentence is missing in each of the following four paragraphs. Read each paragraph carefully and circle the letter of the best topic sentence for that paragraph.

Ninety-five percent of the population in China had been illiterate. He knew that Canadian public schools would take care of our English, but he had to be the watchdog to nurture our Chinese knowledge. Only the Cantonese tongue was ever spoken by him or my mother. When the two oldest girls arrived from China, the schools of Chinatown received only boys. My father tutored his daughters each morning before breakfast. In the midst of a foreign environment, he clung to a combination of the familiar old standards and what was permissible in the newly learned Christian ideals.

a. Education has always been a priority in our family.
b. My father made sure that his sons received a proper education.
c. Learning Cantonese was an essential part of my education.
d. My father believed that the girls deserved educational opportunities just as much as the boys in the family.

How to hold a pair of chopsticks (palm up, not down); how to hold a bowl of rice (one thumb on top, not resting in an open palm); how to pass something to elders (with both hands, never one); how to pour tea into the tiny, handleless porcelain cups (seven-eighths full so that the top edge would be cool enough to hold); how to eat from a centre serving dish (only the piece in front of your place; never pick around); not to talk at table; not to show up outside of one's room without being fully dressed; not to be late, ever; not to be too playful—in a hundred and one ways, we were moulded to be trouble-free, unobtrusive, quiescent, cooperative.

a. From a very young age, I was taught proper table manners.
b. Very early in my life, the manners of a Chinese lady were taught to me.
c. Many Chinese customs differ from the customs in Canada.
d. Learning manners in a Chinese-Canada household.

I was never hungry. Though we had no milk, there was all the rice we wanted. We had hot and cold running water—a rarity in Chinatown, as well as our own bathtub. Others in the community used the YWCA or YMCA facilities, where for twenty-five cents, a family could draw six baths. Our sheets were pieced from dishtowels, but we had sheets. I was never neglected, for my mother and father were always at home. During school vacation periods, I was taught to operate many types of machines—tacking (for pockets), overlocking (for the raw edges of seams), buttonhole, double seaming; and I learned all the stages in producing a pair of jeans to its final inspection, folding, and tying in bundles of a dozen pairs by size, ready for pickup. Denim jeans are heavy—my shoulders ached often. My father set up a modest nickel-and-dime piecework reward for me, which he recorded in my own notebook, and he paid me regularly.

a. Learning the family trade.
b. Life in Chinatown for most people was very hard.
c. Learning how to sew was an important part of my upbringing.
d. Life was often hard, but there was little reason for unhappiness.

Mother would clean our living quarters very thoroughly, decorate the sitting room with flowering branches, fresh oranges, and arrange candied fruits or salty melon seeds for callers. All of us would be dressed in bright new clothes, and relatives or close friends, who came to call, would give each of us a red paper packet containing a good luck coin—usually a quarter. I remember how my classmates would gleefully talk of *their* receipts. But my mother made us give our money to her, for she said that she needed it to reciprocate to others.

a. I always enjoyed dressing up for Chinese holidays.
b. Each holiday was unique and had its own special blend of traditions and festivities.
c. The Chinese New Year, which would fall sometime in late January or early February, was the most special time of the year.
d. There was much work to be done during times of celebration.

How can you tell a topic sentence from a title?

The topic sentence works like a title by announcing to the reader what the paragraph is about. However, keep in mind that the title of an essay or book is usually a single word or short phrase, whereas the topic sentence of a paragraph must *always* be a complete sentence.

Title: Backpacking in the mountains
Topic sentence: Backpacking in the mountains last year was an exciting
                              experience.

Title: The stress of registration
Topic sentence: Registration can be stressful.

EXERCISE 1   Distinguishing a Topic Sentence from a Title

Each of the following ten examples is either a title (T) or a topic sentence (TS). In each of the spaces provided, identify the example by writing T or TS.

_____ 1. The benefits of postsecondary education

_____ 2. The outstanding achievements of the rower Silken Lauman

_____ 3. The president's cabinet faced two major problems

_____ 4. The basis of the Arab-Israeli Conflict

_____ 5. The Japanese diet is perhaps the healthiest diet in the world

_____ 6. The astounding beauty of the Rocky Mountains at dusk

_____ 7. The finest sports car on the market

_____ 8. Fast-food restaurants are popular with families having small children

_____ 9. The expense of maintaining a car

_____ 10. Maintaining a car is expensive

EXERCISE 2   Distinguishing a Topic Sentence from a Title

Each of the following ten examples is either a title (T) or a topic sentence (TS). In each of the spaces provided, identify the example by writing T or TS.

_____ 1. Dreams can be frightening

_____ 2. The advantages of getting a job after high school

_____ 3. *Grumpy Old Men* was an unusual movie because it portrayed the unpopular subject of growing old

_____ 4. The home of my dreams

_____ 5. Walking on the beach at sunset calms me down after a stressful day at work

_____ 6. Making your own clothes requires great patience as well as skill

_____ 7. Selecting the right camera for an amateur

_____ 8. Finding the right place to study was my most difficult problem at college

_____ 9. The worst bargain of my life

_____ 10. The old car I bought from my friend's father turned out to be a real bargain

EXERCISE 3   Distinguishing a Topic Sentence from a Title

Each of the following ten examples is either a title (T) or a topic sentence (TS). In each of the spaces provided, identify the example by writing T or TS.

_____ 1. How to make friends at school and still have time to study

_____ 2. With the widespread use of computers, word processing skills are needed for many jobs

_____ 3. The disadvantages of living alone

_____ 4. The fight to keep our neighbourhood park

_____ 5. The peacefulness of a solitary weekend at the beach

_____ 6. Our investigation into the mysterious death of Walter D.

_____ 7. The flea market looked promising

_____ 8. The two main reasons why divorce is common

_____ 9. The single life did not turn out to be as glamorous as I had hoped

_____ 10. The increasing popularity of board games

How do you find the topic in a topic sentence?

To find the topic in a topic sentence, ask yourself what subject the writer is going to discuss. In the first sentence that follows, the topic is underlined for you. Underline the topic in the second example.

Backpacking in the mountains last year was an exciting experience.

Registration can be stressful.

EXERCISE 1   Finding the Topic in the Topic Sentence

Find the topic in each of the following topic sentences. For each example, ask yourself this question: What topic is the writer going to discuss? Then underline the topic.

1. Remodelling an old house can be frustrating.
2. University work demands more independence than high school work.
3. A well-made suit has three easily identified characteristics.
4. Growing up near a museum had a profound influence on my life.
5. My favourite room in the house would seem ugly to most people.
6. A student who goes to school full time and also works part time has to make careful use of every hour.
7. One of the disadvantages of skiing is the expense.
8. Spanking is the least successful way to discipline a child.

9. An attractive wardrobe does not have to be expensive.

10. The first year of school is usually the most demanding.

EXERCISE 2   Finding the Topic in the Topic Sentence

Find the topic in each of the following topic sentences. For each example, ask yourself this question: What topic is the writer going to discuss? Then underline the topic.

1. Taking care of a house can easily be a full-time job.

2. Many television news programs are more interested in providing entertainment than newsworthy information.

3. One of the undisputed goals in teaching is to be able to offer individualized instruction.

4. Whether it's a car, a house, or a college, bigger isn't always better.

5. Violence on television is disturbing to most child psychologists.

6. In today's economy, carrying at least one credit card is probably advisable.

7. Much highway advertising is not only ugly but also distracting for the driver.

8. Figuring out a semester course schedule can be a complicated process.

9. In recent years, we have seen a dramatic revival of interest in quilting.

10. The grading system at university is quite different from that of the high school in my hometown.

EXERCISE 3   Finding the Topic in the Topic Sentence

Find the topic in each of the following topic sentences. For each example, ask yourself this question: What topic is the writer going to discuss? Then underline the topic.

1. To my surprise, the basement had now been converted into a small studio apartment.

2. Of all the prime ministers, Pierre Trudeau probably enjoys the greatest popularity.

3. Scientists cannot yet explain how an identical twin often has an uncanny knowledge of what the other twin is doing or feeling.

4. If you don't have a car in Ottawa, you have undoubtedly discovered the limitations of the public transportation system.

5. When we met for dinner that night, I was shocked at the change that had come over my friend.

6. According to the report, current tax laws greatly benefit those who own real estate.

7. Alanis Morissette, the famous singer, began her career on television.

8. As we rode into town, the streets seemed unusually empty.

9. Canada Post offers its employees many long-term benefits.

10. Many people claim that clipping coupons can save them as much as 30 percent of their food bill.

What is a controlling idea?

A topic sentence should contain not only the topic but also a controlling idea.

> The *controlling idea* of a topic sentence is the attitude or point of view that the writer takes toward the topic.
>
> Example: Backpacking trips are *exciting*.

A particular topic, therefore, could have any number of possible controlling ideas, all depending on the writer's attitude. Three writers on the same topic of backpacking might have different points of view:

A family backpacking trip can be much more *satisfying* than a trip to an amusement park.

or

Our recent backpacking trip was a *disaster*.

or

A backpacking trip *should be a part of every teenager's experience*.

How do you find the controlling idea of a topic sentence?

When you look for the controlling idea of a topic sentence, ask yourself this question: What is the writer's attitude toward the topic?

In each of the following examples, underline the topic and circle the controlling idea.

The Hudson's Bay Department Store is my favourite store in town.

The Hudson's Bay Department Store is too expensive for my budget.

EXERCISE 1   Finding the Controlling Idea

Below are ten topic sentences. For each sentence, underline the topic and circle the controlling idea.

1. Vigorous exercise is a good way to reduce the effects of stress on the body.

2. Montreal and Toronto differ in four major ways.

3. Television violence causes aggressive behaviour in children.

4. Athletic scholarships available to women are increasing.

5. Caffeine has several adverse effects on the body.

6. Jim Carrey, the actor, has an amusing personality.

7. Training a parakeet to talk takes great patience.

8. Babysitting for a family with four preschool children was the most difficult job I've ever had.

9. The hours between five and seven in the morning are my most productive.

10. The foggy night was spooky.

EXERCISE 2 Finding the Controlling Idea

Below are ten topic sentences. For each sentence, underline the topic and circle the controlling idea.

1. Piano lessons turned out to be a disaster.

2. The training of Japanese policemen is quite different from Canadian police training.

3. An Olympic champion has five distinctive characteristics.

4. The candidate's unethical financial dealings will have a negative impact on this campaign.

5. A bicycle ride along the coast is a breathtaking trip.

6. The grocery store is another place where people waste a significant amount of money every week.

7. Being an only child is not as bad as people think.

8. Rewarding children with candy or desserts is an unfortunate habit of many parents.

9. A childhood hobby often develops into a promising career.

10. The writing of a dictionary is an incredibly detailed process.

EXERCISE 3 Finding the Controlling Idea

Below are ten topic sentences. For each sentence, underline the topic and circle the controlling idea.

1. Learning to type takes more practice than talent.

2. Shakespeare's plays are difficult for today's students because English has undergone many changes since the sixteenth century.

3. Calgary, Alberta, is one of the cities in the West that is experiencing significant population growth.

4. Half a dozen new health magazines are enjoying popularity.

5. The importance of good preschool programs for children has been sadly underestimated.

6. The disposal of toxic wastes has caused problems for many manufacturers.

7. Body piercing is a contentious issue between parents and kids.

8. Finding an inexpensive method to make salt water drinkable has been a difficult problem for decades.

9. Developing colour film is more complicated than developing black and white.

10. The cloudberry is one of the rare berries of the world.

Choosing your own controlling idea

Teachers often assign one general topic on which all students must write. Likewise, when writing contests are announced, the topic is generally the same for all contestants. Since very few people have exactly the same view or attitude toward a topic, it is likely that no two papers would have the same controlling idea. There could be as many controlling ideas as there are people to write them. The secret of writing a good topic sentence is to find the controlling idea that is right for you.

EXERCISE 1   **Choosing Controlling Ideas to Write Topic Sentences**

Below are two topics. For each topic, think of three different possible controlling ideas, and then write a different topic sentence for each of these controlling ideas. An example is done for you.

Topic: My mother

Three possible controlling ideas:
1. Unusual childhood
2. Silent woman
3. Definite ideas about alcohol

Three different topic sentences:
1. My mother had a most unusual childhood.
2. My mother is a very silent woman.
3. My mother has definite ideas about alcohol.

1. **Topic:** My grandmother

First controlling idea: _____

First topic sentence: _____

_____

Second controlling idea: _____

Second topic sentence: _____

_____

Third controlling idea: _____

Third topic sentence: _____

_____

2. **Topic:** New Brunswick

First controlling idea: _____

First topic sentence: _____

_____

Second controlling idea: _____

Second topic sentence: _____

_____

Third controlling idea: _____

Third topic sentence: _____

_____

EXERCISE 2   Choosing Controlling Ideas to Write Topic Sentences

Below are two topics. For each topic, think of three different possible controlling ideas, and then write a different topic sentence for each of these controlling ideas. An example is done for you.

Topic: The movie *The Matrix*

Three possible controlling ideas:
1. Filled with suspense
2. Reveals the bravery of the characters
3. Explores the importance of teamwork

Three different topic sentences:
1. *The Matrix* is a movie filled with suspense.
2. *The Matrix* is a movie that reveals the bravery of the characters when faced with life and death situations.
3. *The Matrix* is a movie that explores the importance of teamwork.

1. **Topic:** Thanksgiving

   First controlling idea: _____

   First topic sentence: _____

   _____

   Second controlling idea: _____

   Second topic sentence: _____

   _____

   Third controlling idea: _____

   Third topic sentence: _____

   _____

2. **Topic:** Working in a nursing home

   First controlling idea: _____

   First topic sentence: _____

   _____

   Second controlling idea: _____

   Second topic sentence: _____

   _____

   Third controlling idea: _____

Third topic sentence: _____

_____

EXERCISE 3 Choosing Controlling Ideas to Write Topic Sentences

Below are two topics. For each topic, think of three different possible controlling ideas, and then write a different topic sentence for each of these controlling ideas. An example is done for you.

Topic: Fitness and health

Three possible controlling ideas:
1. The growth of new lines of products
2. Increased popularity of health clubs
3. Use of exercise videos and equipment at home

Three different topic sentences:
1. Recent years have seen the creation of entire lines of products devoted to fitness and health.
2. The high level of interest in physical fitness and health has resulted in a widespread growth of health clubs across the country.
3. A person can improve his or her health by exercising at home with a professional video or working out on one of the many pieces of equipment available for private use.

1. **Topic:** Rap music

   First controlling idea: _____

   First topic sentence: _____

   _____

   Second controlling idea: _____

   Second topic sentence: _____

   _____

   Third controlling idea: _____

   Third topic sentence: _____

   _____

2. **Topic:** Junk food

   First controlling idea: _____

   First topic sentence: _____

   _____

   Second controlling idea: _____

   Second topic sentence: _____

   _____

   Third controlling idea: _____

   Third topic sentence: _____

   _____

Mastery and editing tests

TEST 1   **Further Practice Writing the Topic Sentence**

Develop each of the following topics into a topic sentence. In each case, the controlling idea is missing. First, decide on an attitude you might take toward the topic. Then use that attitude to write your topic sentence. When you are finished, underline your topic and circle your controlling idea. Be sure your topic sentence is a complete sentence and not a fragment. An example has been done for you.

Topic: My brother's car accident

Controlling idea: Tragic results

Topic sentence: My brother's car accident had (tragic results) for the entire family.

1. **Topic:** Teaching a child good manners

   Controlling idea: _____

   Topic sentence: _____

   _____

   _____

2. **Topic:** Two years in teacher's college

   Controlling idea: _____

   Topic sentence: _____

   _____

   _____

3. **Topic:** Living with your in-laws

   Controlling idea: _____

   Topic sentence: _____

   _____

   _____

4. **Topic:** Moving to a new location

   Controlling idea: _____

   Topic sentence: _____

   _____

   _____

5. **Topic:** Going on a diet

   Controlling idea: _____

   Topic sentence: _____

   _____

   _____

TEST 2   **Further Practice Writing the Topic Sentence**

Develop each of the following topics into a topic sentence. In each case, the controlling idea is missing. First, decide on an attitude you might take toward the topic. Then use that attitude to write your topic sentence. When you are finished, underline your topic and circle your controlling idea. Be sure your topic sentence is a complete sentence and not a fragment.

1. **Topic:** Camping

   Controlling idea: _____

   Topic sentence: _____

   _____

   _____

2. **Topic:** Vegetarians

   Controlling idea: _____

   Topic sentence: _____

   _____

   _____

   _____

3. **Topic:** Noisy neighbours

   Controlling idea: _____

   Topic sentence: _____

   _____

   _____

4. **Topic:** Driving lessons

   Controlling idea: _____

   Topic sentence: _____

   _____

   _____

5. **Topic:** Public transit

   Controlling idea: _____

   Topic sentence: _____

   _____

   _____

TEST 3   **Further Practice Writing the Topic Sentence**

Develop each of the following topics into a topic sentence. In each case, the controlling idea is missing. First, decide on an attitude you might take toward the topic. Then use that attitude to write your topic sentence. When you are finished, underline your topic and circle your controlling idea. Be sure your topic sentence is a complete sentence and not a fragment.

1. **Topic:** Computer programming

   Controlling idea: _____

   Topic sentence: _____

   _____

   _____

2. **Topic:** Tattoos

   Controlling idea: _____

   Topic sentence: _____

   _____

   _____

   _____

3. **Topic:** Allergies

   Controlling idea: _____

   Topic sentence: _____

   _____

   _____

4. **Topic:** Motorcycles

   Controlling idea: _____

   Topic sentence: _____

   _____

   _____

5. **Topic:** Eating out

   Controlling idea: _____

   Topic sentence: _____

   _____

   _____

Working Together

Every topic contains the possibility of more than one controlling idea. For example, the topic of *dating* is rich in possibilities. Think for a few moments and then jot down one or two controlling ideas about dating that come to mind. A class member will then list all the different controlling ideas that members of the class have generated. From this list, pick your favourite controlling idea and compose a topic sentence. Then write a complete paragraph using this topic sentence as your starting point. Be sure all your sentences relate directly to the topic and support the controlling idea so that your paragraph is unified.

If time permits, students can do some peer editing by reading each other's paragraphs. In this case, students should look particularly for any sentences that are off the track and that do not relate to the controlling idea. Such sentences need to be deleted.

Chapter 15

Working with Paragraphs: Supporting Details

What is a supporting detail?

Once you have constructed a topic sentence including the topic and its controlling idea, you are ready to support your statement with details. The quality and number of these details will largely determine the effectiveness of your writing. You can hold your readers spellbound with your choice of details, or you can lose your readers' interest because your details are not effective.

> A *supporting detail* is a piece of evidence used by the writer to make the controlling idea of the topic sentence convincing and interesting to the reader. A piece of evidence might include a descriptive image, an example taken from history or personal experience, a reason, a fact (such as a statistic), a quotation from an expert, or an anecdote to illustrate a point.
>
> **Poor supporting detail:**   Many people died of the flu in the early 1900s.
>
> **Effective supporting detail:** In 1918, 50,000 people died of the Spanish flu in Canada.

As we work through the chapters that follow, you will have opportunities to become familiar with using all of these kinds of supporting details.

As you choose your supporting details, keep in mind that the readers do not necessarily have to agree with your point of view. However, your supporting details must be good enough so that your readers will at least respect your attitude. Your goal should be to educate your readers. Try to give them understanding about your subject. Don't assume they know about or are interested in your topic. If you provide enough interesting and specific details, your readers will feel they have learned something new about the subject, and this alone is a satisfying experience for most people.

Supporting details will encourage the readers to keep reading, will make your points more memorable, and will give pleasure to the readers who are learning new material or picturing the images you have created.

The following selection is an example of a paragraph that provides effective details in order to support the point of the topic sentence.

Everyone has heard of sure-fire formulas to prevent getting a cold. Popular home methods include a cold shower, regular exercise, and a hot rum toddy. Some people swear by cod-liver oil, tea with honey, citrus fruit juices, or keeping one's feet dry. Canadians spent billions last year for cold and cough remedies. Advertisers have claimed preventive and curative virtues for vitamins, alkalizers, lemon drinks, antihistamines, decongestants, timed-release capsules, antibiotics, antiseptic gargles, bioflavonoids, nose drops and sprays, and a variety of other products. There are at least 300 over-the-counter products, most of which are a combination of ingredients sold for the treatment of symptoms of the common cold. Many of these drugs neither benefit nor harm the cold victim, but there is no doubt that they benefit the drug manufacturers! Now—just as fifty years ago—Canadians on average will suffer two to three colds a year, with the infectious stages lasting about a week, regardless of any physical measure, diet, or drug used. Canadian Public Health Service studies show that, during the winter quarter of the year, 50 percent of the population experiences a common cold; during the summer quarter, the figure drops to 20 percent. The increased incidence of colds in winter reflects the fact that people spend more time indoors, thereby allowing the viruses to travel from person to person. In fact, one is less likely to catch a cold after exposure to the elements than after mixing with a convivial group of snifflers and sneezers at a fireside gathering.

•PRACTICE

Using the lines provided, copy the topic sentence from the previous paragraph. Answer the questions about the supporting details for the topic sentence.

Topic sentence: _____

_____

What are some examples of home remedies?

_____

_____

What are some examples of over-the-counter remedies?

_____

_____

What fact is given?

_____

_____

What expert is named? What is the statistic given by that source?

_____

_____

EXERCISE 1   Finding the Topic Sentence and Supporting Details

In each paragraph below, find the topic sentence and the sentences of supporting details.

1. Saturday afternoon was a blessed time on the farm. First of all, there would now be no mail in till Monday afternoon, so that no distressing business letters could reach us till then, and this fact in itself seemed to close the whole place in, as within an *enceinte* [a circular enclosure]. Secondly, everybody was looking forward to the day of Sunday, when they would rest or play all the day, and the Squatters could work on their own land. The thought of the oxen on Saturday pleased me more than all other things. I used to walk down to their paddock at six o'clock, when they were coming in after the day's work and a few hours' grazing. Tomorrow, I thought, they would do nothing but graze all day.

From Isak Dinesen,
Out of Africa

Topic sentence: _____

_____

First reason: _____

_____

Second reason: _____

_____

Third reason: _____

_____

2. We continue to use pesticides on our food at an alarming rate. There is a 25 percent chance that an average peach bought at your local grocery store contains levels of insecticides that are considered unsafe for children. Who could imagine a salad without lettuce? Yet lettuce crops are typically grown using more pesticides than any other vegetable. It's no wonder that 90 percent of North Americans would buy organic food if the prices were comparable to non-organic alternatives. How long will we poison ourselves with the very food we eat?

From *Shift Magazine*, April 1999, p. 9

Topic sentence: _____

_____

First statistical fact: _____

_____

Second statistical fact: _____

_____

Third statistical fact: _____

_____

EXERCISE 2   Finding the Topic Sentence and Supporting Details

In each paragraph below, find the topic sentence and the sentences of supporting details.

1. Hilda takes an enormous amount of space, though so little time, in my adolescence. Even today, her memory stirs me; I long to see her again. She was three years older than I, and for a short while all I wanted to look like, sound like, dress like. She was the only girl I knew who told me I wrote excellent letters. She made a plaster cast of my face. She had opinions on everything. She took a picture of me, at sixteen, which I have still. She and I were nearly killed, falling off a hillside road in her small car. Hilda was so full of life, I cannot believe her dead.

From Han Suyin,
A Mortal Flower

Topic sentence: _____

_____

First example: _____

_____

Second example: _____

_____

Third example: _____

_____

Fourth example: _____

_____

Fifth example: _____

_____

Sixth example: _____

_____

2. If hockey has its rabid dads, figure skating has its snotty moms. Those are the stereotypes, at least, and while most figure skating parents are supportive and gracious, there are enough of the contentious kind to dampen the fun. Horror stories abound of figure skating moms who berate, even fire coaches on a whim. Who take over the management of a club and push it in a direction that benefits their children only. And then there is the infamous *glare,* a tactic some parents use to psych out their kids' competitors. "Parents will stare you down and make you feel so uncomfortable that you make a mistake," says a teenage female skater. "They're just jealous because you can beat their kids. But it still hurts."

From "Bane of the Bleachers" by Susan McClelland, *Maclean's,* March 26, 2001, p. 25

Topic sentence: _____

_____

First piece of evidence: _____

_____

Second piece of evidence: _____

_____

Third piece of evidence and supporting information: _____

_____

EXERCISE 3 Finding the Topic Sentence and Supporting Details

In each paragraph below, find the topic sentence and the sentences of supporting details.

1. Police in every major country have pressed for new powers to intercept what travels over the Internet. In 1999, Australia gave its authorities the right to enter homes surreptitiously to hack into suspects' computers. More recently, British and U.S. police won government blessing for their plans to install eavesdropping devices in Internet service providers' premises. The devices— ominously code-named "Carnivore" in the American case—act much like telephone taps, allowing police to intercept e-mail on its way to and from a specified Internet address. Canada has yet to give its police similar authority, but a report released last October by the normally super-secret federal Communications Security Establishment argued that e-mail interception "may be required" for the CSE to protect government computer networks against viruses.

From "Do You Know Who's Watching You?" by Chris Wood,
Maclean's, Feb. 19, 2001, p. 21

Topic sentence: _____

_____

First example: _____

_____

Second example and additional supporting information: _____

_____

Third example: _____

_____

2. Fairness is the ability to see more than one side in a situation, and sometimes it even means having the ability to decide against your own interests. For example, in Halifax, Nova Scotia, a woman was locked in a bitter custody dispute that involved her thirteen-year-old son. The mother loved her son and wanted custody of him, even though she had a major health problem. She listened patiently while her ex-husband argued for full custody of the child. The woman felt that she had presented a good case before the judge, but when the boy was asked for his feelings in the matter, the mother found herself faced with a difficult situation: her son wanted to live with his father. Fairness to the child led the mother to give up her fight. Fairness, she discovered, is often painful because it means recognizing what is right instead of insisting on your own personal bias.

Topic sentence: _____

_____

Anecdote: _____

_____

_____

_____

_____

_____

Avoid restating the topic sentence

You should be able to recognize the difference between a genuine supporting detail and a simple restatement of the topic sentence. The following is a poor paragraph because all its sentences merely restate the topic sentence.

The wedding day was the highest point in a girl's life—a day to which she looked forward all her unmarried days and to which she looked back for the rest of her life. All the events of the day were unlike any other day in her life before or after. Everyone would remember this day. Each event was unforgettable. The memories would last a lifetime. A wedding was the beginning of living "happily ever after."

By contrast, this paragraph, "From Popping the Question to Popping the Pill" by Margaret Mead, has good supporting details:

> The wedding day was the highest point in a girl's life—a day to which she looked forward all her unmarried days and to which she looked back for the rest of her life. The splendour of her wedding, the elegance of dress and veil, the cutting of the cake, the departure amid a shower of rice and confetti, gave her an accolade of which no subsequent event could completely rob her. Today people over fifty years of age still treat their daughter's wedding this way, prominently displaying the photographs of the occasion. Until very recently, all brides' books prescribed exactly the same ritual they had prescribed fifty years before. The etiquette governing wedding presents—gifts that were or were not appropriate, the bride's maiden initials on her linen—was also specified. For the bridegroom the wedding represented the end of his free, bachelor days, and the bachelor dinner the night before the wedding symbolized this loss of freedom. A woman who did not marry—even if she had the alibi of a fiancé who had been killed in war or had abilities and charm and money of her own—was always at a social disadvantage while an eligible bachelor was sought after by hostess after hostess.

EXERCISE 1   Distinguishing a Supporting Detail from a Restatement of the Main Idea

Each of the following topic sentences is followed by four additional sentences. Three of these additional sentences contain acceptable supporting details, but one of the sentences is simply a restatement of the topic sentence. In the space provided, identify each sentence as SD for supporting detail or R for restatement.

1. I am surprised when I think how neat I used to be before school started.

    _____ a. In my closet, I had my clothes arranged in matching outfits with shoes, hats, and even jewellery to go with them.

    _____ b. I always used to take great pride in having all my things in order.

    _____ c. If I opened my desk drawer, compartments of paper clips, erasers, staples, pens, pencils, stamps, and rulers greeted me without one lost penny or safety pin out of place.

    _____ d. On top of my chest of drawers sat a comb and brush, two oval frames with pictures of my best friends, and that was all.

2. Iceland has a very barren landscape.

    _____ a. One-tenth of the island is covered by ice.

    _____ b. There is not a single forest on the entire island.

    _____ c. Nearly everywhere you look in Iceland, you see vast desolate areas.

    _____ d. Three-fourths of the island is uninhabitable.

3. Until recently, books have been the most important method of preserving knowledge.

    _____ a. Without books, much of the knowledge of past centuries would have been lost.

    _____ b. Leonardo da Vinci kept notebooks of his amazing inventions and discoveries.

_____ c. During the Middle Ages, monks spent their entire lives copying books by hand.

_____ d. The National Library in Ottawa, Ontario, is given a copy of every book published in Canada.

4. Most people no longer wonder whether cigarette smoking is bad for their health.

_____ a. Following the evidence from over 30,000 studies, a federal law requires that cigarette manufacturers place a health warning to all smokers on their packages.

_____ b. Studies have shown that smoking presently causes nearly 80 percent of lung cancer deaths in this country.

_____ c. Few authorities today have any doubts about the connection between cigarette smoking and poor health.

_____ d. We know that 30 percent of the deaths from coronary heart disease can be attributed to smoking.

5. When the Mexican earthquake struck in 1985, scientists and city planners learned a great deal about the kinds of buildings that can survive an earthquake.

_____ a. Buildings that had foundations resting on giant rollers suffered very little damage.

_____ b. Buildings that were made only of adobe material simply fell apart when the earthquake struck.

_____ c. Many of the modern buildings were designed to vibrate when earthquakes occur, so these received the least amount of shock.

_____ d. After the earthquake was over, officials realized why some buildings were destroyed while others suffered hardly any damage at all.

EXERCISE 2   Recognizing a Supporting Detail from a Restatement of the Main Idea

Each of the following topic sentences is followed by four additional sentences. Three of these additional sentences contain acceptable supporting details, but one of the sentences is simply a restatement of the topic sentence. In the space provided, identify each sentence as SD for supporting detail or R for restatement.

1. Recent statistics show that insomnia is the most common sleep disorder, and it affects one in four adults.

_____ a. Insomnia can be defined as having difficulty falling asleep, difficulty staying asleep, waking up too early in the morning, or having non-refreshing sleep at night.

_____ b. It often takes a long time for people to realize that their sleepless nights and exhausting days are worthy of medical attention.

_____ c. One-quarter of adults suffer from insomnia.

_____ d. Thirty percent of patients seen for insomnia were also diagnosed with depression.

[P. Saunders. "Insomnia: A Naturopathic Medical Approach."
Wellness Options, February–March 2001, pp. 18–19.]

2. Today, people are realizing the disadvantages of using credit cards too often.

_____ a. People should think twice before using their cards.

_____ b. Interest rates on credit cards can reach alarming rates.

_____ c. Credit cards encourage buying on impulse, rather than planning a budget carefully.

_____ d. Many credit card companies charge an annual fee for the privilege of using cards.

3. Road rage takes place more often than people think.

_____ a. Failing to signal a lane change, disobeying traffic signs and signals, tailgating, and speeding are all behaviours that may be recognized as road aggression.

_____ b. When the media focus on the extreme instances of road rage, people find it easy to sit back and say, "That's not me."

_____ c. According to a recent study conducted by the Steel Alliance and Canada Safety Council in 2000, 85 percent of drivers surveyed committed at least one act of aggressive driving over the preceding year.

_____ d. Drivers in British Columbia are more likely to tailgate and change lanes without signalling; Ontario drivers are more likely to drive through red lights.

[J. Cleland and Therese Zarb. "Steer Away from Road Rage." *Wellness Options*, February–March 2001, pp. 36–38.]

4. Since World War II, the status of women in Japan has changed.

_____ a. In 1947, women won the right to vote.

_____ b. The women's position in Japanese society has altered over the past forty-five years.

_____ c. Many Japanese women now go on to get a higher education.

_____ d. Women can now own property in their own name and seek divorce.

5. Certain factors that cannot be changed have been shown to contribute to heart attacks and stroke.

_____ a. Three out of four heart attacks and six out of seven strokes occur after the age of sixty-five, so age is definitely a factor.

_____ b. Heart attacks and strokes have many causes, some of which we can do nothing about.

_____ c. Canadian males run a greater risk of having high blood pressure, a major cause of heart attacks and strokes.

_____ d. Men are at greater risk than women in their chance of suffering from cardiovascular disease.

How do you make supporting details specific?

Students often write paragraphs that are made up only of general statements. When you read such paragraphs, you doubt the author's knowledge and you suspect that the point being made may have no basis in fact. Here is one such paragraph that never gets off the ground.

Doctors are terrible. They cause more problems than they solve. I don't believe most of their treatments are necessary. History is full of the mistakes doctors have made. We don't need all those operations. We should never ingest all those drugs doctors prescribe. We shouldn't allow them to give us all those unnecessary tests. I've heard plenty of stories that prove my point. Doctors' ideas can kill you.

Here is another paragraph on the same topic. This topic is much more interesting and convincing because the writer has made use of supporting details rather than general statements.

Evidence shows that "medical progress" has been the cause of tragic consequences and even death for thousands of people. X-ray therapy was thought to help patients with tonsillitis. Now many of these people are found to have developed cancer from these X-rays. Not so long ago, women were kept in bed for several weeks following childbirth. Unfortunately, this cost many women their lives since they developed fatal blood clots from being kept in bed day after day. One recent poll estimates that 30,000 people each year die from the side effects of drugs that were prescribed by doctors. Recently, it was reported that 25 percent of the tests done by clinical laboratories were done poorly. All this is not to belittle the good done by the medical profession, but to impress on readers that it would be foolish to rely totally on the medical profession to solve all our health problems.

This paragraph is much more likely to be of real interest. Even if you would like to disprove the author's point, it would be very hard to dismiss these supports, which are based on facts and information that can be researched. Because the author sounds reasonable, you can respect the writer even if you have a different position on the topic.

In writing effectively, the ability to go beyond the general statement and get to the accurate pieces of information is what counts. A writer tries to make his or her reader an expert on the subject. Readers should go away excited to share with the next person they meet the surprising information they have just learned. A writer who has a statistic, a quotation, an anecdote, a historical example, or a descriptive detail has the advantage over all other writers, no matter how impressive these writers' styles may be.

Good writing, therefore, is filled with supporting details that are specific, correct, and appropriate for the subject. Poor writing is filled with generalizations, stereotypes, vagueness, untruths, and even sarcasm and insults.

EXERCISE 1   Creating Supporting Details

Below are five topic sentences. Supply three supporting details for each one. Be sure each detail is specific and not general or vague.

1. The first semester in college or university can be overwhelming.

   a. _____

   b. _____

   c. _____

2. Designer clothing is a bad investment.

   a. _____

   b. _____

c. _____

3. Dr. Kline is an easy teacher.

    a. _____

    b. _____

    c. _____

4. It is difficult to stop snacking between meals.

    a. _____

    b. _____

    c. _____

5. My sister is the sloppiest person I know.

    a. _____

    b. _____

    c. _____

EXERCISE 2   Creating Supporting Details

Below are five topic sentences. Supply three supporting details for each one. Be sure each detail is specific and not general or vague.

1. December has become a frantic time at our house.

    a. _____

    b. _____

    c. _____

2. My best friend can often be very immature.

    a. _____

    b. _____

    c. _____

3. Each sport has its own peculiar injuries associated with it.

    a. _____

    b. _____

    c. _____

4. My car is on its "last wheel."

    a. _____

    b. _____

    c. _____

5. Watching too much television has serious effects on family life.

    a. _____

    b. _____

    c. _____

EXERCISE 3   Creating Supporting Details

Below are five topic sentences. Supply three supporting details for each one. Be sure each detail is specific and not general or vague.

1. Maintaining a car is a continual drain on one's budget.

   a. _____

   b. _____

   c. _____

2. Climate can affect a person's mood.

   a. _____

   b. _____

   c. _____

3. Last year I redecorated my bedroom.

   a. _____

   b. _____

   c. _____

4. Prince Edward Island is the best place for a family vacation.

   a. _____

   b. _____

   c. _____

5. The amateur photographer needs to consider several points when selecting a camera.

   a. _____

   b. _____

   c. _____

Working Together

What makes one university or college different from another? What characteristics distinguish the school you are now attending from other schools you have known or heard about?

Divide into groups. Each person should take a few moments to think about and then jot down what he or she finds special about the school. Next, work as a group to compare ideas so that each person can expand his or her own list. When each person is satisfied that there is enough material, students can then proceed to write paragraphs providing several supporting details on the subject of what makes your school special. Be sure to begin with a topic sentence.

If time permits, read each other's paragraphs. For each paper ask yourselves these questions:

1. Is there a topic sentence?

2. Did the student stick to the controlling idea? Do all the sentences support the main idea or should some sentences be deleted in order to achieve unity?

3. What is a strength that you could give for each paper? Pick one suggestion for improvement.

Chapter 16

Developing Paragraphs: Illustration

What is illustration?

In Chapter 14, we learned that after writing a topic sentence, the sentences that follow need to contain specific details that will support the main idea. One pattern of development often used is to give **illustrations** (or **examples**) to make an abstract or general idea clear to every reader.

> *Illustration* (or exemplification) is a method for developing a writer's ideas. It provides one or more examples to help the reader understand and remember the point the writer wishes to make.

Three ways to illustrate a point

1. Give one or more brief examples without grouping them in any way:

   As a child I had pen pals from all over the world. There was my cousin Britt-Marie from Sweden, Ying from Hong Kong, Simone from France, Etsuko from Japan, and several children from Kenya.

2. Arrange all the examples into groups:

   As a child I had pen pals all over the world. From Europe was my cousin Britt-Marie of Sweden and Simone from the south of France. From the Pacific came the beautiful monthly letters of Etsuko in Kyoto, Japan, and an occasional postcard from Ying in Hong Kong. Finally, from Africa came a number of charming letters from several schoolchildren in Kenya.

3. Present one or two illustrations that are longer and more developed than a simple mention of examples: (This method is often called **extended example** and may take the form of a story, sometimes called an **anecdote**, using the principles of narration.)

   Let me tell you how my love of getting mail from children around the world changed the course of my life.

   Such a story might even continue for several paragraphs, but remember that the story or anecdote is supposed to prove a point; do not get sidetracked.

Working with illustration: Where does the writer find examples?

Personal experiences and one's own knowledge of the world

Writers find supporting examples for their work everywhere, beginning with their own experience. What you have observed and what has happened to you are two excellent sources of examples for your own writing. All of us have gained a great deal of knowledge either formally or informally, and you can call upon that knowledge when you look for examples to illustrate your points.

Interviews and surveys

Another source for examples is to interview other people or take an informal survey. Gathering this kind of material can enrich your writing by presenting very specific information and facts about your main idea. We see and hear interviews on television and radio every day, as people from all walks of life tell their stories on every topic imaginable. We are accustomed to seeing professional interviewers asking questions, but you can also gain examples in this way by talking to your friends and classmates and learning from them.

Outside research from books and magazines

A third method of finding specific examples for your work is to do outside research. This usually involves going to a library and finding information from books and magazines. This kind of research is necessary for term papers and many other kinds of college or university work, and it always requires a careful listing of the sources that are used.

Using your imagination to create hypothetical examples

There is a final way to obtain examples, and it is a method that does not require any outside sources. This is your own imagination. Writers often find it very useful to create imaginary examples or situations that can provide the specific details for them when they need examples in their writing. Humorous writers do this all the time when they tell jokes. You, too, can use your imagination to generate examples when your writing does not require strictly factual information. The hypothetical example is also useful to illustrate a point. This example often begins with a phrase such as "Imagine the following situation . . ." or "Put the case that . . ." or "What if this were to happen . . ."

EXERCISE 1   The Sources for Illustrations

On page 287 are three paragraphs. Each one develops an idea by using illustration. Read each paragraph and decide what the source was for the illustration. Choose from the following list:

> Example from personal experience or knowledge
>
> Made up or hypothetical example
>
> Information from an interview or survey you conduct yourself
>
> Outside research (using material found in books or articles)

PARAGRAPH 1

Most students today believe they must learn how to use the computer if they are to be competitive in the job market. A case in point is my composition class. Out of the 23 students surveyed, all but two felt they must be computer literate or they might not be able to get the jobs they want. Three of the students currently own their own computers and claim they are able to get their work done more easily. Two of these three students actually have part-time jobs, one in the library and one in the history department where they both enter data on computers. This seems to show that these students already are at an advantage over the rest of the students who are still learning to use the computer.

Type of example: _____

PARAGRAPH 2

Most students today believe they must learn how to use the computer if they are to be competitive in the job market. If a person, just to illustrate, wants a career in auto mechanics and thinks he has no need to learn how to use a computer, the person is likely to be surprised. What if the auto mechanic needs to operate a sophisticated computer to determine certain malfunctions in the cars he is repairing? What if the office staff expects the mechanic to understand how to enter data on their computer and also expects the person to know how to read the computer printout of information? What if he must go to school periodically to learn the newest technology, and everyone sits in a room filled with computers for the class instead of underneath an actual car?

Type of example: _____

PARAGRAPH 3

Most students today realize they must learn how to use computers in order to be competitive in the job market. Last semester, I took my first computer course. To my great pleasure, I found that my new skills helped me not only write compositions but also practise my math. I discovered that I could go on-line and talk all over the world with people who have similar interests to my own. In addition, I was able to use the computer to access information from the Internet. Since I plan to be a teacher, I will be able to use my computer skills making tests and worksheets, researching information for class, and helping students make discoveries for themselves.

Type of example: _____

EXERCISE 2   The Sources for Illustrations

Below is a topic sentence. Write a paragraph in which you support the idea with one or more illustrations. Label the source of your illustration from one of the following:

Example from firsthand experience or knowledge

Made up or hypothetical example

Information from an interview or survey you conduct yourself

Outside research (using material found in books or articles)

Topic sentence: Many advertising claims are deceptive.
Your paragraph:

_____

_____

_____

_____

_____

_____

_____

_____

_____

_____

_____

_____

_____

Type of example used: _____

EXERCISE 3   The Sources for Illustrations

Below is a topic sentence. Write a paragraph in which you support the idea with one or more illustrations. Label the source of your illustration from one of the following:

Example from firsthand experience or knowledge

Made up or hypothetical example

Information from an interview or survey you conduct yourself

Outside research (using material found in books or articles)

Topic sentence: Taste in music is very personal. (Consider doing a survey of your class members.)
Your paragraph:

_____

_____

_____

_____

_____

_____

_____

_____

_____

_____

_____

_____

Type of example used: _____

TRANSITIONS FOR ILLUSTRATION

Writers often signal the beginning of an illustration by using a key phrase. Below is a list of phrases commonly used to signal the beginning of an illustration.

Let me give you an example.

For example, . . .

Another example is . . .

To illustrate, . . .

An illustration of this idea is . . .

A case in point is . . .

Take the case of . . .

For instance, . . .

A personal anecdote will illustrate my point.

Order for illustration

1. If the illustration is a *story* or *anecdote,* the author usually uses *time order.*

2. If the illustration is made up of *several descriptive examples,* the author might use *spatial order* (top to bottom, right to left, etc.).

3. If the illustrations call for a certain *logical order,* this logic will determine the sequence.

4. If there seems to be no special order necessary, authors often place their *strongest or most important example last,* since this is what the reader is likely to remember best.

EXERCISE 1   Analyzing Paragraphs Using Examples

Read the following paragraph and answer the questions about the paragraph.

Being a connoisseur of junk has wonderfully mucked up my entire life. You know the song about favourite things like raindrops on roses and whiskers on kittens? Well, I've got my own list of favourite things: I like the insides of filthy bus stations, unsavoury characters, a Dr. Pepper can floating on the sun-flecked water, Jujubes, the greasy tug and tang of beef jerky wrapped in cellophane, the kitchen drawer beside the phone, the Sunday clutter around the house, the noble whiff of manure, the sweaty odour of a person you love, the smoke-filled room in which I get to inhale the equivalent of eleven cigarettes without breaking my promise to quit, the pigeon droppings in the square, the grease under the finger nails of a gas station attendant (if you can still find one), the rusty Brillo on the sink, the bathroom glass placidly growing bacteria for the whole family, *People* magazine, a dog-eared paperback, a cold pork chop eaten at the refrigerator door.

Questions

1. State the main idea in your own words.

   _____

2. How many examples are given in the paragraph? _____

3. Underline the examples in the paragraph.

4. Does the author use any words or phrases to signal any of the examples? If so, circle each one.

5. If there is more than one example, can you suggest any order for them?

   _____

EXERCISE 2   Analyzing Paragraphs Using Examples

Read the following paragraph and answer the questions about the paragraph.

The Canadian electoral system is based on the simple principle that a candidate gets elected to Parliament if he or she wins the most number of votes. However, advocates for electoral reform in Canada point out that the percentage of the popular vote received by a political party only rarely bares any semblance to the number of seats a party wins in the House of Commons. For example, after the 2000 Canadian federal election the Liberal Party formed a majority in the House of Commons, winning 57 percent of the seats (or 172 out of a possible 301). However, the Liberals received only 41 percent of the popular vote. The Canadian Alliance Party won 25.5 percent of the popular vote, but this translated into 67 (or 22 percent) of the seats in the House of Commons. Finally, the Progressive Conservative Party suffered the greatest imbalance between the number of seats it received versus its percentage of the popular vote. The PCs won a little over 12 percent of the popular vote but won only four percent of the seats (12 to be exact) in the House of Commons.

Questions

1. State the main idea in your own words.

_____

2. How many examples are given in the paragraph? _____

3. Underline the examples in the paragraph.

4. Does the author use any words or phrases to signal any of the examples? If so, circle each one.

5. If there is more than one example, can you suggest any order for the examples?

_____

EXERCISE 3   Analyzing Paragraphs Using Examples

Read the following paragraph and answer the questions about the paragraph.

One of the most wonderful aspects of Sabatini's teaching was his desire to give encouragement. Even if the student did not have a great voice or did not show true promise, Sabatini would find something to praise, some little ray of hope that might help the student continue in the right direction. Let me relate an anecdote that will demonstrate this man's positive approach. One day, I was called in to Sabatini's studio to play the piano for a new pupil. This young man had come many miles in order to study with Sabatini and I could see at once that he was very nervous. The fact that he knew just a few words of Italian only made him more apprehensive. I started to play the music for the test aria. As usual, Sabatini sat in his chair with his eyes closed, listening. The young man's voice floated through the room, small and shaky at first, but growing a little more confident as he went on. Finally, after it was over, we all waited for the great man's judgment. Sabatini looked up and spoke through me. "I cannot do much for this young man," he said slowly, "because God has already done so much for him." When I translated this for the student, his face gained a new colour and he smiled for the first time. That day started his period of study with Sabatini, and three years later he made his first appearance in the opera house. I have always known that his great career really began with those first words of encouragement from his teacher.

Questions

1. State the main idea in your own words.

   _____

2. How many examples are given in the paragraph? _____

3. Underline the examples in the paragraph.

4. Does the author use any words or phrases to signal the use of an illustration? If so, circle each one.

5. If there is more than one example, can you suggest any order for the examples?

   _____

Writing the paragraph using illustration step by step

To learn a skill that makes so many demands, such as writing does, one approach is to work step by step, focusing on one issue at a time. In this way, anxiety is often reduced, and the writer will not miss a crucial point or misunderstand a part of the whole process. There certainly are other ways to go about writing an effective paragraph, but here is one logical method you can use to achieve good results.

STEPS FOR WRITING A PARAGRAPH USING ILLUSTRATION

1. Compose your topic sentence being sure to consider carefully what you want for your controlling idea.

2. Consider the options for examples: personal experience, hypothetical examples, surveys, interviews, library research. What type of examples will fit your idea best? At this stage brainstorming with a group of classmates is usually very helpful.

3. Decide how many examples you will provide in this paragraph: one extended example with several sentences or several brief examples of one sentence each.

4. If you have more than one example, decide on the order to present them. Many writers order their examples by starting with the least important and ending with the most important.

5. Write down each example using complete sentences. Does each example support your main idea? If not, your paragraph will lack unity and the example should be deleted.

6. Write a final sentence that concludes what you want to say about this idea.

7. Finally, copy your sentences into standard paragraph form. If using a computer, indent five spaces to begin the paragraph and double space.

8. Always give a final reading to check for spelling, other errors, and the possibility that you might have left out something. (Writers usually want to make several changes at this final stage.)

EXERCISE 1   **Writing the Paragraph Using Illustration Step by Step**

This exercise will guide you through the construction of a paragraph using illustration. Start with the topic suggested below. Use the eight steps to help you work through each stage of the writing process.

Topic: Childhood memories

You know from experience that your family and friends talk a great deal about events from their childhoods. These events, for better or worse, have shaped their lives in important ways. So many of the essays and articles found in books and magazines contain the stories and lessons learned from childhood. Using this general subject of childhood memories, choose a controlling idea that will allow you to use one or more rich examples from your childhood that the readers in your class might find interesting, informative, or amusing.

1. Topic sentence: _____

   _____

2. Which type of example (or types of examples) would you like to use? _____

   _____

3. How many examples will you give? _____

4. List the order of your examples. (One good example may be enough. Probably no more than three or four brief examples would fit in one paragraph.)

   1. _____

   2. _____

   3. _____

   4. _____

5. Write down each example.

   _____

   _____

   _____

   _____

   _____

   _____

   _____

   _____

   _____

   _____

   _____

   _____

   _____

   _____

   _____

_____

_____

_____

_____

6. Write the sentence that will conclude your paragraph.

_____

_____

7. On a separate piece of paper, copy your sentences into standard paragraph form.

8. Reread and if possible ask someone else to read to check for spelling and other errors. Is your paragraph unified? Do all sentences support the main idea? (Writers usually want to make several changes at this final stage.)

EXERCISE 2   Writing the Paragraph Using Illustration Step by Step

This exercise will guide you through the construction of a paragraph using illustration. Start with the topic suggested below. Use the eight steps to help you work through each stage of the writing process.

Topic: How to convince a family member to change a bad habit

Few of us live in the perfect family situation where every family member is helpful, productive, and happy. We struggle to encourage our loved ones to better themselves and thus make everyone's life in the family happier. What examples can you offer that would help a family member change a bad habit?

1. Topic sentence: _____

   _____

2. Which type of example (or types of examples) would you like to use? _____

   _____

3. How many examples will you give? _____

4. List the order of your examples. (One good example may be enough. Probably no more than three or four brief examples would fit in one paragraph.)

   1. _____

   2. _____

   3. _____

   4. _____

5. Write down each example.

   _____

   _____

   _____

   _____

_____

_____

_____

_____

_____

_____

_____

_____

_____

_____

_____

_____

_____

6. Write the sentence that will conclude your paragraph.

_____

_____

_____

7. On a separate piece of paper, copy your sentences into standard paragraph form.

8. Reread and if possible ask someone else to read to check for spelling and other errors. Is your paragraph unified? Do all sentences support the main idea? (Writers usually want to make several changes at this final stage.)

EXERCISE 3   Writing the Paragraph Using Illustration Step by Step

This exercise will guide you through the construction of a paragraph using illustration. Start with the topic suggested below. Use the eight steps to help you work through each stage of the writing process.

Topic: Art

What good is art? How does art affect our lives? What contact do you have with art in your everyday life? Do we have to go to an art gallery to appreciate fine art? Is a Hallmark card a work of art? Is your living room a work of art? Are there art works on display on your campus that you have opinions about? Talk about these questions with your classmates and then think of what you might want to say about art.

1. Topic sentence: _____

_____

2. Which type of example (or types of examples) would you like to use? _____

_____

3. How many examples will you give? _____

4. List the order of your examples. (One good example may be enough. Probably no more than three or four brief examples would fit in one paragraph.)

1. _____

2. _____

3. _____

4. _____

5. Write down each example.

_____

_____

_____

_____

_____

_____

_____

_____

_____

_____

_____

_____

_____

_____

_____

_____

_____

_____

6. Write the sentence that will conclude your paragraph.

_____

_____

_____

7. On a separate piece of paper, copy your sentences into standard paragraph form.

8. Reread and if possible ask someone else to read to check for spelling and other errors. Is your paragraph unified? Do all sentences support the main idea? (Writers usually want to make several changes at this final stage.)

On your own: Writing paragraphs using illustration from model paragraphs

Assignment 1

Topic: Things are not always what they seem

Write a paragraph that takes something many people find "cute" and give an example that shows the opposite is true. The following paragraph is taken from *Grand Canyon,* a book by the naturalist and essayist Joseph Wood Krutch.

> ### MODEL PARAGRAPH
>
> Quite frequently it is the "cute" animals who create problems under even the slightly unnatural conditions of a park. Take, for instance, the chipmunks and the ground squirrels. No creature is more endearing, and the fact that some species eat the flower stalks of the agave, a spectacularly beautiful flowering plant, is not serious so long as the ground squirrel population is kept down by foxes. But once the fox has been exterminated, the agave also is threatened with extinction. Even the trays of seed put out to attract birds for the benefit of visitors mean that the chipmunks who come uninvited multiply so alarmingly that they, like the beggar deer, have to be periodically transported to remoter areas where artificial overpopulation is not a problem.

Ten suggested topics

cute:

1. Puppies (or other baby animals)
2. Kids
3. Party dresses
4. Stories
5. Teachers
6. Houses
7. Dolls
8. Greeting cards
9. Couples
10. Restaurants

Assignment 2

Topic: Shopping

Most people have very strong feelings about having to do certain shopping tasks. Write a paragraph that gives one or more examples of your worst shopping task(s) or your favourite shopping task(s). The following paragraph is taken from Phyllis Rose's essay "Shopping and Other Spiritual Adventures in America Today."

MODEL PARAGRAPH

I try to think of the opposite, a kind of shopping in which the object is all-important, the pleasure of shopping at a minimum. For example, consider the purchase of blue jeans. I buy new blue jeans as seldom as possible because the experience is so humiliating. For every pair that looks good on me, fifteen look grotesque. But even shopping for blue jeans at Bob's Surplus on Main Street—no frills, bare-bones shopping—is an event in the life of the spirit. Once again I have to come to terms with the fact that I will never look good in Levi's. Much as I want to be mainstream, I never will be.

Ten suggested topics   shopping:

1. For weekly groceries
2. For a bathing suit
3. For a hat that fits
4. For a very fussy relative
5. By catalogue
6. On the home shopping network
7. For the person who never says thank you
8. When you haven't got enough money to get what you really want
9. For a gift for your in-laws
10. For holiday gifts

Assignment 3

Topic: Expectations

We enter into relationships believing that people will behave in a certain expected way. Oftentimes we are sadly disappointed. Write a paragraph in which you give one or more examples of how you expect people to act when they are in certain relationships. The following paragraph is from a piece of advice written by the famous columnist Ann Landers.

MODEL PARAGRAPH

Parents have the right to expect their children to pick up after themselves and perform simple household chores. For example, every member of the family over six years of age should clean the bathtub and the sink so they will be in respectable condition for the next person. He or she should also run errands and help in the kitchen if asked—in other words, carry a share of the load without feeling persecuted. The days of "hired help" are, for the most part, gone. And this is good. Boys as well as girls should be taught to cook and clean, do laundry, and sew on buttons. This is not "sissy stuff." It makes for independence and self-reliance.

Ten suggested topics Expectations of:

1. Husbands and wives

2. Engaged couples

3. Teachers

4. Students

5. Diners

6. Customers

7. Patients

8. Employers

9. Coworkers

10. Friends

Assignment 4 **Topic:** Remedies to cure what ails us

Health food stores are enjoying great popularity, partly because so many people believe that natural products can alleviate a wide range of complaints. Write a paragraph in which you give examples of popular trends for solving an everyday problem. In the following paragraph, Joyce Ludlum provides several examples of currently available remedies that people are using in place of traditional prescriptions.

MODEL PARAGRAPH

Many stores today are selling newly accepted natural remedies for all types of human ailments. For instance, an herb called *astragalus* is being used by people with AIDS as a natural way to boost their immune systems. Other people concerned about their immune systems but only worried about colds or flu use a plant extract called *echinacea* to help them resist sickness. People who want to lose weight also are seeking out help from natural remedies. One of the most popular examples of remedies for overweight people is the Chinese herb *ma huang*. This is a powerful substance and can be dangerous for some since it may cause heart attacks or strokes, especially if it is used with caffeine. One of the cures most sought after is the cure for cancer, and again there are natural substances that hold out some promise of relief. For example, shark cartilage is believed by many to stop the growth of cancerous tumours or even eliminate them altogether. Many users of herbs and other natural healing substances take these supplements to improve their general health. For instance, *ginseng* is used throughout the world as a revitalizing tonic, and garlic has been said to combat infections, prevent blood clots, and lower blood pressure. There are many claims for different natural remedies, but we do not always have proof that they work as well as some people say they do.

Ten suggested topics   Remedies for:

1. Relaxation
2. The common cold
3. The "blues"
4. The hiccoughs
5. Thumbsucking
6. Kicking the smoking habit
7. Shyness
8. Writer's block
9. Insomnia
10. Wanderlust

Working Together

Life would be very lonely without special people to share our good times (and not so good times); therefore, every friend is a treasure.

Divide into groups for a brief discussion on the topic, "What is a friend?" Students should take notes on each other's ideas. Then each student should think back over his or her own life and select three people who were friends. Write three paragraphs, one for each of these three friends. Include your analysis of the qualities that made each person a friend. Did all of these friendships last? If not, why not? These paragraphs could later form the basis for an essay on friendship.

Developing Paragraphs: Description

What is description?

Writers frequently use description as a method of supporting the topic sentence of a paragraph. For example, the openings of many novels begin with paragraphs of description. Authors want their readers to be able to imagine the setting for their stories. In this chapter, we will examine the kinds of specific details that writers use in order to build effective descriptive paragraphs. We will also study the need to create an overall impression in our writing. Too many images, or images not carefully chosen, will greatly weaken the writing. Finally, as with all writing, we must consider the most logical method for putting the details in order.

When you write descriptively, the use of **sensory images** will largely determine whether or not your reader will be able to imagine what you are describing.

Sensory images are those details that relate to our senses: sight, smell, touch, taste, or hearing.

Not descriptive: It was morning in Harrington.

Descriptive: As thick fog rolled down the hills and into the sleepy village of Harrington, the early morning chirping of birds and the calls of one lone wolf fell strangely silent.

When you use details that relate to at least some of the five senses, you help your reader more clearly imagine the physical places, people, and objects in your writing.

Effective descriptive writing also gives the reader a definite sense that the details have been chosen to produce an overall impression.

The *dominant impression* is the overall impression created by a descriptive piece of writing. This impression is often summed up by one word or phrase in the topic sentence.

Topic sentence without a dominant impression: It was morning in Harrington.

Topic sentence with a dominant impression: Early morning in Harrington was *eerie*.

A third important consideration in descriptive writing is the question of how to put the supporting details for that topic sentence into a logical order.

> ***Order*** in descriptive writing is often a *spatial order.* Details can be given as one's eyes might move, for example, from top to bottom, left to right, outside to inside, or around in a circle.

The following example of descriptive writing shows all of the elements of an effective description. As you read this description of a typical neighbourhood delicatessen, note the specific details and the sensory images the writer uses. After you have read the whole description, ask yourself what dominant impression the writer wants us to have of the place.

The delicatessen was a wide store with high ceilings that were a dark brown colour from many years of not being painted. The rough wooden shelves on both sides of the store were filled from floor to ceiling with cans of fruits and vegetables, jars of pickles and olives, and special imported canned fish. A large refrigerator case against one wall was always humming loudly from the effort of keeping milk, cream, and several cases of soft drinks and beer cool at all times. At the end of the store was the main counter with its cold cuts, freshly made salads, and its gleaming white metal scale on top. Stacked beside the scale today were baskets of fresh rolls and breads, which gave off an aroma that contained a mixture of onion, caraway seed, and pumpernickel. Behind the scale was the friendly face of Mr. Rubino, who was in his store seven days a week, fourteen hours or more each day. He was always ready with a smile or a friendly comment, or even a sample piece of cheese or smoked meat as a friendly gesture for his "growing customers," as he referred to us kids in the neighbourhood.

The three terms defined above are essential for the skills you will be developing in this chapter. These skills are:

- How to create a topic sentence with a *dominant impression*
- How to support the topic sentence with details that use *sensory images* allowing the reader to imagine what is being described
- How to put the details in a logical *order,* which in descriptive writing is usually some kind of *spatial order*

Working with description: Selecting the dominant impression

When you use a number of specific, sensory images as you write a description, you should do more than simply write a series of sentences that deal with a single topic. You should also create a dominant impression in your reader's mind. Each individual sentence that you write is part of a picture that becomes clear when the reader finishes the paragraph.

For example, when you describe a place, the dominant impression you create might be one of warmth, friendliness, or comfort; or it could be one of formality or elegance. When you write a description of a person, your reader could receive the dominant impression of a positive, efficient individual who is outgoing and creative, or of a person who appears to be cold, distant, or hostile. All the sentences in the paragraph should support the dominant impression you have chosen.

Picking a dominant impression is essential in writing any descriptive paragraph. Here is a short list of possible dominant impressions for you to use as a guide while you work through this unit.

POSSIBLE DOMINANT IMPRESSIONS FOR DESCRIPTIONS OF PLACE				
crowded	cozy	inviting	cheerful	dazzling
romantic	restful	dreary	drab	uncomfortable
cluttered	ugly	tasteless	unfriendly	gaudy
stuffy	eerie	depressing	spacious	sunny

POSSIBLE DOMINANT IMPRESSIONS FOR DESCRIPTIONS OF PEOPLE				
creative	angry	independent	proud	withdrawn
tense	shy	aggressive	generous	sullen
silent	witty	pessimistic	responsible	efficient
snobbish	placid	bumbling	bitter	easygoing

EXERCISE 1   Selecting the Dominant Impression

Each of the following places could be the topic for a descriptive paragraph. Fill in each blank to the right of the topic with an appropriate dominant impression. Use the guide above if you need help. Remember, there is no single right answer.

Topic   **Dominant Impression**

1. A high school gym on grad night   _____

2. Your barber or hairdresser's shop   _____

3. The room where you are now sitting   _____

4. The grocery store nearest you   _____

5. A hardware store   _____

6. The post office on Saturday morning   _____

7. An overcrowded waiting room   _____

8. Quebec City in the spring   _____

9. The home of your best friend   _____

10. The kitchen in the morning   _____

EXERCISE 2   Selecting the Dominant Impression

Each of the following persons could be the topic for a descriptive paragraph. Fill in each blank to the right of the topic with an appropriate dominant impression. Use the guide above if you need help. Remember, there is no one right answer.

Topic	Dominant Impression
1. An actor being interviewed on television	_____
2. An old woman in a nursing home	_____
3. A librarian	_____
4. A bank clerk on a busy day	_____
5. A farmer	_____
6. A politician running for office	_____
7. A taxi driver	_____
8. A shoe salesperson	_____
9. A bride	_____
10. A soldier just discharged from the service	_____

Revising vague dominant impressions

Certain words in the English language have become so overused that they no longer have any specific meaning for a reader. Careful writers avoid these words because they are almost useless in descriptive writing. Here is a list of the most commonly overused words:

good, bad
nice, fine, okay
normal, typical
interesting
beautiful

The following paragraph is an example of the kind of writing that results from the continued use of vague words:

I had a typical day. The weather was nice and my job was interesting. The food for lunch was okay; supper was really good. After supper I saw my girl-friend, who is really beautiful. That's when my day really became fun.

Notice that all of the details in the paragraph are vague. The writer has told us what happened, but we cannot really see any of the details that are mentioned. This is because the writer has made the mistake of using words that have lost much of their meaning.

• PRACTICE

On a separate piece of paper rewrite this vague paragraph you have just read. Replace the vague words with details that are more specific.

The next group of exercises will give you practice in recognizing and eliminating overused words.

EXERCISE 1   **Revising Vague Dominant Impressions**

In each of the spaces provided, change the underlined word to a more specific dominant impression. An example has been done for you. You might want to work in groups to think of words that are more specific.

> **Vague:**   The tablecloth was <u>beautiful</u>.

> **Revised:** The tablecloth was of <u>white linen with delicate blue embroidery</u>.

1. The sky was <u>beautiful</u>.   _____

2. The water felt <u>nice</u>.   _____

3. Walking along the beach was <u>fun</u>.   _____

4. The storm was <u>bad</u>.   _____

5. The parking lot was <u>typical</u>.   _____

6. The main street is <u>interesting</u>.   _____

7. The dessert tasted <u>good</u>.   _____

8. My brother is <u>normal</u>.   _____

9. Our house is <u>fine</u>.   _____

10. My job is <u>okay</u>.   _____

EXERCISE 2   **Revising Vague Dominant Impressions**

In each of the spaces provided, change the underlined word to a more specific dominant impression. Working in groups may be helpful.

1. It was a really <u>nice</u> date.   _____

2. The window display was <u>beautiful</u>.   _____

3. The boat ride was <u>fine</u>.   _____

4. The circus was <u>fun</u>.   _____

5. The lemonade was <u>awful</u>.   _____

6. The play was <u>bad</u>.   _____

7. His new suit looked <u>okay</u>.   _____

8. The dance class was <u>fine</u>.   _____

9. Her new watch was <u>nice</u>.   _____

10. It was a <u>good</u> lecture.   _____

Working with description: Sensory images

One of the basic ways all good writers communicate experiences to their readers is by using sense impressions. We respond to writing that makes us see an object, hear a sound, touch a surface, smell an odour, or taste a flavour. When a writer uses one or more of these sensory images in a piece of writing, we tend to pay more attention to what the writer is saying, and we tend to remember the details of what we have read.

For example, if you come across the word *door* in a sentence, you might or might not pay attention to it. However, if the writer tells you it was a *brown wooden door* that was rough to the touch and that creaked loudly when it opened, you would hardly be able to forget it. The door would stay in your mind because the writer used sensory images to make you aware of it.

• PRACTICE

The following sentences are taken from the description of Mr. Rubino's delicatessen, a description that you read on page 304. Notice how in each sentence the writer uses at least one sensory image to make the details of that sentence remain in your mind. As you read each of the sentences, identify what physical sense the writer appeals to when a sensory image is used.

1. A large refrigerator case against one wall was always humming loudly from the effort of keeping milk, cream, and several cases of soft drinks and beer cool at all times.

   Physical senses: _____

   _____

2. Stacked on top of the counter were baskets of fresh rolls and breads, which gave off an aroma that contained a mixture of onion, caraway seed, and pumpernickel.

   Physical senses: _____

   _____

3. He was always ready with a sample piece of cheese or smoked meat as a friendly gesture.

   Physical senses: _____

   _____

When you use sensory images, you will stimulate the readers' interest, and these images will stay in their minds.

EXERCISE 1   Recognizing Sensory Images

The following paragraph contains examples of sensory images. Find the images and list them in the spaces provided.

> I knew how a newspaper office should look and sound and smell—I worked in one for thirteen years. Its city room, wide as a city block, was dirty and dishevelled. Reporters wrote on ancient typewriters that filled the air with clatter; copy editors laboured on coffee-stained desks over what the reporters had written. Crumpled balls of paper littered the floor and filled the wastebaskets—failed efforts to write a good lead or a decent sentence. The walls were grimy—every few years they were painted over in a less restful shade of eye-rest green—and the atmosphere was hazy with the smoke of cigarettes and cigars. At the very centre the city editor, a giant named L. L. Engelking, bellowed his displeasure with the day's work, his voice a rumbling volcano in our lives. I thought it was the most beautiful place in the world.
>
> From William Zinsser,
> *Writing with a Word Processor*

Sensory Images

Sight: _____

_____

_____

Sound: _____

_____

Smell: _____

_____

EXERCISE 2   Recognizing Sensory Images

The following paragraph contains examples of sensory images. Find the images and list them in the spaces provided.

The lake ice split with a sound like the crack of a rifle. Thick slabs of ice broke apart, moving ponderously, edge grinding against edge, up-thrusting in jagged peaks, the green-grey water swirling over half-submerged floes. In an agony of rebirth, the splitting and booming of the ice reverberated across the thawing land. Streams raced toward the lake, their swift currents carrying fallen branches and undermining overhanging banks of earth and softened snow. Roads became mires of muck and slush, and the meadows of dried, matted grass oozed mud.

From Nan Salerno with Rosamond Vanderburgh,
Shaman's Daughter

Sensory Images

Sight: _____

_____

_____

Sound: _____

_____

Touch: _____

_____

EXERCISE 3   Recognizing Sensory Images

The following paragraph contains examples of sensory images. Find the images and list them in the spaces provided.

Behind the closed doors one can hear vague sounds. The most dominant one is, perhaps, that of the men coughing and spitting. Almost all of the men smoke quite heavily, some of them rolling their own cigarettes, sitting in their underwear on the edges of their beds. There is also the sound of radios and of the very tiny portable television sets which sit on tables or on top of the nearly empty refrigerators. Few people eat very much. Many of the rooms do not contain stoves, or ones with workable ovens. Tomato soup is heated on top of hotplates and filled with crackers. The smell of burnt toast is often present.

From Alistair MacLeod,
No Great Mischief

[A. MacLeod. *No Great Mischief.* Toronto: McClelland and Stewart Ltd., 1999, pp. 5–6.]

Sensory Images

Sight: _____

_____

Sound: _____

_____

Touch: _____

_____

Taste: _____

_____

Smell: _____

_____

EXERCISE 1   Creating Sensory Images

Each of the following topic sentences contains an underlined word that names a physical sense. For each topic sentence, write three sentences that give examples of sensory images. For example, in the first sentence the sensory image of sound in the vicinity of a hospital could be explained by writing sentences that describe ambulance sirens, doctors being called over loudspeaker systems, and the voices of people in the waiting room.

1. I knew I was walking past the hospital emergency room from the sounds I could <u>hear</u>.

   Three sentences with sensory images:

   a. _____

   _____

b. _____

_____

c. _____

_____

2. I can't help stopping in the bakery every Sunday morning because the <u>smells</u> are so good.

Three sentences with sensory images:

a. _____

_____

b. _____

_____

c. _____

_____

3. The best part of my vacation last year was the <u>sight</u> that greeted me when I got up in the morning.

Three sentences with sensory images:

a. _____

_____

b. _____

_____

c. _____

_____

EXERCISE 2   Creating Sensory Images

Each of the following topic sentences contains an underlined word that names a physical sense. For each topic sentence, write three sentences that give examples of sensory images.

1. It is a luxury to wear clothing made with natural fibres because the <u>feeling</u> is quite different from polyesters.

Three sentences with sensory images:

a. _____

_____

b. _____

_____

c. _____

_____

2. I knew the garbage strike had gone on for a long time when I had to <u>hold my nose</u> walking down some streets.

   Three sentences with sensory images:

   a. _____

   _____

   b. _____

   _____

   c. _____

   _____

3. A lake in the summertime is a relaxing place to be because the <u>sounds</u> you hear all day are so subdued.

   Three sentences with sensory images:

   a. _____

   _____

   b. _____

   _____

   c. _____

   _____

EXERCISE 3   Creating Sensory Images

Each of the following topic sentences contains an underlined word that names a physical sense. For each topic sentence, write three sentences that give examples of sensory images.

1. Going to a rave is an overwhelming experience because of the different sounds you <u>hear</u> there.

   Three sentences with sensory images:

   a. _____

   _____

   b. _____

   _____

   c. _____

   _____

2. My friend Bill says he loves the <u>feel</u> of the chocolate, the nuts, and the coconut when he eats that candy bar.

   Three sentences with sensory images:

   a. _____

   _____

b. _____

_____

c. _____

_____

3. I could <u>see</u> that the old woman standing on the corner was very poor.

Three sentences with sensory images:

a. _____

_____

b. _____

_____

c. _____

_____

Coherence in description: Putting details in space order

In descriptive paragraphs, the writer often chooses to arrange supporting details according to space. With this method, you place yourself at the scene and then use a logical order such as moving from nearby to farther away, right to left, or top to bottom. Often you move in such a way that you save the most important detail until last in order to achieve the greatest effect.

In the paragraph on the delicatessen given on page 304, the writer first describes the ceilings and walls of the store, then proceeds to the shelves and large refrigerator, and ends by describing the main counter of the deli with its owner, Mr. Rubino, standing behind it. By ordering the details in this way, the reader is led from the edges of the room to focus on what is most important—Mr. Rubino behind his counter. A description of a clothes closet might order the details differently. Perhaps the writer would begin with the shoes standing on the floor and finish with the hats and gloves arranged on the top shelf, an arrangement that goes from the ground up.

Here is a paragraph from Ernesto Galarza's autobiography, *Barrio Boy*. The writer is describing the one-room apartment where he and his family lived in Mazatlán, Mexico.

> The floor was of large square bricks worn smooth and of grey mortar between. The ceiling was the underside of the tile resting on beams that pointed from back to front. Families who had lived there before had left a helter-skelter of nails, bolts, and pegs driven into the walls. The kerosene lamp hung from a hook on the centre beam.

Notice that the writer begins with a description of the floor, then gives us an idea of what the ceiling is like, and ends with a detailed picture of the walls. We are able to follow the writer through the description because there is a plan and a sense of logic. No matter which method of space order you choose in organizing details in a descriptive paragraph, be sure the results allow your reader to see the scene in a logical order.

EXERCISE 1   Working for Coherence: Using Space Order

Each of the following topic sentences is followed by four or more descriptive sentences that are not in order. Put these descriptive sentences in order by placing a number (1, 2, 3, 4, or 5) in the space provided before each sentence.

1. The Gooderham flatiron building, one of Toronto's most unique landmarks, was recently renovated.

   (*Order the material from top to bottom.*)

   _____ With the restoration completed, visitors can enjoy dinner and drinks in the pub that now occupies the basement of the building.

   _____ The red sandstone brick of the walls, which was produced locally, had to be sandblasted to clean it of the decades of soot that had come, first from train and then automobile exhaust.

   _____ The roof of the circular turret is covered in copper that has turned a lovely turquoise colour.

   _____ As part of the restoration, the wrought iron rails and fixtures that run along the tops of the walls were repaired and painted.

   _____ At the very top of the cone-shaped roof sits a delicate bronze ornament that sparkles in the sun.

2. The young woman was a teen of the nineties.

   (*Order the material from top to bottom.*)

   _____ She wore an oversized sweater that she had borrowed from her father.

   _____ Her shoes were white tennis sneakers.

   _____ From her ears dangled silver and turquoise earrings.

   _____ Her short blond hair was clean and styled attractively.

   _____ The black cotton stretch pants flattered her slim figure.

3. My aunt's kitchen is a very orderly place.

   (*Order the material from near to far.*)

   _____ As usual, in the centre of the table sits a vase with a fresh yellow daffodil.

   _____ Nearby on the refrigerator, a magnet holds the week's menu.

   _____ Sitting at the kitchen table, I am struck by the freshly pressed linen tablecloth.

   _____ Looking across the room through the stained glass doors of her kitchen cupboards, I can see neat rows of dishes, exactly eight each, matching the colours of the tablecloth and wallpaper.

EXERCISE 2   Working for Coherence: Using Space Order

Each of the following topic sentences could be expanded into a fully developed paragraph. In the spaces provided, give the appropriate supporting details for the topic sentence. Be sure to give your supporting details in a particular order. That is, the details should go from top to bottom, from outside to inside, from close to far, or around the area you are describing.

1. The airport terminal was as busy inside as it was outside.

    a. _____

    _____

    b. _____

    _____

    c. _____

    _____

    d. _____

    _____

2. The student lounge is a quiet and relaxing place in our school.

    a. _____

    _____

    b. _____

    _____

    c. _____

    _____

    d. _____

    _____

3. The motel lobby was obviously once very beautiful, but it was beginning to look shabby.

    a. _____

    _____

    b. _____

    _____

    c. _____

    _____

    d. _____

    _____

EXERCISE 3   Working for Coherence: Using Space Order

Each of the following topic sentences could be expanded into a fully developed paragraph. In the spaces provided, give the appropriate supporting details for the topic sentence. Be sure to give your supporting details in a particular order. That is, the details should go from top to bottom, from outside to inside, from close to far, or around the area you are describing.

1. The shopping mall was supposed to be restful, but the noise and the bright lights gave me a headache.

   a. _____

   _____

   b. _____

   _____

   c. _____

   _____

   d. _____

   _____

2. The pizza shop is so tiny that people are not likely to stay and eat.

   a. _____

   _____

   b. _____

   _____

   c. _____

   _____

   d. _____

   _____

3. The bus was filled with a strange assortment of people.

   a. _____

   _____

   b. _____

   _____

   c. _____

   _____

   d. _____

   _____

Writing the descriptive paragraph step by step

To learn a skill with some degree of ease, it is best to follow a step by step approach so that various skills are isolated. This will ensure that you are not missing a crucial point or misunderstanding a part of the whole. There certainly are other ways to go about writing an effective paragraph, but here is one method you can use to achieve successful results. You will learn that writing, like most skills, can be developed by using a logical process.

STEPS FOR WRITING THE DESCRIPTIVE PARAGRAPH

1. Study the given topic, and then plan your topic sentence, especially the dominant impression.

2. List at least ten details that come to your mind when you think about the description you have chosen.

3. Then choose the five or six most important details from your list. Be sure these details support the dominant impression.

4. Put your list in order.

5. Write one complete sentence for each of the details you have chosen from your list.

6. Write a concluding statement that offers some reason for describing this topic.

7. Finally, copy your sentences into standard paragraph form.

EXERCISE 1　Writing the Descriptive Paragraph Step by Step

The following exercise will guide you through the construction of a descriptive paragraph. Start with the suggested topic. Use the seven steps to help you work through each stage of the writing process.

Topic: A place you have lived

1. Topic sentence: _____

   _____

2. Make a list of possible supporting details.

   a. _____

   b. _____

   c. _____

   d. _____

   e. _____

   f. _____

   g. _____

h. _____

i. _____

j. _____

3. Circle the five or six details you believe are the most important for the description.

4. Put your selected details in order by numbering them.

5. Using your final list, write at least one sentence for each detail you have chosen.

a. _____

_____

b. _____

_____

c. _____

_____

d. _____

_____

e. _____

_____

f. _____

_____

6. Write a concluding statement.

_____

_____

_____

7. On a separate piece of paper, copy your sentences into standard paragraph form.

EXERCISE 2   Writing the Descriptive Paragraph Step by Step

The following exercise will guide you through the construction of a descriptive paragraph. Start with the suggested topic. Use the seven steps to help you work through each stage of the writing process.

Topic: A person you admire

1. Topic sentence: _____

   _____

2. Make a list of possible supporting details.

   a. _____

   b. _____

   c. _____

   d. _____

   e. _____

   f. _____

   g. _____

   h. _____

   i. _____

   j. _____

3. Circle the five or six details you believe are the most important for the description.

4. Put your selected details in order by numbering them.

5. Using your final list, write at least one sentence for each detail you have chosen.

   a. _____

   b. _____

   c. _____

   d. _____

   e. _____

   f. _____

6. Write a concluding statement.

   _____

   _____

   _____

7. On a separate piece of paper, copy your sentences into standard paragraph form.

EXERCISE 3   Writing the Descriptive Paragraph Step by Step

The following exercise will guide you through the construction of a descriptive paragraph. Start with the suggested topic. Use the seven steps to help you work through each stage of the writing process.

Topic: An ideal gift for a child

1. Topic sentence: _____

   _____

2. Make a list of possible supporting details.

   a. _____

   b. _____

   c. _____

   d. _____

   e. _____

   f. _____

   g. _____

   h. _____

   i. _____

   j. _____

3. Circle the five or six details you believe are the most important for the description.

4. Put your selected details in order by numbering them.

5. Using your final list, write at least one sentence for each detail you have chosen.

   a. _____

   b. _____

   c. _____

   d. _____

   e. _____

   f. _____

6. Write a concluding statement.

   _____

   _____

7. On a separate piece of paper, copy your sentences into standard paragraph form.

On your own: Writing descriptive paragraphs from model paragraphs

A description of a person

Assignment 1

Describe a person whose appearance made a deep impression on you. If you saw this person only once, indicate the details that made him or her stay in your mind. If you choose to describe a person with whom you are more familiar, select the most outstanding details that will help your reader have a single, dominant impression. In the model paragraph, Scott Russell Sanders remembers the men from his rural and working class childhood.

MODEL PARAGRAPH

The bodies of the men I knew were twisted and maimed in ways visible and invisible. The nails of their hands were black and split, the hands tattooed with scars. Some had lost fingers. Heavy lifting had given many of them finicky backs and guts weak from hernias. Racing against conveyor belts had given them ulcers. Their ankles and knees ached from years of standing on concrete. Anyone who had worked for long around machines was hard of hearing. They squinted, and the skin of their faces was creased like the leather of old work gloves. There were times, studying them, when I dreaded growing up. Most of them coughed, from dust or cigarettes, and most of them drank cheap wine or whiskey, so their eyes looked bloodshot and bruised. The fathers of my friends always seemed older than the mothers. Men wore out sooner. Only women lived into old age.

Ten suggested topics

1. An elderly relative

2. A hard-working student

3. An outstanding athlete

4. A loyal friend

5. An overworked waitress

6. A taxi driver

7. A fashion model

8. A gossipy neighbour

9. A street vendor

10. A rude salesperson

A description of a time of day

Assignment 2

Write a paragraph in which you describe the sights, sounds, and events of a particular time of day in a place you know well. In the model paragraph that follows, John Riley has chosen to describe an especially busy time of day, the morning, when activity can be frantic in a household.

> ## MODEL PARAGRAPH
>
> I remember the turmoil of mornings in our house. My brothers and sisters rushed about upstairs and down trying to get ready for school. Mom would repeatedly tell them to hurry up. Molly would usually scream down from her bedroom, "What am I going to do? I don't have any clean underwear!" Amy, often in tears, sat at the kitchen table still in her pajamas trying to do her math. Paul paced back and forth in front of the mirror angrily combing his unruly hair, which stuck up in all directions, while Roland threatened to punch him if he didn't find the pen he had borrowed the night before. Mother was stuffing sandwiches into bags while she sighed, "I'm afraid there isn't anything for dessert today." No one heard her. Then came the yelling up the stairs, "You should have left ten minutes ago." One by one, these unwilling victims were packed up and pushed out the door. Mother wasn't safe yet. Somebody always came back frantic and desperate. "My flute, Mom, where's my flute, quick! I'll get killed if I don't have it today." Every crisis apparently meant the difference between life and death. Morning at our house was like watching a troop preparing for battle. When they had finally gone, I was left in complete silence while my mother slumped on a chair at the kitchen table. She paid no attention to me.

Ten suggested topics

1. A Saturday filled with errands

2. The dinner hour at my house

3. Lunchtime in a cafeteria

4. A midnight raid on the refrigerator

5. Christmas morning

6. TGIF (Thank Goodness It's Friday)

7. Getting ready to go out on a Friday night

8. My Sunday-morning routine

9. Coming home from school or work

10. Watching late-night movies

A description of a place

Assignment 3

Write a paragraph in which you describe a place you know well or remember clearly. The model paragraph that follows is from *The Airtight Cage,* a classic study by Joseph Lyford of an urban neighbourhood in a state of change.

MODEL PARAGRAPH

The wreckers would put a one-story scaffold in front of the building to protect automobiles and pedestrians, then begin at the top, working down story by story, gutting the rooms, ripping out woodwork, electrical wiring, plumbing, and fixtures. Once this was done, the men would hammer the shell of the house with sledges. Sections of brick wall would shudder, undulate for a second and dissolve into fragments that fell in slow motion. When the fragments hit the ground, the dust rocketed several feet into the air. The heaps of brick and plaster, coils and stems of rusty pipe attracted children from all over the area. On weekends and after 4 P.M. on weekdays, they would scamper from building to building, dancing in the second-, third-, and fourth-story rooms where fronts and backs had been knocked out, bombing each other with bricks and bits of concrete. Sometimes when they were dashing in and out of clouds of smoke and dust, with ruined buildings in the background, the children looked as if they were taking a town over under heavy artillery fire. The city eventually assigned a guard to stop the children, but apparently there were too many of them to handle and the pandemonium continued.

Ten suggested topics

1. A large department store
2. A sports stadium
3. A coffee shop
4. A pizza parlour
5. A shoe store
6. A club
7. A lively street corner
8. A college bookstore
9. A gymnasium
10. A medical clinic

A description of a time of year

Assignment 4

Write a paragraph in which you describe a particular time of year. Make sure that all of the details you choose relate specifically to that time of year. In the model paragraph that follows, from "Boyhood in Jamaica" by Claude McKay, the writer remembers springtime on his native island.

MODEL PARAGRAPH

Most of the time there was hardly any way of telling the seasons. To us in Jamaica, as elsewhere in the tropics, there were only two seasons—the rainy season and the dry season. We had no idea of spring, summer, autumn, and winter like the peoples of northern lands. Springtime, however, we did know by the new and lush burgeoning of grasses and the blossoming of trees, although we had blooms all the year round. The mango tree was especially significant of spring, because it was one of the few trees that used to shed its leaves. Then, in springtime, the new leaves sprouted—very tender, a kind of sulphur brown, as if they had been singed by fire. Soon afterwards the white blossoms came out and we knew that we would be eating juicy mangoes by August.

Ten suggested topics

1. A winter storm
2. A summer picnic
3. Summer in the city
4. A winter walk
5. Jogging in the spring rain
6. Sunbathing on a beach
7. Signs of spring in my neighbourhood
8. The woods in autumn
9. Ice skating in winter
10. Halloween night

Working Together

The following personal advertisement appeared in a local newspaper:

> Young man seeks neat, responsible roommate to share off-campus apartment for next academic year. Person must be a non-smoker and respect a vegetarian who cooks at home. Furniture not needed, but CD player would be welcome!

Finding the right roommate in a college dormitory, finding the right person with whom to share an apartment, or finding the right long-term companion may be difficult. People's personal habits have a way of causing friction in everyday life. Divide into groups for a brief discussion of the kinds of problems one finds in sharing the same space with another person.

1. Imagine that you must write a paragraph or two in which you provide a character description of yourself for an agency that will match you up with a roommate. As you write, be sure you include information about your hobbies, habits, attitudes, and any other personal characteristics that could make a difference in the kind of person the agency will select for you.

2. Imagine that you must write a paragraph or two in which you provide a character sketch of the person you would like the agency to find for you.

3. Write your own description of what you imagine would be the "roommate from Hell."

Developing Paragraphs: Narration

What is narration?

> ***Narration*** is the oldest and best-known form of verbal communication. It is, quite simply, the telling of a story.

Every culture in the world, past and present, has used narration to provide entertainment as well as information for the people of that culture. Since everyone likes a good story, the many forms of narration, such as novels, short stories, soap operas, and full-length movies, are always popular.

The following narrative paragraph, taken from Helen Keller's autobiography, tells the story of this young girl's realization that every object has a name. The paragraph shows the enormous difficulties faced by a seven-year-old girl who was unable to see, hear, or speak.

> The morning after my teacher came she led me into her room and gave me a doll. The little blind children at the Perkins Institution had sent it and Laura Bridgman had dressed it; but I did not know this until afterward. When I had played with it a little while, Miss Sullivan slowly spelled into my hand the word "d-o-l-l." I was at once interested in this finger play and tried to imitate it. When I finally succeeded in making the letters correctly, I was flushed with childish pleasure and pride. Running downstairs to my mother I held up my hand and made the letters for doll. I did not know that I was spelling a word or even that words existed; I was simply making my fingers go in monkey-like imitation. In the days that followed I learned to spell in this uncomprehending way a great many words, among them *pin*, *hat*, *cup* and a few verbs like *sit*, *stand*, and *walk*. But my teacher had been with me several weeks before I understood that everything has a name.

Working with narration: Using narration to make a point

At one time or another you have met a person who loves to talk on and on without making any real point. This person is likely to tell you everything that happened in one day, including every cough and sideways glance. Your reaction to the unnecessary and seemingly endless supply of details is probably one of fatigue and hope for a quick getaway. This is not narration at its best! A good story is almost always told to make a point: it can make us laugh, it can make us understand, or it can change our attitudes.

When Helen Keller tells the story of her early experiences with her teacher, she is careful to use only those details that are relevant to her story. For example, the doll her teacher gave her is an important part of the story. Not only does this doll reveal something about Helen Keller's teacher and her other friends, but it also reveals the astounding fact that Helen began to understand that objects have names. We see the beginning of Helen's long struggle to communicate with other people.

EXERCISE 1   Using Narration to Make a Point

Each of the following examples is the beginning of a topic sentence for a narrative paragraph. Complete each sentence by providing a controlling idea that could be the point for the story.

1. Since my family is so large (or small), I have had to learn to _____

    _____

2. When I couldn't get a job, I realized _____

    _____

3. After going to the movies every Saturday for many years, I discovered _____

    _____

4. When I arrived at the room where my business class was to meet, I found ___

    _____

5. When my best friend got married, I began to see that _____

    _____

EXERCISE 2   Using Narration to Make a Point

Each of the following examples is the beginning of a topic sentence for a narrative paragraph. Complete each sentence by providing a controlling idea that could be the point for the story.

1. When I looked more closely at the man, I realized that _____

    _____

2. When the Prime Minister finished his speech, I concluded that _____

    _____

3. By the end of the movie, I decided that _____

    _____

4. After I changed the course as well as the teacher, I felt _____

    _____

5. When I could not get past the office secretary, I realized that _____

    _____

EXERCISE 3   Using Narration to Make a Point

Each of the following examples is the beginning of a topic sentence for a narrative paragraph. Complete each sentence by providing a controlling idea that could be the point for the story.

1. When the art teacher tore up my sketches in front of the class, I decided _____

   _____

   _____

2. When there were no responses to my ad, I concluded _____

   _____

3. After two days of trying to sell magazine subscriptions, I knew _____

   _____

4. After I had actually performed my first experiment in the lab, I understood

   _____

   _____

5. The first time I tried to cook a dinner for a group of people, I found out ___

   _____

   _____

Coherence in narration: Placing details in order of time sequence

Ordering details in a paragraph of narration usually follows a time sequence. That is, you tell what happened first, then next, and next, until finally you get to the end of the story. An event could take place in a matter of minutes or over a period of many years.

In the following paragraph, the story takes place in a single day. The six events that made the day a disaster are given in the order in which they happened. Although some stories flash back to the past or forward to the future, most use the natural chronological order of the events.

> My day was a disaster. First, it had snowed during the night, which meant I had to shovel before I could leave for work. I was mad that I hadn't gotten up earlier. Then I had trouble starting my car, and to make matters worse, my daughter wasn't feeling well and said she didn't think she should go to school. When I eventually did arrive at school, I was twenty minutes late. Soon I found out the secretary had forgotten to type the exam I was supposed to give my class that day. I quickly had to make another plan. By three o'clock, I was looking forward to getting my paycheque. Foolish woman! When I went to pick it up, the girl in the office told me that something had gone wrong with the computers. I would not be able to get my cheque until Tuesday. Disappointed, I walked down the hill to the parking lot. There I met my final defeat. In my hurry to park the car in the morning, I had left my parking lights on. Now my battery was dead. Even an optimist like me had the right to be discouraged!

EXERCISE 1   Working for Coherence: Using Details in Order of Time Sequence

Each of the topics below is followed by supporting details. These supporting details are not given in any order. Put the events in order according to time sequence by placing the appropriate number in the space provided.

1. A fight in my apartment building

    _____ Some of the neighbours became so frightened that they called the police.

    _____ The man and the woman began to fight around six o'clock.

    _____ When the police came, they found the couple struggling in the kitchen.

    _____ The neighbours heard the man's voice shouting angrily.

    _____ There were no arrests, but the police warned both individuals not to disturb the peace again.

2. An important invitation

    _____ On the day of the party Louise asked her boss if she could leave an hour or two early in order to have time to get ready.

    _____ When Louise was invited to the party, she was very excited.

    _____ Four days before the party, she finally got up enough nerve to call Bob and ask him to go with her.

    _____ One week before the party she bought a new dress even though she could not afford one.

    _____ Still holding the invitation, she searched through her closet, but all her dresses looked so dull and unfashionable.

EXERCISE 2   Working for Coherence: Using Details in Order of Time Sequence

Each of the topics below is followed by supporting details. These supporting details are not given in any order. Put the events in order according to time sequence by placing the appropriate number in the space provided.

1. From the life of Roberta Bondar, first female Canadian astronaut

    _____ In December 1983, Dr. Bondar was selected to be one of the first six Canadian astronauts ever and began training soon after.

    _____ She was born in Sault Ste. Marie, Ontario, in 1945.

    _____ During junior and middle school, she displayed a strong interest in science and space.

    _____ She earned her doctorate and later a medical degree from McMaster University in Hamilton, Ontario.

    _____ After she completed her training with NASA, Bondar was designated a prime payload specialist whose job it was to study the effects of zero gravity on human physiology.

_____ Bondar flew on the space shuttle *Discovery* in January 1992 where she performed experiments in the Spacelab.

_____ Since returning from her successful mission, Bondar has been awarded many honours for her exceptional efforts in Canada's space program.

2. From the life of Anderson Ruffin Abbot, Canada's first black medical doctor

_____ While working in the hospitals, he met and became very good friends with President Abraham Lincoln.

_____ Anderson Ruffin Abbot died on December 29, 1913, and is buried in the Toronto Necropolis, one of the oldest cemeteries in Canada.

_____ Abbot was educated at the Toronto Academy, where he finally graduated at the age of 23.

_____ In 1863, he joined the Union Army in the U.S. Civil War because he became angered by the kidnapping of runaway slaves from the United States who had made their way to Canada via the underground railroad.

_____ He was born in Toronto on April 17, 1837.

_____ During the U.S. Civil War, he was appointed surgeon to the U.S. Army and was put in charge of Camp Baker and Freedman's Hospitals in Washington, D.C.

_____ Following President Lincoln's assassination in 1865, Mrs. Lincoln presented Abbot with the shawl worn by the President during his first inauguration ceremony.

[M. Filey. *Toronto Sketches 3*. Toronto: Dundurn, 1994, pp. 144–45.]

EXERCISE 3   Working for Coherence: Using Details in Order of Time Sequence

Each of the topics below is followed by supporting details. These supporting details are not given in any order. Put the events in order according to time sequence by placing the appropriate number in the space provided.

1. The novel *The English Patient* by Michael Ondaatje

_____ While in the villa, Hana is asked to take care of a fatally wounded Hungarian count, Laszlo Almásy. She realizes that he is a man with many secrets.

_____ During the Second World War in Italy, Hana, a French-Canadian nurse, sees a close friend of hers get killed by a mine. Traumatized by her experiences, Hana withdraws to an abandoned villa in the Italian countryside.

_____ Almásy dies just as the war ends. Although they must return to their own countries, Kip and Hana realize that they have been changed by the time they shared with Almásy.

_____ Hana and Almásy are later joined in the villa by Caravaggio, a mysterious thief who was captured and tortured during the war, and Kip, a Sikh soldier in the British army. Hana and Kip fall in love.

_____ Before he dies, Almásy tells the others of a desert expedition before the war, where he met and fell passionately in love with Katharine Clifton, the wife of one of his colleagues. He tells of their affair and of how prejudice and misunderstanding led to Katharine's death and his own fatal accident.

2. The novel *Great Expectations* by Charles Dickens

_____ Pip realizes Miss Havisham has had nothing to do with his inheritance.

_____ Pip, an orphan, is born and raised in a small English village by a blacksmith, Joe Gargery, and his sister.

_____ After his adventure with the convict, Pip works in a mansion near his home for a Miss Havisham, a crazed old woman who still wears the wedding dress she wore on the day her bridegroom failed to show up for the wedding.

_____ One day, Pip sees a stranger in the marshes near his home. The man asks Pip to bring him food and a filing iron—he is an escaped convict.

_____ Pip is contacted by a lawyer, who tells him that he must leave Miss Havisham and go to London, all expenses paid, to begin life as a gentleman.

_____ On his twenty-first birthday, Pip receives a visitor; it is the convict, Abel Magwitch, whom he had helped years before—it is he who has given Pip the money.

Transitions and time order

> Words and phrases that help a reader move smoothly from one idea to another and make the proper connection between those ideas are called *transitions.*

Although transitions must not be overused, they are important tools for every writer. Here is the Helen Keller paragraph you studied earlier, but this time printed with each of the transitional words and phrases in boldface.

The morning after my teacher came she led me into her room and gave me a doll. The little blind children at the Perkins Institution had sent it and Laura Bridgman had dressed it; but I did not know this **until afterward.** When I had played with it **a little while,** Miss Sullivan slowly spelled into my hand the word "d-o-l-l." I was **at once** interested in this finger play and tried to imitate it. When I **finally** succeeded in making the letters correctly, I was flushed with childish pleasure and pride. Running downstairs to my mother I held up my hand and made the letters for doll. I did not know that I was spelling a word or even that words existed; I was simply making my fingers go in monkey-like imitation. **In the days that followed** I learned to spell in this uncomprehending way a great many words, among them *pin, hat, cup* and a few verbs like *sit, stand,* and *walk.* But my teacher had been with me **several weeks** before I understood that everything has a name.

Notice how the time transitions used in this paragraph make the order of events clear. "*The morning after* my teacher came" gives the reader the sense that the action of the story is being told day by day. In the second sentence Helen Keller gives information she learned later—*afterward*. The writer then tells us that when she played with the doll *a little while*, she suddenly—*at once*—became interested in the connection between an object and the word for that object. This realization was one of the central lessons in young Helen Keller's education, and it became the starting point for all of her later learning. She uses two more transitional phrases to tell us about the beginning of this education: *In the days that followed*, we learn, she mastered a great many words, although it took her *several weeks* before she learned the even more important concept that everything had a name. Much of the meaning of this paragraph would not have been clear without the careful use of these time transitions.

EXERCISE 1   Working with Transitions

Using the transitions given in the list below or using ones you think of yourself, fill in each of the blanks in the following student paragraph.

at once	later, later on	after a little while
immediately	now, by now	first, first of all
soon afterward	finally	then
suddenly	in the next moment	next

I arrived at Aunt Lorinda's in the middle of a heat wave. It was 32°C in the shade and very humid. Aunt Lorinda as usual greeted me with the list of activities she had scheduled for the day. _____ we went to the attic to gather old clothes for the Salvation Army. I nearly passed out up in the attic. Sweat poured down my face. Aunt Lorinda, in her crisp cotton sundress, looked cool and was obviously enjoying herself. "If you see something you want, take it," she said graciously. "It's so nice of you to give me a hand today. You're young and strong and have so much more energy than I." _____ her plans included the yard work. I took off my shirt and mowed the lawn while my eighty-year-old aunt trimmed hedges and weeded the flower beds. _____ it was time to drive into the dusty town and do errands. Luckily, Auntie stayed behind to fix lunch and I was able to duck into an air-conditioned coffee shop for ten minutes' rest before I dropped off the old clothes at the Salvation Army. I wasn't anxious to find out what help I could be to my aunt in the afternoon. I hoped it wouldn't be something like last year when I had to put a new roof on the old shed in the backyard. I could feel the beginning of a painful sunburn.

EXERCISE 2   Working with Transitions

Below is a narrative paragraph. Make a list in the spaces provided of all the transitions of time that give order to the paragraph.

In the meantime, Jason skated along feeling in the best of moods. He was aware every moment that he was wearing his new pair of roller blades, and several times he even visibly smiled from so much inner pleasure. He hardly noticed when suddenly he found himself skating down his own street. Immediately, neighbourhood children spotted him and ran up to him calling to him by name, "Jason, Jason, where did you get those skates?" In a short time, Jason found himself surrounded by nine or ten children who were running along side of him. Finally, with a flair, he turned, stopped dead and blurted out happily, "It's my birthday today!"

_____   _____

_____   _____

_____   _____

_____   _____

_____   _____

EXERCISE 3   Working with Transitions

Below is a narrative paragraph from a story by the Russian writer Ivan Turgenev. Make a list of all the transitions of time that give order to the paragraph.

> I went to the right through the bushes. Meantime the night had crept close and grown up like a storm cloud; it seemed as though, with the mists of evening, darkness was rising up on all sides and flowing down from over-head. I had come upon some sort of little, untrodden, overgrown path; I walked along it, gazing intently before me. Soon all was blackness and silence around—only the quail's cry was heard from time to time. Some small night-bird, flitting noiselessly near the ground on its soft wings, almost flapped against me and scurried away in alarm. I came out on the further side of the bushes, and made my way along a field by the hedge. By now I could hardly make out distant objects; the field showed dimly white around; beyond it rose up a sullen darkness, which seemed moving up closer in huge masses every instant. My steps gave a muffled sound in the air that grew colder and colder. The pale sky began again to grow blue—but it was the blue of night. The tiny stars glimmered and twinkled in it.

_____   _____

_____   _____

_____   _____

_____   _____

_____   _____

Writing the narrative paragraph step by step

To learn a skill that has so many different demands, the best approach is to work step by step so that one aspect can be worked on at a time. This will ensure that you are not missing a crucial point or misunderstanding a part of the whole. There certainly are other ways to go about writing an effective paragraph, but here is one logical method you can use to achieve results.

STEPS FOR WRITING THE NARRATIVE PARAGRAPH

1. Study the given topic and then plan your topic sentence with its controlling idea.

2. List all the events that come to your mind when you think about the story you have chosen.

3. Then choose the five or six most important events from your list.

4. Put your list in order.

5. Write one complete sentence for each of the events you have chosen from your list.

6. Write a concluding statement that gives some point to the events of the story.

7. Finally, copy your sentences into standard paragraph form.

EXERCISE 1   Writing the Narrative Paragraph Step by Step

This exercise will guide you through the construction of a complete narrative paragraph. Start with the suggested topic. Use the seven steps above to help you work through each stage of the writing process.

Topic: Every family has a favourite story they like to tell about one of their members, often something humorous that happened to one of them. There are also crises and tragic moments in the life of every family. Choose a story, funny or tragic, from the life of a family you know.

1. Topic sentence: _____

    _____

2. Make a list of events.

    a. _____

    b. _____

    c. _____

    d. _____

    e. _____

    f. _____

    g. _____

    h. _____

    i. _____

    j. _____

3. Circle the five or six events you believe are the most important for the point of the story.

4. Put your final choices in order by numbering each of them.

5. Using your final list, write at least one sentence for each event you have chosen.

   a. _____

   _____

   b. _____

   _____

   c. _____

   _____

   d. _____

   _____

   e. _____

   _____

   f. _____

   _____

6. Write a concluding statement. _____

   _____

   _____

   _____

   _____

   _____

7. On a separate piece of paper, copy your sentences into standard paragraph form.

EXERCISE 2 Writing the Narrative Paragraph Step by Step

This exercise will guide you through the construction of a complete narrative paragraph. Start with the suggested topic. Use the seven steps on page 335 to help you work through each stage of the writing process.

Topic: Tell the story of an incident you witnessed. This incident could reveal an unusual act of bravery or compassion, or it could reveal a shocking lack of sensitivity. What did you observe the person doing? How did other people react? What did you do or wish that you had done in response to this incident?

1. Topic sentence: _____

   _____

2. Make a list of events.

   a. _____

   b. _____

   c. _____

   d. _____

e. _____

f. _____

g. _____

h. _____

i. _____

j. _____

3. Circle the five or six events you believe are the most important for the point of the story.

4. Put your final choices in order by numbering each of them.

5. Using your final list, write at least one sentence for each event you have chosen.

a. _____
   _____

b. _____
   _____

c. _____
   _____

d. _____
   _____

e. _____
   _____

f. _____
   _____

6. Write a concluding statement. _____
   _____
   _____
   _____
   _____

7. On a separate piece of paper, copy your sentences into standard paragraph form.

On your own: Writing narrative paragraphs from model paragraphs

The story of how you faced a new challenge

Assignment 1   Write a paragraph telling the story of a day or part of a day in which you faced an important challenge of some kind. It could have been a challenge you faced in school, at home, or on the job. The following paragraph by the journalist Betty Rollin is an example of such an experience.

MODEL PARAGRAPH

When I awoke that morning I hit the floor running. I washed my face, brushed my teeth, got a pot of coffee going, tightened the sash on my bathrobe, snapped my typewriter out of its case, placed it on the kitchen table, retrieved my notes from the floor where they were stacked in Manila folders, unwrapped a pack of bond paper, put the top sheet in the typewriter, looked at it, put my head on the keys, wrapped my arms around its base and cried.

Ten suggested topics

1. The day I started a new job

2. My first day in history class

3. The day I began my first term paper

4. The day I tried to wallpaper my bedroom

5. The morning of my big job interview

6. Facing a large debt

7. Trying to re-establish a friendship gone sour

8. The day I started driving lessons

9. Coping with a death in the family

10. The day I faced a deadline

The story of an unpleasant fight or argument

Assignment 2

Write a paragraph in which you tell the story of a fight or confrontation you either witnessed or became involved in. Choose an experience that left a deep impression on you. What are the important details of the incident that remain most clearly in your mind? The following paragraph is from Albert Halper's short story "Prelude."

MODEL PARAGRAPH

But the people just stood there afraid to do a thing. Then while a few guys held me, Gooley and about four others went for the stand, turning it over and mussing and stamping on all the newspapers they could find. Syl started to scratch them, so they hit her. Then I broke away to help her, and then they started socking me too. My father tried to reach me, but three guys kept him away. Four guys got me down and started kicking me and all the time my father was begging them to let me up and Syl was screaming at the people to help. And while I was down, my face was squeezed against some papers on the sidewalk telling about Austria and I guess I went nuts while they kept hitting me, and I kept seeing the headlines against my nose.

Ten suggested topics   A confrontation between

1. A police officer and a guilty motorist
2. A teacher and a student
3. An angry customer and a store clerk
4. A frustrated parent and a child
5. A manager and an unhappy employee
6. A judge and an unwilling witness
7. A museum guard and a careless tourist
8. A politician and an angry citizen
9. A mugger and a frightened victim
10. An engaged couple about to break up

You won't believe what happened to me today!

Assignment 3   Tell the story of a day you found yourself in a difficult or frustrating situation. The following example is from the novel *Fifth Business* by Robertson Davies.

MODEL PARAGRAPH

Walking up the street ahead of me were the Reverend Amasa Dempster and his wife; he had her arm and was leaning toward her in the protective way he had. I was familiar with this sight, for they always took a walk at this time, after dark and when most people were at supper, because Mrs. Dempster was going to have a baby, and it was not the custom in our village for pregnant women to show themselves boldly in the streets—not if they had any position to keep up, and of course the Baptist minister's wife had a position. Percy had been throwing snowballs at me, from time to time, and I had ducked them all; I had a boy's sense of when a snowball was coming, and I knew Percy. I was sure that he would try to land one last, insulting snowball between my shoulders before I ducked in our house. I stepped briskly—not running, but not dawdling—in front of the Dempsters just as Percy threw, and the snowball hit Mrs. Dempster on the back of the head. She gave a cry and, clinging to her husband, slipped to the ground; he might have caught her if he had not turned at once to see who had thrown the snowball.

Ten suggested topics   1. When I ran out of money

2. When I ran out of gas
3. When I was accused of something I didn't do
4. When I was stopped by the police (or by some other authority)
5. When I was guilty of . . .
6. When something terrible happened just before a big date

7. When the weather didn't cooperate

8. When I locked myself out of the house

9. When I couldn't reach my family by phone

10. When my computer died the night before a paper was due

A memorable experience from childhood

Assignment 4

Write a paragraph in which you remember a special moment from your childhood. The following example is from George Orwell's novel *Coming Up for Air*.

MODEL PARAGRAPH

It was an enormous fish. I don't exaggerate when I say it was enormous. It was almost the length of my arm. It glided across the pool, deep under water, and then became a shadow and disappeared into the darker water on the other side. I felt as if a sword had gone through me. It was by far the biggest fish I'd ever seen, dead or alive. I stood there without breathing, and in a moment another huge thick shape glided through the water, and then another and then two more close together. The pool was full of them. They were carp, I suppose. Just possibly they were bream or tench, but more probably carp. Bream or tench wouldn't grow so huge. I knew what had happened. At some time this pool had been connected with the other, and then the stream had dried up and the woods had closed round the small pool and it had just been forgotten. It's a thing that happens occasionally. A pool gets forgotten somehow, nobody fishes in it for years and decades and the fish grow to monstrous sizes. The brutes that I was watching might be a hundred years old. And not a soul in the world knew about them except me. Very likely it was twenty years since anyone had so much as looked at the pool, and probably even old Hodges and Mr. Farrel's *bailiff* had forgotten its existence.

---

bailiff: in England, a person who looks after a large estate

Ten suggested topics

1. The first time I went swimming

2. My first time on a roller coaster (or on another ride)

3. A frightening experience when I was home alone

4. My most memorable Halloween (or other holiday)

5. The best birthday party I ever had

6. My first bicycle (or car)

7. The greatest present I ever received

8. A memorable visit to a favourite relative

9. My first time travelling alone

10. The first time I went camping

Working Together

Aesop is believed to have been a Greek slave who lived about 2,500 years ago. He created over 200 fables, many of which have become part of our international literary heritage. The following example of his work is a classic fable, one that has a timeless moral.

Once, a schoolboy stole a writing tablet belonging to a classmate. He took the tablet to his mother who, instead of blaming him, actually praised him. On another occasion he showed her some clothing he had stolen. Again she praised him, this time even more highly. As he grew toward adulthood, the young man's thievery became more and more risky. One day he was caught in a serious crime, arrested, and sentenced to death. As he was led off to be executed, with his hands tied behind him, his mother walked with him, beating her breast and crying out in sorrow. The young man turned to her and asked her to come closer, as he had something to say to her. When she was near to him, he took her earlobe in his teeth and bit it savagely. His mother was stunned, and cried out in protest against what he had done. Was it not enough that he had committed all of those other crimes? Will he now attack his own mother? "You should have corrected me the day I first stole from my classmate in school," her son replied. "If you had, I would not have ended up in the hands of the executioner today."

Moral: Offenders who are not punished go from bad to worse.

Sometimes a writer's purpose is to teach a lesson, as Aesop does in the fable you have just read. Create a fable of your own by writing a short narrative account of an incident that could teach your readers a lesson. You might want to set your fable in a modern city or town and have your characters (a fable usually has only one or two) perform actions that will lead to a moral at the end. For example, you might want to teach a lesson about greed by showing the different actions of two people when they find money in the street; or you could illustrate a lesson about human ambition by describing two students studying for the same career.

Be sure to imitate Aesop by placing a short moral at the end of your fable. Keep in mind that your fable might make a very good lesson to read out loud to the children in your family. What lesson would you like them to learn?

Test the effectiveness of your fable by reading it out loud in class. Do your classmates have suggestions that are useful for revising your fable?

Developing Paragraphs: Process

What is process?

> *Process* is the method that explains how to do something or that shows how something works. There are two kinds of process writing: *directional* and *informational.* A process that is directional actually shows you, step by step, how to do something; a process that is informational is not intended to be carried out.

Your daily life is filled with activities that involve process. For example, if you wanted to show someone how to brew a perfect cup of coffee, you would take the person through each step of the process, from selecting and grinding the coffee beans to pouring the finished product. Instructions on a test, directions on how to get to a wedding reception, or your favourite spaghetti recipe are a few examples of the kinds of process writing you see and use regularly. You can find examples of *directional* process writing everywhere you look, in newspapers, magazines, and books, as well as on the containers and packages of products you use every day.

On the other hand, a process that is *informational* tells you how something is or was done for the purpose of informing you about the process. For example, in a history course it might be important to understand how a general planned his strategy during the First World War. Of course, you would not use this strategy yourself. The purpose is for information.

The following paragraph describes the various stages that scientist David Suzuki went through in the process of developing his awareness of environmental issues. Notice that each step is given in its proper sequence. Words such as *first, next,* and *finally* can be used to show that a writer is developing an idea by using process. In the paragraph, the words that signal the *steps* or *stages* of the process have been italicized:

> David Suzuki's thoughts examine the shortcomings of modern society by emphasizing the negative effects it has on nature. For Suzuki, we cannot continue to pollute or otherwise harm the environment because, in the long run, we are only harming ourselves. Suzuki *first* developed a real love for nature through the camping and fishing trips he used to take with his father. There were many of these trips. The *next stage* in the development of his awareness

came when he entered university. He planned to study medicine but became more interested in the study of genetics. This completely absorbed him, and he loved conducting laboratory research. *At this point,* he began to realize the limits of scientific knowledge. He noticed that scientists tended to look at the world like a "fractured mosaic"; they didn't look at the big picture or how phenomena connected and related to one another. He *began* to question the role of science in society. *Eventually,* he concluded that scientists must play an active role educating people about the dangers they face when they neglect their responsibility for preserving nature. *Finally,* he established the David Suzuki Foundation as an educational centre designed to increase awareness of our need to protect the environment.

Working with process: Don't overlook any one of the steps

The writer of the process essay is almost always more of an authority on the subject than the person reading the essay. In giving directions or information on how something was done or is to be done, it is possible to leave out a step that you think is so obvious that it is not worth mentioning. The reader, on the other hand, does not necessarily fill in the missing step as you did. An important part of process writing, therefore, is understanding your reader's level of ability. All of us have been given directions that, at first, seemed very clear. However, when we actually tried to carry out the process, something went wrong. A step in the process was misunderstood or missing. The giver of the information either assumed we would know certain parts of the process or didn't stop to think through the process completely. The important point is that directions must be complete and accurate. Here is one further consideration: If special equipment is required in order to perform the process, the directions must include a clear description of the necessary tools.

EXERCISE 1   **Is the Process Complete?**

In each of the following processes, figure out what important step or steps of information have been omitted. Imagine yourself going through the process using only the information provided.

How to Make a Swedish Spice Cake

1. Butter an 8-inch tube pan and sprinkle with 2 tbsp. of fine dry bread crumbs.

2. Cream ½ cup of butter; add 1 cup of firmly packed brown sugar and cream until light and fluffy.

3. Beat 2 egg yolks in a small bowl until light and add to the creamed mixture.

4. Sift together 1½ cups all purpose flour, 1 tsp. baking power, 2 tsp. ground cardamon, and 2 tsp. of ground cinnamon.

5. Add the dry ingredients to the creamed ingredients mixing alternately with ½ cup of light cream.

6. Beat egg whites stiff and fold into batter.

7. Turn in prepared pan, bake, and serve unfrosted.

Missing step or steps: _____

_____

_____

_____

_____

How to Plan a Wedding

1. Make an appointment with the minister or other authority involved, to set a date for the wedding.

2. Discuss plans with both families as to the budget available for the wedding; this will determine the size of the party and where it is to be held.

3. Reserve the banquet hall as much as eight months in advance.

4. Choose members of the wedding party and ask them whether they will be able to participate in the ceremony.

5. Begin to choose the clothing for the wedding party, including your own wedding gown or suit.

6. Enjoy your wedding!

Missing step or steps: _____

_____

_____

_____

_____

EXERCISE 2   Is the Process Complete?

In each of the following processes, figure out what important step or steps of information have been omitted. Imagine yourself going through the process using only the information provided.

How to Prepare for an Essay Exam

1. Read the chapters as they are assigned well in advance of the test.

2. Take notes in class.

3. Ask the teacher what format the test will take if the teacher has not described the test.

4. Get a good night's sleep the night before.

5. Bring any pens or pencils that you might need.

6. Arrive at the classroom a few minutes early in order to get yourself settled and to keep yourself calm.

Missing step or steps: _____

_____

_____

_____

_____

_____

_____

How to Wrap a Present

1. Gather all the materials needed: box for gift, wrapping paper, tape, scissors, and ribbon.

2. Measure the amount of paper needed, and cut off excess.

3. Place box top side down on paper.

4. Bring one long side of wrapping paper up and tape it to the box.

5. Bring the other long side of the paper up over the box to the far edge. Pull tight. Fold the paper under so that it fits exactly along the far edge of the box. Tape securely.

6. Tie ribbon, make bow, and attach the card.

You can see that illustrations with directions like these would be very helpful.

Missing step or steps: _____

_____

_____

_____

_____

_____

_____

Coherence in process: Order in logical sequence

When you are working with process, it is important not only to make sure the steps in the process are complete but also to present the steps in the right sequence. For example, if you are describing the process of cleaning a mixer, it is important to point out that you must first unplug the appliance before you actually remove the blades. The importance of this step is clear when you realize that a person could lose a finger if this part of the process were missing. Improperly written instructions have caused serious injuries and even death.

EXERCISE 1   **Coherence in Process: Order in Logical Sequence**

The following steps describe the process of refinishing hardwood floors. Put the steps into their proper sequence.

_____   Keep sanding until you expose the hard wood.

_____   Apply a coat of polyurethane finish.

_____   When the sanding is done, clean the floor thoroughly with a vacuum sweeper to remove all the sawdust.

_____   Allow the finish to dry for three days before waxing and buffing.

_____   Take all furnishings out of the room.

_____   Do the initial sanding with a coarse sandpaper.

_____   The edger and hand sander are used after the machine sanding to get to those hard-to-reach places.

_____   Put the second coat of polyurethane finish on the following day, using a brush or a roller.

_____   Change to a fine sandpaper for the final sanding.

_____   Any nails sticking out from the floor should be either pulled out or set below the surface of the boards before you start the sanding machine.

EXERCISE 2   **Coherence in Process: Order in Logical Sequence**

The following steps describe the process of making a filing system that works. Put the steps into their proper sequence.

_____   When your mind begins to blur, stop filing for that day.

_____   Now label the file folder and slip the piece of paper in.

_____   Gather together all materials to be filed so that they are all in one location.

_____   Alphabetize your file folders and put them away into your file drawer, and you are finished for that session.

_____   Add to these materials a wastebasket, folders, labels, and a pen.

_____   Pick up the next piece of paper and go through the same procedure, the only variation being that this new piece of paper might fit into an existing file, rather than one with a new heading.

_____   Pick up an item on the top of the pile and decide whether this item has value for you. If it does not, throw it away. If it does, go on to the next step.

_____   Finally, to maintain your file once it is established, each time you consult a file folder, riffle through it quickly in order to throw out material no longer useful.

_____   If the piece of paper is worth saving, ask yourself the question, "What is this paper about?"

Transitions for process

Writers of process, like writers of narration, usually order their material by time sequence. Although it would be tiresome to use "and then" for each new step, a certain number of transitions are necessary for the process to read smoothly and coherently. Here is a list of transitions frequently used for a process paragraph.

TRANSITIONS FOR PROCESS

the first step	while you are . . .	the last step
in the beginning	as you are . . .	the final step
to start with	next	finally
to begin with	then	at last
first of all	the second step	eventually
	after you have . . .	

EXERCISE 1   Using Transitions to Go from a List to a Paragraph

Select one of the four processes given on pages 344–346. Use this list to write a process paragraph that includes transitional devices to make the paragraph smooth and coherent.

_____

_____

_____

_____

_____

_____

_____

_____

_____

_____

_____

_____

_____

EXERCISE 2 **Using Transitions to Go from a List to a Paragraph**

Select one of the four processes listed on pages 344–346. Use this list to write a process paragraph that includes transitional devices to make the paragraph smooth and coherent.

_____

_____

_____

_____

_____

_____

_____

_____

_____

_____

Writing the process paragraph step by step

To learn a skill that has so many different demands, the best approach is to work step by step so that one aspect can be worked on at a time. This will ensure that you are not missing a crucial point or misunderstanding a part of the whole. There certainly are other ways to go about writing an effective paragraph, but here is one logical method you can use to achieve results.

STEPS FOR WRITING THE PROCESS PARAGRAPH

1. After you have chosen your topic and controlling idea, plan your topic sentence.

2. List as many steps or stages in the process as you can.

3. Eliminate any irrelevant steps; add equipment needed or explain any special circumstances of the process.

4. Put the steps in order.

5. Write at least one complete sentence for each of the steps you have chosen from your list.

6. Write a concluding statement that says something about the results of completing the process.

7. Finally, copy your sentences into standard paragraph form.

EXERCISE 1   Writing the Process Paragraph Step by Step

This exercise will guide you through the construction of a complete process paragraph. Start with the topic suggested below. Use the seven steps to help you work through each stage of the writing process.

Topic: How to lose weight

Perhaps no topic has filled more bookstores or magazine pages than the "lose ten pounds in two days" promise. The wide variety of diet plans boggles the mind. Here is your chance to add your own version.

1. Topic sentence: _____

2. Make a list of possible steps.

    a. _____

    b. _____

    c. _____

    d. _____

    e. _____

    f. _____

    g. _____

    h. _____

    i. _____

    j. _____

3. Eliminate any irrelevant steps; add equipment needed or explain any special circumstances.

4. Put your steps in order by numbering them.

5. Using your final list, write at least one sentence for each step you have chosen.

    a. _____

    _____

    b. _____

    _____

    c. _____

    _____

    d. _____

    _____

    e. _____

    _____

    f. _____

    _____

    g. _____

    _____

6. Write a concluding statement. _____

_____

_____

7. On a separate piece of paper, copy your sentences into standard paragraph form.

EXERCISE 2   Writing the Process Paragraph Step by Step

This exercise will guide you through the construction of a complete process paragraph. Start with the topic suggested below. Use the seven steps to help you work through each stage of the writing process.

Topic: How to pick a college or university

Sometimes an individual goes through an agonizing process before he or she is finally seated in a classroom. The factors that go into selecting a college or university can be extremely complicated. Give advice to a prospective student on how to go about finding the right school.

1. Topic sentence: _____

2. Make a list of possible steps.

a. _____

b. _____

c. _____

d. _____

e. _____

f. _____

g. _____

h. _____

i. _____

j. _____

3. Eliminate any irrelevant steps; add equipment needed or explain any special circumstances.

4. Put your steps in order by numbering them.

5. Using your final list, write at least one sentence for each step you have chosen.

a. _____

_____

b. _____

_____

c. _____

_____

d. _____

_____

e. _____

_____

f. _____

_____

g. _____

_____

6. Write a concluding statement. _____

_____

_____

7. On a separate piece of paper, copy your sentences into standard paragraph form.

EXERCISE 3   Writing the Process Paragraph Step by Step

This exercise will guide you through the construction of a complete process paragraph. Start with the topic suggested below. Use the seven steps to help you work through each stage of the writing process.

Topic: How to manage a budget

Imagine you are the expert who has been hired by a couple to help them sort out their money problems. They bring in a reasonable salary, but still they are always spending more than they earn.

1. Topic sentence: _____

2. Make a list of possible steps.

a. _____

b. _____

c. _____

d. _____

e. _____

f. _____

g. _____

h. _____

i. _____

j. _____

3. Eliminate any irrelevant steps; add equipment needed or explain any special circumstances.

4. Put your steps in order by numbering them.

5. Using your final list, write at least one sentence for each step you have chosen.

a. _____

_____

b. _____

_____

c. _____

_____

d. _____

_____

e. _____

_____

f. _____

_____

g. _____

_____

6. Write a concluding statement. _____

_____

_____

7. On a separate piece of paper, copy your sentences into standard paragraph form.

On your own: Writing process paragraphs from model paragraphs

Informational: How something scientific works

Assignment 1   Write a paragraph in which you describe a scientific process. You could tell how a simple radio works, or you could describe how a snake sheds its skin. The following paragraph gives a description of a modern scientific process that increases the world's supply of drinking water. After you have chosen a topic, look for specific information in encyclopedias, textbooks, or other sources to help you explain the process.

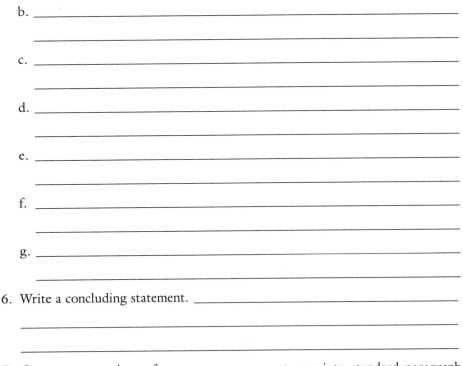

MODEL PARAGRAPH

The Anse method of converting sea water to fresh water is a cheap and efficient way to produce drinkable water from the sea. First, you cover an area of water with a sheet of black plastic. Air-filled channels in the plastic keep it raised slightly above the water. Underneath this plastic is another sheet of plastic that floats on the water; this plastic has small holes that allow sea water to seep up between the two layers of plastic. The heat of the sun, striking the upper layer of the plastic, causes the water to evaporate, leaving the salt behind. The hot air, filled with water, is then forced through a pipe and into an underground collection chamber by wind that is channelled between the plastic sheets by air ducts built on top of the plastic. When the hot air enters the collection chamber, the water in the air condenses, leaving fresh water on the bottom of the submerged chamber. This fresh water can then be pumped out of the chamber and used.

Ten suggested topics

1. How leather is made
2. How metamorphosis happens
3. How an airplane flies
4. How stars are formed
5. How photosynthesis occurs
6. How the human heart works
7. How a bee makes honey
8. How a camera works
9. How a piano works
10. How a book is produced

Directional: How to care for your health

Assignment 2

Write a paragraph in which you show steps you could take for your mental or physical health. Concern for health and physical fitness is enjoying great popularity, bringing in big profits to health-related magazines, health clubs, health-food producers, and sports equipment manufacturers. The following paragraph tells us how to get a good night's sleep.

MODEL PARAGRAPH

The process of getting a good night's sleep depends on several factors. First, the conditions in your bedroom must be correct. Be sure that the room temperature is around 18°C and that the room is as quiet as possible. Next, pay attention to your bed and how it is furnished. A firm mattress is best, and wool blankets are better than blankets made of synthetic material. In addition, pillows that are too soft can cause stiffness of the neck and lead to a poor night's sleep. Also, keep in mind that what you eat and how you eat are part of the process of preparing for bed. Do not go to bed hungry, but do not overeat, either. Avoid candy bars or cookies; the sugar they contain acts as a stimulant. Finally, do not go to bed until you are sleepy; do something relaxing until you are tired.

Ten suggested topics

1. How to plan a healthful diet
2. How to care for someone who is ill
3. How to plan a daily exercise program
4. How to choose a sport that is suitable for you
5. How to live to be one hundred
6. How to pick a doctor
7. How to make exercise and diet foods fun
8. How to stop eating junk food
9. How to deal with depression
10. How to find a spiritual side to life

Informational: An explanation of how something works

Assignment 3   Write a paragraph in which you explain a complicated or interesting process. The task may be something that is frequently done in human society or that occurs in the world of nature. The following paragraph, which describes how a mosquito bites a human, is an example of a process that is informational.

MODEL PARAGRAPH

On six long legs, she puts down so lightly that you feel nothing. Sensors on her feet detect the carbon dioxide that your skin exhales. Down comes the long proboscis; up go the long back legs, as though to balance it. The little soft lobes at the tip of the proboscis are spread to test the surface. It will do. A sudden contraction of the legs with the weight of the body behind it bends the proboscis backward in an arc while the six sharp blades it has unsheathed are thrust into your skin. Two of the blades are tipped with barbs. These work alternately, shove and hold, shove and hold, pulling the insect's face down and carrying their fellows deeper into your skin.

Ten suggested topics
1. How cheese is made
2. How an eclipse occurs
3. How an airplane flies
4. How the human heart works
5. How to make the perfect cappuccino
6. How the ancient Egyptians built the pyramids
7. How a bill becomes a law
8. How a city prepares for hosting the Olympics
9. How Henry Ford mass-produced the automobile
10. How glass is made

Directional: How to write school assignments

Assignment 4   Your writing in school takes many forms. Write a paragraph in which you show the process of writing a specific assignment related to school. The following paragraph, adapted from Donald Murray's *Write to Learn*, shows the several steps you need to follow in the writing of a term paper.

MODEL PARAGRAPH

Doing a term paper involves both careful research on a topic and a methodical approach to the writing of the material. First, consult the important and up-to-date books and articles related to your subject. Next, find out the style of writing that your instructor wants; also find out details about length, organization, footnoting, and bibliography that will be part of the presentation of your paper. Then write a draft of the paper as quickly as you can, without using notes or bibliography; this will help you see your ideas and how they can be further developed. Before you go any further, review what you have written to see if you have begun to develop a point of view about your subject or an attitude toward your topic. Finally, write a draft of your paper that includes all of the important information about your subject, a draft that includes your footnotes and your bibliography.

Ten suggested topics   1. How to prepare an oral report

2. How to write a résumé

3. How to write a letter of application (for a school or for a job)

4. How to write a science experiment

5. How to write a book review

6. How to revise an essay

7. How to take classroom notes

8. How to take notes from a textbook

9. How to write a letter home, asking for money

10. How to write a story for the school newspaper

Working Together

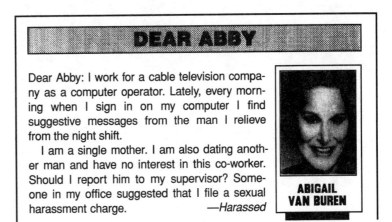

DEAR ABBY

Dear Abby: I work for a cable television company as a computer operator. Lately, every morning when I sign in on my computer I find suggestive messages from the man I relieve from the night shift.

I am a single mother. I am also dating another man and have no interest in this co-worker. Should I report him to my supervisor? Someone in my office suggested that I file a sexual harassment charge.　　　　　*—Harassed*

ABIGAIL VAN BUREN

1. If you were the one to advise this person, what would you tell her to do? Explain the process she should follow in order to solve this problem.

    In order to better answer this question, the class could divide into groups to consider the following questions:

    a) Should she confront the man who is harassing her?

    b) Should she go to her supervisor? Should she have told her coworkers about the problem?

    c) Should she share her problem with the man she is dating?

    d) Should she avoid the problem and quit her job?

    e) How important is evidence for a person in this situation? How and when should she gather documentation for a possible formal action?

    f) Does she need a lawyer? Does she need to consider the consequences of a formal action?

2. Sexual harassment is not the only problem workers or students might face. In a brief discussion with your classmates, list some other common complaints workers or students might have. Are there steps that need to be followed in order to successfully resolve all such problems? Following the class discussion, write your own paragraph describing the steps you feel are necessary to deal with such situations.

Chapter 20

Developing Paragraphs: Comparison or Contrast

What is comparison or contrast?

One method of developing a subject in writing is to compare it to another item to show its similarities or to contrast it with another item to show how it differs. This method is used when we need to demonstrate our understanding of a complex subject and make some conclusion that is usually judgmental.

Placing one item next to another and pointing out the similarities is called a *comparison;* pointing out the differences, is called a *contrast.* The entire process of looking at both similarities and differences, however, is often referred to as *comparison.* In this chapter, we will distinguish between the two terms.

> *Comparison* or *contrast* in writing is the careful look at the similarities and/or differences between people, objects, or ideas, usually in order to make some conclusion or judgment about what is being compared or contrasted.

We use comparison or contrast in a variety of ways every day. In the grocery store, we consider similar products before we decide to buy one of them; we listen to two politicians on television and think about the differences between their positions before we vote for one of them; and we read college catalogues and talk to our friends before we make a final choice as to which school we should attend.

When we compare or contrast two items, we want to be able to see very clearly the points of comparison or contrast so that we may judge which item is better or worse than the other. The process of comparison gives us a deeper understanding of the subject and enables us to make well-researched decisions rather than being at the mercy of a clever salesperson or being convinced by a good price or some other feature that might strike us at first glance.

Let's think about the selection of a word processing program, an expensive purchase that many individuals and companies will make. A shopper must consider price, availability of help for installing and troubleshooting, compatibility with available computers, specific features that differentiate the package from other programs available, how "user-friendly" the program is, what the specific needs are now and what they might be in the future, and how current or popular the program is among other software users. Also, it is a good idea to seek out advice from others who are more expert on the available programs. All of this research is basically comparison and contrast. Especially with such a complex and expensive purchase as computer software, we can see that comparison and contrast becomes not only a useful tool, but an essential one.

Working with comparison or contrast: Choosing the two-part topic

The problem with writing a good comparison or contrast paragraph usually centres on the fact that you now have a two-part topic. This demands very careful attention to the topic sentence. While you must be careful to choose two subjects that have enough in common to make them comparable, you must also not choose two things having so much in common that you cannot possibly handle all the comparable points in one paragraph or even ten paragraphs. For example, a student trying to compare the French word *chaise* with the English word *chair* might be able to come up with only two sentences of material. With only a dictionary to consult, it is unlikely that the student would find enough material for several points of comparison. On the other hand, contrasting Canada with Europe would present such an endless supply of points to compare that the tendency would be to give only general facts that your reader would already know. When the subject is too broad, the writing is often too general. A better two-part topic might be to compare travelling by train in Europe with travelling by train in Canada.

Once you have chosen a two-part topic that you feel is not too limiting and not too broad, you must remember that a good comparison or contrast paragraph should devote an equal or nearly equal amount of space to each of the two parts. If the writer is only interested in one of the topics, the danger is that the paragraph will end up being very one-sided.

Here's an example of a one-sided contrast:

While Canadian trains go to only a few towns, are infrequent, and are often shabby and uncomfortable, the European train is much nicer.

The next example is a better written contrast that gives attention to both topics:

While Canadian trains go to only a few large cities, run very infrequently, and are often shabby and uncomfortable, European trains go to virtually every small town, are always dependable, and are clean and attractive.

EXERCISE 1   Evaluating the Two-Part Topic

Study the following topics and decide whether each topic is *too broad* for a paragraph, or whether it is *suitable* as a topic for a paragraph of comparison or contrast. Mark your choice in the appropriate space to the right of each topic.

Topic	Too Broad	Suitable
1. Australia and England	_____	_____
2. Indian elephants and African elephants	_____	_____
3. Canadian wine and French wine	_____	_____
4. Wooden furniture and plastic furniture	_____	_____
5. Wood and plastic	_____	_____
6. Photography and oil painting	_____	_____
7. Heart surgeons and plastic surgeons	_____	_____
8. Taking digital photographs and photographs using film	_____	_____
9. Doctors and lawyers	_____	_____
10. Windows computers and Mac computers	_____	_____

EXERCISE 2   **Working with Comparison or Contrast**

Each of the suggested comparison or contrast topics below is followed by a more specific topic that has not been completed. Complete each of these specific topics by supplying details of your own. Each topic you complete should be one that you could develop as an example of comparison or contrast.

1. Compare two friends:

   My friend _____ with my friend _____

2. Compare two kinds of coats:

   _____ coats with _____ coats

3. Compare two kinds of diets:

   The _____ diet and the _____ diet

4. Compare two kinds of floors:

   _____ floors with _____ floors

5. Compare two kinds of entertainment:

   Watching _____ with looking at _____

6. Compare two kinds of rice:

   _____ rice with _____ rice

7. Compare two places where you can study:

   Studying in the _____ with studying in the _____

8. Compare the wedding customs of two groups:

   What _____ do at a wedding with what _____ do at a wedding

9. Compare two textbooks:

   A textbook that has _____ with a textbook that contains _____

10. Compare two politicians:

    A local politician who _____ with a national politician who _____

EXERCISE 3   **Working with Comparison or Contrast**

Each of the suggested comparison or contrast topics below is followed by a more specific topic that has not been completed. Complete each of these specific topics by supplying details of your own. Each topic you complete should be one that you could develop as an example of comparison or contrast.

1. Compare two kinds of popular board games people play:

   Playing _____ with playing _____

2. Compare two ways of looking at movies:

   Watching movies on _____ with going to _____

3. Compare two careers:

   A career in _____ with a career as a _____

4. Compare two ways of paying for a purchase:

Using _____ to buy something, with using _____ to buy something

5. Compare two different lifestyles:

   Living the life of a _____ with living as a _____

6. Compare two places to go swimming:

   Swimming in a _____ with swimming in a _____

7. Compare a no-frills product with the same product sold under a standard brand name (such as no-frills corn flakes with Kellogg's corn flakes):

   A no-frills _____ with _____

8. Compare two popular magazines:

   _____ with _____

9. Compare two hobbies:

   _____ with _____

10. Compare two kinds of tests given in school:

   The _____ kind of test with the _____ kind of test

Coherence in comparison or contrast: Two approaches to ordering material

The first method for ordering material in a paragraph of comparison or contrast is known as the *point-by-point method.* When you use this method, you compare a point of one topic with a point of the other topic. For example, here is a paragraph from Julius Lester's *All Is Well.* In the paragraph, the writer uses the point-by-point method to compare the difficulties of being a boy with the difficulties of being a girl:

> Now, of course, I know that it was as difficult being a girl as it was a boy, if not more so. While I stood paralyzed at one end of a dance floor trying to find the courage to ask a girl for a dance, most of the girls waited in terror at the other, afraid that no one, not even I, would ask them. And while I resented having to ask a girl for a date, wasn't it also horrible to be the one who waited for the phone to ring? And how many of those girls who laughed at me making a fool of myself on the baseball diamond would have gladly given up their places on the sidelines for mine on the field?

Notice how, after the opening topic sentence, the writer uses half of each sentence to describe a boy's situation growing up and the other half of the same sentence to describe a girl's experience. This technique is effective in such a paragraph, and it is most often used in longer pieces of writing in which many points of comparison are made. This method helps the reader keep the comparison or contrast carefully in mind at each point.

The second method for ordering material in a paragraph of comparison or contrast is known as the *block method.* When you use this approach, you present all of the facts and supporting details about your first topic, and then you give all of the facts and supporting details about your second topic. Here, for example, is another version of the paragraph you studied above, but this time it is written according to the block method:

Now, of course, I know that it was as difficult being a girl as it was being a boy, if not more so. I stood paralyzed at one end of the dance floor trying to find the courage to ask a girl for a dance. I resented having to ask a girl for a date, just as I often felt foolish on the baseball diamond. On the other hand, most of the girls waited in terror at the other end of the dance floor, afraid that no one, not even I, would ask them to dance. In addition, it was a horrible situation for the girls who had to wait for the phone to ring. And how many of those girls who waited on the sidelines would have traded places with me on the baseball diamond?

Notice how the first half of this version presents all of the details about the boy, while the second part of the paragraph presents all of the information about the girls. This method is often used in shorter pieces of writing because with a shorter piece it is possible for the reader to keep the blocks of information in mind.

Looking at the two paragraphs in outline form will help you see the shape of their development.

Point-by-point method

Topic sentence

"Now, of course, I know that it was as difficult being a girl as it was a boy, if not more so."

First point, first topic: "While I stood paralyzed at one end of a dance floor trying to find the courage to ask a girl for a dance . . ."

First point, second topic: ". . . most of the girls waited in terror at the other, afraid that no one, not even I, would ask them."

Second point, first topic: "And while I resented having to ask a girl for a date, . . ."

Second point, second topic: ". . . wasn't it also horrible to be the one who waited for the phone to ring?"

Third point, first topic: "And how many of those girls who laughed at me making a fool of myself on the baseball diamond . . ."

Third point, second topic: ". . . would have gladly given up their places on the sidelines for mine on the field?"

Block method

Topic sentence

"Now, of course, I know that it was as difficult being a girl as it was a boy, if not more so."

First topic, points one, two, and three:
"I stood paralyzed at one end of the dance floor trying to find the courage to ask a girl for a dance. I resented having to ask a girl for a date, just as I often felt foolish on the baseball diamond."

Second topic, points one, two, and three:
"On the other hand, most of the girls waited in terror at the other end of the dance floor, afraid that no one, not even I, would ask them to dance. In addition, it was a horrible situation for the girls who had to wait for the phone to ring. And how many of those girls who waited on the sidelines would have traded places with me on the baseball diamond?"

You will want to choose one of these methods before you write a comparison or contrast assignment. Keep in mind that although the block method is most often used in shorter writing assignments, such as a paragraph, you will have the chance to practise the point-by-point method as well.

EXERCISE 1   Working for Coherence: Recognizing the Two Approaches to Ordering Material

Each of the following passages is an example of comparison or contrast. Read each paragraph carefully and decide whether the writer has used the point-by-point method or the block method. Also indicate whether the piece emphasizes similarities or differences. Indicate your choices in the spaces provided after each example.

1. Female infants speak sooner, have larger vocabularies, and rarely demonstrate speech defects. (Stuttering, for instance, occurs almost exclusively among boys.) Girls exceed boys in language abilities, and this early linguistic bias often prevails throughout life. Girls read sooner, learn foreign languages more easily, and, as a result, are more likely to enter occupations involving language mastery. Boys, in contrast, show an early visual superiority. They are also clumsier, performing poorly at something like arranging a row of beads, but excel at other activities calling on total body coordination. Their attentional mechanisms are also different. A boy will react to an inanimate object as quickly as he will to a person. A male baby will often ignore the mother and babble to a blinking light, fixate on a geometric figure, and, at a later point, manipulate it and attempt to take it apart.

        _____ Point-by-Point   _____ Block

        _____ Similarities   _____ Differences

2. General James Wolfe has been described as an unlikely warrior. He was thin and pale and suffered from rheumatism and constant bladder infections. He hailed from a common background and lacked the finesse of many of his contemporaries. Ironically, he spent some time in France trying to refine his manners. He was, however, a bold military tactician who, very early in his career, developed a reputation for recklessness and brutality. The Marquis de Montcalm, on the other hand, had distinguished himself in numerous battles during his long career as a soldier in the French army. Despite the fact that he had been wounded several times, he was a robust and passionate individual. Montcalm came from an aristocratic family and was educated by a private tutor throughout his adolescence. As a commander, he had preferred traditional military tactics and believed strongly that war should be conducted in a civilized manner.

        _____ Point-by-Point   _____ Block

        _____ Similarities   _____ Differences

3. I first realized that the act of writing was about to enter a new era five years ago when I went to see an editor at *The Globe and Mail.* As I was ushered through the vast city room I felt that I had strayed into the wrong office. The place was clean and carpeted and quiet. As I passed long rows of desks, I saw that almost every desk had its own computer terminal and its own solemn occupant—a man or a woman typing at the computer keyboard or reading what was on the terminal screen. I saw no typewriters, no paper, no mess. It was a cool and sterile

environment; the drones at their machines could have been processing insurance claims or tracking a spacecraft in orbit. What they didn't look like were newspaper people, and what the place didn't look like was a newspaper office. I knew how a newspaper office should look and sound and smell—I worked in one for thirteen years. The paper was the *The Toronto Star,* and its city room, wide as a city block, was dirty and dishevelled. Reporters wrote on ancient typewriters that filled the air with clatter; copy editors laboured on coffee-stained desks over what the reporters had written. Crumpled balls of paper littered the floor and filled the wastebaskets—failed efforts to write a good lead or a decent sentence. The walls were grimy—every few years they were painted over in a less restful shade of eye-rest green—and the atmosphere was hazy with the smoke of cigarettes and cigars. At the very centre the city editor bellowed his displeasure with the day's work, his voice a rumbling volcano in our lives. I thought it was the most beautiful place in the world.

_____ Point-by-Point   _____ Block

_____ Similarities   _____ Differences

4. We went fishing the first morning. I felt the same damp moss covering the worms in the bait can, and saw the dragonfly alight on the tip of my rod as it hovered a few inches from the surface of the water. It was the arrival of this fly that convinced me beyond any doubt that everything was as it always had been, that the years were a mirage and there had been no years. The small waves were the same, chucking the rowboat under the chin as we fished at anchor, and the boat was the same boat, the same colour green and the ribs broken in the same places, and under the floor-boards the same freshwater leavings and debris—the dead helgramite, the wisps of moss, the rusty discarded fishhook, the dried blood from yesterday's catch. We stared silently at the tips of our rods, at the dragonflies that came and went. I lowered the tip of mine into the water, tentatively, pensively dislodging the fly, which darted two feet away, poised, darted two feet back, and came to rest again a little farther up the rod. There had been no years between the ducking of this dragonfly and the other one—the one that was part of memory. I looked at the boy, who was silently watching his fly, and it was my hands that held his rod, my eyes watching. I felt dizzy and didn't know which rod I was at the end of.

_____ Point-by-Point   _____ Block

_____ Similarities   _____ Differences

5. The streets are littered with cigarette and cigar butts, paper wrappings, particles of food, and dog droppings. How long before they become indistinguishable from the gutters of medieval towns when slop pails were emptied from the second-story windows? Thousands of women no longer attend evening services in their churches. They fear assault as they walk the few steps from bus or subway station to their apartment houses. The era of the medieval footpad has returned, and, as in the Dark Ages, the cry for help brings no assistance, for even grown men know they would be cut down before the police could arrive.

_____ Point-by-Point   _____ Block

_____ Similarities   _____ Differences

EXERCISE 2   **Using the Point-by-Point and Block Methods for Comparison or Contrast**

The third passage, given on pages 364–365, uses the block method to make its points of contrast. Rewrite the material using the point-by-point approach.

EXERCISE 3   **Using the Point-by-Point and Block Methods for Comparison or Contrast**

Use the list below to write a comparison or contrast paragraph on life in the city compared with life in a suburban area. Review the list provided and add to it any of your own ideas. Omit any you do not wish to use. Then, selecting either the block method or the point-by-point method, write a comparison or contrast paragraph.

Topic sentence: If I could move back to the city from the suburbs, I know I would be happy.

The following points provide details that relate to living in the city and living in a suburban community:

Topic I
Advantages of the City

A short ride on the bus or subway gets you to work.

Men are as visible as women in the neighbourhood.

Variety in the architecture and ethnic diversity

Families and single people

Local shopping for nearly everything

Mingle with people walking in the neighbourhood daily

Topic II
Disadvantages of the Suburbs

Commuting to work from the suburb to the city is often long and exhausting.

Because most men in the suburbs work in the city, few of them are active in the suburban community.

Sameness of people and streets is monotonous.

Mostly families

Mostly mall shopping

Little walking, use cars to go everywhere

Notice that the writer who created this list emphasized the disadvantages of the suburbs, in contrast to the advantages of the city. No mention was made, for example, of crime in the city. A writer could create another list, this time from the point of view of a person who prefers the suburbs.

Working for coherence: Using transitions

A number of words and phrases are useful to keep in mind when writing the comparison or contrast paper. Some of them are used in phrases, some in clauses.

COMMON TRANSITIONS		
Transitions for Comparison	**Transitions for Contrast**	
similar to	on the contrary	though
similarly	on the other hand	unlike
like	in contrast with	even though
likewise	in spite of	nevertheless
just like	despite	however
just as	instead of	but
furthermore	different from	otherwise
moreover	whereas	except for
equally	while	and yet
again	although	still
also		
too		
so		

Notice the different uses of *like* and *as*:

Like is a preposition and is used in the prepositional phrase *like me*.

> My sister is just *like* me.

As is a subordinate conjunction and is used in the clause below with a subject and a verb.

> My sister sews every evening, *as* does her older daughter.

EXERCISE 1   Using Transitions in Comparisons and Contrasts

Each of the following examples is made up of two sentences. Read both sentences and decide whether the idea being expressed is one of comparison or contrast. Next, combine the two sentences by using a transition you have chosen from the list above. Then write your new sentence on the lines provided. You may reword your new sentence slightly in order to make it grammatically correct. An example has been done for you.

> Mr. Johnson is a teacher.
>
> His wife is a teacher.

First you decide that the two sentences show a comparison. Then you combine the two by using an appropriate transition:

> Mr. Johnson is a teacher just like his wife.

> *or*

> Mr. Johnson is a teacher; his wife is too.

1. Dr. Rappole has a reputation for excellent bedside manners.

    Dr. Connolly is very withdrawn and speaks so softly that it is almost impossible to understand what he has said.

    Your combined sentence: _____

    _____

    _____

2. In Canada, soccer has recently become the most popular sport of young children.

    Soccer has always been immensely popular in Brazil.

    Your combined sentence: _____

    _____

    _____

3. Hemingway's book *Death in the Afternoon* deals with the theme of man against nature.

    The same writer's novel *The Old Man and the Sea* deals with the theme of man against nature.

    Your combined sentence: _____

    _____

    _____

4. Amy is carefree and fun-loving, with little interest in school.

    Janet, Amy's sister, is so studious and hard-working that she is always on the honour roll.

    Your combined sentence: _____

    _____

    _____

5. The apartment had almost no furniture, was badly in need of painting, and felt chilly even though I was wearing a coat.

    The other apartment was attractively furnished, had been freshly painted, and was warm enough so that I had to take off my coat.

    Your combined sentence: _____

    _____

    _____

EXERCISE 2   Using Transitions in Comparisons and Contrasts

First, identify each of the following examples as comparison or contrast. Then combine the two sentences by using a transition from the list on page 367. Finally, write your new sentence on the lines provided.

1. MuchMusic plays videos that are popular with a yonger, hipper audience.

   MuchMoreMusic plays videos that people over the age of thirty enjoy.

   Your combined sentence: _____

   _____

   _____

2. Shakespeare's *Romeo and Juliet* is a famous love story that takes place in Italy.

   West Side Story is a modern-day version of Shakespeare's love story that takes place in New York City.

   Your combined sentence: _____

   _____

   _____

3. The French Revolution was directed by the common people.

   The Russian Revolution was directed by an elite group of thinkers.

   Your combined sentence: _____

   _____

   _____

4. Some scientists believe that dinosaurs became extinct because they ran out of food.

   Some scientists think that dinosaurs were victims of radiation from a meteor from outer space.

   Your combined sentence: _____

   _____

   _____

5. The Museum of Modern Art in New York City shows paintings, photographs, movies, and many other forms of twentieth-century art.

   The Metropolitan Museum of Art in New York City contains sculptures, paintings, and other forms of art that date from the beginning of recorded history.

   Your combined sentence: _____

   _____

   _____

EXERCISE 3   Using Transitions in Comparisons and Contrasts

First, identify each of the following examples as comparison or contrast. Then combine the two sentences by using a transition from the list on page 367. Finally, write your new sentence on the lines provided.

1. A ballet dancer trains for years in order to master all aspects of dancing.

   A football player puts in years of practice in order to learn the game from every angle.

   Your combined sentence: _____

   _____

   _____

2. George Brown College is a large urban college that has the resources of a big city as part of its attraction for faculty and students.

   Malaspina College is a small college that has beautiful surroundings as part of its attraction.

   Your combined sentence: _____

   _____

   _____

3. Ice cream, a popular dessert for many years, has many calories and added chemicals to give it more flavour.

   Tofuti is a dessert made of processed soybeans that is low in calories and contains no harmful additives.

   Your combined sentence: _____

   _____

   _____

4. Ted Rogers gave much of his time and money for education and the arts.

   Ed Mirvish supported the arts by building theatres in Toronto.

   Your combined sentence: _____

   _____

   _____

5. *The Nature of Love and Unidentified Human Remains* is a play that has a single setting for all of its action.

   Love and Human Remains, a film based on the play, is a movie that is able to use many different settings to present all of its action.

   Your combined sentence: _____

   _____

   _____

Writing the comparison or contrast paragraph step by step

To learn a skill that has so many different demands, the best approach is to work step by step so that one aspect can be worked on at a time. This will ensure that you are not missing a crucial point or misunderstanding a part of the whole. There certainly are other ways to go about writing an effective paragraph, but here is one logical method you can use to achieve results.

> **STEPS FOR WRITING THE COMPARISON OR CONTRAST PARAGRAPH**
>
> 1. After you have chosen your two-part topic, plan your topic sentence.
>
> 2. List all your ideas for points that could be compared or contrasted.
>
> 3. Then choose the three or four most important points from your list.
>
> 4. Decide whether you want to use the point-by-point method or the block method of organizing your paragraph.
>
> 5. Write at least one complete sentence for each of the points you have chosen from your list.
>
> 6. Write a concluding statement that summarizes the main points, makes a judgment, or emphasizes what you believe is the most important point.
>
> 7. Finally, copy your sentences into standard paragraph form.

EXERCISE 1   Writing the Comparison or Contrast Paragraph Step by Step

This exercise will guide you through the construction of a comparison or contrast paragraph. Start with the suggested topic. Use the seven steps to help you work through each stage of the writing process.

> **Topic:** Compare or contrast how you spend your leisure time with how your parents or friends spend leisure time.

1. Topic sentence: _____

   _____

2. Make a list of possible comparisons or contrasts.

   a. _____

   b. _____

   c. _____

   d. _____

   e. _____

   f. _____

   g. _____

   h. _____

   i. _____

   j. _____

3. Circle the three or four comparisons or contrasts that you believe are most important and put them in order.

4. Choose either the point-by-point method or the block method.

5. Using your final list, write at least one sentence for each comparison or contrast you have chosen.

    a. _____
    _____

    b. _____
    _____

    c. _____
    _____

    d. _____
    _____

    e. _____
    _____

    f. _____
    _____

    g. _____
    _____

6. Write a concluding statement. _____
    _____
    _____

7. On a separate piece of paper, copy your sentences into standard paragraph form.

EXERCISE 2   Writing the Comparison or Contrast Paragraph Step by Step

This exercise will guide you through the construction of a comparison or contrast paragraph. Start with the suggested topic. Use the seven steps to help you work through each stage of the writing process.

Topic: Compare or contrast going to work with going on to college or university immediately after high school.

1. Topic sentence: _____
    _____

2. Make a list of possible comparisons or contrasts.

    a. _____
    b. _____
    c. _____

     d. _____

     e. _____

     f. _____

     g. _____

     h. _____

     i. _____

     j. _____

3. Circle the three or four comparisons or contrasts that you believe are most important and put them in order.

4. Choose either the point-by-point method or the block method.

5. Using your final list, write at least one sentence for each comparison or contrast you have chosen.

     a. _____

       _____

     b. _____

       _____

     c. _____

       _____

     d. _____

       _____

     e. _____

       _____

     f. _____

       _____

     g. _____

       _____

6. Write a concluding statement. _____

   _____

   _____

7. On a separate piece of paper, copy your sentences into standard paragraph form.

EXERCISE 3 Writing the Comparison or Contrast Paragraph Step by Step

This exercise will guide you through the construction of a comparison or contrast paragraph. Start with the suggested topic. Use the seven steps to help you work through each stage of the writing process.

    Topic: Compare or contrast the styles of two television personalities (or two public figures often in the news).

1. Topic sentence: _____

_____

2. Make a list of possible comparisons or contrasts.

   a. _____
   b. _____
   c. _____
   d. _____
   e. _____
   f. _____
   g. _____
   h. _____
   i. _____
   j. _____

3. Circle the three or four comparisons or contrasts that you believe are most important and put them in order.

4. Choose either the point-by-point method or the block method.

5. Using your final list, write at least one sentence for each comparison or contrast you have chosen.

   a. _____
   _____
   b. _____
   _____
   c. _____
   _____
   d. _____
   _____
   e. _____
   _____
   f. _____
   _____
   g. _____
   _____

6. Write a concluding statement. _____

_____

_____

_____

7. On a separate piece of paper, copy your sentences into standard paragraph form.

On your own: Writing comparison or contrast paragraphs

Contrasting two different perceptions toward a topic

Assignment 1　Write a paragraph in which you contrast two perceptions toward a topic. The following paragraph contrasts the Disney film depiction of the Pocahontas story with what we know to be more historically correct about the real Pocahontas.

> **MODEL PARAGRAPH**
>
> The Disney version of the Pocahontas story is not an accurate portrayal of what we know to be true. A seventeenth-century portrait of Pocahontas reveals her to be buxom, full-faced, and strong, not the Barbie-like glamour girl of Disney. John Smith, too, is portrayed inaccurately in the film. Far from the young blond heroic figure shown in the movie, John Smith was in actuality a bearded and weathered-looking man of thirty when he met Pocahontas. The dramatic version of romance and rescue is another historical inaccuracy of the Disney film. Most historians contend that the supposed "rescue" of John Smith was in fact a farce. The Powhatans, historians claim, may have been adopting Smith into their tribe through a ritual that required a little play acting. So, while Pocahontas may have rescued Smith, the circumstances of that rescue may have been very different from the film's depiction. Furthermore, there is no historical evidence to support romance between Pocahontas and John Smith as the movie shows. The unfortunate reality was that Pocahontas was taken captive by the English and forced to marry an English tobacco planter named John Rolfe. The ending of the film is certainly the final blow to what we know to be fact. Pocahontas did not, as Disney suggests, stay in North America while John Smith sailed into the distance toward his native England. Instead, she travelled to England with Rolfe, her new husband. On the return trip to her native North America, at the young age of twenty-two, Pocahontas fell ill, probably with smallpox, and died.

Ten suggested topics　Compare or contrast two perceptions you have had of the same topic. Choose from one of the topics suggested below or a topic you think of yourself.

1. A sports figure's public image, versus his or her private personality

2. A politician's promises before an election with those after an election

3. A "friend" before you win the lottery and after

4. Attitudes toward smoking twenty years ago contrasted with attitudes today

5. A person's reputation in the past with his or her reputation today

6. An actor or musician on television or stage with the same actor offstage

7. Baseball years ago and baseball now

8. Attitudes toward AIDS when the virus was first discovered contrasted with attitudes toward the disease today

9. Traditional portrayal of Native Americans (in old films, for example) with portrayals today

10. How a member of your family acts at home, contrasted with how that same person acts in public

Comparing two cultures

Assignment 2   Write a paragraph in which you compare two cultures, or an aspect of culture that may be observed in two societies. The following paragraph was written by Brenda David, an American teacher who worked with schoolchildren in Milan, Italy, for several years.

> ## MODEL PARAGRAPH
>
> All young children, whatever their culture, are alike in their charm and innocence—in being a clean slate on which the wonders and ways of the world are yet to be written. But during the three years I worked in a school in Milan, I learned that American and Italian children are different in several ways. First, young American children tend to be active, enthusiastic, and inquisitive. Italian children, on the other hand, tend to be passive, quiet, and not particularly inquisitive. They usually depend on their parents to tell them what to do. Second, American children show their independence while their Italian counterparts are still looking to their parents and grandparents to tell them what to do or not do. Third, and most important to those who question the influence of environment on a child, the American children generally surpass their Italian schoolmates in math, mechanical, and scientific abilities. But American children are overshadowed by their Italian counterparts in their language, literature, art, and music courses. Perhaps the differences, which those of us at the school confirmed in an informal study, were to be expected. After all, what priority do Americans give to the technological skills? And what value do Italians—with the literature of poets and authors like Boccaccio, the works of Michelangelo, and the music of the world-famous LaScala opera at Milan—place on the cultural arts?

Ten suggested topics   Compare or contrast:

1. Mexican cooking with Chinese cooking

2. Marriage customs in Africa and in Canada

3. Attitudes toward women's roles in Saudi Arabia and in Canada

4. Folk dancing in two countries

5. Raising children in China and raising them in Canada

6. Urban people with small-town people

7. The reputation of a place with the reality of the place as you found it

8. The culture of your neighbourhood with the general culture of our society

9. The culture you live in now with the culture in which your parents were raised

10. Medical care in our society with the medical care of another society

Comparing a place then and now

Assignment 3   Write a paragraph in which you compare the appearance of a place you knew when you were growing up with the appearance of that same place now. The following paragraph compares a small city as it was some years ago and how it appeared to the writer on a recent visit.

MODEL PARAGRAPH

As I drove up Swede Hill, I realized that the picture I had in my mind all these years was largely a romantic one. It was here that my father had boarded, as a young man of eighteen, with a widow who rented rooms in her house. Now the large old wooden frame houses were mostly two-family homes; no single family could afford to heat them in the winter. The porches which had once been beautiful and where people had passed their summer evenings had peeling paint and were in poor condition. No one now stopped to talk; the only sounds to be heard were those of cars whizzing past. The immigrants who had come to this country and worked hard to put their children through school were now elderly and mostly alone, since their educated children could find no jobs in the small city. From the top of the hill I looked down fondly upon the town built on the hills and noticed that a new and wider highway now went through the town. My father would have liked that; he would not have had to complain about Sunday drives on Foote Avenue. In the distance I could see the large shopping mall which now had most of the business in the surrounding area and which had forced several local businesses to close. Now the centre of town no longer hummed with activity, as it once had. My town was not the same place I had known, and I could see that changes were taking place that would eventually transform the entire area.

Ten suggested topics   Compare or contrast a place as it appears now with how it appeared some years ago:

1. A barber shop or beauty salon
2. A house of worship
3. A local "corner store"
4. A friend's home
5. Your elementary school
6. A local bank
7. A downtown shopping area
8. A restaurant or diner
9. An undeveloped place such as an open field or wooded area
10. A favourite local gathering place

Comparing male attitudes and female attitudes

Assignment 4   Some observers believe that males share similar attitudes toward certain subjects, while females seem to have a similar way of thinking on certain other topics. Some observers believe that such conclusions are nothing more than stereotypes and that people should not be divided in this way. The following paragraph reports that recent studies indicate a possible biological basis for some of the differences between males and females.

MODEL PARAGRAPH

Recent scientific research has shown that differences in behaviour between males and females may have their origins in biological differences in the brain. Shortly after birth, females are more sensitive than males to certain types of sounds, and by the age of five months a female baby can recognize photographs of familiar people, while a boy of that age can rarely accomplish this. Researchers also found that girls tend to speak sooner than boys, read sooner than they do, and learn foreign languages more easily than boys do. On the other hand, boys show an early visual superiority over girls and they are better than girls at working with three-dimensional space. When preschool girls and boys are asked to mentally work with an object, the girls are not as successful as the boys. In this case, as in several others, the girls are likely to give verbal descriptions while the boys are able to do the actual work in their minds.

Ten suggested topics   In a paragraph, compare or contrast what you believe are male and female attitudes on one of the following topics:

1. Cooking

2. Sports

3. The nursing profession

4. Child care

5. The construction trade

6. Military careers

7. A career in science

8. Hobbies

9. Friendship

10. Clothing

Working Together

1. Below is a typical advertisement from a 1943 *Good Housekeeping* magazine. Read it carefully and then discuss it with your class. How many aspects of this advertisement seem out of date by modern standards? In how many ways would a modern day advertisement for a similar product be different?

2. The 1943 advertisement is followed by a modern ad for a dishwashing detergent. Write a paragraph in which you contrast the two advertisements. Before you begin to write, be sure to list all of the differences you can observe.

Developing Paragraphs: Cause and Effect

What is cause and effect?

People have always looked at the world and asked the questions, "Why did this happen?" or "What will be the result?" Ancient societies created beautiful myths and legends to explain the origin of the universe and our place in it, while modern civilization has emphasized scientific methods of observation to find the cause of a disease or to determine why the planet Mars appears to be covered by canals. When we examine the spiritual or physical mysteries of our world, we are trying to discover the connections or links between events. In this chapter, we will refer to connections between events as *causal relationships.*

Causal relationships are part of our daily lives and provide a way of understanding the cause, result, or consequence of a particular event. The search for cause or effect is a bit like detective work. Probing an event is a way of searching for clues to discover what caused an event or what result it will have in the future.

For example, we might ask the question, "Why did the car break down just after it came back from the garage?" as a way of searching for the cause of the car's new problem. Or we might ask, "What will be the side effects of taking a certain medicine?" This search for connections can be complex. Often the logical analysis of a problem reveals more than one possible explanation. Sometimes the best one can do is find possible causes or probable effects. In the exercises that follow, you will be asked to search for causes, effects, and connections that are causal relationships.

• PRACTICE

Become familiar with the causal relationship by thinking through a few typical situations signalled by the following expressions:

1. If . . . . then

   If you _____, **then** you will _____

   _____ .

2. The cause or reason . . . . the result, consequence, or effect

   Because I _____ , the **result** was that I _____

   _____ .

3. The problem . . . . the solution

   _____ could be **solved** by _____ .

EXERCISE 1   Finding Causes and Effects in Paragraphs

Below are two paragraphs about the same topic: headaches. One paragraph considers causes and the other looks at some of the effects recurring headaches have on people's lives. In each case, list the causal relationships suggested in the paragraph.

1. CAUSE: Explaining WHY

> Headaches can have several causes. Many people think that the major cause of headache is nervous tension, but there is strong evidence that suggests diet and environment as possible factors. Some people get headaches because they are dependent on caffeine. Other people may be allergic to salt, or they may have low blood sugar. Still other people are allergic to household chemicals including polishes, waxes, bug killers, and paint. If they can manage to avoid these substances, their headaches tend to go away. When a person has recurring headaches, it is worthwhile to look for the underlying cause, especially if the result of that search is freedom from pain.

What causes a headache?

1. _____

2. _____

    a. _____

    b. _____

    c. _____

3. _____

    a. _____

    b. _____

    c. _____

    d. _____

2. EFFECT: Understanding or predicting RESULTS, CONSEQUENCES, EFFECTS, SOLUTIONS

> Recurring headaches can have several disruptive effects on a person's life. Severe headaches are more than temporary inconveniences. In many cases, these headaches make a person nauseous to the point that he or she must go to bed. Sleep is often interrupted because of the pain. This worsens the physical and emotional state of the sufferer. For those who try to maintain a normal lifestyle, drugs are often relied on to get through the day. Such drugs, of course, can have other negative side effects. Productivity on a job can certainly be reduced, even to the point of regular absences. Finally, perhaps the most distressing aspect of all this is the seemingly unpredictable occurrence of these headaches. The interruption to a person's family life is enormous: cancelling plans in the last minute and straining relationships with friends and family. It is no wonder that many of these people feel discouraged and even depressed.

What are some of the effects of headaches?

1. _____
2. _____
3. _____
4. _____
5. _____
6. _____
7. _____

EXERCISE 2 Separating the Cause from the Effect

In each sentence, separate the cause, problem, or reason from the effect, solution, or result. Remember the cause is not necessarily given first.

1. More than half of the mothers with children under one year of age work outside the home, which has resulted in the unprecedented need for daycare in this country.

   cause _____

   _____

   effect _____

2. In 2000, two-thirds of all preschool children had mothers who worked, and four out of five school-age children had working mothers, facts that led to increased strains on the daycare system.

   cause _____

   _____

   effect _____

3. In one national survey, over half the working mothers reported that they had either changed jobs or cut back on their hours in order to be more available to their children.

   problem _____

   solution _____

4. Many mothers who work do so only when their children are in school, while other mothers work only occasionally during the school year because they feel their children need the supervision of a parent.

   cause _____

   effect _____

   _____

5. Many mothers experience deep emotional crises as a result of their need to combine the financial obligations of their home with their own emotional needs as parents.

   problem _____

   result _____

Working with cause and effect: Recognizing relationships and connections between events

Here is an example of a possible error in logic:

> Every time I try to write an essay in the evening, I have trouble getting to sleep. Therefore, writing must prevent me from sleeping.

In this case, writing may indeed be a stimulant that prevents the person from sleeping. However, if the person is serious about finding the cause of insomnia, he or she must observe whether any other *factors* may be to blame. For instance, if the person is drinking several cups of coffee while writing each evening, this could be a more likely cause of why the person is not sleeping.

EXERCISE 1   Looking for the Causal Relationship

Study each of the following situations. In each case, if the sequence of events is merely coincidental or chronological, put a "T" for "time" in the space provided. If the relationship is most likely causal, put a "C." Be able to explain your answers in class.

_____   1. Every time I carry my umbrella, it doesn't rain. I am carrying my umbrella today; therefore, it won't rain.

_____   2. We put the fertilizer on the grass. A week later the grass grew two inches and turned a deeper green.

_____   3. On Tuesday morning, I walked under a ladder. On Wednesday morning, I walked into my office and was told I had lost my job.

_____   4. The child grew up helping her mother cook. In adulthood, she became a famous chef.

_____   5. Tar and nicotine from cigarettes damage the lungs. People who smoke cigarettes increase their chances of dying from lung cancer.

_____   6. A political scandal was exposed in the city on Friday. On Saturday night, only twenty-four hours later, a power blackout occurred in the city.

_____   7. Increasing numbers of tourists came to the island last year. The economy of the island reached new heights.

_____   8. Many natural disasters have occurred this year. The world must be coming to an end.

_____   9. The factory in a certain town decided to relocate to another country. The town officials invited different industries to consider moving to the town.

_____   10. A woman sings beautifully. She must have an equally beautiful personality.

EXERCISE 2   Underlying Causes

Below are five topics. For each topic, give a possible immediate or direct cause and then give a possible underlying cause. Discuss your answers in class. An example has been done for you.

Causes for a Disease

Immediate or direct cause: contact with a carrier of the disease

Underlying cause: weakened immune system due to poor nutrition

1. Causes for being selected out of several candidates for a position

   Immediate cause _____

   Underlying cause _____

2. Causes for immigrants coming to Canada

   Immediate cause _____

   Underlying cause _____

3. Causes for spanking a child

   Immediate cause _____

   Underlying cause _____

4. Causes for an unreasonable fear you have

   Immediate cause _____

   Underlying cause _____

5. Causes for a bad habit you have

   Immediate cause _____

   Underlying cause _____

EXERCISE 3   Immediate or Long-Term Effects

Below are five topics. For each topic give an immediate effect and then give a possible long-term effect. Discuss your answers in class. An example has been done for you.

Possible Effects of Using Credit Cards

Immediate effect: money available on the spot for purchases

Long-term effect: greater cost due to interest payments

1. Effects of horror movies on young children

   Immediate effect _____

   Long-term effect _____

2. Effects of tuition increases in community colleges

   Immediate effect _____

   Long-term effect _____

3. Effects of increased spot checks on people's driving habits

   Immediate effect _____

   Long-term effect _____

4. Effects of a microwave oven on how a family lives

   Immediate effect _____

   Long-term effect _____

5. Effects of having a family member with special needs

   Immediate effect _____

   Long-term effect _____

Working for coherence: Using transitions

Several transitions and expressions are particularly useful when writing about causes or effects. You will need to feel comfortable using these words and expressions, and you will need to know what punctuation is required.

COMMON TRANSITIONS

common transitions for *cause*:

  because

  caused by

  results from

  the reason is that . . . + a complete sentence

  since

common transitions for *effect*:

  accordingly

  as a result, resulted in

  consequently

  for this reason

  so, so that

  then, therefore, thus

EXERCISE 1   Using Transitional Words and Expressions of Cause

Use each of the following words or phrases in a sentence that demonstrates your understanding of its use for expressing **cause** relationships.

1. to be caused by

_____

_____

2. because (of)

_____

_____

3. resulted from

_____

_____

4. the reason is that + clause (subject and verb)

_____

_____

5. since

_____

_____

EXERCISE 2   Using Transitional Words and Expressions for Effect

Use each of the following words or phrases in a complete sentence to demonstrate your understanding of how the word or phrase is used to point to an effect.

1. accordingly

_____

_____

2. as a result

_____

_____

3. results in

_____

_____

4. consequently

_____

_____

5. for this reason

_____

_____

6. so

_____

_____

7. therefore

_____

_____

Writing the cause or effect paragraph step by step

To learn a skill that has so many different demands, the best approach is to work step by step so that one aspect can be worked on at a time. This will ensure that you are not missing a crucial point or misunderstanding a part of the whole. There certainly are other ways to go about writing an effective paragraph, but here is one logical method you can use to achieve results.

STEPS FOR WRITING THE CAUSE OR EFFECT PARAGRAPH

1. After you have chosen your topic, plan your topic sentence.

2. Brainstorm by jotting down all possible causes or effects. Ask others for their thoughts. Do research if necessary. Consider long-range effects or underlying causes.

3. Then choose the three or four best points from your list.

4. Decide on the best order for these points. (One way to organize them is from least important to most important.)

5. Write at least one complete sentence for each of the causes or effects you have chosen from your list.

6. Write a concluding statement.

7. On a separate piece of paper or at the computer, copy your sentences into standard paragraph form.

EXERCISE 1   Writing the Cause Paragraph Step by Step

This exercise will guide you through the cause paragraph. Start with the suggested topic. Use the seven steps to help you work through each stage.

> **Topic:** Why do so many Canadians enroll their children in French immersion classes?

1. Topic sentence: _____

_____

2. Make a list of possible causes. (Consider underlying causes.)

   a. _____

   b. _____

   c. _____

   d. _____

   e. _____

3. Cross out any points that may be illogical or merely coincidental.

4. Put your list in order.

5. Using your final list, write at least one sentence for each of the causes you have found.

   a. _____

   _____

   b. _____

   _____

   c. _____

   _____

   d. _____

   _____

6. Write a concluding statement. _____

   _____

   _____

   _____

   _____

   _____

   _____

7. On a separate piece of paper, copy your sentences into standard paragraph form.

EXERCISE 2   Writing the Effect Paragraph Step-by-Step

This exercise will guide you through the effect paragraph. Start with the suggested topic. Use the seven steps to help you work through each stage.

   Topic: What are the effects of teenagers having part-time jobs after school?

1. Topic sentence: _____

   _____

2. Make a list of possible effects. (Consider long-range effects.)

   a. _____

   b. _____

   c. _____

   d. _____

   e. _____

3. Cross out any points that may be illogical, merely coincidental, or the result of only time sequence.

4. Put your list in order.

5. Using your final list, write at least one sentence for each of the effects you have found.

a. _____

_____

b. _____

_____

c. _____

_____

d. _____

_____

6. Write a concluding statement. _____

_____

_____

_____

7. On a separate piece of paper, copy your sentences into standard paragraph form.

On your own: Writing cause and effect paragraphs from model paragraphs

The causes of a social problem

Assignment 1   Write a paragraph about the causes of a social problem that is of concern to you. The following paragraph looks at possible causes for placing an elderly relative in a nursing home.

MODEL PARAGRAPH

   Industrialized societies have developed homes for the elderly who are unable to care for themselves. In spite of much criticism, these homes have a growing percentage of our nation's elderly. Why do some people feel forced into placing parents into a nursing home? The most immediate cause is that following some serious illness, there is often no place for the elderly person to go where he or she can be cared for. In the family of today, it is often the case that both partners work outside the home so no one is home during the day to care for the person. Hiring a nurse to be in the home every day is beyond the budget of nearly every family. Even when a family member can be home to care for the elderly person, the problems can be overwhelming. The older person can be too heavy for one or even two to manage. Bathing, particularly, can be dangerous in these circumstances. In addition, many elderly people have to be watched very carefully because of their medical condition. Many families do not have the proper training to meet these needs. Finally, elderly people who may be senile and difficult can often intrude on a family's life to the point that a caregiver may never be able to leave the house or get a proper night's rest. Perhaps a better system of visiting nursing care could help some families keep their loved ones in their homes longer.

Ten suggested topics

1. The causes of homelessness

2. The causes of prostitution

3. The causes of teenage runaways

4. The causes of high school dropouts

5. The causes of divorce

6. The causes of child abuse

7. The causes of tax cheating

8. The causes of high stress among college students

9. The causes of long life

10. The causes of the increase in childless couples

The causes that led to a particular historical event

Assignment 2

Write a paragraph about the causes that led to a particular event in history. The following model paragraph describes the causes that led to the French Revolution.

MODEL PARAGRAPH

Several reasons can account for the outbreak of the French Revolution in eighteenth-century France. First was people's widespread feeling of resentment against the nobility and the clergy, groups that paid almost no taxes. The nobility held all the highest posts in the government, and the clergy had the right to impose new taxes on the people, facts that added to the people's resentment. In addition, the upper classes used lawyers to rediscover old laws that led to even more oppression of the lower classes. Secondly, people from the middle class who had been successful in business found themselves cut off from higher positions by the nobles, who wanted to restrict the number of people in the upper class. Thirdly, the rising economic situation at the end of the eighteenth century led to even more discontent as clergy and nobles, unable by law to enter commerce or industry, increased their pressure for tax money on the lower classes. Finally, the most immediate cause of the revolution was the French government's growing financial crisis, beginning in 1789. Because France had helped the American colonies in their struggle against England during the American Revolution, the French government could not balance its budget. The combination of social and economic injustice, along with the inability of the French upper classes to change, eventually led to the explosive situation known to history as the French Revolution.

Ten suggested topics

1. Causes for the growing disenchantment with the British royal family

2. Causes of the Quiet Revolution in the 1960s in Quebec

3. Causes for the Gulf War in 1991

4. Causes for Canadian Confederation in 1867

5. Causes for the victory (or loss) of a particular political candidate in a recent election

6. Causes for the increase in white-collar crime

7. Causes for the growth of the feminist movement starting in the 1970s

8. Causes for the Great Depression of the 1930s

9. Causes for the rise of neo-Nazism in Germany in 1992

10. Causes for the loss of many jobs in the early 1990s in the United States

The effects of a substance or activity on the human body

Assignment 3   Write a paragraph about what happens to the human body when it uses a substance or engages in some activity. The following model paragraph is from Norman Taylor's *Plant Drugs That Changed the World*.

MODEL PARAGRAPH

The ordinary cup of coffee, of the usual breakfast strength, contains about one and a half grains of caffeine (100 mg). That "second cup of coffee" hence means just about three grains of caffeine at one sitting. Its effects upon the nervous system, the increased capacity for thinking, its stimulating effects on circulation and muscular activity, not to speak of its sparking greater fluency—these are attributes of the beverage that few will give up. If it has any dangers, most of us are inclined to ignore them. But there is no doubt that excessive intake of caffeine at one time, say up to seven or eight grains (i.e., 5 or 6 cups), has harmful effects such as restlessness, nervous irritability, insomnia, and muscular tremor. The lethal dose in man is unknown, for there are no records of it. Experimental animals die in convulsions after overdoses, and from such studies it is assumed that a fatal dose of caffeine in man may be about 150 grains (i.e., one-half ounce). That would mean about one hundred cups of coffee!

Ten suggested topics
1. The effects of alcohol on the body
2. The effects of regular exercise
3. The effects of overeating
4. The effects of a strict diet
5. The effects of fasting
6. The effects of drug abuse
7. The effects of sunburn
8. The effects of allergies
9. The effects of a sedentary lifestyle
10. The effects of vitamins

Working Together

Read the following analysis of the causes for the decline of Central America's Mayan culture. The entire class should listen as the excerpt is read out loud and then the class should divide into groups. Each group will list the immediate and the underlying causes for the decline of Mayan civilization. One person from each group will then read the group's complete list of immediate and underlying causes. After a complete listing is agreed upon, make a judgment on how positive scientists are about the underlying causes of this historic event.

In the last few years scholars have made great strides in translating the Mayas' previously indecipherable writing system. From the emerging texts and from recent excavations has emerged a new, at times bewildering, picture of the Maya civilization at its peak, from A.D. 250 to 900. Great as their cultural and economic achievements manifestly were, they had anything but a peaceful society.

Indeed, the latest feeling among scholars is that the increasing militarism of Maya society may have undermined the ecological underpinnings of the economy. Some of them speculate that siege warfare concentrated population in urban centres, caused desperate farmers to abandon previously successful practices of diversified agriculture, and led to overexploitation of the forest.

Dr. Arthur A. Demarest, an archeologist at Vanderbilt University here who directs an ambitious Maya dig in Guatemala, said the evidence from stone art and texts points to the surprising conclusion that "the Maya were one of the most violent state-level societies in the New World, especially after A.D. 600."

Various writings and artifacts, Dr. Demarest said, indicate continual raiding and warfare between the elites of adjacent city-states and also the practice of ritual bloodletting and human sacrifice. The prestige of ruling dynasties, and hence their power, seemed to depend on their success in battle and the sacrifice of prisoners of war.

Dr. Linda Schele, a Maya scholar at the University of Texas at Austin, writes in this month's issue of *Natural History* magazine, "We don't know if the early Maya went to war mainly to acquire territory, take booty, control conquered groups for labour, take captives for sacrifice in sanctification rituals or a combination of these."

Whatever the specific goal, archeologists think that for centuries the wars were limited to ritualized conflicts between the elite troops of two rulers. The losing ruler was sometimes decapitated with great ceremony, as depicted in Maya art.

Developing Paragraphs: Definition and Classification

What is definition?

> You define a term in order to explain its meaning or significance. The starting point for a good definition is to group the word into a larger *category* or *class.*

For example, the trout is a kind of fish; a doll is a kind of toy; a shirt is an article of clothing. Here is a dictionary entry for the word *family.*

> **family** (fam´e -le, fam´le) *n., pl.* **-lies.** *Abbr.* **fam.** 1. The most instinctive, fundamental social or mating group in man and animal, especially the union of man and woman through marriage and their offspring; parents and their children. 2. One's spouse and children. 3. Persons related by blood or marriage; relatives; kinfolk. 4. Lineage; especially, upper-class lineage. 5. All the members of a household; those who share one's domestic home.

To what larger category does the word *family* belong? The family, according to this entry, is a kind of *social group.*

> Once the word has been put into a larger class, the reader is ready to understand the *identifying characteristics* that make it different from other members in the class.

What makes a *trout* different from a *bass,* a *doll* different from a *puppet,* a *shirt* different from a *sweater*? Here a definition can give examples. The dictionary definition of *family* identifies the family as a married man and woman and their children. Four additional meanings provide a suggestion of some variations.

When you write a paragraph or an essay that uses definition, the dictionary entry is only the beginning. In order for your reader to understand a difficult term or idea, you will need to expand this definition into what is called *extended definition.* It is not the function of a dictionary to go into great depth. It can only provide the basic meanings and synonyms.

> Extended definition, however, seeks to analyze a concept so that the reader will have a more complete understanding.

For instance, you might include a historical perspective. When or how did the concept begin? How did the term change or evolve over the years, or how do different cultures understand the term? You will become involved in the word's connotations. **Extended definition,** or **analysis** as it is sometimes called, uses more than one method to arrive at an understanding of a term.

The following paragraph, taken from *Sociology: An Introduction* by John E. Conklin, is the beginning of a chapter on the family. The author's starting point is very similar to the dictionary entry.

> In every society, social norms define a variety of relationships among people, and some of these relationships are socially recognized as family or kinship ties. A family is a socially defined set of relationships between at least two people who are related by birth, marriage, or adoption. We can think of a family as including several possible relationships, the most common being between husband and wife, between parents and children, and between people who are related to each other by birth (siblings, for example) or by marriage (a woman and her mother-in-law, perhaps). Family relationships are often defined by custom, such as the relationship between an infant and godparents, or by law, such as the adoption of a child.

The author began this definition by putting the term into a larger class. *Family* is one type of social relationship among people. The writer then identifies the people who are members of this group. Family relationships can be formed by marriage, birth, adoption, or custom, as with godparents. The author does not stop here. The extended definition explores the functions of the family, conflicts in the family, the structure of the family, and the special characteristics of the family.

The writer could also have defined *family* by **negation.** That is, he could have described what a family is *not:*

A family is not a corporation.
A family is not a formal school.
A family is not a church.

When a writer defines a concept using negation, the definition should be completed by stating what the subject is:

A family is not a corporation, but it is an economic unit of production and consumption.
A family is not a formal school, but it is a major centre for learning.
A family is not a church, but it is where children learn their moral values.

EXERCISE 1   Working with Definition: Class

Define each of the following terms by placing it in a larger class. Keep in mind that when you define something by class, you are placing it in a larger category so that the reader can see where it belongs. Use the dictionary if you need help. An example has been done for you.

Chemistry is *one of the branches of science* that deals with a close study of the natural world.

1. Mythology is _____

2. Nylon is _____

3. An amoeba is _____

4. A tricycle is _____

5. Cabbage is _____

6. Democracy is _____

7. Asbestos is _____

8. A piccolo is _____

9. Poetry is _____

10. A university is _____

EXERCISE 2   Working with Definition: Distinguishing Characteristics

Using the same terms as in Exercise 1, give one or two identifying characteristics that differentiate your term from other terms in the same class. An example is done for you.

Chemistry studies the structure, properties, and reactions of matter.

1. Mythology _____

_____

_____

2. Nylon _____

_____

_____

3. An amoeba _____

_____

_____

4. A tricycle _____

_____

_____

5. Cabbage _____

_____

_____

6. Democracy _____

_____

_____

7. Asbestos _____

_____

_____

8. A piccolo _____

_____

_____

9. Poetry _____

_____

_____

10. A university _____

_____

_____

EXERCISE 3   Working with Definition: Example

Help define each of the following terms by providing one example. Examples always make writing more alive. An example has been done for you.

Term: Chemistry

Example: Chemistry studies an element like hydrogen. This element is the simplest in structure of all the elements, with only one electron and proton; it is colourless, highly flammable, the lightest of all gases, and the most abundant element in the universe.

1. Mythology

_____

_____

_____

2. Friendship

_____

_____

_____

3. Philanthropist

_____

_____

_____

4. Planet

_____

_____

_____

5. Gland

_____

_____

_____

6. Greed

_____

_____

_____

7. Volcano

_____

_____

_____

8. Patriotism

_____

_____

_____

9. Terrorism

_____

_____

_____

10. Equality

_____

_____

_____

EXERCISE 4   Working with Definition: Negation

Define each of the following terms by using negation to construct your definition. Keep in mind that such a definition is not complete until you have also included what the topic is that you are defining.

1. A *disability* is not _____

   but it is _____

2. The *perfect car* is not _____

   but it is _____

3. *Drugs* are not _____

   but they are _____

4. *Freedom* is not _____

   but it is _____

5. A *good job* is not _____

   but it is _____

6. *Exercise* is not _____

   but it is _____

7. A *university* is not _____

   but it is _____

8. A *politician* is not _____

   but he or she is _____

9. The *ideal pet* is not _____

   but it is _____

10. A *boring person* is not _____

    but he or she is _____

On your own: Writing a paragraph using definition

Defining a term

Write a paragraph in which you define a term. Use one or more of the techniques you have studied—*class, identifying characteristics, example,* and *negation*—as well as any further analysis, historical or cultural, that will help the reader. The following paragraph by Susan Sontag defines AIDS by starting with a negation.

MODEL PARAGRAPH

Strictly speaking, AIDS—acquired immune deficiency syndrome—is not the name of an illness at all. It is the name of a medical condition, whose consequences are a spectrum of illnesses. In contrast to syphilis and cancer, which provide prototypes for most of the images and metaphors attached to AIDS, the very definition of AIDS requires the presence of other illnesses, so-called opportunistic infections and malignancies. But though not in that sense a single disease, AIDS lends itself to being regarded as one—in part because, unlike cancer and like syphilis, it is thought to have a single cause.

Ten suggested topics

1. Photosynthesis

2. Ecology

3. Symphony

4. Football

5. Paranoia

6. Courage

7. Algebra

8. Democracy

9. Masculinity or femininity

10. Justice

What is classification?

> *Classification* is the placing of items into separate categories for the purpose of helping us to think about these items more clearly. This can be extremely useful and even necessary when large numbers of items are being considered.

In order to classify things properly, you must always take the items you are working with and put them into *distinct categories,* making sure that each item belongs in only one category. For example, if you wanted to classify automobiles into imported automobiles, Canadian-made automobiles, and used automobiles, this would not be an effective use of classification because an imported automobile or a Canadian-made automobile could also be a used automobile. When you classify, you want each item to belong in only one category.

A classification should also be *complete.* For example, if you were classifying motorcycles into the two categories of new and used, your classification would be complete because any item can only be new or used. Finally, a classification should be *useful.* If you are thinking of buying a motorcycle, or if a friend is thinking of buying one, then it might be very useful to classify them in this way because you or your friend might save a great deal of money by deciding to buy a used machine.

The following paragraph is taken from Judith Viorst's essay "Friends, Good Friends—and Such Good Friends" and shows the writer classifying different kinds of friends.

There are medium friends, and pretty good friends, and very good friends indeed, and these friendships are defined by their level of intimacy. And what we'll reveal at each of these levels of intimacy is calibrated with care. We might tell a medium friend, for example, that yesterday we had a fight with our husband. And we might tell a pretty good friend that this fight with our husband made us so mad that we slept on the couch. And we might tell a very good friend that the reason we got so mad in that fight that we slept on the couch had something to do with that girl who works in his office. But it's only to our very best friends that we're willing to tell all, to tell what's going on with that girl in his office.

In this paragraph, the writer gives us four distinct types of friends, beginning with "medium friends," going on to "pretty good friends" and "very good friends," and ending with "very best friends." Her classification is complete because it covers a full range of friendships, and of course it is useful because people are always interested in the types of friends they have.

EXERCISE 1 Working with Classification: Finding the Basis for a Classification

For each of the following topics, pick three different ways that topic could be classified. You may find the following example helpful.

Topic: Ways to choose a vacation spot

Basis for classification: By price (first class, medium price, economy), by its special attraction (the beach, the mountains, the desert, etc.), by the accommodations (hotel, motel, cabin, trailer)

1. Topic: Cars

   Ways to divide the topic: _____

   _____

2. Topic: Houses

   Ways to divide the topic: _____

   _____

3. Topic: Neighbourhoods

   Ways to divide the topic: _____

   _____

4. Topic: Religions

   Ways to divide the topic: _____

   _____

5. Topic: Soft drinks

   Ways to divide the topic: _____

   _____

6. Topic: Dating

   Ways to divide the topic: _____

   _____

7. Topic: Floor coverings

   Ways to divide the topic: _____

   _____

8. Topic: Medicines

   Ways to divide the topic: _____

   _____

9. Topic: Snack foods

   Ways to divide the topic: _____

   _____

10. Topic: Relatives

    Ways to divide the topic: _____

    _____

EXERCISE 2   Working with Classification: Making Distinct Categories

First pick a basis for classifying each of the following topics. Then break it down into distinct categories. Divide the topic into as many distinct categories as you think the classification requires.

Keep in mind that when you divide your topic, each part of your classification must belong to only one category. For example, if you were to classify cars, you would not want to make *sports cars* and *international cars* two of your categories because several kinds of sports cars are also international cars.

1. Clothing stores

   Distinct categories:

   _____   _____   _____

   _____   _____   _____

2. Television commercials

   Distinct categories:

   _____   _____   _____

   _____   _____   _____

3. Sports

   Distinct categories:

   _____   _____   _____

   _____   _____   _____

4. Doctors

   Distinct categories:

   _____   _____   _____

   _____   _____   _____

5. Hats

   Distinct categories:

   _____   _____   _____

   _____   _____   _____

6. Courses in the English department of your school

   Distinct categories:

   _____   _____   _____

   _____   _____   _____

7. Pens

   Distinct categories:

   _____   _____   _____

   _____   _____   _____

8. Dances

   Distinct categories:

   _____   _____   _____

   _____   _____   _____

9. Mail

   Distinct categories:

   _____   _____   _____

   _____   _____   _____

10. Music

Distinct categories:

_____   _____   _____

_____   _____   _____

On your own: Writing a paragraph using classification

Classifying material (placing items into distinct categories)

Write a paragraph classifying or grouping a number of items into distinct categories. Your choice of how to group these items might be based on a criterion such as size, quality, usefulness, or value. The following paragraph by Diane Ackerman uses colour as the criterion to group various trees as they appear in the autumn.

> ### MODEL PARAGRAPH
>
> Not all leaves turn the same colours. Elms, weeping willows, and the ancient ginkgo all grow radiant yellow, along with hickories, aspens, bottle-brush buckeyes, cottonweeds, and tall, keening poplars. Basswood turns bronze, birches bright gold. Water-loving maples put on a symphonic display of scarlets. Sumacs turn red, too, as do flowering dogwoods, black gums, and sweet gums. Though some oaks yellow, most turn a pinkish brown. The farmlands also change colour, as tepees of cornstalks and bales of shredded-wheat-textured hay stand drying in the fields. In some spots, one slope of a hill may be green and the other already in bright colour, because the hillside facing south gets more sun and heat than the northern one.

As you plan your paragraph, keep in mind the following points. Does the classification help to organize the material? Are you sure the classification is complete and that no item could belong to more than one category? Is there some purpose for your classifying the items as you did? (For example, will it help someone make a decision or understand a concept?)

Ten suggested topics

1. Parents
2. Governments
3. Dogs
4. Careers
5. Parties
6. Summer jobs
7. Movies
8. Classmates
9. Coworkers
10. Restaurants

Working Together

Brainstorming can be wonderfully helpful when several people put their heads together! Divide into groups and brainstorm on one of the topics given below. After the members of each group have thought of everything they can, come together as a class and put your classifications on the board. Compare and contrast them. What makes one grouping of categories more successful than another? Can you use each other's material?

Suggested topics for brainstorming:

1. Fads

   What is a "fad"? Classify as many different types of fads as you can.

   or

2. Friendship

   What is "friendship"? Classify as many different types of friendships as you can.

Your instructor may now ask each student to write his or her own paragraph using this material.

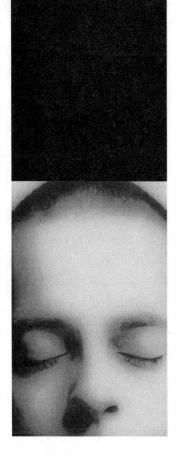

APPENDICES

CONTENTS

IRREGULAR VERBS

Alphabetical listing of principal parts of irregular verbs

Simple Form	Past Form	Past Participle
arise	arose	arisen
bear	bore	borne
beat	beat	beat or beaten
become	became	become
begin	began	begun
bend	bent	bent
bet	bet	bet
bind	bound	bound
bite	bit	bitten, bit
bleed	bled	bled
blow	blew	blown
break	broke	broken
breed	bred	bred
bring	brought	brought
build	built	built
burst	burst	burst
buy	bought	bought
cast	cast	cast
catch	caught	caught
choose	chose	chosen
cling	clung	clung
come	came	come
cost	cost	cost
creep	crept	crept
cut	cut	cut
deal	dealt	dealt
dig	dug	dug
dive	dived, dove	dived
do	did	done
draw	drew	drawn
drink	drank	drunk
drive	drove	driven
eat	ate	eaten
fall	fell	fallen

Simple Form	Past Form	Past Participle
feed	fed	fed
feel	felt	felt
fight	fought	fought
find	found	found
fit	fit	fit
flee	fled	fled
fling	flung	flung
fly	flew	flown
forbid	forbade, forbad	forbidden
forget	forgot	forgotten
forgive	forgave	forgiven
freeze	froze	frozen
get	got	gotten
give	gave	given
go	went	gone
grind	ground	ground
grow	grew	grown
hang	hung, hanged	hung, hanged
have	had	had
hear	heard	heard
hide	hid	hidden
hit	hit	hit
hold	held	held
hurt	hurt	hurt
keep	kept	kept
kneel	knelt	knelt
know	knew	known
lay (to put)	laid	laid
lead	led	led
leave	left	left
lend	lent	lent
let	let	let
lie (to recline)	lay	lain
lose	lost	lost
make	made	made
mean	meant	meant
meet	met	met
mistake	mistook	mistaken
pay	paid	paid
prove	proved	proved, proven
put	put	put
quit	quit	quit

Simple Form	Past Form	Past Participle
read	*read	*read
ride	rode	ridden
ring	rang	rung
rise	rose	risen
run	ran	run
say	said	said
see	saw	seen
seek	sought	sought
sell	sold	sold
send	sent	sent
set	set	set
sew	sewed	sewn, sewed
shake	shook	shaken
shave	shaved	shaved, shaven
shed	shed	shed
shine	shone	shone
shoot	shot	shot
show	showed	shown, showed
shrink	shrank, shrunk	shrunk, shrunken
shut	shut	shut
sing	sang	sung
sink	sank	sunk
sit	sat	sat
slay	slew	slain
sleep	slept	slept
slide	slid	slid
sling	slung	slung
slink	slunk	slunk
slit	slit	slit
sow	sowed	sown, sowed
speak	spoke	spoken
speed	sped, speeded	sped, specded
spend	spent	spent
spin	spun	spun
spit	spat	spat
split	split	split
spread	spread	spread
spring	sprang	sprung
stand	stood	stood
steal	stole	stolen

* Pronunciation changes in past and past participle forms.

Simple Form	Past Form	Past Participle
stick	stuck	stuck
sting	stung	stung
stink	stank, stunk	stunk
strike	struck	struck
string	strung	strung
swear	swore	sworn
sweep	swept	swept
swim	swam	swum
swing	swung	swung
take	took	taken
teach	taught	taught
tear	tore	torn
tell	told	told
think	thought	thought
throw	threw	thrown
wake	woke, waked	woken, waked
wear	wore	worn
weave	wove	woven
weep	wept	wept
wet	wet	wet
win	won	won
wind	wound	wound
wring	wrung	wrung
write	wrote	written

Words can be divided into categories called *parts of speech.* Understanding these categories will help you work with language more easily, especially when it comes to revising your own writing.

Nouns

A *noun* is a word that names persons, places, or things.

Common Nouns	Proper Nouns
officer	Michael Johnson
station	Union Station
magazine	*Maclean's*

Nouns are said to be *concrete* if you can see or touch them.

> window
>
> paper
>
> river

Nouns are said to be *abstract* if you cannot see or touch them. These words can be concepts, ideas, or qualities.

> meditation
>
> honesty
>
> carelessness

To test for a noun, it may help to ask these questions.

- Can I make the word plural? (Most nouns have a plural form.)
- Can I put the article *the* in front of the word?
- Is the word used as the subject or object of the sentence?

Pronouns

> A *pronoun* is a word used to take the place of a noun. Just like a noun, it is used as the subject or object of a sentence.

Pronouns can be divided into several classes. Here are some of them:

PRONOUNS

Note: Personal pronouns have three forms depending on how they are used in a sentence: as a subject, object, or possessive.

Personal Pronouns

	Subjective		*Objective*		*Possessive*	
	Singular	**Plural**	**Singular**	**Plural**	**Singular**	**Plural**
1st person	I	we	me	us	my (mine)	our (ours)
2nd person	you	you	you	you	your (yours)	your (yours)
3rd person	he	they	him	them	his (his)	their (theirs)
	she		her		her (hers)	
	it		it		its (its)	

Relative Pronouns	*Demonstrative Pronouns*	*Indefinite Pronouns*			
who, whom, whose	this	**Singular**			
which	that	everyone	someone	anyone	no one
that	these	everybody	somebody	anybody	nobody
what	those	everything	something	anything	nothing
whoever, whichever		each	another	either	neither

Singular or **Plural** (depending on meaning)

all	more	none
any	most	some

Plural

both	few	many	several

Adjectives

> An *adjective* is a word that modifies a noun or pronoun. Adjectives usually come before the nouns they modify, but they can also come in the predicate.

The adjective comes directly in front of the noun it modifies:

The *unusual* package was placed on my desk.

The adjective occurs in the predicate but refers back to the noun it modifies:

The package felt *cold*.

Verbs

> A *verb* is a word that tells what a subject is doing as well as the time (past, present, or future) of that action.

Verbs can be divided into three classes:

1. *Action Verbs*

> *Action verbs* tell us what the subject is doing and when the subject does the action.

The action takes place in the present:

> The athlete *runs* five miles every morning.

The action takes place in the past:

> The crowd *cheered* for the oldest runner.

2. *Linking Verbs*

> A *linking verb* joins the subject of a sentence to one or more words that describe or identify the subject.

The linking verb *was* identifies *He* with the noun *dancer*:

> He *was* a dancer in his twenties.

The linking verb *seemed* describes She as *disappointed*:

> She *seemed* disappointed with her job.

COMMON LINKING VERBS

be (am, is, are, was, were, have been)	
act	grow
appear	look
become	seem
feel	taste

3. *Helping Verbs* (also called *auxiliaries*)

> A *helping verb* is any verb used before the main verb.

The helping verb could show the **tense** of the verb:

It *will* rain tomorrow.

The helping verb could show the **passive voice:**

The new civic centre *has been* finished.

The helping verb could give a **special meaning** to the verb:

Annie Lennox *may be* singing here tonight.

COMMON HELPING VERBS

can, could
may, might, must
shall, should
will, would
forms of the irregular verbs *be, have,* and *do*

Adverbs

> An *adverb* is a word that modifies a verb, an adjective, or another adverb. It often ends in -ly, but a better test is to ask yourself if the word answers one of the questions *how, when,* or *where.*

The adverb could modify a *verb:*

The student walked *happily* into the classroom.

The adverb could modify an *adjective:*

It will be *very* cold tomorrow.

The adverb could modify another *adverb:*

Winter has come *too* early.

Here are some adverbs to look out for:

COMMON ADVERBS

Adverbs of Frequency	Adverbs of Degree
often	even
never	extremely
sometimes	just
seldom	more
always	much
ever	only
	quite
	surely
	too
	very

Prepositions

A *preposition* is a word used to relate a noun or pronoun to some other word in the sentence. The preposition with its noun or pronoun is called a *prepositional phrase.*

The letter is *from* my father.

The envelope is addressed *to* my sister.

Read through the following list of prepositions several times so that you will be able to recognize them. Your instructor may ask you to memorize them.

COMMON PREPOSITIONS

about	below	in	since
above	beneath	inside	through
across	beside	into	to
after	between	like	toward
against	beyond	near	under
along	by	of	until
among	down	off	up
around	during	on	upon
at	except	outside	with
before	for	over	within
behind	from	past	without

Conjunctions

A *conjunction* is a word that joins or connects other words, phrases, or clauses.

A conjunction connecting *two words:*

> Sooner *or* later, you will have to pay.

A conjunction connecting *two phrases:*

> The story was on the radio *and* in the newspaper.

A conjunction connecting *two clauses:*

> Dinner was late *because* I had to work overtime at the office.

CONJUNCTIONS

Coordinating Conjunctions	*Subordinating Conjunctions*
and	after
but	although
or	as, as if, as though
nor	because
for (meaning "because")	before
yet	how
so	if, even if
	provided that
	since
	unless
	until
	when, whenever
	where, wherever
	while

Correlative Conjunctions	*Adverbial Conjunctions* (also known as "conjunctive adverbs")
either . . . or	
neither . . . nor	To add an idea: furthermore
both . . . and	moreover
not only . . . but also	likewise
	To contrast: however
	nevertheless
	To show results: consequently
	therefore
	To show an alternative: otherwise

Interjections

> An *interjection* is a word that expresses a strong feeling and is not connected grammatically to any other part of the sentence.

Oh, I forgot my keys.

Well, that means I'll have to sit here all day.

Study the context

Since one word can function differently or have different forms or meanings, you must often study the context in which the word is found to be sure of its part of speech.

for functioning as a preposition:

The parent makes sacrifices *for* the good of the children.

for functioning as a conjunction meaning *because*:

The parent worked two jobs, *for* her child needed a good education.

ANSWER KEY TO SELECTED EXERCISES

Appendix C

Step 2   Creating Effective Sentences

Chapter 2   Finding Subjects and Verbs in Simple Sentences

Practice (page 18)

1. <u>man</u> — noun (*common, concrete*)
2. <u>Mark</u> — noun (*proper*)
3. <u>He</u> — pronoun (*personal, subjective*)
4. <u>room</u> — noun (*common, concrete*)
5. <u>wind</u> — noun (*common, concrete*)
6. <u>idea</u> — noun (*abstract*)
7. <u>dinner</u>, <u>nap</u> — nouns (*common, concrete, compound subject*)

Exercise 1   Finding the Subject of a Sentence (pages 18–19)

1. <u>lamps</u>, <u>lights</u>
2. <u>People</u>
3. <u>musicians</u>
4. <u>Anticipation</u>
5. <u>music</u>
6. <u>mood</u>
7. <u>Many</u>
8. <u>evening</u>
9. <u>fans</u>
10. <u>children</u>

Exercise 2   Finding the Subject of a Sentence (page 19)

1. <u>trail</u>
2. <u>Brent</u>, <u>friends</u>
3. <u>expedition</u>
4. <u>eagle</u>
5. <u>hiker</u>
6. <u>This</u>
7. <u>passes</u>
8. <u>rope</u>
9. <u>Everyone</u>
10. <u>Pride</u>, <u>confidence</u>

Exercise 3   Finding the Subject of a Sentence (page 19)

1. <u>auditorium</u>
2. <u>presenters</u>
3. <u>chair</u>
4. <u>Gloria Jenkins</u>
5. <u>She</u>
6. <u>Everyone</u>

7. <u>audience</u>
8. <u>applause</u>
9. <u>People</u>
10. <u>Mr. George Sanders</u>

Exercise 2   Finding Subjects in Sentences with Prepositional Phrases (page 22)

1. <u>cell phones</u> are a way
2. <u>you</u> will find people talking
3. <u>you</u> never have to say goodbye
4. <u>they</u> were too big and cumbersome
5. <u>cell phones</u> are considered status symbols
6. the <u>use</u> of cell phones has created a new series of problems
7. <u>patrons</u> must turn off their cell phones and pagers as a courtesy
8. <u>many</u> must remind their students to turn off their cell phones
9. The growing <u>number</u> may lead to laws prohibiting their use
10. a quiet <u>night</u> has become a thing

Exercise 3   Finding Subjects in Sentences with Prepositional Phrases (page 23)

1. <u>Maggie</u> looked
2. the <u>cost</u> had risen dramatically
3. <u>she</u> planned a carpool
4. <u>ownership</u> meant increased recreational opportunities
5. <u>Maggie</u> could go
6. <u>Maggie</u> sorted
7. the <u>advertisements</u> were often misleading
8. <u>sellers</u> often hid their cars' problems
9. <u>Maggie</u> searched
10. <u>Maggie</u> settled

Exercise 1   Finding Hidden Subjects (pages 24–25)

    1. How can <u>you</u> get rid
(*You*) 2. Hold a garage sale!
    3. <u>Bob L. Berko</u> warns
    4. garage <u>sales</u> require careful planning and skillful dealings
    5. Why are some garage <u>sales</u> more successful than others?
    6. Here are some tried and true <u>methods</u>
(*You*) 7. Advertise and carefully price all items ahead
(*You*) 8. Improve the chances

9. the best <u>items</u> should go
10. There is a <u>treasure</u>

Exercise 2   Finding Hidden Subjects
(page 25)

1. <u>astronomers</u> have established the existence
2. Why should <u>this</u> be
3. our solar <u>system</u> would no longer be unique
4. the <u>likelihood</u> would be increased
5. <u>Planets</u>, however, cannot support life
6. two Swiss <u>astronomers</u> announced their observations
7. There was some <u>skepticism</u>
8. Then two American <u>astronomers</u> took a look and confirmed the discovery
9. This new <u>planet</u> is orbiting the star
10. Here is its <u>distance</u>: 40 light years

Exercise 3   Finding Hidden Subjects
(pages 25–26)

1. There is a <u>part</u> that is still virtually unexplored
2. The <u>territory</u> north is Canada's North
(*You*) 3. Look
4. lies a <u>spot</u> that is the precise geographic centre
5. however, lives <u>less than one percent</u>
6. the <u>North</u> looks bare, desolate, and inhospitable
7. How could <u>artists</u> find inspiration?
8. the <u>solitude</u> and <u>simplicity</u> are challenges
9. Why have so many <u>people</u> begun to settle?
10. The <u>North</u> may finally succumb

Exercise 1   Finding Action Verbs (page 27)

1. <u>Zoe</u> (signed up) for another season of Little League. (**past**)
2. Last year <u>she</u> (played) outfield. (**past**)
3. Her red <u>jersey</u> (carried) the name of a local restaurant on the back. (**past**)
4. The other four <u>girls</u> on the team slowly (dropped out) or (did) not (show up) for practice. (**past**)
5. The <u>boys</u> generally (ignored) Zoe. (**past**)
6. <u>She</u> sat slightly apart from the others on the bench and (warmed up) alone. (**past**)
7. Zoe's <u>mom</u> (worked) as a construction worker. (**past**)
8. Zoe's <u>mother</u> (understood) her daughter's feelings. (**past**)
9. Often the only woman on the job site, <u>she</u> also (faced) the isolation of crossing gender boundaries. (**past**)
10. In new or unusual roles, <u>people</u> often (pay) an unfair price. (**present**)

Exercise 2   Finding Action Verbs
(pages 27–28)

1. Many <u>people</u> (love) folk music. (**present**)
2. Folk music <u>enthusiasts</u> (travel) to festivals around the country. (**present**)
3. <u>Cape Breton</u> (offers) traditional Celtic music. (**present**)
4. <u>Ashley MacIsaac</u> (plays) a new style of Celtic music. (**present**)
5. The <u>island</u> of Cape Breton (hosts) an annual Celtic music festival. (**present**)
6. Scottish <u>people</u> (settled) in Cape Breton two hundred years ago. (**past**)
7. <u>They</u> (maintained) a very strong musical tradition. (**past**)
8. Scottish <u>musicians</u> (learn) the old music styles from their Canadian cousins. (**present**)
9. <u>Cape Breton</u> (attracts) music lovers from around the world. (**present**)
10. Many <u>fiddlers</u> (prefer) the traditional Celtic music style. (**present**)

Exercise 1   Finding Linking Verbs
(pages 28–29)

1. My mood (has) never (been) worse.
2. I (was) tired in the morning.
3. I (felt) as dreary as the rainy weather outside.
4. My apartment (seemed) messy and cluttered.
5. Even after my shower, my world (appeared) gloomy.
6. Even my dog (looked) depressed.
7. The coffee in the local diner (tasted) burnt.
8. I (grew) resigned to a bad day.
9. My work day (seemed) endless.
10. In spite of all this, I (feel) hopeful about tomorrow.

Exercise 2   Finding Linking Verbs (page 29)

1. Her grad night (was) fabulous.
2. Monique (looked) lovely in her prom gown.
3. Her mother (had been) very helpful.

4. Everything (seemed) in order.

5. The limousine (appeared) right on time.

6. The hall (was) decorated with lights.

   (was decorated is the verb phrase)

7. The food (tasted) extra special.

8. The band (sounded) professional.

9. Everyone (felt) so grown up.

10. Grad night (seemed) to be a complete success.

Exercise 1   Finding Helping Verbs (page 30)

1. The <u>country</u> of Argentina (can claim) the highest consumption of beef in the world.
2. Argentina's four billion dollar beef <u>industry</u> (has) always (been) an important national symbol.
3. Argentina's grass-fed <u>cattle</u> (are considered) leaner and lower in cholesterol than North American grain-fed cattle.
4. Even so, <u>concerns</u> about health and an economic <u>recession</u> (may be changing) the country's diet.
5. Many <u>Argentines</u> (have begun) to eat lighter and cheaper.
6. <u>Necessity</u> (will force) even the most dedicated meat-eaters to try new kinds of foods.
7. Clearly, <u>some</u> (do) not (wish) to alter their eating habits.
8. Not surprisingly, however, many <u>Argentines</u> (have found) <u>they</u> actually (like) tofu and pasta salads.
9. <u>Argentina</u> (will) not (let) its national symbol of beef fade away without a fight.
10. Beef <u>producers</u> (must sell) more beef abroad due to decreased local consumption.

Exercise 2   Finding Helping Verbs (pages 30–31)

1. <u>You</u> (should record) your dreams in a journal.
2. Your <u>dreams</u> (will reveal) your innermost concerns.
3. Elderly <u>people</u> (can) often (recall) events from twenty-five years ago.
4. <u>Dreams</u> (could be put) to good use.
5. <u>Imagination</u> (might be developed) through dreams.
6. <u>Dreams</u> (are) usually (forgotten) shortly after waking.
7. <u>Children</u> (may) not (know) the difference between dreams and reality.

8. <u>They</u> (may create) imaginary friends.
9. <u>Dreams</u> (have brought) contentment to many people's lives.
10. A dream <u>book</u> (could be) your most valuable possession.

Exercise 1   Identifying Parts of Speech (page 31)

1. verb
2. noun
3. adjective
4. adverb
5. adverb
6. noun
7. pronoun
8. preposition
9. preposition
10. noun

Exercise 2   Identifying Parts of Speech (page 32)

noun
adjective
preposition
preposition
pronoun
noun
verb
verb
verb
noun

Exercise 3   Identifying Parts of Speech (page 32)

1. adjective
2. noun
3. verb
4. noun
5. preposition
6. verb
7. verb
8. preposition
9. noun
10. preposition

Mastery and editing tests

Test 1   Finding Subjects and Verbs in Simple Sentences (page 33)

1. <u>Jacques Cartier</u>, the French explorer, (learned) of the medicinal properties of common North American herbs and plants.
2. In the winter of 1535, <u>scurvy</u> (killed) many of the men on his expedition to Canada.

3. Scurvy, a disease caused by a deficiency in vitamin C, leads to a swelling of the gums and improper healing of wounds.

4. The Hurons, a native peoples who lived nearby, saved Cartier's men by giving them herbal tea made from the foliage of white cedar.

5. The natives of North America have helped Europeans by showing them how to use local herbs and plants to cure a variety of illnesses.

6. Fevers, stomach ailments, and rheumatism are everyday sicknesses that can be cured with the right herbs and plants.

7. Echinacea, commonly known as the purple coneflower, is one such herb.

8. It had been used by natives to cure snakebites, sore throats, and toothaches for thousands of years prior to Europeans settling in North America.

9. How do the medicinal properties of this herb work?

10. There are new studies that suggest echinacea may stimulate the immune system to help fight some viral and bacterial infections.

Test 2   Finding Subjects and Verbs in Simple Sentences (page 33)

1. A certain amount of stress can be a good thing.

2. In many cases, stress motivates us.

3. When does stress become distress?

4. Your own self-awareness is the best place to start.

5. Have there been changes in your sleep or appetite?

6. Are you using alcohol or drugs too much?

7. Anxious people feel trapped by pressure and disappointment.

8. There is usually help from your family and friends.

9. Many can offer you their observations and advice.

10. Clinical depression, a more serious condition, usually responds well to the right combination of psychotherapy and the right medicine.

Test 3   Finding Subjects and Verbs in Simple Sentences (page 34)

1. The X-ray can be used to illuminate and cure illness.

2. It can also bring some risk from misuse.

3. Consumers should stay vigilant about unnecessary X-rays.

4. Both the benefits and the risks must be balanced.

5. Modern imaging techniques can spare patients unnecessary surgery.

6. In the 1970s, for example, bad stomach pain triggered exploratory surgery for appendicitis.

7. Intense doses of radiation can also kill cells.

8. When is the use of intense doses of radiation a benefit?

9. In cancer treatments, radiation therapy is often beneficial.

10. With massive exposure, however, chromosomes or bone marrow could be damaged.

Test 4   Finding Subjects and Verbs in Simple Sentences (page 34)

1. Most people, at one time or another, suffer from fatigue.

2. There could be many reasons for fatigue.

3. It is the body's way of warning us.

4. How can a person figure out the reason?

5. Sensations of sleepiness or feelings of physical weakness are separate symptoms with different causes.

6. Too much work and not enough sleep can cause fatigue.

7. Anemia, a condition of too little hemoglobin in the blood, can be diagnosed with a blood test.

8. Has anyone heard of obstructive sleep apnea or snoring sickness?

9. Infections such as mononucleosis, hepatitis, and Lyme disease are notorious for their exhausting effects.

10. After a tragedy such as the death of a spouse, profound fatigue is natural.

Test 5   Finding Subjects and Verbs in Simple Sentences (page 35)

1. chronic lateness may be considered a serious problem

2. Students will often fail their classes

3. Teachers must warn these students

4. Those same students often show up late

5. Their social lives can be negatively affected

6. Friends can become angry

7. Why does anyone put up with these kinds of friends?

8. Parents and counsellors search

9. Constant reminders may only annoy these people or even slow them down.

10. the individual must suffer the consequences

Crossword Puzzle: Reviewing the Terms for Sentence Parts (page 36)

```
P R O P E R . . I . W . I
R . F E D . L I N K I N G
Y . T . . U . C . L . . N
. B O S T O N . A R T . O
T . V . O . C . . E . . R
H . . . S H O U L D . . .
A R R A Y . U . A . . . N
T . . Y . O . T . T . A T
. Y O U N G . . W I L L .
. U . . R . E . . . L . .
A P P O S I T I V E . . I
```

Chapter 3   Making Subjects and Verbs Agree

Practice (page 38)
1. laughs
2. amuses
3. like
4. memorizes
5. enjoy

Practice (page 38)
1. doesn't
2. were
3. doesn't
4. Were
5. doesn't

Exercise 1   Making the Subject and Verb Agree (page 39)

	Subject	Verb
1.	Tandy	loves
2.	brother	is
3.	rehearsals	begin
4.	actors	worry
5.	Tandy	calls
6.	She	is
7.	we	plan
8.	Michael	doesn't
9.	We	hope
10.	I	am

Exercise 2   Making the Subject and Verb Agree (pages 39–40)

	Subject	Verb
1.	Exercise	is
2.	It	provides
3.	forms	are
4.	You	have
5.	training	strengthens
6.	exercise	burns
7.	Swimming	offers
8.	Exercise	does
9.	music	makes
10.	exercise	has

Exercise 3   Making the Subject and Verb Agree (page 40)

	Subject	Verb
1.	Television	offers
2.	television	is
3.	Sesame Street	teaches
4.	Jeopardy	expands
5.	shows	cater
6.	television	provides
7.	You	learn
8.	programs	make
9.	shows	inform
10.	Television	brings

Exercise 1   Agreement with Hidden Subjects (page 41)
1. Here is a story about school uniforms.
2. Interest in requiring uniforms is growing throughout the country.
3. A few provinces, among them Alberta and British Columbia, are considering laws to allow schools to have uniforms if they wish.
4. The government of Ontario has passed a law allowing the majority of parents in a school district to set the student dress code.
5. Why do some people, including parents, object to these new laws?
6. Some parents believe that the behaviour of children cannot be changed by changing the clothes they wear.
7. Others feel that school dress codes encourage respect and unity among students.
8. School uniforms are often based on the colours of a particular school.
9. My little sister hopes that she does not have to wear a school uniform.
10. The colours of her school are brown and yellow.

Exercise 2   Agreement with Hidden Subjects (page 41)
1. Knowledge of household safety measure is important.
2. Where is the closest escape route?
3. Parents should, as early as possible, teach their children about safety.
4. Children as well as adults in a house need to practise safety procedures.
5. What are some common safety tips everyone should know?
6. Batteries in the smoke detector warn you about a smoky situation.

7. "Stop, drop, and roll" <u>are</u> steps to follow when there is a fire.
8. <u>(You)</u> Always <u>know</u> how to gain access in the fire escape.
9. Every family <u>member</u>, especially young children, <u>is</u> expected to memorize the home telephone number and house address.
10. In the home, there <u>are</u> safety <u>procedures</u> to reduce the chances of a disaster.

Exercise 3 Agreement with Hidden Subjects (page 42)

	Subject	Verb
1.	topics	are
2.	one	is
3.	meteorologist	does
4.	Adults	want
5.	Farmers	need
6.	Pilots	rely
7.	number	tends
8.	region	has
9.	predictions	are
10.	umbrellas	are

Exercise 1 Subject-Verb Agreement with Group Nouns (page 43)

Some answers can vary depending on interpretation.

1. was
2. makes
3. was
4. sit
5. line
6. stand
7. gesture
8. gasp
9. run
10. prepares

Exercise 2 Subject-Verb Agreement with Group Nouns (page 43)

Some answers can vary depending on interpretation.

1. decides
2. takes
3. show
4. are
5. demonstrates
6. cooperates
7. sell
8. gets
9. is
10. comes

Exercise 3 Subject-Verb Agreement with Group Nouns (page 44)

Some answers can vary depending on interpretation.

1. decides
2. plans
3. expects
4. are
5. wants
6. prefer
7. is
8. make
9. have
10. gets

Exercise 1 Subject-Verb Agreement with Indefinite Pronouns (page 45)

1. knows
2. argue
3. remain
4. is, proves
5. agrees
6. is
7. is
8. is
9. recommend
10. are

Exercise 2 Subject-Verb Agreement with Indefinite Pronouns (page 45)

1. wants
2. complain
3. are
4. Doesn't
5. take
6. have
7. is
8. tells
9. has
10. are

Exercise 3 Subject-Verb Agreement with Indefinite Pronouns (page 46)

1. is
2. think
3. find
4. knows
5. is
6. has
7. depend
8. is
9. tries
10. is

Exercise 1   Subject-Verb Agreement with Compound Subjects (page 47)
1. consume
2. is
3. eat
4. increases
5. is
6. disappear
7. feels
8. want
9. is
10. need

Exercise 2   Subject-Verb Agreement with Compound Subjects (page 47)
1. are
2. attract
3. discourage
4. keeps
5. have
6. is
7. is
8. enjoy
9. prefer
10. upsets

Exercise 3   Subject-Verb Agreement with Compound Subjects (pages 47–48)
1. are
2. contain
3. provide
4. change
5. needs
6. is
7. lead
8. increase
9. promotes
10. contribute

Exercise 1   Subject-Verb Agreement with Unusual Nouns (pages 48–49)
1. come
2. is
3. light
4. is
5. is
6. has
7. are
8. allow
9. affects
10. show

Exercise 2   Subject-Verb Agreement with Unusual Nouns (page 49)
1. requires
2. reveals

3. wants
4. live
5. fear
6. treat
7. shed
8. seem
9. is
10. are

Mastery and editing tests

Test 1   Making the Subject and Verb Agree (pages 49–50)

	Subject	Verb
1.	study	reveals
2.	who	have
3.	Both	are
4.	group	believes
5.	One	is
6.	who	smoke
7.	cigarettes	are
8.	companies	give
9.	Addictions	are
10.	Concern	is

Test 2   Making the Subject and Verb Agree (page 50)

	Subject	Verb
1.	Canada	wants
2.	One	is
3.	Everybody	feels
4.	politicians/artists	hope
5.	Economics	affects
6.	offices	are
7.	desire	has
8.	People	worry
9.	Teachers	strive
10.	Solutions	have

Test 3   Making the Subject and Verb Agree (pages 50–51)

	Subject	Verb
1.	price	has
2.	decision	requires
3.	She	doesn't
4.	operator/guard	sees
5.	committee	agrees
6.	chips/pop	make up
7.	One	is
8.	raccoons	were
9.	assignments	were
10.	Everyone	takes

Chapter 4 Correcting the Fragment in Simple Sentences

Practice Putting a Conversation into Complete Sentences (page 56)

1. There you are again!
2. You are late, as usual.
3. I had an emergency.
4. What happened this time?
5. I had car trouble.
6. You have had more bad luck, haven't you?
7. Yes. I had a flat tire this time.
8. I wonder what will happen next.

Exercise 1 Understanding Fragments (page 57)

1. a. needs a subject
2. b. needs a verb
3. a. needs a subject
4. c. needs a subject and a verb
5. d. a complete thought
6. a. needs a subject
7. b. needs a verb
8. c. needs a subject and a verb
9. a. needs a subject
10. d. a complete thought

Exercise 2 Understanding Fragments (page 58)

1. a. subject
2. b. verb
3. c. subject and verb
4. b. verb
5. c. subject and verb
6. c. subject and verb
7. b. verb
8. b. verb
9. c. subject and verb
10. d. a complete thought

Exercise 3 Understanding Fragments (pages 58–59)

1. b. verb
2. b. verb
3. c. subject and verb
4. b. verb or c. subject and verb
5. b. verb
6. c. subject and verb
7. b. verb
8. c. subject and verb
9. d. a complete thought
10. a. subject

Exercise 1 Changing Fragments into Sentences (pages 59–60)

1. Her boyfriend came to dinner for the first time.
2. The author at the conference gave a fascinating lecture.
3. The neighbour's dog barked all night.
4. The elevator could not go above the twentieth floor.
5. The salesperson considered her hours to be too long.
6. She called her mother every week.
7. Sweetly the songbird sang.
8. Too many girls live on our dormitory floor.
9. My high school art teacher inspired me to paint.
10. The taxicab driver deposited the luggage on the sidewalk.

Exercise 2 Changing Fragments into Sentences (pages 60–61)

1. The police quickly arrived at the scene.
2. A crowd was out of control.
3. There were too many obstacles between the dance floor and the exit.
4. Thick smoke in the stairway restricted visibility.
5. The fire began in the middle of the night.
6. Now the dancers were gasping for breath.
7. Only one exit from the rave was unlocked.
8. There was the danger of trampling each other.
9. These people will be more careful in the future about dancing at crowded raves.
10. The officials who inspected the club had not made a careful inspection.

Exercise 3 Changing Fragments into Sentences (page 61)

1. The bicycle race is held annually in France.
2. Athletes from all over the world come to compete.
3. They race hundreds of miles across France.
4. The race lasts for a gruelling five straight days.
5. The incredible energy required for the race amazes the spectators.
6. In the towns along the route the townspeople are lined up to watch.
7. The publicity of the race brings out thousands of spectators.
8. They are all crowding to catch a glimpse of the cyclists.
9. The cyclists are encouraged by children who put banners out for them.
10. Many spectators handed water to tired racers.

Exercise 1   Finding Fragments That Belong to Other Sentences (page 62)

Passage 1   Snow was very dangerous for airplane pilots. (Until the invention of radar) The distance from an airplane to a snowfield below was almost impossible to judge. Sometimes a "whiteout" seemed to be a mile beneath a plane when actually it was only fifty feet. Some pilots have seen snow come up to their cockpit. (Before they know it) They are at a complete stop with their engines still running.

Passage 2   The dandelion is the enemy of every gardener, but it is also a powerful herb. (With wonderful medicinal properties) Perhaps it received its name from the French words *dent de lion*, or *lion's tooth*. The leaves of the plant have jagged edges. (Like the lion's teeth) Others disagree. They say the plant's yellow flower is like the colour of a lion.

Passage 3   Pictures from everyday life are among the most impressive objects to survive from ancient Egypt. We see farmers labouring in the fields. (And craftsmen working in their studios) Sometimes the colours are as fresh as ever. The pictures show a deep love for life and for the things of the earth.

Exercise 2   Finding Fragments That Belong to Other Sentences (pages 62–63)

Passage 1   Mr. Howell loves gardening. He devotes long hours to working in his garden. (Behind the garage in the back yard) His garden is the pride of the neighbourhood. Sometimes he enters garden competitions. He usually comes home happy. (With a first place trophy)

Passage 2   Photography can be a wonderful hobby. The only equipment required is a camera. (And a good pair of eyes to view the world around you) This hobby can lead to a career. (Along with the possibility of good earnings) Consider photography for either pleasure or profit.

Passage 3   Demasduwit, or Mary March as she was named in English, was a Beothuk. In March 1819 a group of armed settlers from Notre Dame Bay encountered a small party of Beothuk at Red Indian Lake. A fight ensued, in which the settlers captured Demasduwit. She was renamed Mary March. (Her second name referring to the month of her capture) The settlers took her in the hope that she could be taught to speak English and might become an agent of contact with her people. When the time came for her to return to the Beothuk, Demasduwit discovered she had tuberculosis. Instead of taking her back alive, a military expedition returned her body. (Which they left in early February at the deserted Beothuk camp where she had been captured the previous year)

Exercise 3   Finding Fragments That Belong to Other Sentences (page 63)

Passage 1   During the War of 1812, invading American armies met some of their fiercest opposition from the French in Quebec. (Then called Lower Canada) Charles-Michel de Salaberry, commander of the resistance against the American invaders, was from an old French-Canadian family. De Salaberry chose to confront the Americans on the banks of the Châteauguay River. His three hundred volunteers faced an army of three thousand. The Americans fired the first volley, but the Canadians held their ground. They returned fire. (From their entrenched positions) The Americans fell back across the border. The French Canadians repelled another American attack a few weeks later. At a place called Crysler's Farm, a small force of French defeated a much larger American army. This ended American plans to conquer Lower Canada.

Passage 2   The construction of the Canadian Pacific Railway in the 1880s played an important part in Canadian history. It connected the country from coast to coast. However, the contribution of Chinese labourers in its construction is often overlooked. In total, some 15,700 Chinese were recruited to work on the railroad. They did some of the hardest and most dangerous work. (Including digging tunnels and handling explosives.) They were also treated unfairly. These workers were paid $1.00 a day and had to pay for their own camping gear. In contrast, white labourers were paid $1.50 to $2.50 a day and did not have to pay for their gear. Many Chinese workers often died from exhaustion due to the hard work. Some perished in explosions. (Or were buried in collapsed tunnels.) The Chinese labourers helped to link Canada from coast to coast.

Exercise 1   Identifying Phrases (page 65)
1. prepositional
2.` noun
3. infinitive
4. noun
5. verb
6. prepositional
7. prepositional
8. verb
9. verb
10. infinitive

Exercise 2   Identifying Phrases (page 66)
1. noun
2. prepositional
3. verb
4. verb
5. infinitive
6. prepositional
7. noun
8. verb
9. prepositional
10. noun

Exercise 3   Identifying Phrases (page 66)
1. noun
2. prepositional
3. participial
4. prepositional
5. verb
6. verb
7. prepositional
8. infinitive
9. gerund
10. verb

Mastery and editing tests

Test 2   Correcting Fragments (pages 73–74)
1. prepositional
2. participial or gerund or verb
3. infinitive
4. prepositional
5. prepositional
6. infinitive
7. participial or gerund or verb
8. participial or gerund or verb
9. infinitive
10. prepositional

Test 3   Recognizing and Correcting the Fragment (page 74)
1. The moon rose high in the sky. All of us worked quickly to pitch the tent, and then we made a fire.
2. Raising the drinking age to twenty-one saves the lives of all drivers, the drinkers and the nondrinkers. Every province should raise the drinking age to twenty-one.
3. Companies do a lot of research before they name a new product. Based on the results of a market research team, a company makes its final selection.
4. The day of my eighteenth birthday, my parents made reservations at a fine restaurant. My father came home early from work.
5. Francie loved to see her mother grind the coffee. Her mother would sit in the kitchen with the coffee mill clutched between her knees, grinding away with a furious turn of her left wrist. The room filled up with the rich odour of freshly ground coffee.

Test 4   Recognizing and Correcting the Fragment (page 75)

Hint: 6 fragments

We called it our house. It was only one room. With about as much space as a tent. Painted in a pastel colour with a red tiled roof. The front window reaching nearly from the sidewalk to the roof. We could look up and down the street. Sitting indoors on the window seat. Our kitchen was a small narrow area. With the brick stove and two benches to serve as shelves. Three steel bars and a short piece of lead pipe from a scrap heap to make a grate.

We called it our house. It was only one room. It had about as much space as a tent. It was painted in a pastel colour and had a red tiled roof. The front window reached nearly from the sidewalk to the roof. We could look up and down the street when we were sitting indoors on the window seat. Our kitchen was a small narrow area with a brick stove and two benches to serve as shelves. Three steel bars and a short piece of lead pipe from a scrap heap made a grate.

Test 5   Recognizing and Correcting the Fragment (pages 75–76)

Hint: 5 fragments

The snow came down all night long. <u>And well into the next day.</u> <u>By the time.</u> The snow storm ended. My mother woke me up. <u>Saying that it was time for me to get up and shovel the driveway.</u> <u>When I ran out of the kitchen door.</u> I saw that the car had been snowed in. I then realized that my job was going to be harder than ever. <u>Somewhere underneath all that snow.</u> There lay the snow shovel.

The snow came down all night long and well into the next day. By the time the snow storm ended, my mother woke me up, saying that it was time for me to get up and shovel the driveway. When I ran out of the kitchen door, I saw that the car had been snowed in. I then realized that my job was going to be harder than ever. Somewhere underneath all that snow, there lay the snow shovel.

Chapter 5   Combining Sentences Using the Three Methods of Coordination

Practice (page 80)

1. The <u>streets</u> <u>were</u> slippery, (yet) the <u>trucker</u> <u>drove</u> fast.
2. The <u>night</u> <u>was</u> cold and damp, (and) the <u>rain</u> <u>froze</u> in patches on the roads.
3. (Either) he <u>had</u> an emergency, (or) he <u>was</u> careless and irresponsible.
4. The <u>light</u> ahead <u>was</u> red, (but) the <u>driver</u> <u>didn't slow</u> down.

Exercise 1   Combining Sentences Using Coordinating Conjunctions (pages 81–83)

1. Relationship: reason
   Conjunction: for
   Alicia and Greg thought about breaking up, for they could not agree on many things.
2. Relationship: adds an idea
   Conjunction: and
   Alicia thought Greg was too possessive, and Greg thought Alicia did not care enough.
3. Relationship: contrast
   Conjunction: but
   Alicia's mother wanted her to date other boys, but Greg was completely against that idea.
4. Relationship: reason
   Conjunction: for
   Alicia and Greg argued frequently, for they both had strong personalities.
5. Relationship: add an idea
   Conjunction: and

Greg did not like many of Alicia's friends, and Alicia did not care for Greg's friends.
6. Relationship: contrast
   Conjunction: but
   Alicia wanted to go away to college, but Greg wanted her to stay home for college.
7. Relationship   show a choice
   Conjunction: or
   They could try to talk with other couples, or they could seek professional counselling.
8. Relationship: contrast
   Conjunction: yet
   The couple did not get along well together, yet they did not really want to separate.
9. Relationship: contrast
   Conjunction: but
   Dating can be stressful, but it has its rewards.
10. Relationship: contrast
    Conjunction: but
    Deciding to date is easy, but deciding to break up is more difficult.

Practice (page 85)

1. <u>Jennifer</u> <u>was</u> too tired during the week to meet me (; consequently,) I <u>met</u> her for lunch on Saturday.
2. <u>I</u> <u>suggested</u> roller blading (; otherwise,) <u>I</u> <u>proposed</u> we see a movie.
3. <u>We</u> <u>didn't own</u> roller blades (; however,) <u>we</u> <u>could have rented</u> them.
4. <u>We</u> <u>spent</u> at least an hour trying to decide what to do (; meanwhile,) the <u>time</u> <u>was passing</u>.
5. <u>Jennifer</u> <u>didn't want</u> to spend any money (; therefore,) <u>we</u> <u>ended up</u> taking a walk through the park just like every other Saturday afternoon.

Exercise 1   Combining Sentences Using Adverbial Conjunctions (pages 85–87)

1. Iceland is often thought to be covered by ice; however, it is gloriously green.
2. The country is small; in fact, it is 31,000 square kilometres larger than New Brunswick.
3. The population numbers about a quarter million; therefore, it is the most sparsely populated country in Europe.
4. Miles of rich tundra cover the landscape; in addition, deep lakes, bubbling hot springs, and tumbling waterfalls await the traveller.
5. Iceland has more lava than any place on earth; indeed, some of it is in furious eruption.

6. Iceland is closer to Toronto than Vancouver; however, Canadians are surprisingly ignorant of the place.
7. The history of Iceland goes back 11,000 years; moreover, nearly every Icelandic citizen is steeped in this history.
8. The Icelandic language has remained virtually unchanged for over 1,000 years; thus, children and adults delight in reading the ancient legends of the country with their real life heroes, trolls, and witches.
9. The whole of Iceland lies close to the Arctic Circle; however, the Gulf Stream warms its shores and softens its climate.
10. Iceland uses its underground hot springs to heat its many greenhouses; consequently, Icelanders can enjoy fresh tropical fruit all year long.

Mastery and editing tests

Test 1   Combining Sentences Using Coordination (pages 91–92)

1. The Guess Who was playing at the Air Canada Centre, and my friend Eddie said he could get tickets.
2. My anticipation began to grow; in fact, my stereo played all their albums that day.
3. Most old rock stars lose their appeal as they age, and their music loses its excitement.
4. The Guess Who has been playing for thirty years, but I didn't know what to expect.
5. We went to Toronto by train; otherwise, we would have been stuck in traffic.
6. The concert didn't start on time; it began one hour late.
7. The first band was loud, but The Guess Who was more subdued.
8. I'd seen them only in pictures, so I was shocked at how chubby they were.
9. They weren't just good musicians; musical stories were spun before my eyes.
10. I didn't know if I'd enjoy their music; however, I now have a new appreciation for subtlety.

Test 2   Combining Sentences Using Coordination (pages 92–93)

1. The Stampeders and Lions played a football game for the Western Conference final last week, and I knew it would be an exciting game.
2. As champions, the winner would represent the West in the Grey Cup; as a result, the loser would have to wait until next year to try again.

3. I couldn't wait for the contest to start; meanwhile, all my friends planned a party for game time.
4. The Stampeders had a tough, gritty, and angry team; therefore, they wore down their foes.
5. The Lions' offence showed balance and flair, so they were able to move the ball and score points.
6. In a monumental clash, both teams played well; in fact, the momentum swung to each side like a pendulum.
7. The Lions outplayed the Stampeders, but they couldn't put the Stampeders away.
8. The Stampeders converted only three out of ten second downs into first downs; however, they converted all four third downs that they attempted.
9. Mistakes by the Lions proved to be too costly; consequently, the Stampeders won by the slimmest of margins.
10. The loss ensured that the Lions wouldn't advance to the Grey Cup, so they would have to wait until next year.

Test 3   Combining Sentences Using Coordination (pages 93–94)

1. There is a hole in the ozone layer; therefore, the environment is in danger of global warming.
2. Plant life is being negatively affected around the world, and an increase of a few degrees in average temperatures can have serious effects.
3. Many nations are concerned about the effects of global warming, so they are making the scientific study of global warming a priority.
4. World farming is negatively affected by global warming, yet nations continue to pollute the environment.
5. A continual change in temperature patterns can affect our seasons; consequently, we may no longer have four distinct seasons.
6. Canadians are used to reasonably priced fresh produce, and they cannot imagine paying high prices for imported foods on a daily basis.
7. Wetlands contain a wide variety of plant and animal life, and their disappearance could seriously upset the ecological balance of nature.
8. A hole in the ozone layer allows dangerous ultraviolet rays to penetrate our atmosphere,

but people still flock to the beaches in search of the perfect suntan.

9. Changes in world temperatures will change the ways we live; nevertheless, we continue to pollute our environment and do further damage.
10. We all live on this planet called Earth, and we all have a responsibility to protect it.

Test 4   Combining Sentences Using Coordination (page 95)

Susan was asked to create an advertisement for the violin concert, so she designed a flyer. She figured she needed 100 copies to post around town; therefore, she went to the print shop. Susan presented the flyer to the man behind the counter; he determined it was suitable for reproduction. It could be reproduced on a copier, or it could be reproduced on a printing press. The printing press would generate higher quality; the copier, however, would be quicker. Both time and quality were factors; thus, she had a decision to make. Susan decided to let cost be the determining factor, so she inquired about the difference in price. Copies were five cents each, yet the cost of using the press wasn't fixed. As more copies were made, the cost per copy decreased; therefore, at some point using the press would become more cost effective. The cost effective point, she was told, was 150, so Susan chose to use the copier.

Test 5   Combining Sentences Using Coordination (page 95)

Two hours after dinner, Jeanne and John were still hungry, so they asked Dad for a pizza. Dad had had a long day; furthermore, no pizza shops were delivering at that late hour. His first answer was no; however, the persistence of a six-year-old and nine-year-old can be very persuasive. Reluctantly, Dad agreed to make the trip; besides, he was getting hungry himself. The car had trouble starting; meanwhile, Dad was beginning to have an increasing sense of doom about the trip. The children were hyperactive in the car; moreover, they expected Dad to determine who was responsible for their backseat fight. At the pizza shop, their bickering continued; accordingly, on their way home they fought over who could hold the pizza. Dad advised them to take turns. John held the pizza for awhile, but the heat on his bare legs became too much for him. Suddenly he yanked the pizza box off his scorched lap. The pizza flew out of the box and landed cheese down on top of Jeanne; nonetheless, their anticipation of pizza proved greater than their dismay. At home both children enjoyed eating the now cheeseless pizza.

Chapter 6   Combining Sentences Using Subordination

Exercise 1   Recognizing Dependent and Independent Clauses (page 98)
1. DC
2. IC
3. DC
4. IC
5. IC
6. DC
7. DC
8. IC
9. DC
10. IC

Exercise 2   Recognizing Dependent and Independent Clauses (page 98)
1. DC
2. IC
3. DC
4. IC
5. IC
6. DC
7. IC
8. DC
9. IC
10. DC

Exercise 3   Recognizing Dependent and Independent Clauses (page 99)
1. IC
2. DC
3. DC
4. IC
5. DC
6. IC
7. DC
8. DC
9. IC
10. DC

Exercise 1   Using Subordinating Conjunctions (page 101)
1. a. Monica left the game after she watched the halftime show.
   b. After she watched the halftime show, Monica left the game.
2. a. I was very pleased when my husband returned to university this fall.
   b. When my husband returned to university this fall, I was very pleased.

Exercise 1   Combining Sentences Using Subordination (pages 102–103)
1. She decided to move when the traffic became too noisy.

2. I fixed dinner while Andrea did her homework.

3. If you do your chores, I'll give you your allowance.

4. Although I felt sleepy, I decided to watch the late movie anyway.

5. You should not eat ice cream unless you wish to gain weight.

Exercise 2   Combining Sentences Using Subordination (pages 103–104)

1. He was eating breakfast when the results of the election came over the radio.

2. The town council voted against the plan because they believed the project was too expensive.

3. I will see Margaret Atwood tonight since she is speaking at the university.

4. The worker hoped for a promotion even though not one person in the department had received a promotion last year.

5. As the worker hoped for a promotion, he made sure all his work was done accurately and on time.

Exercise 3   Combining Sentences Using Subordination (pages 104–105)

1. a. Since the computer was on sale, the businessperson decided to purchase it.
   b. The businessperson decided to purchase the computer since it was on sale.

2. a. After the play ended at 10 p.m., the couple went out for dessert.
   b. The couple went out for dessert after the play ended at 10 p.m.

3. a. When the new school term begins in September, you can expect larger class sizes.
   b. You can expect larger class sizes when the new school term begins in September.

4. a. While he recovered from a broken leg, he read more than twenty novels.
   b. He read more than twenty novels while he recovered from a broken leg.

5. a. Before the family decided on a ski vacation, they considered several alternatives.
   b. The family considered several alternatives before they decided on a ski vacation.

Practice   Identifying Essential and Nonessential Clauses (page 106)

1. My cousin's Bar Mitzvah reception, which was held at a lake resort, lasted late into the night.

2. The band that my uncle hired for the night played a variety of music.

3. Everyone who came to the event danced until dawn.

4. Even the folks who didn't like rock music enjoyed themselves on the dance floor.

5. The caterer, whose food was delicious, joined in the train of dancers parading around the room.

Practice   Combining Sentences Using a Relative Pronoun (page 107)

1. The shoes that I bought last week are very expensive.

2. The exercise equipment that I use every day at the local YWCA is very effective.

3. The librarian who is sitting at the reference table is busy at the moment.

4. Here is the new atlas that I told you about.

5. Mrs. Faigle, who is your adviser, is the older woman on the stage.

Exercise 3   Combining Sentences Using Relative Pronouns (pages 109–110)

1. Chris Hadfield, who was born in Sarnia, Ontario, was the first Canadian to go on a space walk.

2. Hadfield's mission was to install the Canadarm2, which was designed by Canadian engineers, on the International Space Station.

3. The Canadarm2, which weighs 1.5 tonnes and spans over 17 metres, is a robot claw installed on the space station to help in its construction.

4. Getting the Canadarm2 installed and working was critical to the construction schedule, which is expected to continue until 2006.

5. The crew, which was made up of people from four different countries, had to test the effectiveness of the Canadarm2.

6. Hadfield commanded the original Canadarm that is attached to the space shuttle.

7. Canadarm2, which was commanded from inside the space station, lifted a pallet over the cargo bay of the space shuttle.

8. Hadfield, who is an experienced pilot and skilled technician, then manoeuvred the shuttle's arm to reach over and grasp the pallet.

9. This "handshake," which took place between the two robot Canadarms, was the highlight of the mission.

10. The space shuttle crew, which was made up of many talented people, returned to earth safely.

Mastery and editing tests

Test 1 Combining Sentences Using a Subordinating Conjunction or a Relative Pronoun (pages 110–111)

1. The elderly woman lives alone with three cats that sleep on the floor beside her bed.
2. The crowd was asked to move back because the paramedics needed more space.
3. The dancer walked across the room in tap shoes, which made a distinct clicking sound.
4. My sister, whose name is Eileen, is extremely generous with her time.
5. His talent was evident even though his costume was tattered and dirty.
6. The bank manager would not smile until he realized our common interests.
7. Although I begin a new job tomorrow, I stayed awake reading a novel.
8. The baseball player, who was trying to catch a fly fall, tripped and sprained his ankle.
9. Immediately his face, which generally showed no emotion at all, screwed up with pain.
10. As I was reading a book, the cat jumped into my lap.

Test 2 Combining Sentences Using a Subordinating Conjunction or a Relative Pronoun (pages 111–112)

1. Ahmed, who likes jazz music the best, chose to play the saxophone.
2. When the sun finally emerged from behind the clouds, all the puddles dried up.
3. The monks, who dined in silence, sat down to lunch.
4. The books, which were arranged in alphabetical order, were put on the shelf.
5. Although the computer is brand new, something is wrong with the disk drive.
6. While the tea is brewing, I will make a sandwich.
7. I can't go with you to the gym tonight because I have a math test.
8. Daniel Lanois, who is a famous Canadian producer, produced CDs for U2.
9. When the clock read twelve o'clock, the cuckoo popped out.
10. The children's clothes are dirty because yesterday they played soccer.

Test 3 Combining Sentences Using a Subordinating Conjunction or a Relative Pronoun (pages 112–113)

1. Our best friend, whose name is Muneer, lives far away.

2. Although we don't see each other very often, we write many letters.
3. He likes to collect stamps that are very colourful.
4. Betty, who lives in Halifax, came to visit us.
5. Although her parents usually arrive on time, today they were late.
6. You cannot go out because you must clean your room.
7. Even though not many people study weaving, Marco is.
8. Since fall is my favourite season, I would like to travel then.
9. Ballet, which is very beautiful to watch, demands great discipline.
10. Ballerinas, who practise for many hours every day, are very graceful.

Test 4 Combining Sentences Using a Subordinating Conjunction or a Relative Pronoun (pages 113–115)

1. Although the CN Tower has an observation deck, it is closed for repair.
2. The ferryboat, which has not been popular for a long time, is making a comeback.
3. Earth, which is the third planet from the sun, lies between Venus and Mars.
4. My favourite shirt, which my girlfriend made for me, has a rip in the sleeve.
5. I wanted an invitation to the poetry reading because the poet was one of my favourites.
6. I bought a cup of coffee that smelled better than it tasted.
7. Although Banff National Park contains pristine wilderness, parts of it are experiencing urban problems.
8. Even though I share an apartment with my sister, I have my own room.
9. The airline lost my suitcase when I flew to Nunavut to visit my sister.
10. While wheat is grown in Saskatchewan, tobacco is grown in Ontario.

Chapter 7   Correcting the Run-On

Exercise 1   Revising Run-Ons (pages 122–123)

1. Two simple sentences:
   I read Margaret Atwood's *Alias Grace* again.
   It's one of my favourite books.

   Two kinds of compound sentences:
   a. I read Margaret Atwood's *Alias Grace* again, for it's one of my favourite books.
   b. I read Margaret Atwood's *Alias Grace* again; it's one of my favourite books.

Complex sentence:
I read Margaret Atwood's *Alias Grace* again since it's one of my favourite books.

2. Two simple sentences:
She has written over a dozen books. Most of her novels deal with the lives of women.

Two kinds of compound sentences:
a. She has written over a dozen books, and most of her novels deal with the lives of women.
b. She has written over a dozen books; most of her novels deal with the lives of women.

Complex sentence:
She has written over a dozen books, most of which deal with the lives of women.

3. Two simple sentences:
Margaret Atwood has written books on many topics. She has won numerous awards for her writing.

Two kinds of compound sentences:
a. Margaret Atwood has written books on many topics, and she has won numerous awards for her writing.
b. Margaret Atwood has written books on many topics; in fact, she has won numerous awards for her writing.

Complex sentence:
Margaret Atwood has written books on many topics, for which she has won numerous awards.

Exercise 2   Revising Run-Ons
(pages 124–125)

1. Two simple sentences:
Pier 21 in Halifax, Nova Scotia, was recently renovated. It was restored as a museum.

Two kinds of compound sentences:
a. Pier 21 in Halifax, Nova Scotia, was recently renovated; in fact, it was restored as a museum.
b. Pier 21 in Halifax, Nova Scotia, was recently renovated, and it was restored as a museum.

Complex sentence:
When Pier 21 in Halifax, Nova Scotia, was recently renovated, it was restored as a museum.

2. Two simple sentences:
The new museum at Pier 21 is wonderful. It brings to life the experiences of so many past immigrants to Canada.

Two kinds of compound sentences:
a. The new museum at Pier 21 is wonderful, for it brings to life the experiences of so many past immigrants to Canada.
b. The new museum at Pier 21 is wonderful; it brings to life the experiences of so many past immigrants to Canada.

Complex sentence:
The new museum at Pier 21 is wonderful because it brings to life the experiences of so many past immigrants to Canada.

3. Two simple sentences:
For many, Pier 21 was the gateway to a new life in Canada. Many who landed there went on to make a positive impact in their new country.

Two kinds of compound sentences:
a. For many, Pier 21 was the gateway to a new life in Canada; in fact, many who landed there went on to make a positive impact in their new country.
b. For many, Pier 21 was the gateway to a new life in Canada; many who landed there went on to make a positive impact in their new country.

Complex sentence:
Because Pier 21 was the gateway to a new life in Canada, many who landed there went on to make a positive impact in their new country.

Exercise 3   Revising Run-Ons
(pages 125–126)

1. Two simple sentences:
Examinations are one way to measure knowledge. They are not always the best method.

Two kinds of compound sentences:
a. Examinations are one way to measure knowledge, but they are not always the best method.
b. Examinations are one way to measure knowledge; however, they are not always the best method.

Complex sentence:
Although examinations are one way to measure knowledge, they are not always the best method.

2. Two simple sentences:
Alcohol and tobacco are dangerous to health. They should be avoided.

Two kinds of compound sentences:
a. Alcohol and tobacco are dangerous to health, and they should be avoided.

b. Alcohol and tobacco are dangerous to health; consequently, they should be avoided.

Complex sentence:
Because alcohol and tobacco are dangerous to health, they should be avoided.

3. Two simple sentences:
Reading broadens your mind. You should read every day.

Two kinds of compound sentences:
a. Reading broadens your mind, so you should read every day.
b. Reading broadens your mind; therefore, you should read every day.

Complex sentence:
Since reading broadens your mind, you should read every day.

Mastery and editing tests

Test 4   Editing for Run-Ons (page 128)

In 1985, Joshua Slocum was the first solo sailor to sail around the world without radar. He was the first to circle the world alone, and he did it without any of the technological aids that help protect sailors today. He told time with a tin clock that lost its minute hand halfway through the journey. He had the humility to acknowledge that his adventures were tame compared with the writing of earlier explorers. Born in Nova Scotia, Slocum had been around the world five times on tall ships before his solo voyage, and he commanded a ship by the age of 30. He was out of work in 1892 when a captain offered to give him a sailboat that needed some repairs. Really, the boat needed rebuilding, which Slocum proceeded to do. Three years later he sailed from Boston, headed east. He planned to sail through the Mediterranean, but he reversed his course, crossed back toward South America and continued west. He entered the Strait of Magellan in February 1896. It took him two months to pass through because he was set back by winds so heavy that his mainsail was torn to rags. Slocum's journey took three years. With stops at various island ports, he raised money by giving talks and enjoyed the local hospitality. His story is a tale of the intelligence, skill, and fortitude that drove a master navigator.

Test 5   Editing for Run-Ons (page 129)

1. Many parents worry that their children are not reading; others worry about what they are reading.
2. Most children are not reading anything at all, and the home is filled with the sounds from stereos and television sets.

3. Children should have library cards, and parents should accompany them regularly to the library to pick out books.
4. Children need to see their parents reading magazines, books, and newspapers that reflect the tastes and interests of the adults in a home.
5. Books can be bonds between children and their parents, so parents should read aloud to their children as often as possible.
6. What do you think of parents who are not involved in the school? They are usually quick to go to make a complaint about a teacher.
7. Maps are wonderful geography lessons, and they remind children they are not at the centre of the world.
8. Some parents think their child is gifted, but it is a mistake to let your child think this.
9. Memorizing poetry should be encouraged because we learn the rhythms of our language and strengthen our speech and writing.
10. A child who doesn't read will be at the mercy of other people; reading encourages children to think through many issues that they might not normally experience themselves.

Chapter 8   Making Sentence Parts Work Together

Practice (page 132)
1. I
2. me

Exercise 1   Choosing the Correct Pronoun in Comparisons (page 132)
1. they
2. ours
3. I
4. ours
5. we
6. theirs
7. them
8. her
9. she
10. him

Practice (page 133)
1. I
2. me

Exercise 2   Choosing the Correct Pronoun in Compound Constructions (page 133)
1. me
2. I
3. her

4. me
5. she
6. she
7. He, I
8. me
9. he
10. me

Practice (page 134)
1. whom
2. whom
3. who
4. who

Exercise 3   Choosing the Correct Pronoun Using Who/Whom (page 134)
1. Who
2. Whoever
3. whom
4. Who
5. whoever
6. who
7. Whose
8. Whoever
9. who
10 Whose

Exercise 1   Choosing Correct Pronoun Forms (page 134)
1. He
2. they
3. them
4. whomever
5. hers
6. Whose
7. They
8. I
9. Whoever
10. theirs

Exercise 2   Choosing Correct Pronoun Forms (page 135)
1. he
2. me
3. whoever
4. he
5. Whoever
6. Who
7. they
8. mine
9. him
10. I

Exercise 3   Choosing Correct Pronoun Forms (page 135)
1. I
2. they
3. whom

4. who
5. I
6. her
7. me
8. who
9. us
10. they

Practice 1 (page 137)
1. All the participants should bring their recommendations for the conference to the meeting.
2. These types of envelopes are required by the Post Office.
3. They didn't care what they were eating.
4. If the angler hopes to catch anything, he must rise early.
5. This group of plants appears to be poisonous.

Practice 2 (page 138)
1. We love quiz shows because we can demonstrate what we know.
2. As I studied science, I found that self-examination helped prepare me for quiz show questions.
3. Game show contestants need to rehearse their responses in order to remember them.
4. Quiz shows can be enjoyable for you if you have a sense of curiosity.
5. When preparing for a quiz show, you must remember that you must practise, practise, practise.

Practice 3 (page 139)
1. The tenant asked the superintendent, "Will you bring back my receipt?"
2. The pharmacist said the prescription could not be refilled.
3. The venetian blind dropped onto the air conditioner and damaged it.
4. The newspaper says the heat wave will continue for at least another week.
5. We don't enjoy the daily newspaper anymore because the news coverage has become too sensational.

Exercise 1   Making Pronouns and Antecedents Agree (pages 139–140)
1. Her dance instructor mailed the dance recital video to her.
2. The workers want their salaries increased.
3. When a business does not computerize its functions, it pays a price in lost business.
4. The female graduate has more job options available to her than in the past.
5. All people want their own dreams fulfilled.

6. The nurse said that those kinds of inoculations are given here.
7. If the hikers expect to sleep tonight, they should put up their tents.
8. These styles of dresses look terrific on you.
9. The magazine says you must return the entry form before the end of the month.
10. The students look forward to their summer break.

Exercise 2   Making Pronouns and Antecedents Agree (pages 140–141)

1. Every student must have an I.D. card to use the library.
2. If you want to get a seat, you have to be there early.
3. When children fly alone, they usually get special attention from the flight attendant.
4. Those sorts of movies depress me.
5. Those nurses are in danger of having their jobs eliminated.
6. These helium balloons will float away if you don't hold onto them.
7. This type of fabric tends to run in the wash.
8. General Mills has a new cereal out now that I like.
9. All the girls were given corsages for their dresses.
10. The teacher gave her special pen to the girl.

Exercise 3   Making Pronouns and Antecedents Agree (pages 141–142)

1. You should try rock climbing if you like adventure.
2. Her friend forwarded Allison's blue sweater to her.
3. The iron scorched the shirt, which had to be thrown away.
4. The article said that nicotine is a carcinogen.
5. It also said pregnant women shouldn't expose their babies to smoke.
6. I usually do well on this kind of test.
7. Girls must bring their gym clothes on Tuesdays and Thursdays.
8. Jack created a copy of Carlos' demo tape for him.
9. The government ought to do something about the national debt.
10. Sue told Sarah, "I won the lottery."

Practice (page 143)

1. My favourite sweater is misshapen, worn, and stained.
2. They love travelling overseas, visiting the sights, and eating in fine restaurants.

3. He admires doctors who donate their medical skills to the needy and who willingly encourage new research.

Exercise 1   Revising Sentences for Parallel Structure (pages 143–144)

1. The Barbara Gowdy book was exciting, startling, and horrifying.
2. Clothes were thrown on the chairs, across the sofa, and on the floor.
3. Reading, decorating, and painting with water colours are three hobbies she enjoys.
4. He appeared drained, worn, and sleepy after the long search for his dog.
5. The house was empty and lifeless.
6. Aruba is always breezy and sunny.
7. The table was solid oak, carved with beautiful details, and reasonably priced.
8. The collector enjoys buying the stamps, studying their history, and putting them in albums.
9. The old book is torn, water stained, and mouldy.
10. The people of the community are not only pleased but also proud.

Exercise 2   Revising Sentences for Parallel Structure (pages 144–145)

1. The editor told her the writing was interesting and accurate, but not concise.
2. The journalist researched the story, wrote a first draft, and took it to the editor for changes.
3. She was undecided about continuing in her present job, quitting to look for a new job, or asking her supervisor for some changes.
4. William is not only a gifted painter, but also a capable teacher of children.
5. The child's demeanour, his actions, and his conversation amused me.
6. Employers should look for people who are competent, honest, and cooperative.
7. The gambler must either stop going to the casinos or risk the ruination of her entire family.
8. The young lawyer would rather work seven days a week than spend one day with his mother-in-law.
9. The kitchen faced a brick wall, had no ventilation, and was painted an ugly dark colour.
10. I would rather visit the East coast that go to Alberta this year.

Exercise 3   Revising Sentences for Parallel Structure (pages 145–146)

1. She's a good singer, a fine dancer, and a talented actress.

2. I would rather watch television than do homework.

3. On each table were a vase of flowers, a bowl of fruit, and a bucket of ice.

4. The composition displayed the student's imagination and wit.

5. On my trip to Winnipeg, I plan to visit relatives, to do some sightseeing, and to eat at a fine restaurant.

6. Gardening, golfing, and sewing curtains are three of my grandmother's favourite hobbies.

7. She seemed exhausted, ill, and hungry after the journey.

8. He cleaned the cellar, washed the windows, and painted the back door.

9. The movie was expensive, too long, and boring.

10. The counsellor makes everyone feel comfortable, speaks in a gentle voice, and gets everyone to participate.

Exercise 1   Revising Misplaced or Dangling Modifiers (pages 148–149)

1. Holding his bowling ball in one hand, Maurice fed the baby.

2. While I was reading the newspaper, the chipmunk scurried across the patio.

3. Walking up the steps of the cathedral, we could hear the organ music faintly.

4. When I was leaving for work this morning, the children reminded me of our plan to play baseball when I got home.

5. Since he was quite blind, the darkness posed no unusual problem for him.

6. After painting the house all day, Joey was refreshed by a dip in the pool.

7. When you are cooking spaghetti, a strainer is helpful.

8. The police returned the purse, which had been found in the park, to the owner.

9. Use great caution when you are crossing the railroad tracks.

10. I had to pull out a tick that I found in my leg.

Exercise 2   Revising Misplaced or Dangling Modifiers (pages 149–150)

1. I petted the little spaniel pup that was wagging his tail.

2. I called the police to help me get the baby out of the stroller where it was stuck.

3. His sadness vanished while he was hiking on the trail.

4. While we are working late at night, the coffeepot is often perking.

5. Disappointed and discouraged, he cheered up after a good brisk walk.

6. I was surprised how the car looked after it was polished.

7. Encouraged by the teacher's help, the student found it easier to organize the paper.

8. I was moved by his words, and tears came to my eyes.

9. Taking the math test, I wrote my answers in ink rather than pencil.

10. In my closet I found an overdue book that needed to be returned to the library.

Exercise 3   Revising Misplaced or Dangling Modifiers (pages 150–151)

1. Wearing her evening gown, Dolores fed the bird.

2. The Tyrrell Museum in Drumheller, Alberta, was my destination.

3. Expecting to hear the weather report, I turned on the radio by 6 a.m.

4. A variety of plant life that had been thought extinct was discovered in the Amazon.

5. Walking outside in our neighbourhood, we could hear the six o'clock whistle.

6. While I was cleaning my binocular lens, the rare bird disappeared.

7. My mother caught sight of her children dangling from the playground monkey bars.

8. I heard the cat next door meowing all night.

9. After I cleaned my apartment, my dog scratched the door to go out.

10. The marathon, which promised all proceeds would go to charity, caused a traffic slowdown.

Mastery and editing tests

Test 1   Making Sentence Parts Work Together (pages 151–152)

1. He and I enjoyed our camping trip.

2. If you are afraid of heights, you mustn't look down.

3. My duties at work include making telephone calls, working on the computer, and picking up the mail.

4. When we went shopping today, we saw the man who is always singing.

5. They went biking in Italy, hiking in England, and grape picking in France.

6. These kinds of trips seem to be getting popular.

7. Jean and I called for more information.

8. In France, there are many beautiful castles to visit.

9. Did anyone bother to finish the assignment?

10. Wouldn't you prefer to eat a peanut butter sandwich than to drink that vegetable juice?

Test 2   Making Sentence Parts Work Together (pages 152–153)

1. Jonathan created his art project quicker than I.
2. Amy told Nancy, "I don't like my shoes."
3. I love to go to the theatre and to spend time at a museum.
4. They love going to Kelly's class because they can always get up and sing.
5. To whom should I address this letter?
6. Our cats like eating, sleeping, and stretching when they wake up.
7. My mom asked my brother and me if we wanted to go to the museum today.
8. The critics say *Mamma Mia!* at the Royal Alxeandra Theatre is a great success.
9. My daily chores are making my bed and washing the dishes.
10. My daughter's favourite teddy bear has a yellow hat, a blue coat, and red shoes.

Test 3   Making Sentence Parts Work Together (pages 153–154)

My adviser and I met to discuss my career options. Later, the Career Centre turned out to be a better source of guidance than he. These kinds of choices are complicated. According to the centre, the first year of college should be a chance to explore a variety of possible careers. The centre suggested that I take advantage of computer training, internship programs, and visits to the campus by experts. Since the new generation of students is likely to change careers several times, versatility, the counsellor said, will be one key to success. I found out what was necessary to get a job in several fields in which I am interested. Internships open doors. They can lead to a job opportunity. When hiring new employees, employers always demand job experience. I was told to constantly explore the job market. I also need to keep abreast of developments in my field even after I have a job. As I walked back to my dorm after this discussion, my future career seemed more promising.

Test 4   Making Sentence Parts Work Together (page 154)

1. Jeremy finally decided to change jobs. He told himself that the move was a good one.
2. His wife is not as convinced as he. The new company is smaller than the one he is leaving.
3. The offer was given to whoever could qualify. Jeremy told Ron, "You need to review before you take the test."

4. Those kinds of tests can be tricky. People can freeze and not be able to do their best.
5. Everyone worked on his or her exam carefully. All those taking the test wanted to get the job.
6. After the applicants took the exam, the results were calculated. The applicants were told a letter would be sent to them shortly.
7. The letter said Jeremy had received the highest score. The job was his if he wanted it.
8. The new job would mean moving the family to a new location, leaving all their friends, and getting a big pay raise.
9. The job, which is in North Bay, Ontario, will be a challenge. Everyone says they will like the city.
10. Moving is a big adjustment. Jeremy hopes his wife and he will be happy.

Test 5   Making Sentence Parts Work Together (pages 154–155)

1. Some parts of the world cannot take water for granted; the people must be grateful for what water there is.
2. The Middle East is an example of these kinds of situations. Water there is usually a problem.
3. If you look at a map of Saudi Arabia, most of the land is not suitable for farming.
4. Oil production can be controlled, but not water.
5. In the dry lands of the Middle East, short rivers called wadis can be dry all year and suddenly fill up with water.
6. The oasis, which is all over the Middle East, is a more dependable water source.
7. Water needs have led governments to hire engineers, build dams, and plan for the future.
8. If engineers take salt water from the sea, they can produce fresh water by a special process.
9. For the nomadic people in these areas, who have only a herd of animals, the search for water makes life hard.
10. We are surprised how many cities grew up in these areas; however, the reason, we remember, is that the locations of the cities made them important centres for trade.

Chapter 9   Practising More with Verbs

Practice 1 (page 158)

1. hit
2. fit

3. spread
4. cut
5. come

Practice 2 (page 159)
1. brought
2. caught
3. led
4. fought
5. crept

Practice 3 (page 160)
1. sprang
2. risen
3. driven
4. bitten
5. written

Exercise 1   Irregular Verbs (page 161)
1. drunk
2. came
3. spent
4. blew
5. bent
6. wept
7. came
8. known
9. set
10. sank

Exercise 2   Irregular Verbs (page 161)
1. drove
2. bitten
3. hurt
4. sent
5. sprang
6. quit
7. swam
8. hidden
9. bet
10. spread

Exercise 3   Irregular Verbs (page 162)
1. began
2. flown
3. thought
4. written
5. rose
6. kept
7. felt
8. shrunk
9. grown

Exercise 1   More Practice with Irregular Verbs (page 162)
1. arose
2. bore
3. dealt
4. chose

5. felt
6. gotten
7. seen
8. spoken
9. stuck
10. found

Exercise 2   More Practice with Irregular Verbs (page 163)
1. saw
2. came
3. sat
4. drank
5. left
6. gone
7. froze
8. quit

Exercise 3   More Practice with Irregular Verbs (page 163)
1. bound
2. bought
3. dug
4. woven
5. rang
6. fallen
7. swore
8. stole
9. taken
10. slid
11. stuck

Practice (page 166)
1. has worked
2. had dreamed
3. has interested
4. has planned
5. have spread
6. had lived
7. has become

Practice   Sequence of Tenses (pages 167–168)
1. has stopped
2. has
3. will give
4. had been
5. liked
6. will be
7 will be
8. had studied
9. would turn
10. had gone

Exercise 1   Correcting Unnecessary Shift in Verb Tense (pages 168–169)
1. will return
2. was feeling
3. are

4. asked
5. was shivering
6. noticed
7. was driving
8. doesn't
9. worries
10. provides

Exercise 2 Correcting Unnecessary Shift in Verb Tense (pages 169–170)

1. In the beginning of the play, the characters' motives were clear; by the end, I was as confused as the rest of the audience.
2. The actors met with the audience after the play, but they didn't explain what motivated their characters.
3. While discussing the play with the actors, the director lost his notes and spoke from memory.
4. One actor talked about preparing for his role while another talked about his techniques for memorizing.
5. I thought the play was wonderful because the actors were so authentic in their portrayals.
6. While viewing the production, the woman seated next to me dropped her purse and asked me for help.
7. She asked me to check under my seat, but I said nothing was there.
8. After I leave the theatre, I take a taxicab home.
9. The play finishes before 11 p.m., and I am stranded without a ride.
10. Overall, the evening is a success, and I decide to visit the theatre again.

Exercise 3 Correcting Unnecessary Shift in Verb Tense (page 170)

The writer Alistair MacLeod was born in North Battleford, Saskatchewan, in 1936. He lived on the Prairies until the age of ten when his parents moved back to the family farm on Cape Breton Island in Nova Scotia. He completed his studies in the United States at Notre Dame University and became deeply interested in the art of writing. He began to gather international acclaim for his short stories while spending most of his energy teaching and raising a family of seven children. He lectured at the University of Windsor until his retirement a few years ago. His only novel, *No Great Mischief*, took him ten years to complete and won him a major international literary award.

Practice (page 171)

1. The roof of the car was pounded by the rain.

2. In the 1700s, fashionable men and women wore powdered wigs.
3. The decision was announced by the Prime Minister in the Commons.
4. A huge tornado hit Edmonton last year.
5. Various people proposed many new ideas over the years.

Practice (page 172)

1. The writing required that (Alice) first (define) several words.
2. It was necessary that (she go) to the library for help.
3. If she were focused, (she would finish) the work quickly.
4. The librarian suggested that (Alice consult) a particularly good medical encyclopedia in the reference section.
5. Alice wishes that this (librarian were) always (available) for advice.

Mastery and editing tests

Test 1 Editing for Correct Verbs (page 173)

I would be so happy if Carlos were given a promotion. He has worked in this company since 1985. He has brought out the best in people no matter in which department he works. I requested he be considered for the promotion. The supervisor said today that she already made up her mind last week. I hope to change her mind. Carlos always does his work accurately and fast. Furthermore, when a colleague of his became ill last year, Carlos did all of the colleague's work in addition to his own without one complaint. Just now I have written a formal letter on his behalf.

Test 2 Editing for Correct Verbs (page 173)

We hurried toward the gate at Toronto's Skydome because we would have been late for the baseball game. I did not know at this time, but we passed beneath the artwork of one of Canada's most famous artists, Michael Snow. The 14 large shiny figures of sports fans make up a single sculpture known as "The Audience" and are located at the northeast and northwest corners of the Skydome. Other examples of Michael Snow's art can be found in some of the most famous galleries and museums in the world. You can also view some of his art if you walk around downtown Toronto. For example, the fibreglass replicas of Canada geese that hang from the ceiling of the Eaton Centre were also created by Michael Snow. Since the 1950s, he has been one of Canada's best known artists. As we approached the Skydome that day, I would never have thought that I would be looking at famous art. I only wanted to see a baseball game.

Test 3   Editing for Correct Verbs (pages 173–174)

The leader is announcing that the presentation will resume after the lunch period finishes. She says that we shouldn't miss the two o'clock lecture. The Director of Consumer Affairs will present the lecture. Although we have invited her many times before, she has never spoken to our group until now. She has been in her position since 1990 and can speak with a great deal of experience. The video equipment, which has lain in the storage area all week, will be set up. I asked that the director speak about several issues that are of concern to us. The announcer reminded us that the director's work last year had a great effect on the safety of children's car seats. I remember that after the lecture last year, the audience asked many questions. My friend and I prepared several questions that we had wanted to ask, but on the way to lunch we lost our notes and had to go back to the auditorium to look for them.

Test 4   Editing for Correct Verbs (page 174)

Maxine should have gone to camp last summer; instead, she stayed at home, looking for things to do. I saw her walking to the candy store every day, sometimes alone, sometimes with a friend. Her mother wished she had gone, and she told her so, but Maxine didn't listen. Maybe her judgment will improve after the summer ends. Her father told her that if she wanted to go to camp next year, he will pay for it. Since 1990, he has been sending his children to camp, and he sees no reason why Maxine should miss out on it. Camp was a benefit for the rest of the children; now the youngest child has to make up her mind to get that benefit.

Test 5   Editing for Correct Verbs (page 174)

In the fifth century, Venice was built on low mud islands between the mouths of two rivers. The city, half on land and half in the water, has been called "The Bride of the Adriatic" since the sixteenth century. The setting of this city is unique. One hundred and seventy canals make up the streets and avenues. Gondolas are ridden by tourists the same way taxicabs serve as transportation in other cities. This Italian city is rich in tradition, a tradition that dates back well over a thousand years. Venetian architects built magnificent palaces and churches. They are filled with priceless treasures that ought not be lost. Students by the thousands have spent time in Venice studying the beautiful sculpture and paintings. Venetian libraries also

hold priceless relics and manuscripts. The city may be a rich museum, but it is also a city with modern problems. Erosion, pollution, and tides are taking a toll on the structures. There are churches that are world famous, but their paintings and statues suffer from the toxic fumes of the motor boats that constantly make waves in the city's canals. I wish we were able to publicize all of the problems of this famous place so something could be done. We don't want to read in the newspaper someday that Venice has sunk into the sea. I suggest the best prize for our newspaper's annual essay contest be a romantic two week trip to Venice for two.

Chapter 10   Using Correct Capitalization and Punctuation

Exercise 1   Capitalization (page 179)
1. When my family visited Sweden, we stayed near Stockholm in a little town called Tumba.
2. The town is situated in the southeast part of the country.
3. I was very glad to be there on June 24 to participate in their spring holiday called Midsummer Day.
4. The weather was beautiful, and a cool breeze came from the Baltic Sea.
5. My cousin asked me, "Have you ever been sailing?"
6. I had only watched people sailing on Lake Ontario.
7. We decided to explore some of the 24,000 islands that attract tourists every year.
8. Not only was Cousin Lars an outstanding engineer, he was also an experienced sailor.
9. My parents, who were less adventurous, enjoyed taking the steamboat called the Cinderella to visit the island where the king and queen live.
10. Before we left, I visited Uppsala University, the country's oldest and largest university, founded in 1477.

Exercise 2   Capitalization (pages 179–180)
Michael Ondaatje was born in Sri Lanka in 1943. In 1954, he moved to London, England, with his mother. After relocating to Canada in 1962, he studied at the University of Toronto and at Queen's University in Kingston, Ontario. He is best known for his novel *The English Patient*, which was the first novel by a Canadian author to win the prestigious Booker Prize. The book was set in Italy, during the final months of the Second World War. Later, the book was adapted for screen, and it won nine Academy Awards in 1996. Although

most of us know him as a novelist, Ondaatje began his writing career with four books of poetry. Ondaatje currently resides in Toronto with his wife, Linda Spalding. Together they edit the literary journal *Brick*.

Exercise 3 Capitalization (page 180)

The 18th Century is sometimes called the Golden Age of Piracy. When the War of the Spanish Succession ended, unemployed sailors in France and England were tempted to support themselves by robbing the treasures off the ships of the Spanish fleet, the ships that brought treasures from the Spanish colonies in the West Indies back to Spain. One of the "gentleman pirates" was Major Stede Bonnet, a wealthy landowner from Barbados, who became a pirate simply for adventure. He counted among his friends a man by the name of Edward Teach, better known to us today as Blackbeard. Bonnet equipped a sloop called the Revenge, and in 1717, he began to raid ships in the Atlantic Ocean near the coast of Virginia. He was hanged for piracy in November 1718. The only female pirates known to history were Mary Read and Anne Bonny, captured on Calico Jack's ship in 1720 and brought to trial at St. Jago de la Vega, Jamaica. Contrary to popular belief, pirates seldom killed their victims, and there is no record that pirates ever forced people to walk the plank.

Practice 1 (page 181)

1. Anyone who listens to the radio, watches television, and reads books, newspapers, and magazines cannot help but be aware of statistics.
2. Statistics appear in the claims of advertisers, in predictions of election results and opinion polls, in cost-of-living indexes, and in reports of business trends and cycles.
3. On the basis of statistics, important decisions are made in the fields of government, industry, and education.
4. Statistical data are usually collected by consulting existing source material, by setting up a survey and collecting data at firsthand from individuals or organizations, and by conducting scientific experiments that measure or count under controlled conditions.
5. The results of statistical investigation may be stated in a simple sentence, presented in the form of a numerical table, or shown in the form of a graph or chart.

Practice 2 (page 182)

1. The satirical news shows, *This Hour Has 22 Minutes,* is one of my favourite programs, but I especially like one segment on it called "Talking to Americans."
2. Rick Mercer plays a TV reporter who travels through the United States, and he asks average Americans questions that are designed to test their knowledge of Canada.
3. Some Americans do not want to admit their ignorance about Canada, nor do they want to pass up a chance to be on TV.
4. The degree of American ignorance about Canada is remarkable, for some people actually think that the Canadian government operates out of a giant igloo.
5. The show illustrates the fact that Canadians may know a lot about the United States, yet Americans know almost nothing about their neighbours to the north.

Practice 3 (pages 182–183)

1. Before World War II, people with disabilities had little chance to find employment in industry.
2. With the severe labour shortage at that time, employers took a second look at the remaining population.
3. Recognizing many physically challenged people were well trained and capable, industrial leaders began to hire these people.
4. As a matter of fact, the physically disabled men and women turned out to be a significant asset rather than a liability.
5. Yes, statistics show that physically challenged workers are more enthusiastic about their jobs, have fewer absences, have fewer accidents on the job, and are less likely to shift from one job to another than the general population of workers.

Practice 4 (page 184)

1. The McMichael Art Gallery, which is located in Kleinburg, Ontario, is home to many beautiful paintings.
2. It has, among other works, paintings by my favourite artist Lawren Harris.
3. The gallery, a large wooden house overlooking the East Humber River Valley, was first built by Robert and Signe McMichael in 1951.
4. Robert McMichael, a wealthy businessman, collected art by Canadian artists.
5. Now, of course, McMichael's collection has become a national treasure.

Practice 5 (page 184)

1. I think, Denise, your paper was very well written.
2. Helen, when does your flight arrive?

3. I insist, Mr. Senator, on your putting more thought into this matter.
4. Honey, why don't we eat out tonight?
5. Dad, could I borrow the car on Friday?

Practice 6 (page 184)
1. 3,640,722
2. 41,555
3. 298,066,400
4. 987
5. 6,432

Practice 7 (page 185)
1. "I hope," she pleaded, "you'll agree to our terms."
2. "Perhaps," I answered, "but we will need time to study the document."
3. "You won't," she added, "get a better offer."
4. I responded, "We never make a hasty decision."
5. "Well, then," she concluded, "I'll hope to hear from you soon."

Practice 8 (page 185)
1. Waking, the woman felt the sun on her face.
2. If you will swallow, you ears will clear.
3. Whoever this is, is certainly making a mistake.
4. For Melinda, Timothy Findley is her favourite writer.
5. Studying in groups often helps, teachers say.

Exercise 1   Using the Comma Correctly (page 185)

In Peru, a country known for its different landscapes, Lake Titicaca has the special distinction of being the highest navigable lake in the world. It is 12,500 feet above sea level. It is also South America's largest lake and is about half the size of Lake Ontario. In early June before the tourists arrive, the weather is cold but beautiful. To tell the truth, that is the best time to visit. The lake, which is a famous tourist attraction, seems more breathtaking when only the indigenous people are to be seen. In the early morning, you might ride a boat illuminated by candles out to the islands of the Uros Indians, or you might visit the hilly island of Taquile. There you would see the men dressed in traditional sandals, black trousers, ruffled-sleeved white shirts, short black and white vests, a pin striped white wrap around the waist, and red and white caps flopped to one side.

Exercise 2   Using the Comma Correctly (page 186)

At the time of Confederation, many Canadians considered lacrosse Canada's national sport. The National Lacrosse Association, founded in 1867, and its slogan, *Our Country and Our Game,* certainly clamed that status. Lacrosse was also closely associated with the game of baggataway, which was played by several First Nations. On the very day of Canada's creation, Kahnawake took the Dominion lacrosse title, which was considered a world championship at the time, by defeating the Montreal Lacrosse Club. The First Nations in eastern North America originated the sport, but non-Natives had altered the game by drawing up new "rules." Even so, the Kahnawake team defeated the Montreal team while playing under the non-Native rules. Lacrosse had a sporadic history before 1914. After an enthusiastic beginning in the 1860s, it ebbed in the early 1870s as a result, they say, of the presence of "rowdy" or undesirable elements at many of the matches. The game revived in the 1880s but also changed from amateur to professional. Around the same time, lacrosse also became a national sport, although the sport didn't boast a national association until 1912.

Exercise 3   Using the Comma Correctly (page 186)

Dedication and perseverance mark the career of African-Canadian jazz pianist Oscar Peterson. Born in Montreal on August 15, 1925, Peterson was the fourth in a family of five children. Peterson's father, a porter with the Canadian Pacific Railway, learned to play piano on his own. He also encouraged his children to become proficient musicians. Oscar's long and distinguished career really began to take off when Norman Ganz, the legendary jazz producer, discovered Oscar playing at a club in Montreal. Oscar then impressed those who came to see him at New York's Carnegie Hall. Since the 1950s, he has been considered the best jazz pianist in the world and has toured throughout North America, Europe, and Asia. In 1993, Oscar suffered a serious stroke. He could not play for two years; however, he overcame this setback and is still touring, recording, and composing today. He has since received a Grammy Award for Lifetime Achievement and an International Jazz Hall of Fame Award, proof that Oscar Peterson is still regarded as one of the greatest jazz musicians ever to play.

Exercise 1   Using the Apostrophe (page 188)
1. the <u>water's</u> flow
2. the <u>president's</u> office
3. the <u>people's</u> hopes
4. the <u>children's</u> nursery
5. the briefcase is <u>yours</u>
6. <u>everybody's</u> work

7. They <u>won't</u> open today.
8. the <u>1900's</u>
9. <u>Jennifer's and Michelle's</u> personalities
10. the <u>critics'</u> reviews

Exercise 2   Using the Apostrophe (pages 188–189)

1. The school's playground is empty.
2. The town's marketplace was crowded.
3. The lawyers' fees seemed excessive.
4. We've tried to convince him without success.
5. What's for dinner?
6. Who's responsible for this mess?
7. My sister-in-law's advice is generally good.
8. You will find those sweaters in the men's department.
9. Watson's and Dana's test scores were the highest in the class.
10. My aunt and uncle's home is warm and inviting.

Exercise 3   Using the Apostrophe (page 189)

Everybody's talking about Jim's new car. Its design is based on an old Italian model first built in the 1930's (*or* 1930s). It's strange to observe a model you've seen only in old movies. I don't think there are too many of his friends who won't be thrilled to accept an invitation for a ride. All his friends' cars are either American or Japanese—Hondas, Chevys, and Fords. His parents' generosity allowed him to buy the car, but now Jim realizes the upkeep will cost half his week's pay. Now he'll ask his supervisor about his chances for a small raise.

Practice 1 (page 190)

1. "After the Race" is a short story included in the book *Dubliners* (or <u>Dubliners</u>) by James Joyce.
2. In an address to the press Club in Washington, D.C., Pierre Trudeau said, "Living next to you is like sleeping with an elephant."
3. The director told his actors that they would have to learn their parts in twenty-four hours.
4. The word "night" should never be spelled "nite."
5. He saw the article "Digging Near the Nile" in last month's issue of *Archeology* (or <u>Archeology</u>).

Practice 2 (page 191)

1. A good way to understand a play is to read it; a better way is to see the play produced.
2. The old pipes in the street must be replaced; otherwise, the water main will burst.

3. The interviewer spoke with Millicent Silver, a musician; James O'Leary, a journalist; and Charles Bedford, an architect.
4. The bank teller was very polite; however, he would not release the cheque.
5. Boats are increasingly being made of fibreglass; perhaps wooden boats will become obsolete.

Practice 3 (page 192)

1. Three tennis players were on television that afternoon: Monica Seles, Martina Hingis, and Anna Kournikova.
2. The actress has what every actress needs: vanity.
3. The fruit store has several varieties of lettuce such as iceberg and romaine.
4. The institute will prepare you in three important areas: office skills, personal grooming, and interview techniques.
5. The clock went off at 6:10 this morning, but I continued to sleep.

Practice 4 (Page 193)

1. Scientists announced recently (*Nature*, February 2001) that there are 30,000 genes that make up the human genetic code.
2. Scientists have also identified genetic defects (more than 3,200) that are linked to various diseases.
3. No technique—at least not in my lifetime—seems to offer more promise than gene replacement therapy.
4. In Muscular Dystrophy, muscle cells without the protein called dystrophin (see photo above) waste away.
5. Unfortunately—and this has been a big blow to genetic researchers—nobody has yet been cured by the experiments with this therapy.

Exercise 1   Using All Punctuation Marks Correctly (page 193)

1. The Spanish word for "goodbye" is "adios."
2. I spoke to the man in French; he spoke back to me in Greek.
3. My professor could speak the following languages: Russian, German, and Chinese.
4. All foreign words are explained (see the glossary at the back of the book).
5. Have you read Judy Rebick's essay, "Kick 'em Again"?
6. "Please," I begged, "let me visit Ecuador."
7. The man spoke with a distinct accent; however, I could not guess his first language.
8. Most children in Canada—and I think this is a mistake—do not take the study of Canadian history seriously.

9. We were hoping to visit cities such as Lima, Bogota, and Quito.

10. The train departs at 5:40; therefore, we must leave for the station as soon as possible.

Exercise 2   Using All Punctuation Marks Correctly (page 194)

1. Emily Carr (1871–1945) was unusual for her time.

2. Women in the nineteenth century learned painting to be refined; ladies were never encouraged to be serious artists.

3. Emily went off to San Francisco, London, and Paris to study painting seriously; in fact, she emerged as one of Canada's prominent painters.

4. She wrestled with the artist's dilemma: should she paint in the traditional style of the day, or should she experiment with creative styles?

5. I recently bought a calendar that has many of Carr's works reproduced: "Totem Poles," completed in 1912; "Blue Sky," completed in 1934; "Mountain Forest," completed in 1936; and "Rushing Sea of Undergrowth," painted in 1936.

6. Many of her paintings depicted the wilderness and islands of coastal British Columbia (native village sites were also favourite subjects for her to paint).

7. The lack of interest in her work made Carr give up painting in 1916; however, other Canadian painters, some of whom were members of the famous Group of Seven, saw her work and encouraged her to continue painting.

8. At the age of 70, when advised for health reasons to slow down, Carr turned seriously to writing; she received the Governor General's award for her book, *Klee Wyck*.

9. Painting was an act of self-discovery for Carr: she wrote in her journal, "I always feel, when looking at a painting straight in the eye, I could have put more into it."

10. She is, and I'm serious, my favourite artist.

Exercise 3   Using All Punctuation Marks Correctly (pages 194–195)

1. Helen plays the saxophone; her brother plays the trumpet.

2. I'll take the following items: five legal pads, a box of paper clips, and a box of number two pencils.

3. She never spoke to her neighbours; in fact, she seldom went out of her house.

4. Winning the prizes were Mr. Hovan, chemistry professor; Ms. Lopez, sociologist; and Dr. Madison, research scientist at the lab.

5. "I found out," Peter said, "that your father was Greek."

6. There is nothing I can do for you today; however, if you come back tomorrow I'll see what I can do.

7. Women did not act on the stage in Shakespeare's time; young boys usually played the female roles.

8. Fewer Canadians now live on farms (see chart on page 546).

9. He called collect—believe it or not—just to tell me a joke.

10. I read George Grant's well-known book, Lament for a Nation.

Mastery and editing tests

Test 1   Editing for Correct Capitalization and Punctuation (page 195)

1. The plural form for the word "mouse" is "mice."

2. According to his birth certificate, he was born in Charlottetown, PEI, on June 20, 1965.

3. The train leaves at 8:30 and nobody's ready.

4. Moira, who is my best friend, will meet us at the theatre.

5. If it rains—and we pray it doesn't—the program will be cancelled.

6. Ladies and gentlemen, I am honoured to present the mayor of our great city.

7. My uncle read the newspaper; my aunt cooked dinner.

8. "My dear," said the father kindly, "you are soon going to feel better."

9. When she returned to work, her office coworkers welcomed her back.

10. He grew up west of the Rocky Mountains, but he now lives in Halifax.

Test 2   Editing for Correct Capitalization and Punctuation (page 195)

1. After the guests went home, the dirty dishes remained.

2. The word "and" is a conjunction.

3. She wrote the article for Canadian Geographic magazine while she was still director of the Museum of Natural History.

4. While still a Baptist minister, Tommy Douglas became Premier of Saskatchewan.

5. The term paper was handed in on time, and the quality of the thinking and writing was outstanding.

6. Harold agreed to work late because he wanted to finish the report before the weekend.

7. The Johnsons moved to the West last spring.

8. I called Dr. Rosen; however, I was able to speak only to the nurse.

9. Before eating, the dog showed us his tricks.

10. Nancy opened the envelope, read the letter, and shouted for joy.

Test 3   Editing for Correct Capitalization and Punctuation (page 196)

1. Mr. Franklin has retired; Eileen Smith will take over his job.

2. I told Grandmother to expect me by 7:00.

3. "The score is ten to nothing," said the announcer.

4. The woman who is sitting at the desk is the one to ask.

5. Even though she loves to paint, Freida is majoring in business.

6. Willy, the tall fellow on the right, drives up to Whistler, British Columbia, nearly every weekend to go skiing.

7. In history class, we are studying the French Revolution.

8. An interest in expensive clothing, nights out, and pretty girls caused his bank balance to drop dangerously low.

9. The painting by Titian sold for several million dollars, and the museum that purchased it felt it was a bargain.

10. The Norwegian student speaks German as well as English.

Test 4   Editing for Correct Capitalization and Punctuation (page 196)

On February 19, 1927, Edward Samuel Rogers, called Ted Rogers, made history with the launch of his new radio station. As a child, Ted was fascinated with amateur radio. In fact, several rooms of his house were filled with equipment and bulky storage batteries. At the time, radios operated on batteries, which were a real nuisance because they were large, unreliable, and often leaked dangerous sulphuric acid. Working long hours in his small lab on Chestnut Street, Rogers perfected a new way of building radios without batteries. The new "Batteryless Radio" gave a reception that was clearer and better than ever before possible. The station started by Rogers, which is still in existence, was known as CFRB. The initials stood for "Canada's First Rogers' Batteryless."

Test 5   Editing for Correct Capitalization and Punctuation (pages 196–197)

Without a doubt, Prime Minister Trudeau's most controversial decision was to use the War Measures Act. In the October Crisis of 1970, a group of radical separatists in Quebec, known as the FLQ, kidnapped Pierre Laporte, a prominent Quebec politician, and James Cross, a British diplomat. Trudeau then called upon his government to use the War Measures Act. The Act gave the police and the army the powers to do the following: detain people indefinitely without a trial, search houses without warrants, and tap phone lines. Many felt that Trudeau had acted rashly; indeed, this kind of police action seemed unnecessarily severe. It can be argued that the roots of Quebeckers' current mistrust of the Canadian government can be traced back to the October Crisis.

Chapter 11   Review: Using All You Have Learned

Exercise 1   Revising Fragments and Run-Ons (pages 199–200)

1. R Ten years ago, Niagara Falls, Ontario, was not a lively city; it needed a new direction.

2. R Trouble began for the city when the economy began to do poorly; this discouraged a much-needed improvement of its infrastructure.

3. F The downtown, with its casino, new nightclubs, and restaurants, has even more attractions than ever before.

4. R Whenever you walk downtown, you can still hear the roar of the Falls, which echoes throughout the streets of that city.

5. F The large casino is expanding all the time.

6. F Some people complain that the casino is an unethical way for the city to make money.

7. F The wax museum is where people can see replicas of once-popular movie stars and entertainers such as Michael Jackson and Ann-Margret.

8. F The atmosphere on Niagara Falls' Clifton Hill is unlike anywhere else in Canada.

9. C Upscale establishments such as the Rainforest Café are thriving, and it's harder to find cheesy attractions such as the serpent museum.

10. F Stars still shimmer in the night skies through the mists of the Falls.

Exercise 2 Revising Fragments and Run-Ons (pages 200–201)

1. F Scientists have now confirmed there is a planet like ours with a sun like ours elsewhere in the universe.
2. F The planet is only forty light years away from earth.
3. R A light year is the distance light travels in a year, which is six trillion miles.
4. F Some scientists thought that it could not be possible to find such a planet so similar to our own earth.
5. C You should go to an observatory and watch how astronomers prove their findings by using the latest equipment.
6. R The new planet has a temperature of 1,800 degrees; consequently, it could not have life on its surface.
7. R Because planets at these distances are not easy to see, you need the most sophisticated equipment.
8. R Astronomers do not have an easy job schedule, for they must work through the night.
9. F The same question remains about life on other planets.
10. F Meanwhile, scientists predict that they will find other such planets in other solar systems in the near future.

Exercise 3 Revising Fragments and Run-Ons (pages 201–202)

Joy Kogawa is known for her novels, poetry, and essays; she is also known for her activism. She was born in Vancouver in 1935, as a second-generation Japanese-Canadian. She writes about the stories of Japanese-Canadians seeking redress from the Canadian government for the actions against the Japanese-Canadians during the Second World War. When Canada was at war with Japan in 1942, the government committed a great injustice: it forced those Canadians of Japanese descent into special internment camps. As a young girl, Kogawa was one of 20,000 Japanese placed in internment camps in British Columbia. The Japanese-Canadians were released after the war, but they had nothing when they went home, for the Canadian government had taken away their property and their possessions. Kogawa's novel *Obasan* is about her experiences in an internment camp.

Exercise 4 Revising Fragments and Run-Ons (page 202)

In a recent issue of *Nature* magazine, scientists have reported the find of new dinosaur fossils of the biggest meat-eating dinosaur now known, even bigger than the Tyrannosaurus Rex. Seventy percent of the skeleton has been recovered; consequently, scientists can only estimate the creature's size. These fossils were first discovered in Argentina by Ruben Carolini, an automobile mechanic who hunts for dinosaur bones in his spare time. In honour of the discoverer, the dinosaur has been named Giganotosaurus Carolini. This dinosaur resembles Tyrannosaurus Rex, but it is thought to have been somewhat longer and three tons heavier. The two dinosaurs lived in completely different times and places. The newly discovered G. Carolini lived 30 million years before T. Rex. Scientists are interested to know if this new dinosaur was a hunter or a scavenger.

Exercise 5 Revising Fragments and Run-Ons (page 202)

Last spring a talk show host presented a daytime show on laser peels. Viewers watched a procedure that took less than two minutes. In front of the television cameras and the live audience, the host had the wrinkles zapped away from around his eyes. These high-energy laser beams are said to be quick, painless, safe, and without scarring. Add this new technology to face-lifts, dermabrasion, collagen injections, and chemical peels! More than 30,000 laser peels have been performed since 1992. Lasers were first used by dermatologists to remove port-wine stains in the late 1970s. For many people, this means they can now look as young as they feel, but the healing process can be painful and messy. Most physicians believe this is a much more precise method of rejuvenating the skin because it's so much more accurate, so much more predictable, and so much safer than other methods. One note of caution: any physician can buy the equipment with little or no training. Therefore, you should always check out the doctor's experience. A practitioner without experience could zap too deep and cause tissue damage. Following a laser zap, you must scrupulously avoid the sun for several months. Afterwards, always wear a sunscreen. One bad point about laser technology is the expense: a full-face laser peel costs from $2,000 to $6,000. Sorry, no long-term scientific studies have been conducted to prove their safety.

Mastery and editing tests

Test 1 Editing Sentences for Errors (page 203)

In a Victorian farmhouse on the eastern shore of Georgian Bay, John Watson walks down to the dock and pulls in the nets with the day's catch of perch, the local specialty. Here John and his wife have one goal: to live simply. After working for many years in city jobs, this retired couple spend their time tasting the good local fish, creating their own vegetable garden, and enjoying the visits of friends from time to time. Mrs. Watson is well versed in the art of preparing gourmet fare, but today she favours simple foods. "Why make the difficult meals when a simple meal is bound to please?" she says. Meals are served out on the porch facing the bay. Mrs. Watson does all the cooking herself—no fast food meals. When the boats are in harbour, it's only a short walk from the house to find out what the fishing is like.

Test 2   Editing Sentences for Errors (pages 203–204)

Virtually all societies have maintained some beliefs about witchcraft or sorcery. Before the witch craze, European beliefs were similar to those found on other continents. Witches and sorcerers were sometimes feared, sometimes persecuted, but often respected and recognized as people who served a useful role in the social order. For instance, they provided charms and amulets to protect people from harm or sickness, or they would act as oracles to decide the innocence or guilt of accused people. Magic directed against political leaders, however, was regarded as treason.

Belief in witches was a continuing preoccupation of villagers, but not an obsession. The penalties for unauthorized or malicious practice of witchcraft were commensurate with those enforced for other kinds of assault on individuals or their property.

Before C.E. 1000, the church's *Canon Episcopi* law tended to hold that it was both un-Christian and illegal to believe in the reality of witches. Witchcraft was not treated as part of the conspiracy theory of the demonic versus God, except for the *Canon*'s claim that women who believed themselves able to use love incantations or to fly at night with the pagan goddess Diana were suffering from delusions planned by the devil. The *Canon* asserted that the folkloric practice associated with such beliefs would disappear as all people became Christian.

Between C.E. 1000 and 1480, witches and sorcerers (along with other manifestations of supernatural beings) were redefined. Rather than harmless and misunderstood relics of pagan life, they became agents of the devil. In fact, many of the accusations made against witches in this period (incest, infanticide, and cannibalism) were the same as those that had been levelled against the early Christians by pagans. The process whereby folklore, witchcraft beliefs, ritual magic, and devil worship became one overall conspiracy was neither smooth nor gradual: it was contested in some areas and embraced in others.

Test 3   Editing Sentences for Errors (page 204)

Some books describe the common bedbug as harmless, but that only means that it causes no pain and produces no more that a mild reaction on the skin. While this may be true, people have been trying to get rid of bedbugs for many centuries. The ancient Greeks recommended hanging the feet of a deer at the foot of the bed. A better remedy was to place each leg of the bed in a bowl of water, preventing bugs from invading the bed (although it did not get rid of the bedbugs that were already living in the mattress). Some people, trying to figure out the behaviour patterns of bedbugs, have watched them leave a bed, climb up the wall, walk across the ceiling, and drop down on the waiting victim. Nearly a century ago, it was estimated that four million people in London were plagued with bedbugs. In Germany alone, seven hundred exterminators were busy all the time trying to get rid of them. No matter what kinds of sprays were used, including the formulas of such specialists as Southall and Tiffin, bedbugs promptly reinvaded rooms where victory had been declared.

Test 4   Editing Sentences for Errors (page 204)

Recently, a debate has started in Canada on the legalization of marijuana for medicinal purposes. Marijuana, it is claimed, relieves symptoms related to the following illnesses: epilepsy, glaucoma, multiple sclerosis, and chronic pain. People suffering from nausea and vomiting associated with some cancer and AIDS therapies have found that smoking marijuana brings relief from these side effects. In one case, a man suffering from AIDS has been given the right to cultivate and possess marijuana to treat his health condition. The Ministry of Health and Welfare has agreed to develop a plan that would include tests on medical marijuana; however, the recreational use of the drug will still be considered illegal. Although the vast majority of Canadians polled recently favour legalizing marijuana for medical purposes, the Government of Canada is quick to point out that the drug has not been approved as a therapeutic product in any country.

Test 5   Editing Sentences for Errors (page 205)

The 1976 Olympic Summer Games were held in Montreal, Quebec. They were the first Olympic Games to be held in Canada and will be remembered for, among other things, their planning errors, labour unrest, and construction delays. Most importantly, however, the Montreal Games ended up costing 10 times more than originally estimated. At the time, the Mayor of Montreal, Jean Drapeau, said that the price would not exceed $124 million. A special lottery, Olympic stamps, and a series of commemorative coins would help raise the necessary cash to pay for the construction of new facilities. The final cost for the 1976 Olympics, however, was about $1.5 billion, a tab that won't be paid off until 2005. In addition, the giant stadium built for the occasion was poorly designed. Although it is impressive to look at, it is an uncomfortable venue for audiences going to see concerts or sporting events. The stadium continues to be a financial burden. A few years ago, a large piece of concrete fell off the exterior of the stadium; however, nobody was hurt in the incident. The lessons learned during the 1976 Olympics helped the organizers of the 1988 Winter Olympics, which were held in Calgary, Alberta. The 1988 Winter Games were on time and budget, and the world-class facilities constructed for the Games are still used to train athletes.

Step 3   Understanding the Power of Words

Chapter 12   Choosing Words That Work

Exercise 1   Using Words Rich in Meaning (pages 209–210)

1. E
2. D
3. C
4. A
5. B

1. E
2. C
3. D
4. A
5. B

Exercise 2   Using Words Rich in Meaning (page 210)

old

1. extremely old
2. out-of-date
3. being in the style or fashion of former times
4. primitive, antiquated

car

1. a means of carrying or transporting something
2. a car that is not in good running order
3. a more formal word for "car"
4. an old and perhaps dilapidated car

weak

1. lacking in strength
2. physically weak; fragile
3. ill
4. unable to function

like

1. take pleasure in
2. to enjoy, especially a food or drink
3. to be lavish or excessive in one's affection
4. respect

Exercise 3   Using Words Rich in Meaning (page 211)

careful with money

1. not generous to others
2. wisely economical
3. being extremely economical
4. unwilling to spend money

coarse

1. not in good taste; improper
2. offensive language or behaviour
3. indecent or repulsive behaviour or language
4. not refined

plan

1. to plan secretly against something or someone
2. to plan in an original way; to invent
3. to plan with others, secretly
4. to make a devious plan against something or someone

firm

1. excessively firm, perhaps causing discomfort
2. having a serious disposition (personality or behaviour)
3. strong and dependable
4. unwilling or unable to change; unbending

Exercise 1   Denotation/Connotation (page 212)

1. village
2. wanders; meanders
3. unique; quaint
4. echo
5. travel; journey
6. thunderous; booming
7. desired; craved
8. stood; gathered

9. sizzling; frying
10. delicious

Exercise 2 Denotation/Connotation (pages 212–213)

1. jammed negative: "jammed" suggests that it will be difficult to move
2. meter maid negative: a civil servant whose only function is to write parking tickets
3. strewn negative: "strewn" suggests a mess
4. merchant positive: "merchants" sounds respectable
5. cruisers positive: "cruisers" suggests large, powerful cars

Exercise 3 Denotation/Connotation (page 213)

1. slippery negative: dishonest
2. to hog negative: to take
3. chummy here, negative; to be too friendly
4. glaring negative: obvious
5. swallowed negative: to accept without thinking

Exercise 1 Revising Wordy Sentences (page 215)

1. A large percentage of the people in the waiting room are becoming impatient.
   Most people in the waiting room are becoming impatient.
2. With respect to the matter before the board, I wish to appeal the decision.
   I wish to appeal the board's decision.
3. Her field of work afforded her many advantages.
   Her work provided many advantages.
4. The circumstances are such that I do not think we will go there again.
   We will not go there again.
5. I think he would be happy to have a job along the lines of television writing.
   He would like a job in television writing.
6. Regarding the doctor's fee, I think I should protest at least part of it.
   I should protest at least part of the doctor's fee.
7. There are several reasons I have for not wanting to go with her: the first is that I have no time; the second is that I have already seen the movie.
   I do not want to go with her because I have no time and I have seen the movie.
8. I spoke to him concerning the matter of my future plans.
   I spoke to him about my future plans.
9. It is necessary that each member of the team registers for participation in the race.
   Each team member needs to register to race.
10. In terms of the refund, I would expect the full refund as soon as possible.
    I expect a full refund soon.

Exercise 2 Revising Wordy Sentences (pages 215–216)

1. Dating practices continue on and obey their own laws no matter how much adults try to regulate them.
   Dating practices continue despite adult attempts to regulate them.
2. There are enormous differences between dating a century ago and dating now.
   Dating a century ago differs from dating now.
3. Back then, the chances for young people to be alone were few in number.
   Then, young people had few chances to be alone.
4. The basic fundamentals of dating were that you had to inform the parents and you had to put up with a chaperone.
   The fundamentals of dating required you to inform the parents and put up with a chaperone.
5. A chaperone was a person, usually an aunt or grandmother, who would chaperone a dating situation, to make sure that the situation was in control.
   A chaperone, usually an aunt or grandmother, supervised the date.
6. Now all of those restrictions have disappeared from view.
   Now those restrictions have disappeared.
7. They started to go when the automobile began to be used throughout the whole country.
   They declined with the invention of the automobile.
8. When World War II came, it appears that the rules for dating changed even more, as society tried to adapt to a stressful time.
   With the stress of World War II, the rules for dating changed even more.
9. After the war, the women's liberation movement was an advance forward in the relations between the sexes.
   After the war, the women's liberation movement advanced the relations between the sexes.

10. Today, the <u>basic important essentials</u> of dating <u>seem to be</u>: ask out whoever you want whenever you want.
Today, the essentials of dating are: ask out whoever you want whenever you want.

Exercise 3   Revising Wordy Sentences (pages 216–217)

1. In <u>the scientific century</u>, the twentieth century, we have seen the birth and development of the <u>modern</u> computer.
The twentieth century saw the birth and development of the computer.

2. Computers, <u>it seems to me</u>, are not the only mechanical marvels <u>of our age</u>.
Computers are not the only modern mechanical marvels.

3. The phonograph, also known as the gramophone, <u>has been with us throughout the century</u>, having come into general use about 1905 <u>or so</u>.
The phonograph, also known as the gramophone, came into general use about 1905.

4. The movies also came into vogue <u>about that time</u>, bringing <u>with them</u> an <u>enthralling new means of entertainment</u> for <u>vast numbers of people</u>.
The movies also came into vogue then, bringing new entertainment for people.

5. <u>There is another</u> major invention, of course, <u>which</u> is the automobile.
Another major invention is, of course, the automobile.

6. However, we are using computer-related inventions with <u>more and more frequency in recent years</u>.
However, we are using computer-related inventions more frequently.

7. <u>The fact is that</u> the washing machines <u>we operate</u>, the radios <u>we play</u>, the remote controls <u>we use for</u> our television sets, <u>all, it turns out</u>, are operated by some sort of computer.
Our washing machines, radios, and remote controls for televisions are all operated by some sort of computer.

8. <u>In my opinion</u>, if you are not <u>into the</u> use of computers, you are not in the twenty-first century.
If you do not use computers, you are not in the twenty-first century.

9. <u>This is a topic about</u> a current <u>subject that interests</u> nearly everyone.
This current topic interests nearly everyone.

10. <u>In this day and age, we have to wonder</u> how many of today's jobs will be taken over by computers in the future.
We wonder how many of today's jobs will be taken over by computers in the future.

Exercise 1   Recognizing Inappropriate Language for Formal Writing (page 218)

1. VIP — an important person
2. stomach for — fondness/desire
3. crazy about — in love with
4. the best man for the job — the best person possible
5. awesome — impressive
6. shut up — refused to incriminate himself
7. no man is an island — no person can live in isolation
8. dropped the ball — failed to follow through
9. listen up — pay attention
10. all men — all people

Exercise 2   Recognizing Inappropriate Language for Formal Writing (pages 218–219)

1. bad vibes — a bad impression
2. lot of guts — courage
3. weatherman's — weather forecaster's or meteorologist's
4. bull — not true
5. loony — strange
6. fireman — firefighter
7. the bomb, eh — attractive, the best
8. off the wall — insane/out of control
9. he tipped — left quietly
10. chairman — chairperson/chair

Exercise 3   Recognizing Inappropriate Language for Formal Writing (page 219)

1. shrink — psychiatrist
2. spooky — disturbing
3. wired — over-excited
4. lady — (omit)
5. going nuts — mentally unbalanced
6. some straight talk — He wanted her to tell him the truth.
7. old wives' tales — superstitions
8. doc — physician
9. pretty penny — high fee
10. O.K. — all right

Working Together (page 225)

1. a. I'm sorry. I don't understand.
   b. Please print legibly.
      I'm sorry, but I'm having trouble reading this. Could you tell me about ...?

c. You will need to write neatly so that your application can be processed more quickly.
d. May I ask your age?
e. Please read the instructions carefully and let me know if you have any questions.
f. Let me explain this procedure to you again.
g. I am sorry that we are so busy today.

Chapter 13 Paying Attention to Look-Alikes and Sound-Alikes

Exercise 1 Group I Words (pages 229–230)
1. oral/aural
2. buy/by
3. eminent/imminent
4. close/clothes
5. course/course
6. complements/compliment
7. foreward/forward
8. passed/past
9. plane/plain
10. presence/presents

Exercise 2 Group I Words (page 230)
Incorrect/Correct
imminent/eminent
buy/by
cloths/clothes
presence/presents
plain/plane
passed/past
complements/compliments
aural/oral
course/coarse
foreward/forward

Exercise 1 Group II Words (pages 232–233)
1. principal principle
2. rein rain
3. site sight
4. stationary stationery
5. two to to
6. vain vane
7. waste waist
8. Whether weather
9. hole whole
10. right rite

Exercise 2 Group II Words (pages 233–234)
1. site
2. reign
3. weather
4. waist
5. stationary
6. principal
7. write
8. whole

9. too
10. vain

Exercise 1 Group III Words (page 235)
1. Who's/whose
2. Your/you're
3. They're/their/there
4. we're/where
5. its/it's
6. your/you're
7. We're/where/were
8. Your/you're
9. Their/there/their
10. you're/your

Exercise 2 Group III Words (pages 235–236)
1. They're
2. there
3. ✓
4. ✓
5. Who's
6. Their
7. they're
8. we're
9. their
10. It's
11. it's
12. They're
13. it's
14. ✓
15. you're

Exercise 1 Group IV Words (page 238)
1. custom
2. dinner
3. desserts
4. councils
5. advise
6. Conscientious
7. choose
8. effect
9. breathe
10. advice

Exercise 2 Group IV Words (pages 238–239)
Incorrect/Correct
1. advise/advice
2. conscious/conscience
3. except/accept
4. desert/dessert
5. costume/custom
6. council/counsel
7. desserted/deserted
8. affects/effects

Exercise 1 Group V Words (page 241)
1. used
2. farther
3. Though
4. lose
5. than
6. quite
7. personnel
8. thorough

9. personal
10. especially

Exercise 2   Group V Words (page 241)

Incorrect/Correct

1. lose/loose
2. Through/Though
3. loose/lose
4. quite/quiet
5. special/especially
6. use/used
7. though/thought
8. thorough/through
9. receipts/recipes

Practice (page 242)

1. rising
2. rises/rose
3. sitting
4. sit
5. lying
6. lay

Practice (page 243)

1. laid, letters
2. laid, newspaper
3. raised, son
4. raised
5. set, chairs
6. setting

Exercise 1   Group VI Words (page 243)

1. set
2. lie
3. set
4. raising
5. sit
6. laid
7. rose
8. lain
9. Set/Lay
10. risen

Exercise 2   Group VI Words (pages 243–244)

1. lying
2. rise
3. lying
4. set/lay
5. rose
6. raised
7. laid
8. risen
9. lain
10. sat

Mastery and editing tests

Test 1   Editing for Words Commonly Confused (page 244)

Incorrect/Correct

1. then/than
2. quite/quiet
3. who's/whose
4. farther/further
5. though/thought
6. past/passed
7. there/their
8. weather/whether
9. foreward/forward
10. choses/chooses

Test 2   Editing for Words Commonly Confused (page 244–245)

Incorrect/Correct

1. set/sit
2. thorough/through
3. sight/site
4. your/you're
5. quiet/quite
6. by/buy
7. waste/waist
8. cloths/clothes
9. especial/special
10. plane/plain

Test 3   Editing for Words Commonly Confused (page 245)

Incorrect/Correct

1. Thought/Though
2. compliment/complement
3. Its/It's
4. to/too
5. advise/advice
6. conscience/conscious
7. affects/effects
8. hole/whole
9. lays/lies
10. breath/breathe

Test 4   Editing for Words Commonly Confused (pages 245–246)

Incorrect/Correct

1. principle/principal
2. immigrate/emigrate
3. coarse/course
4. stationery/stationary
5. looses/loses
6. raise/rise
7. its/it's
8. vane/vain
9. through/thorough
10. to/too

Test 5   Editing for Words Commonly Confused (page 246)

Incorrect/Correct
1. presents/presence
2. its/it's
3. were/where
4. maid/made
5. counsels/consuls
6. personal/personnel
7. sites/sights
8. use/used
9. passed/past
10. lays/lies

Step 4   Creating Effective Paragraphs

Chapter 14   Working with Paragraphs: Topic Sentences and Controlling Ideas

Exercise 1   Finding the Topic Sentence of a Paragraph (pages 254–255)
1. We are the great "Let's junk it" society!
2. Today, the hospital nurse has one of the hardest jobs of all.
3. Anything can happen at an agricultural fair.
4. It was one of the most uncomfortable experiences of my life.
5. During those summer days, the sunporch was the centre of our lives.

Exercise 2   Finding the Topic Sentence of a Paragraph (pages 255–256)
1. Astrology is enjoying increasing popularity all across Canada.
2. These same tourists are not always so aware that an impressive variety of other sights awaits them in this country.
3. The brain is one of the most remarkable organs, a part of the body that we have only begun to investigate.
4. Visiting these houses was an experience that would always stay in our memory.
5. We should always be suspicious of offers that promise us something for little or no effort or money.

Exercise 3   Finding the Topic Sentence of a Paragraph (pages 256–257)
1. c. Learning Cantonese was an essential part of my education.
2. b. Very early in my life, the manners of a Chinese lady were taught to me.
3. d. Life was often hard, but there was little reason for unhappiness.

4. c. The Chinese New Year, which would fall sometime in late January or early February, was the most special time of the year.

Exercise 1   Distinguishing a Topic Sentence from a Title (page 258)
1. T
2. T
3. TS
4. T
5. TS
6. T
7. T
8. TS
9. T
10. TS

Exercise 2   Distinguishing a Topic Sentence from a Title (page 258)
1. TS
2. T
3. TS
4. T
5. TS
6. TS
7. T
8. TS
9. T
10. TS

Exercise 3   Distinguishing a Topic Sentence from a Title (page 259)
1. T
2. TS
3. T
4. T
5. T
6. T
7. TS
8. T
9. TS
10. T

Exercise 1   Finding the Topic in the Topic Sentence (page 259–260)
1. Remodelling an old house can be frustrating.
2. University work demands more independence than high school work.
3. A well-made suit has three easily identified characteristics.
4. Growing up near a museum had a profound influence on my life.
5. My favourite room in the house would seem ugly to most people.
6. A student who goes to school full time and also works part time has to make careful use of every hour.

7. <u>One of the disadvantages of skiing</u> is the expense.

8. <u>Spanking</u> is the least successful way to discipline a child.

9. <u>An attractive wardrobe</u> does not have to be expensive.

10. <u>The first year of school</u> is usually the most demanding.

Exercise 2   Finding the Topic in the Topic Sentence (page 260)

1. <u>Taking care of a house</u> can easily be a full-time job.

2. Many <u>television news programs</u> are more interested in providing entertainment than newsworthy information.

3. One of the undisputed <u>goals in teaching</u> is to be able to offer individualized instruction.

4. Whether it's a car, a house, or a college, <u>bigger</u> isn't always better.

5. <u>Violence on television</u> is disturbing to most child psychologists.

6. In today's economy, <u>carrying at least one credit card</u> is probably advisable.

7. <u>Much highway advertising</u> is not only ugly but also distracting for the driver.

8. <u>Figuring out a semester course schedule</u> can be a complicated process.

9. In recent years, we have seen a dramatic revival of interest in <u>quilting</u>.

10. <u>The grading system at university</u> is quite different from that of the high school in my hometown.

Exercise 3   Finding the Topic in the Topic Sentence (page 260–261)

1. To my surprise, <u>the basement</u> had now been converted into a small studio apartment.

2. Of all the <u>prime ministers, Pierre Trudeau</u> probably enjoys the greatest popularity.

3. Scientists cannot yet explain how an <u>identical twin</u> often has an uncanny knowledge of what the other twin is doing or feeling.

4. If you don't have a car in Ottawa, you have undoubtedly discovered the limitations of the <u>public transportation</u> system.

5. When we met for dinner that night, I was shocked at <u>the change that had come over my friend</u>.

6. According to the report, <u>current tax laws</u> greatly benefit those who own real estate.

7. <u>Alanis Morissette</u>, the famous singer, began her career on television.

8. As we rode into town, <u>the streets</u> seemed unusually empty.

9. <u>Canada Post</u> offers its employees many long-term benefits.

10. Many people claim that <u>clipping coupons</u> can save them as much as 30 percent of their food bill.

Exercise 1   Finding the Controlling Idea (pages 261–262)

1. Vigorous <u>exercise</u> is a good way to reduce the effects of stress on the body.

2. <u>Montreal and Toronto</u> differ in four major ways.

3. <u>Television violence</u> causes aggressive behaviour in children.

4. <u>Athletic scholarships available to women</u> are increasing.

5. <u>Caffeine</u> has several adverse effects on the body.

6. <u>Jim Carey</u>, the actor, has an amusing personality.

7. <u>Training a parakeet to talk</u> takes great patience.

8. <u>Babysitting for a family with four preschool children</u> was the most difficult job I ever had.

9. <u>The hours between five and seven in the morning</u> are my most productive.

10. <u>The foggy night</u> was spooky.

Exercise 2   Finding the Controlling Idea (page 262)

1. <u>Piano lessons</u> turned out to be a disaster.

2. <u>The training of Japanese policemen</u> is quite different from Canadian police training.

3. <u>An Olympic champion</u> has five distinctive characteristics.

4. <u>The candidate's unethical financial dealings</u> will have a negative impact on this campaign.

5. <u>A bicycle ride along the coast</u> is a breath-taking trip.

6. <u>The grocery store</u> is another place where people waste a significant amount of money every week.

7. <u>Being an only child</u> is not as bad as people think.

8. <u>Rewarding children with candy or desserts</u> is an unfortunate habit of many parents.

9. <u>A childhood hobby</u> often develops into a promising career.

10. <u>The writing of a dictionary</u> is an incredibly detailed process.

Exercise 3   Finding the Controlling Idea (pages 262–263)

1. <u>Learning to type</u> takes more practice than talent.

2. <u>Shakespeare's plays</u> (are difficult for today's students because English has undergone many changes since the sixteenth century.)
3. <u>Calgary, Alberta,</u> (is one of the cities in the West that is experiencing significant population growth.)
4. <u>Half a dozen new health magazines</u> (are enjoying popularity.)
5. <u>The importance of good preschool programs for children</u> (has been sadly underestimated.)
6. <u>The disposal of toxic wastes</u> (has caused problems for many manufacturers.)
7. <u>Body piercing</u> (is a contentious issue between parents and kids.)
8. <u>Finding an inexpensive method to make salt water drinkable</u> (has been a difficult problem for decades.)
9. <u>Developing colour film</u> (is more complicated than developing black and white.)
10. <u>The cloudberry</u> (is one of the rare berries of the world.)

Chapter 15 Working with Paragraphs: Supporting Details

Practice (page 272)

Topic sentence: Everyone has heard of sure-fire formulas to prevent getting a cold.

What are some examples of home remedies?

Cold shower, regular exercise, hot rum toddy, cod-liver oil, tea with honey, citrus fruit juices, keeping one's feet dry.

What are some examples of over-the-counter remedies?

Vitamins, alkalizers, lemon drinks, antihistamines, decongestants, timed-release capsules, antibiotics, antiseptic gargles, bioflavonoids, nose drops and sprays.

What fact is given?

A Canadian averages two to three colds a year.

What expert is named? What is the statistic given by that source?

Canadian Public Health Service; 50% of the population have colds during the winter, and 20% have colds during the summer.

Exercise 1 Finding the Topic Sentence and Supporting Details (pages 273–274)

1.

Topic sentence: Saturday afternoon was a blessed time on the farm.

First reason: There would be no mail until Monday afternoon.

Second reason: Everybody looked forward to Sunday, a day of rest or play or a day for Squatters to work their own land.

Third reason: The author liked the thought of the oxen grazing all day on Sunday.

2.

Topic sentence: We continue to use pesticides at an alarming rate.

First statistical fact: There is a 25% chance that a store-bought peach contains unsafe levels of insecticides.

Second statistical fact: Lettuce crops are grown with more pesticides than any other vegetable.

Third statistical fact: 90% of North Americans would buy organic food if the prices were comparable to non-organic products.

Exercise 2 Finding the Topic Sentence and Supporting Details (pages 274–275)

1.

Topic sentence: Hilda takes an enormous amount of space, though so little time, in my adolescence.

First example: I wanted to look, sound, and dress like her.

Second example: She told me I wrote excellent letters.

Third example: She made a plaster cast of my face.

Fourth example: She had opinions on everything.

Fifth example: She took a picture of me, at sixteen, which I have still.

Sixth example: She and I were nearly killed, falling off a hillside road in her small car.

2.

Topic sentence: Those are the stereotypes, at least, and while most figure skating parents are supportive and gracious, there are enough of the contentious kind to dampen the fun.

First piece of evidence: Stories are told of figure skating moms who berate and fire coaches.

Second piece of evidence: Stories are told of moms who take over club management and use it to benefit their children only.

Third piece of evidence and supporting information: Some moms "glare" at other children to distract and intimidate them. Personal experience is offered by a skater.

Exercise 3   Finding the Topic Sentence and Supporting Details (pages 275–276)

1.

Topic sentence: Police in every major country have pressed for new powers to intercept what travels over the Internet.

First example: In 1999, Australian authorities gained the right to enter homes and hack into suspects' computers.

Second example and additional supporting information: British and U.S. police are able to legally install eavesdropping devices (e.g., the American "Carnivore") in Internet service providers' premises.

Third example: The Canadian CSE has argued that e-mail interception may be required for the protection of government networks.

2.

Topic sentence: Fairness is the ability to see more than one side in a situation, and sometimes it even means having the ability to decide against your own interests.

Anecdote: For example, in Halifax, Nova Scotia, a woman was locked in a bitter custody dispute that involved her thirteen-year-old son. The mother loved her son and wanted custody of him, even though she had a major health problem. She listened patiently while her ex-husband argued for full custody of the child. The woman felt that she had presented a good case before the judge, but when the boy was asked for his feelings in the matter, the mother found herself faced with a difficult situation: her son wanted to live with his father. Fairness to the child led the mother to give up her fight. Fairness, she discovered, is often painful because it means recognizing what is right instead of insisting on your own personal bias.

Exercise 1   Distinguishing a Supporting Detail from a Restatement of the Main Idea (pages 277–278)

1. a. SD
   b. R
   c. SD
   d. SD
2. a. SD
   b. SD
   c. R
   d. SD
3. a. R
   b. SD
   c. SD
   d. SD
4. a. SD
   b. SD
   c. R
   d. SD
5. a. SD
   b. SD
   c. SD
   d. R

Exercise 2   Recognizing a Supporting Detail from a Restatement of the Main Idea (pages 278–279)

1. a. SD
   b. SD
   c. R
   d. SD
2. a. R
   b. SD
   c. SD
   d. SD
3. a. SD
   b. R
   c. SD
   d. SD
4. a. SD
   b. R
   c. SD
   d. SD
5. a. SD
   b. R
   c. SD
   d. SD

Chapter 16   Developing Paragraphs: Illustration

Exercise 1   The Sources for Illustrations (pages 286–287)

1. Type of example: information from survey
2. Type of example: hypothetical example
3. Type of example: personal experience

Exercise 1   Analyzing Paragraphs Using Examples (page 290)

1. State the main idea in your own words.
   My favourite things are junky.
2. How many examples are given in the paragraph?
   17
4. Does the author use any words or phrases to signal any of the examples?
   "I've got my own list of favourite things"

Exercise 2   Analyzing Paragraphs Using Examples (pages 290–291)

1. State the main idea in your own words:
   In Canada, the number of votes a party receives is not always reflected in the number of seats the party wins.
2. How many examples are given in the paragraph?   *3*

5. If there is more than one example, can you suggest any order for the examples? *Strongest example last, by gap between percentage of popular vote and number of seats.*

Exercise 3   Analyzing Paragraphs Using Examples (pages 291–292)

1. State the main idea in your own words. *Sabatini was a great teacher because he encouraged his students.*
2. How many examples are given in the paragraph? *1*

Chapter 17   Developing Paragraphs: Description

Exercise 1   Selecting the Dominant Impression (page 305)

1. exciting
2. bright and trendy
3. cluttered
4. dilapidated
5. organized
6. crowded
7. claustrophobic
8. romantic
9. fashionably decorated
10. warm and cozy

Exercise 2   Selecting the Dominant Impression (pages 305–306)

1. egotistical
2. forgetful
3. helpful
4. efficient
5. hard-working
6. aggressive
7. sullen
8. pushy
9. hopeful
10. ecstatic

Exercise 1   Revising Vague Dominant Impressions (page 307)

1. bright blue
2. as warm as a baby's bath
3. a relaxing change of pace
4. destructive to property
5. full of cars and shopping carts
6. picturesque
7. delicious
8. as annoying as my friends' brothers are
9. in good repair
10. fulfilling

Exercise 2   Revising Vague Dominant Impressions (page 307)

1. romantic
2. like a starry night of dark blue and silver

3. peaceful
4. hilarious
5. too sour
6. poorly acted
7. like it was comfortable
8. exhilarating
9. expensive
10. informative

Practice (page 308)

1. see, hear, feel
2. see, smell
3. smell, taste

Exercise 1   Recognizing Sensory Images (pages 308–309)

Sight: coffee-stained desks, crumpled paper, grimy walls, hazy atmosphere

Sound: clattering typewriters, editor's voice

Smell: smoke

Exercise 2   Recognizing Sensory Images (page 309)

Sight: thick slabs of ice, jagged peaks, green-grey water

Sound: "crack of a rifle," "splitting and booming of the ice"

Touch: edges of ice, cold, "roads became mires," "dried, matted grass," oozing mud

Exercise 3   Recognizing Sensory Images (pages 309–310)

Sight: men in underwear sitting on edge of bed, nearly empty refrigerators

Sound: men coughing and spitting, radio, portable televisions

Touch: men rolling cigarettes

Taste: tomato soup, crackers

Smell: burnt toast

Exercise 1   Working for Coherence: Using Space Order (page 314)

1. 5, 4, 2, 3, 1.
2. 3, 5, 2, 1, 4.
3. 2, 3, 1, 4.

Chapter 18   Developing Paragraphs: Narration

Exercise 1   Working for Coherence: Using Details in Order of Time Sequence (page 330)

1. 3, 1, 4, 2, 5.
2. 5, 1, 4, 3, 2.

Exercise 2   Working for Coherence: Using Details in Order of Time Sequence (pages 330–331)

1. 4, 1, 2, 3, 5, 6, 7.
2. 5, 7, 2, 3, 1, 4, 6.

Exercise 3   Working for Coherence: Using Details in Order of Time Sequence (pages 331–332)
1. 2, 1, 5, 3, 4.
2. 6, 1, 3, 2, 4, 5.

Exercise 1   Working with Transitions (page 333)

First, Next, Then

Exercise 2   Working with Transitions (pages 333–334)

in the meantime

every moment

several times

suddenly

immediately

in a short time

Finally

Exercise 3   Working with Transitions (page 334)

Meantime

soon

from time to time

By now

every instant

again

Chapter 19   Developing Paragraphs: Process

Exercise 1   Is the Process Complete? (pages 344–345)

How to Make a Swedish Spice Cake

Missing step or steps:

Preheat the oven to 350°.

Assemble equipment: one large mixing bowl, one small mixing bowl, measuring spoons, measuring cups, and electric beater.

Separate eggs.

Cool cake in pan for 10 minutes; then invert on rack. Cool cake completely before serving.

How to Plan a Wedding

Missing step or steps:

Choose and order invitations.

Send out invitations.

Consult with florist and order flowers.

Consult with caterer and order food and services.

Have fitting for wedding clothes; pick up clothes.

Exercise 2   Is the Process Complete? (pages 345–346)

How to Prepare for an Essay Exam

Missing step or steps:

Review class notes daily.

Begin studying for the test specifically two or three days before the test.

Do final review of reading assignments and notes the day before the test.

How to Wrap a Present

Missing step or steps:

Place the gift inside the box.

On one end of the box, fold the top flap straight down (the top of the package should be facing down), then fold one side in, then the other side in, and then fold the bottom flap up and tape.

Exercise 1   Coherence in Process: Order in Logical Sequence (page 347)

4, 8, 7, 10, 1, 3, 5, 9, 6, 2.

Exercise 2   Coherence in Process: Order in Logical Sequence (page 347)

7, 5, 1, 8, 2, 6, 3, 9, 4.

Chapter 20   Developing Paragraphs: Comparison or Contrast

Exercise 1   Evaluating the Two-Part Topic (page 360)
1. too broad
2. suitable
3. suitable
4. suitable
5. too broad
6. suitable
7. suitable
8. suitable
9. too broad
10. suitable

Exercise 1   Working for Coherence: Recognizing the Two Approaches to Ordering Material (pages 364–365)
1. Block, Differences.
2. Point-by-Point, Similarities.
3. Block, Differences.
4. Point-by-Point, Similarities.
5. Point-by-Point, Similarities.

Exercise 1   Using Transitions in Comparisons and Contrasts (pages 367–368)
1. While Dr. Rappole has a reputation for excellent bedside manners, Dr. Connolly is very withdrawn and speaks so softly that it is

almost impossible to understand what he has said.

2. In Canada, soccer has only recently become the most popular sport of young children; in contrast, soccer has always been immensely popular in Brazil.

3. Like Hemingway's book *Death in the Afternoon*, his novel *The Old Man and the Sea* deals with the theme of man against nature.

4. Amy is carefree and fun-loving, with little interest in school; on the other hand, Janet, Amy's sister, is so studious and hardworking that she is always on the honour roll.

5. The apartment had almost no furniture, was badly in need of painting, and felt chilly even though I was wearing a coat; in contrast, the other apartment was attractively furnished, had been freshly painted, and was warm enough so that I had to take off my coat.

Exercise 2 Using Transitions in Comparisons and Contrasts (pages 368–369)

1. MuchMusic plays videos that are popular with a younger, hipper audience, while MuchMoreMusic plays videos that people over the age of thirty enjoy.

2. Shakespeare's *Romeo and Juliet* is a famous love story that takes place in Italy, in contrast with *West Side Story*, a modern-day version of Shakespeare's love story that takes place in New York City.

3. The French Revolution was directed by the common people whereas the Russian Revolution was directed by an elite group of thinkers.

4. Although some scientists believe dinosaurs became extinct because they ran out of food, other scientists believe that dinosaurs were victims of radiation from a meteor from outer space.

5. The Museum of Modern Art in New York City shows paintings, photographs, movies, and many other forms of twentieth-century art; on the other hand, the Metropolitan Museum of Art in New York City contains sculptures, paintings, and other forms of art that date from the beginning of recorded history.

Exercise 3 Using Transitions in Comparisons and Contrasts (pages 369–370)

1. A ballet dancer trains for years in order to master all aspects of dance, similar to a football player who puts in years of practice in order to learn the game from every angle.

2. George Brown College is a large urban college that has the resources of a big city as part of its attraction for faculty and students; on the other hand, Malaspina College is a small college that has beautiful surroundings as part of its attraction.

3. Ice cream, a popular dessert for many years, has many calories and added chemicals to give it more flavour, but tofuti is a dessert made of processed soybeans that is low in calories and contains no harmful additives.

4. Ted Rogers gave much of his time and money for education and the arts; similarly, Ed Mirvish supported the arts by building theatres in Toronto.

5. Although *The Nature of Love and Unidentified Human Remains* has a single setting for all of its action, *Love and Human Remains*, a film based on the play, is able to use many different settings to present all of its action.

Chapter 21 Developing Paragraphs: Cause and Effect

Exercise 1 Finding Causes and Effects in Paragraphs (pages 382–383)

What causes a headache?
1. Tension
2. Diet
   a. Caffeine
   b. Salt
   c. Sugar
3. Allergies to household chemicals
   a. Polishes
   b. Waxes
   c. Bug killers
   d. Paint

What are some of the effects of headaches?
1. Nausea
2. Sleep problems
3. Reliance on drugs
4. Loss of job productivity
5. Cancelled plans
6. Strained relationships with friends and family
7. Depression

Exercise 2 Separating the Cause from the Effect (page 383)

1. cause: working mothers
   effect: need for daycare
2. cause: the number of children with working mothers
   effect: strains on the daycare system

3. problem: the need for mothers to have time to be with their children
   solution: job changes or decreased hours
4. cause: many mothers feel their children need parental supervision
   effect: they limit their work to the time when the children are attending school
5. problem: conflict between financial needs and parental responsibility
   result: emotional crises

Exercise 1   Looking for the Causal Relationship (pages 384–385)

1. T
2. C
3. T
4. C
5. C
6. T
7. C
8. T
9. C
10. T

Chapter 22   Developing Paragraphs: Definition and Classification

Exercise 1   Working with Classification: Finding the Basis for a Classification (pages 401–402)

1. by price, by dependability, by appearance
2. by location, site, architectural styles
3. locations; types of inhabitants (singles, young families, retirees); proximity to stores, hospitals, and other conveniences
4. location of major groups of believers in world; belief; number of adherents
5. types of ingredients; nutritional value; colours
6. enjoyment level; type of event attended; type of wardrobe worn
7. ease of maintenance; appearance; cost
8. purpose of the medicines; length of time in use; effects on the body
9. nutritional value; taste; fat and sugar contents
10. likability; place in family (immediate family, one generation removed, etc.); frequency of visits

Exercise 2   Working with Classification: Making Distinct Categories (pages 402–404)

1. men's
   children's and infant's
   women's
   teenagers'
2. soap
   soft drinks
   toys
   automobiles
   cereal
   clothing
3. football
   soccer
   volleyball
   basketball
   hockey
   track
4. pediatrician
   anesthesiologist
   neurologist
   cardiologist
   dermatologist
   orthopedic surgeon
5. cowboy hat
   balaclava
   baseball cap
   top hat
   mad bomber hat
   Panama hat
6. The Modern Novel
   The Canadian Short Story
   Introduction to Fiction
   Shakespeare
   Romantic Poetry
   Writing the Term Paper
7. ballpoint pens
   felt tip pens
   calligraphy pens
   fountain pens
   cartridge pens
   quill pen
8. tango
   macarena
   waltz
   electric slide
   cha-cha
   disco
9. letters
   advertisements
   solicitations
   bills
   packages
   post cards
10. jazz
    rhythm and blues
    Broadway show tunes
    alternative
    country
    rock

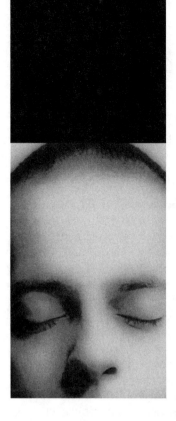

READINGS

CONTENTS

My Life as a High School Dropout
ROBERT FULFORD

Some people achieve incredible accomplishments while facing considerable obstacles. This was the experience of Robert Fulford. Despite living with Attention Deficit Disorder (ADD) all his life, Fulford has become one of Canada's most distinguished writers and critics. He has written books and essays on a wide range of subjects, from history and architecture to visual arts and sports. In the following essay, Fulford examines the impact of ADD on his education and career.

1   No book on sex is complete without an account of those who don't get any, and no discussion of formal education should omit the many citizens who mostly lack it, such as I. The other day, while testifying as an expert witness in a copyright case, I was asked about my education. "Completed Grade 11 in high school," I replied. The lawyer cross-examining me raised his eyebrows and, just to be sure, asked whether I had any further education. No, I said. As he moved on to his next question, my mind floated back to 1950, when I was 18 years old and concluding my career as the most dismal academic failure I had ever met.

2   If this delicate subject comes up, kind friends treat my high school life as mildly comic, a cute eccentricity. I don't discourage that interpretation, but nor do I agree with it. It was, in fact, horrible. One history teacher called me the best student he had ever taught but in the same breath made it clear he didn't expect me to go anywhere, educationally speaking. How right he was. When finally I made my escape, I had some of the worst marks in Malvern Collegiate, which may have been the least-demanding high school in Toronto.

3   Failed Grade 10, repeated it, then passed Grade 11 (in only one year!), then failed again in Grade 12. But I wrote the Grade 13 provincial exams in history and English without taking the courses, and passed them. It has since occurred to me that if only there had been a school that taught nothing but history and English, I might be a high school graduate today.

4   None of this should be considered a complaint; things didn't work out badly. But it appears now that I was living with a condition whose name was then unknown, attention deficit disorder. Since the mid-1990s, ADD has become a suspiciously fashionable diagnosis. Any idea that so quickly invades our collective consciousness, accompanied by convenient drug therapy, should be scrutinized with care. Even so, ADD demands to be taken seriously, and there is no question I displayed, floridly, a crucial tell-tale sign.

5   Aside from a tendency to be easily distracted, my most obvious ADD characteristic was an acute version of something that remains merely chronic in most adolescents: I didn't feel like paying attention to what I didn't feel like paying attention to. It was considered laziness at the time, and part of me still thinks of it that way, but its extreme form falls within the ADD spectrum.

6   Experts in ADD try to state it gently. Dr. Sam Goldstein, a University of Utah child psychologist, says that people with ADD "do not respond well to repetitive, effortful, uninteresting activities that others choose for them." Dr. Gabor Maté of Vancouver, in his engrossing book, *Scattered Minds: A New Look at the Origins and Healing of Attention Deficit Disorder*, says that among people with ADD, "Active attention, the mind fully engaged and the brain performing work, is mustered only in special circumstances of high motivation." Dr. Maté's discovery that he himself suffers from ADD, even though he made his way through medical school, makes his book especially persuasive.

7   The ADD mind can't arouse itself when it should be attending to a subject it finds uninteresting. In those circumstances it is (Dr. Maté says) "immobilizingly difficult" to marshal the brain's motivational apparatus. Immobilized: That was

me when confronted by chemistry, irregular French verbs, geometry and many other mandatory subjects. Anyone could see they weren't that hard and had to be conquered, but I couldn't manage.

8   Still, I was a long-time heavy reader, and my reading was slowly growing serious. I could write a little, and I could type like the wind. Though poorly co-ordinated, I performed better in typing than in any other subject. A student of ADD could easily explain. I wanted passionately to be a newspaperman and had seen newspapermen typing fast, so I simply bulled my way through, emotionally motivated.

9   I had been working part time in the sports department of *The Globe and Mail* during summers and weekends, and the sports editor agreed to take me on, at 18, as the lowliest sports writer. My older colleagues, some stern and some friendly, generously assumed the responsibility of making me reliable enough to remain employed, screaming when necessary. Thirty months later, the paper shifted me to the news pages, at my request, and my education grew more interesting. Whatever law I learned, for instance, was acquired sitting as a reporter in courtrooms. Jury trials were best, because you could hear the same legal principles explained three times, by judge, Crown attorney and defence lawyer. Covering City Hall was even more rewarding. Many aldermen had little idea of what was going on, so the city solicitor had to explain to them the subtleties of "enabling legislation" and "legal non-conforming use" and many other concepts. A man of infinite patience, he did this so slowly even I caught on.

10   Meanwhile, I was pursuing private studies elsewhere. My art education was obtained in galleries and the studios of artists, my literary education in books, magazines and ferocious arguments. Later I became a reviewer of books and read somewhere that literary critics are people who conduct their education in public. In my own case, this was true in a more than usually literal sense.

11   Once or twice I've been asked whether I missed much by failing to go to university. The answer is yes and no. I missed all those subjects a university teaches best: classics, ancient history, the sciences, philosophy. But on the other hand, I wouldn't have studied any of them. I would have picked modern literature, modern history, political science, maybe even journalism—all, in my opinion, subjects you study best at your own pace, according to your own inclination and more or less on your own. At 18 I wasn't nearly smart enough to choose the really useful subjects. That's one of the flaws I long ago noticed in the education system: All the truly vital decisions are made by people too young to know exactly what they're doing. Maybe I should be grateful to ADD for saving me from folly.

Questions for Critical Thinking

1. The first paragraph of this essay tells us of a situation in which Robert Fulford is forced to admit he has not completed high school and has no postsecondary education. What does an education mean to you? How do you define the word "education"? How did Robert Fulford overcome the fact that he had a limited formal education?

2. What are some of the characteristics of ADD as described in the article? How did this affect Fulford's life?

3. Describe Robert Fulford's attitude toward his condition. Generally speaking, does he display any regrets at having ADD? If so, what are they? If not, why not?

4. What is Robert Fulford's purpose in writing this essay? Of what does he hope to convince the reader?

Writing in Response

1. Write an essay that describes how you succeeded at something, giving an account of any physical or mental challenges that you had to overcome. What lessons did you learn from this experience?

2. We often make a distinction between a formal education and an informal one. What do you think is the difference between the two? Is a formal education more important than an informal education? Why or why not?

3. Write an essay describing your own education. What have you learned so far? What do you hope to learn in the future? What were the circumstances surrounding your decision to pursue a postsecondary education?

There Goes the Neighborhood

JIM SHAHIN

Although all neighbourhoods may change over time, some aspects of living in a community remain the same. In the following essay, Jim Shahin's fond memories of his old neighbourhood lead him to realize that while his life has progressed far beyond the little world of his childhood, some truths about living with others in a community will always remain.

1　There is an order to my neighborhood, a rhythm to its life. It is an order and a rhythm I've come to know during the eight years I've lived in my house. But the order has been disrupted and the rhythm set off its beat. The reason is the house next door.

2　The house next door has been empty since before Thanksgiving, maybe Halloween, I don't remember exactly. I only know it's been a while and the suspense is killing me: What's happening with the house? When is somebody going to move in? Who is it going to be?

3　I keep hoping the new occupant will be a family with a kid my son's age and parents we like. But it'll probably be me of twenty years ago—some guy with a loud stereo and weird friends.

4　Please, God, not that. Please, not all-night parties with people hanging out on the front porch drinking keg beer until dawn. Please, no hard rock blasting through the walls causing visitations from the police. And please, please, please, no colored plastic owls with little light bulbs in them illuminating the backyard with its furniture of metal folding chairs and telephone-cable-spool tables.

5　As I look back on those days, I recall the mother's curse: May you have a child just like yourself. A worse fate is to have neighbors in their twenties who are just like you when you were that age.

6　A neighborhood is a delicate thing, but a resilient thing. There are deaths and births and graduations, and tuna casseroles at all of them. Neighborhoods are also indelible. You remember everything about where you grew up—the way the misty light from the street lamp shone on the snow, the person who lived next door, the smell in the bluish evening air of roasting meats at dinner time, the closest kid your age, the mounds of raked leaves piled every year at the same place by the curb. These, anyway, are among the things I remember.

7　There are nice people, like the woman who tipped me a dime every week when I went to collect for my paper route. There are mean people, like the guy across the street who would make a face, shake his fist, and keep our ball if it rolled into his yard. (We started tormenting him by smacking crab apples onto his lawn with a tennis racket.) And there are the just plain weird people, like the guy who went a little nuts one night and, when asked by his neighbor to turn off his porch light because it was shining into their side of the duplex, responded by grabbing a shotgun and marching down the middle of the street blasting it into the air and yelling admonitions, while his wife trailed behind him in her bathrobe hollering, "You tell him, hon!"

8   I remember playing handball, stickball, and football in the street. I remember the enormous sixty-foot blue spruce on the corner of our yard and climbing to the very top and swaying back and forth in the wind and being afraid. I remember beating up a kid who was a year older than me because I caught him beating up my younger brother. I remember my friends with their unlikely names, Itchy and Rusty, and going to their houses and wondering at Rusty's why my family couldn't have hoagies for dinner like this family did and at Itchy's discovering the transcendent delight of peanut butter and butter on toast.

9   I remember the blond girl about five or six years older than me, who I thought was absolutely gorgeous and who baby-sat me. I forgave her because I adored her. She was sitting on my porch baby-sitting one summer evening when suddenly I was overcome with an uncontrollable urge to kiss her. I did. Rather than make me feel like the foolish little kid that I was, she said simply, "I could use a root beer. Let's go inside." And she rose from the lawn chair, all poise and dignity, rolled up the teen magazine she had been reading, and went into the house. I stayed on the porch, frozen with mortification at what I had done. Then I ran off into the neighborhood, hoping it hadn't seen, and looking to it for comfort.

10   As a kid growing up, your neighborhood is the world and it takes a long time before you realize that the world is not your neighborhood. These days, the world of the neighborhood belongs more to Sam, my six-year-old son, than to me. The impressions he is forming of his place will stay with him forever, shaping in some important ways his sense of the world, and I often wonder what those impressions are.

11   We live in an older neighborhood of gently rolling hills, big houses, and large old pecan and live oak trees. Geographically it is small and, depending on your viewpoint, either within walking distance of restaurants, grocery stores, doctors offices, record stores, a nightclub, a liquor store, some fast-food joints, a coffee bar, a vintage-clothes place, a comic-book shop, and assorted other retail outlets, or it is in the ever-tightening vice grip of commercial development.

12   An in-town neighborhood a few blocks from the university, its social mix is diverse. There are retirees, twentysomethings, families, professors, graduate students, state government employees, fast-food workers, rock-and-rollers, and a few people whose lives I think it's probably best I didn't know much about. It is a quiet neighborhood. Few kids live in it. And although it is close to campus, it does not attract the bare-chested, Jeep-riding, beer-swilling crowd.

13   What will Sam remember of all this? Maybe the little girl down the street with whom he sometimes plays. Probably the ice-cream parlor a few blocks away. Undoubtedly the burger joint down the hill.

14   My wife says he'll most likely recall the sound of clomping feet. Built in 1911, our house is two stories, but, like many of the houses in the neighborhood, it was carved into a triplex years ago. We live on the first floor and rent out the two units above us. The floors are hardwood throughout. Great aesthetically. Not so hot acoustically.

15   Maybe, though, it won't be the clomping that Sam remembers. Maybe it'll be the cooing of the doves that one of the tenants keeps. Or maybe it will be the neighborhood itself, its shadings and scents and sounds, or maybe the people who comprise it, such as the large elderly man across the street who, I'm told, is a professor of English at the university and who we usually see doing something industrious like chopping wood, or the guy who walks his dogs so much it seems like it's his job.

16   Or maybe his memories will be of the house next door. Lately, there has been some activity in and around the house. We've seen a beige collie in the backyard on occasion. And we've heard music coming from the house while power drills are running. But no one lives there yet.

17   I haven't seen the guy, only glimpsed his dog and heard his music. He likes his music loud. We can hear it from our porch. It's rock. Hard rock. Hard, loud, depresso, scream, rage rock. The kind of stuff I fear I would be listening to if I was in my twenties.

18   I contemplate the possibilities. Maybe he's a carpenter doing some renovation work for the people who are moving in and he likes to bring his dog to the job site. Or maybe he's the new neighbor, getting the place ready before setting up residence.

19   And I remember my mother's words. And I figure I could do worse. The neighborhood's resilient. So am I.

20   Maybe I'll take him a tuna casserole.

Questions for Critical Thinking

1. The author's title gives the reader one impression of what the essay will be about, but it is not until paragraph 5 that we learn who is being referred to in that title. Why does the writer give us the title he does, and why does he keep us waiting before he reveals his true subject?

2. What are the sources of humour in this essay? Why are we amused at so many of the writer's details?

3. How does the conclusion bring the point of the essay into focus? What is the significance of the tuna casserole at the very end? What exactly is the author's thesis?

4. In paragraphs 6 through 9, Jim Shahin describes the neighbourhood of his youth. Make a list of the kinds of memories he has. In paragraphs 10 through 18, he describes the neighbourhood he now lives in. Does he cover the same topics that he discussed about his childhood neighbourhood? What would be the list of memories you would make of your childhood neighbourhood?

5. If a new neighbour were to move in to the apartment or house next door to you tomorrow, what kind of person would you want that neighbour to be? Take a survey in your class. Is there any agreement about what the ideal neighbour should be like?

Writing in Response

1. Write an essay in which you classify the kinds of neighbours that have moved in and out of your neighbourhood.

2. Write an essay classifying the neighbourhoods you have moved in and out of during your life.

3. Describe the best or the worst neighbour you have ever encountered.

4. Define your neighbourhood for someone who has never seen it. Study Jim Shahin's descriptions to get ideas for the kinds of details you can include.

5. Argue about the benefits of living in a culturally diverse neighbourhood as opposed to living in a neighbourhood with only one ethnic group.

6. Argue about the benefits of living in a neighbourhood with all age groups as opposed to only young families or only retired couples, or all college students.

7. Define what makes a good neighbour.

Virtual Death Machine

KEN MacQUEEN

Once available only in arcades, video games can now be found in many Canadian homes. The following article from *Maclean's* magazine describes the nature of these games, the reasons why people are worried about them, and recent attempts at regulating their content and sale.

1   For a remarkable number of children, happiness is a virtual gun. A scoped rifle for the long shot, though you can't beat a shotgun for close work. Grenades have a certain indiscriminate charm, but if you're into shredding flesh, consider a nail gun for that personal touch. Nothing is more intimate than a knife; you can practically feel them die. But, hey, when things start backing up, and it seems there's a killer or a cop or a civilian or two around every corner, no kid should be without your basic high-calibre assault rifle.

2   The arsenal is loaded into home computers or stacked as video-game cartridges next to the Nintendo or PlayStation. In all, the $12-billion-a-year gaming industry now surpasses Hollywood box-office receipts. Few children—boys outnumber girls by more than three to one—have not been exposed, whether at a friend's home or through schoolyard tales of video conquest. Families that wouldn't consider having a real weapon on the premises would do well to inventory their computer games, says Stephen Kline, a professor of communications at Simon Fraser University. Odds are parents will find a child's garden of mayhem: exotic weapons with endless rounds of ammo; graphics so cinematic that bodies twitch and faces contort when Johnny pulls the trigger; the sounds of trash talk, of clattering shell casings, of body parts splatting. For those who don't like killing in the abstract, "skinning" allows the technologically adept to superimpose a real face on a virtual target. "Until now," says Kline, "the industry has been able to get away with murder."

3   This month, the B.C. government passed what it calls the first legislation in North America to implement a mandatory classification and regulatory system for video games. Ontario, Manitoba and Saskatchewan are also considering stricter controls. "We're not in a hurry to slap on new regulations, but it's not something we have ruled out either," says Brian Kelcey, a spokesman for the Ontario ministry of consumer and business services, which is preparing an internal report on the issue.

4   The B.C. law puts video games on an equal footing with film or video. Minors—who account for more than half the gaming population—can no longer buy, rent or view Mature or Adult-rated video games. Stores must segregate Mature games and display Adult-only games in a separate room. The provincial film-classification branch has authority to ban games if they exceed the same standards that apply to films. And although details are still unclear, arcade games will also be regulated.

5   While industry reaction is mixed, the law has the blessing of a B.C. pressure group, the Coalition Opposing Violent Entertainment. The organization includes the RCMP, the B.C. Teachers' Federation, Media Watch and End the Arms Race. Coalition spokeswoman Jillian Skeet of End the Arms Race says the campaign

against video violence has drawn more interest than her work against real weapons. Still, in her view, there isn't much difference. The perpetrators of several school massacres in the United States were heavy players of the Doom and Quake series of so-called first-person shooter games. While there isn't a direct "causal link," she says, "there is a pattern there that we ignore, I think, to our folly."

6   Kline says there is a generation gap on the issue. Surveys indicate, he says, that about 80 per cent of parents view computers as educational tools. Fewer than one per cent of children say they use educational software. "The kids report that their parents regulate video games less than they regulate TV," he says. Many games are fairly benign, especially strategy games, flying simulations or sports simulations. Yet 58 per cent of the favourite games of B.C. teens are violent, Kline says, and almost one-third of the favourite games for children under 12 are rated Teen or Mature. Kline plays a videotaped interview with a boy of about 10 who seems genuinely puzzled when asked about the games he plays. "It's either about racing or hurting a person," says the boy. "What other goals would you have?"

7   The B.C. law uses an industry-sanctioned, but independently operated, vetting system, the New York–based Entertainment Software Rating Board. The board established its rating guidelines—E, Everyone, T, Teen, M, Mature, A, Adult—in 1994, and they are already printed on most game packages. The board was an industry response to the outcry for regulation over such fight games as 1996's Mortal Kombat Trilogy—a product now too lame and primitive to hold the interest of most gamers. Barry Salmon, spokesman for British Columbia's film-classification office, said the existing ratings are valid, but they were ignored. "If a five-year-old can buy it, what's the point?" Still, he notes the games downloaded off the Net will remain unregulated: "There's no way we can unilaterally affect what's on the Internet."

8   Industry associations in the United States and Canada say regulation is unnecessary as long as families follow the rating system. However, not everyone in the industry considers regulation a threat. "Of course there should be a rating system," says Danielle Michael, director of business development for Radical Entertainment Inc., Vancouver-based game developers. "It just shows the industry is growing up." Radical creates a wide range of action and sports titles—from Jackie Chan: Stuntmaster to NHL Championship 2000—but it does not produce first-person shooters. Still, Michael dismisses the notion that the games present a danger: "I'm a mother and I have no problem with kids playing video games. I think it's better than staring blankly into a TV."

9   Interaction is exactly what makes violent games dangerous, say critics. Children aren't just watching murders and car wrecks, says Skeet; they're causing "things that we would consider in real life to be sociopathic."

10   So, why do kids play them? Kline has developed a surprising theory: because of their parents. Parental fear that the real world is dangerous has severely curtailed the simple joys of unstructured outdoor play. Instead, parents offer the haven of a well-stocked computer room, perhaps a more dangerous place. "The paradox is, I feel that my kids are safe if they're in the bedroom playing on these games, safer than if they were out on the street playing street hockey," says Kline.

11   Critics and industry alike agree that no law can replace a vigilant parent. "Video games are not a babysitter," says Katie Rebak, manager of media and community relations for Rogers Video, which has a nationwide policy of not renting age-inappropriate video games to children. Kline says parents can spend $1,000 on their kids' video system and games and rationalize it as a lesson in hand-eye co-ordination. Or they can spend a couple of bucks on a device that teaches kids far more complex skills. It's called a ball. "And if you go out in the backyard, too," he says, "you might even get to know them a little bit."

Questions for Critical Thinking

1. From reading the first paragraph of this article, what is a common feature of most video games available today? Do you think that the author gives an accurate account of what these video games are like?

2. From the information available in the article (paragraphs 2 and 6), what group of people in society likes playing these video games the most?

3. According to the article (paragraphs 4 and 7), how are authorities planning to regulate the sale of these games? Do you think that these efforts will succeed? What are some of the challenges they face? Can you think of any solutions?

Writing in Response

1. After reading the article, do you think that playing these games has an effect on kids? If so, what effects do they have? Are these effects positive or negative?

2. The author of the article writes: "Critics and industry alike agree that no law can replace a vigilant parent" (paragraph 11). Write an essay describing the steps that parents might take to regulate the video games with which their children play.

3. Censorship is a controversial topic. Provide a definition of censorship, then write an essay discussing its benefits and drawbacks. Do you think the content of these games should be censored?

4. Imagine you are someone who loves to play these video games, and you have read the above article. Write an essay describing the benefits of video games (or other aspects of these games that you like). Are people just overreacting to this issue?

Parking on the Past

SHELLEY DIVNICH HAGGERT

Like many other parts of Canada, the landscape of southern Ontario is rich in history. Although some houses, churches, and inns date back almost two centuries, not all are of national historical importance. In the following essay, Windsor, Ontario, writer Shelley Divnich Haggert considers the personal impact of our vanishing heritage.

1   Tucked away behind the liquor store off Lakeshore Road in Sarnia, Ont., there is a small plot of land enclosed with a chain-link fence. Progress and civilization surround it. On one side lies the liquor store parking lot, while the other sides face single-family homes several decades old. Traffic speeds down Lakeshore, and few people will notice this spot as they pass.

2   Forgotten patches of land are not unusual in our cities, so what makes this one an oddity? My ancestors are buried there. I don't know how old the Kemsley family cemetery is—only that it is the final resting place of my great-great-grandparents and several of their children. The weathered and leaning stones indicate at least one generation before my great-great-grandparents may be buried there as

well. A tall, four-sided stone in the centre displays birth and death dates on all sides, marking as many as seven or eight graves. Many stones are unreadable—time and nature have taken their toll on the engraving. Others have almost sunk out of sight. At some point in time, the family erected the fence to keep the grounds from becoming a place for teens to party. In random patches along that fence, ivy has entwined itself, providing a buffer between the grounds and the outside world. Except for the gravestones, it could be a vacant lot anywhere.

3   I was nine years old when I was first introduced to this piece of my history. Passing through Sarnia, my aunt stopped to let me have a look. I remember that we had to climb the fence—no one seemed to know who has the key. The weeds were knee high, and for the first time I saw poison ivy up close. I don't remember much else about that visit. I just thought it was cool that my family had its own cemetery.

4   A decade later, I was living in Sarnia, and my cemetery appeared on the front page of the Lambton College newspaper. A journalism student had taken it upon himself to investigate this local mystery. There weren't many answers to be found. An elderly cousin appeared to own the property. My great-aunt—who lived in Sarnia—had paid to have the weeds cleared after receiving a notice from the city, and she was the recipient of the tax statements.

5   Another decade or so has passed, and our family has been approached by a lawyer. It seems someone wants to buy the property, or part of it, and turn it into more parking. Some relatives, like me, have expressed shock and dismay; others are pretty apathetic.

6   It's true, sometimes we need to bury the past, but must we pave it over? In the constant battle between progress and preserving our heritage, progress is winning. In my own home town, the François Baby House sits nestled between hotels and parking garages, with Casino Windsor only a few blocks away. From this site, British and Canadian forces launched their successful attack on Detroit in 1812. In the Rebellion of 1837–1838, the Battle of Windsor was fought behind this house. Its future seems secure—since it began housing Windsor's Community Museum it has earned official protection. But the future has marched right to the doorstep; the building can't even be seen until you're almost on top of it.

7   So much of our heritage has been lost. Our children think of Lundy's Lane in Niagara Falls as a place where merry-go-rounds and souvenirs can be found. They don't connect the name with the bloodiest battle ever fought on Canadian soil. It was here that the American invasion was brought to a halt. But once again we've marked the spot with casinos and concrete. Across Canada, the odd plaque commemorates significant people or events that shaped the country—but most people don't stop to read them.

8   And now the push for parking threatens my personal heritage. Eventually developers will pave over the efforts of my great-grandmother, a widow with 10 children, who scraped together dimes to pay for a stone to be placed at her parents' grave years ago.

9   My ancestors were not famous, they didn't win wars or found institutions or anything else that might have earned them a place in the history books. They were too busy eking out a living, feeding children, keeping body and soul together. And there aren't many left who remember them at all. We just know where they lived and where they died. After years of effort just to be average, they were buried in a small plot of land, which now sits in the shadow of the liquor store, just off Lakeshore Road in Sarnia, Ont. Some of them have been there for more than a century. Can't we let them rest?

Questions for Critical Thinking

1. In the first paragraph, the author describes a small plot of land in Sarnia, Ontario. What is the significance of this plot of land to the author? What is the author arguing against? Is the essay interesting and persuasive?

2. Find the paragraph that best expresses the topic and controlling idea of this essay. What are they? Do you have to read to the end to find out what point the author wants to make about the topic? State the author's thesis in your own words.

3. Would it be easy to part with something if it's been in your family for generations? Why or why not? What would make you part with an antique handed down from your great-grandparents?

4. What do you think would explain the different reactions among members of the author's family when they heard the news that someone wanted to buy the old cemetery to turn it into a parking lot (paragraph 5)?

5. Do you know of any places of historical importance in the town where you live? How would you find out about them?

Writing in Response

1. Find out if there are any historical places close to where you live. Research and write an essay on one of them.

2. "If we started saving every old house and building, we'd be slaves to the past and there'd be no progress." Do you agree with this statement? Write an essay on why you do or do not think it is important to preserve old buildings or other sites.

3. If you think it is important to save old buildings and other old sites, should we preserve every old building or just those with historical significance? Why or why not?

Urban Legends

JACK MABLEY

Every culture has its tales and legends, and our modern urban culture is no exception. In this report on urban legends, Jack Mabley reports on some of these well-known city folktales and examines how they continue to be told despite the fact that they are pure myth.

1   Surely you've heard about the cobra in the clothing section. Or the rapist with the hook hand. Or the kidnapping of grandmother's body.

2   These are urban legends, or fairy tales.

3   A girl went into a fast-food place and bought a take-out dinner. When she got home she opened the box, bit into a piece, and found to her horror she had taken a bite of a deep-fried rat.

4   It never happened, though it was repeated thousands of times. It always happened to a friend or a friend of a friend. Scholars in an academic discipline called folklore have interviewed thousands of people trying to pin down this and other urban legends. They have yet to find a legitimate origin of the widely circulated legends.

5   They'd be funny if they weren't so costly. Usually the rumors name a specific store or fast-food place, and these companies have had to spend millions to counteract the rumors. One of the most vicious and most expensive involved the "man-in-the-moon" trademark on Proctor & Gamble products. A rumor went across the country that this symbol somehow involved witchery. It didn't and doesn't.

6   Business suffers when these rumors involve stores or specific products. A bubble gum company in the East had to take out full-page ads to put down a rumor that there were spider eggs in their gum. The company hired investigators to try to discover the origin of the rumor.

7   Sometimes denial of a rumor only accelerates its circulation.

8   The stolen grandmother legend comes in various forms, the most common being about a young couple vacationing in Mexico with one's grandmother.

9   The grandmother dies in Mexico. Fearing complications getting her body back to the States, the couple puts the body in the trunk of their car. They clear customs and after a few miles stop for coffee. When they come out of the restaurant, the car (with the body) has been stolen.

10   A professor of folklore at Indiana University said, "Everybody swears up and down they know the couple it happened to. But when you go to the people they name, they refer you to someone else. It's an endless chain. It always is."

11   The baby-sitter story has countless versions, usually embellished with each telling and retelling. The main one involves a baby-sitter getting threatening phone calls. She asks the operator to trace the calls. The operator tells the baby-sitter to get out of the house in a hurry—the call is being made from an extension phone. The spinners of this fairy tale overlook the fact that it is impossible to make this kind of call.

12   Students were frightened when a rumor swept campuses that a famous psychic predicted twenty-five girls would be slain on campuses by an ax murderer. The psychic denied the prediction, but that did little to alleviate the fear for months.

13   Larry Danielson, an English professor at the University of Illinois and a student of folklore, told us he heard the fried rat rumor "three or four years ago, and just the other night at a dinner party, a faculty wife brought it up."

14   He also heard three or four versions of a story about a man injured in an explosion while smoking near his wife's hair spray. On the way to the hospital he fell out of the stretcher and broke a leg.

15   Rumors generally are "grotesque stories," Danielson said. "They're usually within the realm of possibility and involve grotesque incidents, often with bodily mutilation."

16   Many of the grisly rumors seem to appeal to adolescents, he said, "because they're going through such dramatic physical and psychological changes. They have a lot of anxiety about physical malformations and death."

17   There's the poisonous spider in the clothing from Singapore. The cult leaders hypnotizing children at the supermarket. The teenage girl who reappears every year at the scene of the crash that took her life.

18   Rumors for every purse and purpose. Legendary bunkum.

Questions for Critical Thinking

1. Jack Mabley gives several examples of "urban legends," or stories that turned out to be only rumours. Can you add your own specific examples to those given in the essay? What are the stories currently going round on your campus or in your neighbourhood? Do you believe them?

2. In paragraph 4, the writer notes that people who study folklore "have interviewed thousands of people trying to pin down . . . urban legends." Why do you think these researchers continue to try to pin down these stories?

3. What motivates people to begin rumours? What motivates other people to repeat the stories and make them even more elaborate than when they first heard them?

Writing in Response

1. In the essay, the writer refers to scholars who have studied the entire issue of urban legends. He uses a professor, Larry Danielson, to explain why these legends are created and told over and over again. Why do you think urban legends are so popular? Use the explanation in paragraph 16 of the essay, along with your own theories, to discuss the whole issue of urban legends.

2. Write the history of a rumour or legend in your school or neighbourhood. How did the story begin? What were the results, good or bad, of the spread of this rumour? Was there any truth to the tale?

3. In the essay, the writer points out that more than one company has had to spend a great deal of money fighting some of the rumours that have been circulated about them. Write about various effects rumours can have on a large company or even on a small business. For example, what are the effects of these rumours on the cost of products we buy? (Be sure to include the costs of legal fees and advertising in a company's expenses.) Before you start to write, be sure to make a complete list of all effects that come to mind. Work with a group if possible.

Thin Edge of the Wedge (Island)
LESLEY CHOYCE

Places change over time. In this essay, Lesley Choyce shows us that the physical environment can have an immense impact on the way a place looks. As you read this essay, think about the ways in which your own home has changed over the years.

1   Wedge Island is barely discernible on a road map of Nova Scotia because there are no roads leading there. Although it is not truly an island, its tether to the eastern shore is so tenuous that it remains remote and seemingly adrift. Eroded by the forces of the North Atlantic, it is a mere fragment of what was once a formidable headland. Within a lifetime, it will most likely be reduced to a rubble of stone, an insignificant reef at high tide. But for now, the Wedge exists, a reminder that nothing is permanent on this shore. Geologists define it as a "drowned coast" because the sea is gradually engulfing it. It has been for a long time.

2   Something like a dinosaur's bony spine of boulders leads a wary hiker from the salt-bleached fish shacks on the mainland to the Wedge. If it's a fine July day—blue sky, big and bold above—the hiker might slide his hand along the silky beards of sea oats as he leaves solid land, then dance from rock to rock. Low tide is the best bet to make it there in one piece. Still, waves will spank the rocks from both sides, slap cold saltwater on his shoes and spit clean, frothy Atlantic into his face.

3   Wedge Island is a defeated drumlin, a dagger-shaped remnant of land stretching a good kilometre out to sea. Smashed lobster traps, shreds of polypropylene rope as well as bones of birds and beasts litter the rocks near the shore. Thirty metres up

the red dirt cliff sits a parliament of herring gulls peering down at a rare visitor with some suspicion. If the visitor scurries up the side of crumbling dirt, the gulls will complain loudly at his intrusion, then take to the sky and let him pass.

4   At the top is a grassy peninsula a mere 60 centimetres wide where both sides have been sculpted away by rains and pounding seas. It's a place of vertigo and lost history. The land widens as it extends seaward onto this near-island of full thistles, raspberry bushes and grass that seems cropped short as a putting green.

5   Farther out, at the very tip of the island, bare ribs of bedrock protrude into the sea. This is the same rock you'd find if you could make one giant leap from here across the Atlantic and step ashore on the edge of the Sahara. It is the very rock that was once part of the super-continent that drifted north to crash into this coast, then drag itself away to form Africa.

6   The island is a forgotten domain on the edge of the continent. It is easy to imagine that no man has ever been here before. But on the way back to the main-land, the truth reveals itself on the western shore. Not three metres from the edge of a cliff eight storeys high is a circle of lichen-covered rocks in the grass. A man-made well. The water is deep and long-legged insects skim along its obsidian sur-face. The well is full, nearly to the brim—it seems impossible given its elevation on this narrow wedge of land.

7   Nearby are two dents in the ground, as if some giant had punched down into a massive surface of dough. Those two dents were once the foundations of a farm-house and barn. Nearby fields sprouted cabbage and turnips. A family lived on veg-etables from the stony soil, cod and mackerel from the sea. There were no roads, no cars, nothing but boats for commerce with Halifax. A way of life long gone.

8   The rains and seas will continue to conspire to undo the ribbon of land left between the well's fresh water and the sky. The well's stone walls will collapse. The drumlin's cliff will be pried by ice, and pocked by pelting rain. The sea will slip out stones from beneath the hill, the turf up above will tumble, and eventually the water of the farmer's well will gush out of the heart of the headland and race down to meet the sea.

Questions for Critical Thinking

1. This passage on Wedge Island is very descriptive. Underline each sensory image that makes it vivid. What purpose does the description serve in this essay?

2. The author includes many details about the island's past. Make a list of these details. What do they reveal about the island's history?

3. What does the last paragraph show? Why do you think the author chooses to conclude the essay in this way?

4. Descriptive writing usually depicts the way things look like in space rather than describing events in time. Find transition words or expressions that help the reader follow this descriptive essay easily.

Writing in Response

1. Write a description of a place from your childhood. It can be a house you once lived in or visited, or it can be an attraction such as a museum or an amuse-ment park.

2. Choyce reveals how Wedge Island has changed over many years. Think of a place that you have seen that has also changed significantly. Write an essay in

which you describe these changes. Remember to use descriptive writing techniques.

3. Think of a place you enjoy visiting today, such as a restaurant, nightclub, or park. Imagine how this place will look twenty-five years from now. What details do you think will change? What will remain the same? Write a descriptive essay that reveals the changes that the place will go through.

4. Find an old photograph of someone you know. Imagine the events that led up to the taking of the picture. How has the person changed physically? What do these changes reveal about his or her character? Write a descriptive essay about this photograph.

Summer Reading

MICHAEL DORRIS

Michael Dorris was a Native American professor and writer. His works include both fiction and nonfiction. The following essay describes a summer in the writer's childhood, a time when he had ordinary expectations, but something very extraordinary happened to him.

1   When I was fourteen, I earned money in the summer by mowing lawns, and within a few weeks I had built up a regular clientele. I got to know people by the flowers they planted that I had to remember not to cut down, by the things they lost in the grass or stuck in the ground on purpose. I reached the point with most of them when I knew in advance what complaint was about to be spoken, which particular request was most important. And I learned something about the measure of my neighbors by their preferred method of payment: by the job, by the month—or not at all.

2   Mr. Ballou fell into the last category, and he always had a reason why. On one day he had no change for a fifty, on another he was flat out of checks, on another, he was simply out when I knocked on his door. Still, except for the money part, he was a nice enough old guy, always waving or tipping his hat when he'd see me from a distance. I figured him for a thin retirement check, maybe a work-related injury that kept him from doing his own yard work. Sure, I kept a running total, but I didn't worry about the amount too much. Grass was grass, and the little that Mr. Ballou's property comprised didn't take long to trim.

3   Then, one late afternoon in mid-July, the hottest time of the year, I was walking by his house and he opened the door, motioned me to come inside. The hall was cool, shaded, and it took my eyes a minute to adjust to the muted light.

4   "I owe you," Mr. Ballou began, "but . . . "

5   I thought I'd save him the trouble of thinking up a new excuse. "No problem. Don't worry about it."

6   "The bank made a mistake in my account," he continued, ignoring my words. "It will be cleared up in a day or two. But in the meantime I thought perhaps you could choose one or two volumes for a down payment."

7   He gestured toward the walls and I saw that books were stacked everywhere. It was like a library, except with no order to the arrangement.

8   "Take your time," Mr. Ballou encouraged. "Read, borrow, keep. Find something you like. What do you read?"

9   "I don't know." And I didn't. I generally read what was in front of me, what I could snag from the paperback rack at the drugstore, what I found at the library, magazines, the back of cereal boxes, comics. The idea of consciously seeking out a

special title was new to me, but, I realized, not without appeal—so I browsed through the piles of books.

10   "You actually read all of these?"

11   "This isn't much," Mr. Ballou said. "This is nothing, just what I've kept, the ones worth looking at a second time."

12   "Pick for me, then."

13   He raised his eyebrows, cocked his head, regarded me appraisingly as though measuring me for a suit. After a moment, he nodded, searched through a stack, and handed me a dark red hard-bound book, fairly thick.

14   "*The Last of the Just*," I read. "By André Schwarz-Bart. What's it about?"

15   "You tell me," he said. "Next week."

16   I started after supper, sitting outdoors on an uncomfortable kitchen chair. Within a few pages, the yard, the summer, disappeared, the bright oblivion of adolescence temporarily lifted, and I was plunged into the aching tragedy of the Holocaust, the extraordinary clash of good, represented by one decent man, and evil. Translated from French, the language was elegant, simple, overwhelming. When the evening light finally failed I moved inside, read all through the night.

17   To this day, thirty years later, I vividly remember the experience. It was my first voluntary encounter with world literature, and I was stunned by the undiluted power a novel could contain. I lacked the vocabulary, however, to translate my feelings into words, so the next week, when Mr. Ballou asked, "Well?" I only replied, "It was good."

18   "Keep it, then," he said. "Shall I suggest another?"

19   I nodded, and was presented with the paperback edition of Margaret Mead's *Coming of Age in Samoa*.

20   To make two long stories short, Mr. Ballou never paid me a dime for cutting his grass that year or the next, but for fifteen years I taught anthropology at Dartmouth College. Summer reading was not the innocent pastime I had assumed it to be, not a breezy, instantly forgettable escape in a hammock (though I've since enjoyed many of those, too). A book, if it arrives before you at the right moment, in the proper season, at a point of intermission in the daily business of things, will change the course of all that follows.

Questions for Critical Thinking

1. The author uses narration to develop his ideas about the importance of reading. Summarize the story.

2. Review paragraphs 2 through 6 in the essay and decide why Mr. Ballou could not (or would not) pay Michael Dorris. Do you think he did not have enough money, or was he unwilling to spend money on something other than books?

3. What were the author's reading habits before his encounter with Mr. Ballou? What do you think his reading habits were after this summer experience?

4. The second book Mr. Ballou gave the author was Margaret Mead's *Coming of Age in Samoa,* one of the most important books on anthropology (the study of social and cultural development of people) written in the last century. In the next sentence, Michael Dorris tells us that "for fifteen years I taught anthropology at Dartmouth College." What connection does the writer want us to make?

5. When is it appropriate or acceptable for a person to repay a financial debt, not with money but with some other form of repayment, either in goods or services? When is it not a good idea to try to settle a debt in this way?

6. In the first paragraph, the writer indicates he received no payment from some of his customers, and in the concluding paragraph he mentions that Mr. Ballou never gave him any money for mowing his lawn. The writer did, nevertheless, get paid. Explain.

Writing in Response

1. This story is about an adolescent who had a summer job. Write an essay in which you discuss the lessons that young people can learn by having the responsibility of part-time jobs while they are growing up.

2. Write an essay in which you talk about the people in your neighbourhood and the personalities you have observed through the years you have lived there. What lessons did they teach you or what help did they offer you? You could use description, narration, example, and/or cause and effect to develop your ideas.

3. Michael Dorris concludes his essay by noting that if you come across a book "at the right moment," it could change the direction of your life. Write an essay about something that happened to you that changed your life in an important way.

My Favourite Place
DAVID ADAMS RICHARDS

Travelling often enables us to experience a new place and culture, but it often also makes us re-evaluate the climate and customs of our own homeland. In the following essay by David Adams Richards, the author discovers that Canadians share many similarities with Australians.

1   It was not so hot in Tasmania, it was not hot in Adelaide either, but from Sydney north to Brisbane it was "getting there" as they say back home in the Maritimes. And by the time we reached Coolum Beach, and in our apartment, with a balcony that overlooked miles of gold coloured sand, and almost the entire South Pacific, there was no question of holding it back—Hot was the word. But I have found that the worst thing you can do, as a Canadian, is mention that it is Hot. As Canadians, we should be honour-bound to hop about on burning coals before we give into the bastards by admitting we find it the least bit warm.

2   You see, I was sweating in Brisbane—and they were saying how late the spring was in coming. I happened into a Pizza Hut, which in itself is as warm as most Maritimers can stand. And I decided to make conversation, which is another glaringly fatal flaw Maritimers are known for.

3   "Hot isn't it," I said to a man sitting beside me who looked like he had been baked in a potter's oven sometime in the sixties.

4   He looked at me, screwed up his eyes.

5   "OT?—OT?—where the bloody hell you from mate?"

6   "Canada," I whispered.

7   "Where?"

8   "Can-a-da," I whispered again.

9   "E-y," he said, in direction of the kitchen, "This Can-ad-e-an 'ere thinks it's— OT! Martha—Canada ere thinks it OTT!?"

10   "WOT—OTTT!" laughed a woman from behind the oven, though I didn't manage to see her face. "O—where's he from?"

11   "CANADA."

12   "Ah, that explains it mate," she said somewhat disappointed, as if she was hoping for a raving lunatic to brighten her day, and discovered only a Canadian, wanting a pizza, olives on one side, pepperoni on the other.

13   The man then told me I should watch out for snakes and crocs and spiders. This had all been said to me before, so I tried to look nonchalant, even shrugging at the idea that snakes could get into shopping baskets and elevators. But my friend continued.

14   "We got the great white too mate—WHITE DEATH—a nasty customer he is. Why there are more things can kill you in Australia than anywhere I reckon," he said happily.

15   So I told him if he happened to go to Canada, he better watch our for—icicles falling off buildings. I just blurted that out without thinking, but I knew I'd scared him. Why? Because there is one thing the average Australian cannot imagine—and that is –40 degree weather. Any Canadian should keep this in mind if they ever get into an argument with an Australian over which country is less livable.

16   But we were now at Coolum Beach north of Brisbane. And the ocean was dazzling. Right whales on their journey to the South Pole, breached on the horizon, dolphins skimmed the surface, small towns dotted miles of uninterrupted shore, the stars in the southern sky were infinite. I knew why people lived here.

17   Besides we had been in Australia two months and had not yet been eaten by a snake, though I was almost sure I saw one coming toward me each time I shut off the bedroom light.

18   In fact for all the dire warnings we saw nothing dangerous at all.

19   We did get to see a stuffed salt water crocodile, about seven metres long, with a model of a grown woman standing beside it. Even looking at it could give you a shudder. I told my wife Peg if we went farther north—to Darwin—we could buy "If you get eaten by a croc while in Darwin" insurance, right along with our flight insurance. This is of course true, but Peggy said it was too far to go just for the benefit of the insurance. So we were to stay at Coolum and relax in its unbridled warmth and generosity. I suppose what is most beautiful about Australia, is that the Aussies themselves seem so much like Maritimers, Maritimers with suntans and accents, who were forced into paradise by the British justice system. They are friendly, lovable, and kind. Besides, they know their beer, their sport, their tattoos, and their songs. They also hate almost everything we hate, which is a real indicator of closeness (politics, GST, capital cities, snobbish pretence and biker wars).

20   Not many though have gone swimming in the Bay of Fundy. I could tell this when they called the water we swam in on those fine spring mornings cold.

21   "It's still a bit fresh don't you think mate?"

22   To us Maritimers, it was a bath with large waves, some undertow you had to pay attention to, and a shark net 50 metres off shore. For the first few days I swam, I did not know what the shark net was there for. When I discovered it to be the net that kept sharks from coming in contact with swimmers, I had only one question.

23   "What happens if a shark gets through the net?"

24   "Oh then we ring a bell mate," the lifeguard said.

25   I thought of this next morning when I found myself closer to the net than the shore, and saw the shark net's buoy bobbing in the swell. Looking down I could see 10 metres beneath me. I began to assess my chances.

26   "If a shark got through the net—it would be something like a race," I thought. "The little bell would jingle like we were at a starter's gate. I'd have about a 20-metre head start on the nasty customer. Who would reach the shore first?"

27   Well, what was the point of pondering it too long? Best to go in and get a tan. On one of the most beautiful beaches in the entire world, one could suspend time all afternoon. And life really was too short.

Questions for Critical Thinking

1. The author uses narration to make a point. Describe the sequence of events that makes up the story he tells. What is the point the author wants to make?

2. The author uses dialogue in this essay. How does the dialogue add to the overall tone of the story? What other function does it serve? What do we learn from it?

3. During the story, what do we learn about the author's attitude toward Australians? Use specific examples from the essay that support your answer.

4. Select three or four details about Maritimers that the author discusses; then select three or four details about Australians. What differences can you see between these groups of people? What are the similarities?

5. What does the author's view of Australian wildlife reveal about him? Does his focus on Australian wildlife have any other purpose in this story? Be specific.

6. Does the author's attitude change at all over the course of the narrative? Why or why not?

Writing in Response

1. Many people have travelled throughout Canada or in other parts of the world. Write a story about an important moment during your travels.

2. Narrate a story about an event that changed your life. Remember to choose carefully the details that you decide to include.

3. Write an article for a travel magazine wherein you convince your readers to travel to a particular place. What aspects of this place do you think would make someone want to visit there? Keep your purpose for writing in mind when you write your story.

4. This essay by David Adams Richards contains many humorous elements. How does the author achieve this humour? Write your own story about a humorous event in your life.

The Art of Play: Street Games in the Depression

GLYNN A. LEYSHON

The Great Depression, which lasted throughout the 1930s, was a difficult time for thousands of Canadians. Even during this gloomy period, however, children's natural desire to play and have fun could not be dampened. As you read the following essay by Glynn A. Leyshon, try to compare it with a previous essay in this collection entitled "Virtual Death Machine."

1   The street games of children in the Great Depression were a product of the times. Like most children's games, they were handed down from the previous generation, but because so many people, particularly in the working class, faced extreme financial restrictions in the 1930s, the games were caught in a time warp. While the natural progression of the play activities has tended to grow more and more sophisticated over time, Depression pastimes were a throwback—children were left to

their own devices and initiatives just as they were in an earlier time. There was little or no adult supervision, little or no equipment, and the games were played out on the pavement, in the alleys, and in back lanes....

2   Street games in the 1930s held out a promise of hope for Depression children. Their parents faced consequences of a harsh economy over which they had little or no control. Many ordinary working Canadians had played by the rules of society, had been penalized with unemployment and poverty through no fault of their own, and looked to the future pessimistically. For children, rules and penalties were givens in their games, but within those conventions there was the glimmer of victory. A game would work toward a climax, usually a triumph of skill, speed, or strength, with the occasional soupçon of chance. Fate could be reversed....

3   [A game that] we played as boys in the east end of Hamilton in the '30s [was called] Relievo, known in some places as Ringalievio. Recorded as early as the 1840s, the game involved choosing sides of fairly even proportion, with ages ranging from eight or nine to young teens. The "in" team would select a jail, usually the square of sidewalk immediately under a streetlight (the game was only played at dusk or later), then the "out" team would hide as the "in" team counted.

4   Capturing one of the "out" team required more than a mere sighting. You also had to touch him in some way, either on top of the head, or on both head and butt ("bobbed and tailed") or slapped three times on the back, which was our ritual. The "ins" could hunt as a pack for the single target "outs." If the three strokes failed to touch the back exactly, it did not count as a capture, which became the point of many disputes. "Out" players would struggle mightily even to the point of throwing themselves on their backs and lashing out with their feet to prevent being tagged between the shoulder blades. Once captured, the man had to stand docilely in jail under the light for all to see his shame, unless a teammate could scream out of the darkness, plant a foot in the jail, and holler "Relievo" at the top of his lungs, which signalled the release of all prisoners. Oh, it was exciting!

5   The logical progression of such a game would dictate that the "out" team and the "in" team would change places at some point. But this never happened. There was no time. Most children, especially the younger ones, were under instruction to come in when the streetlight came on. No one seemed to mind being on the "in" team, and in retrospect it was probably because the "ins" found the game as exciting as the "outs." There was certainly no shortage of pounding feet echoing down alleys, exciting chases, shouts of discovery, and cries of surprise or help. As with all games of the era, there were no scores kept, no time limits observed, no adults involved, no equipment, no officials, and no MVPs or postseason banquets. The game was self-directed, self-initiated, and sparked by the need to entertain oneself using only one's own resources.

6   Few kids walk to school today so they could not know the pleasures of playing marbles in the gutter along the way. Up to about age ten, exclusively in the spring, most boys carried marbles to shoot on the way to and from school as well as at noontime. One player would toss his marble into the gutter and draw a line with his toe about five or six feet away. The shooter would stand behind the line, take his agate between thumb and forefinger, and throw it like a dart at the target marble. If he struck the other's marble, he could keep it, whereupon the defeated would pluck another from his bag or pocket and challenge to recoup his loss. Should the shooter miss, he would immediately shout "burnsies." "Burning" consisted of standing with the outside of your foot against your marble and then bringing the opposite foot smartly into contact, much in the manner of a guardsman coming to attention. This propelled the agate a few feet further away. A shout of "no burnsies" meant, naturally, the opposite—the marble would remain where fate had placed it—so that the second shooter would have a closer shot. There was also a rule spelling out the distance between marbles that could constitute a hit. If my marble landed close to yours, and I could touch both with the span

of my hand, that was considered a hit. Playing this way slowed the progress to school, but the amount of practice turned some boys into real sharpshooters....

7   Of course, we played many more games in those days.... There was British Bulldog, Red Rover, Duck-on-a-Rock, Prisoner's Base, Kick the Can, Jimmy Jimmy Longtail, Paper-Scissors-Stone, and Truth or Dare among the other constant and seasonally shifting games with which we Depression children amused ourselves....

8   Were the games we played important? Play is certainly a learning instrument, a way of absorbing the lesson that rules, wisely conceived and fairly administered, lie at the heart of a civil society. But American sociologist Arnold Arnold believes that children learn these lessons best through the games that they initiate, organize, and execute on their own behalf. He despairs that play today involves adults directing children in structured settings toward specific educational goals. Their learning is devoid of the social and experiential aspects that made the play of my contemporaries so valuable. We children of the Depression may have lacked for the material comforts today's young people enjoy, but in the other, less tangible way we were, I think, blessed.

Questions for Critical Thinking

1. In paragraph 2, the author compares the attitudes of adults with those of children in the Depression. What factor does the author suggest accounts for the differences between their outlooks on life?

2. Write down on a separate piece of paper the steps involved in playing Relievo. What was the object of the game for the team of "ins"? What was the object for the team of "outs"? Why do you think children playing Relievo did not bother to keep score?

3. What is the author's tone as he describes a typical game of Relievo? Is it serious? Is it playful? Do you think the author is nostalgic about his childhood? Find evidence in the article to support your view.

4. In paragraph 7, Glynn A. Leyshon lists a series of other games that were popular during the Depression. Did you play any of these games as a child yourself? How would you find out the rules to some of these games? Compare some of the games you used to play as a child with games played by your classmates.

Writing in Response

1. Write an essay about a game that you used to play as a child. What was the object of the game? What were the rules of the game? Were there winners and losers in this game?

2. While we wish that life could be nothing but fun and games, we often have to perform dull but important tasks around the house. Write an essay about your least favourite chore. Describe the process involved and explain why it is your least favourite chore.

3. Throughout the article, the author states that children played games such as Relievo. As people mature, they look to hobbies as an important form of relaxation and entertainment. Write a process essay that describes the steps involved in your favourite hobby.

Neat People vs. Sloppy People

SUZANNE BRITT JORDAN

Sometimes we learn about our vices and virtues best when we are told about them in a humorous way. This is what Suzanne Britt Jordan does in the following essay, as she invites us to look for ourselves in one of two groups: those who are organized and those who can only hope to be.

1   I've finally figured out the difference between neat people and sloppy people. The distinction is, as always, moral. Neat people are lazier and meaner than sloppy people.

2   Sloppy people, you see, are not really sloppy. Their sloppiness is merely the unfortunate consequence of their extreme moral *rectitude*. Sloppy people carry in their mind's eye a heavenly vision, a precise plan, that is so stupendous, so perfect, it can't be achieved in this world or the next.

3   Sloppy people live in Never-Never Land. Someday is their *métier*. Someday they are planning to alphabetize all their books and set up home catalogues. Someday they will go through their wardrobes and mark certain items for tentative mending and certain items for passing on to relatives of similar shape and size. Someday sloppy people will make family scrapbooks into which they will put newspaper clippings, postcards, locks of hair, and the fried corsage from their senior prom. Someday they will file everything on the surface of their desks, including the cash receipts from coffee purchases at the snack shop. Someday they will sit down and read all the back issues of *The New Yorker*.

4   For all these noble reasons and more, sloppy people never get neat. They aim too high and wide. They save everything, planning someday to file, order, and straighten out the world. But while these ambitious plans take clearer and clearer shape in their heads, the books spill from the shelves onto the floor, the clothes pile up in the hamper and closet, the family mementos accumulate in every drawer, the surface of the desk is buried under mounds of paper and the unread magazines threaten to reach the ceiling.

5   Sloppy people can't bear to part with anything. They give loving attention to every detail. When sloppy people say they're going to tackle the surface of the desk, they really mean it. Not a paper will go unturned; not a rubber band will go unboxed. Four hours or two weeks into the excavation, the desk looks exactly the same, primarily because the sloppy person is meticulously creating new piles of papers with new headings and scrupulously stopping to read all the old book catalogues before he throws them away. A neat person would just bulldoze the desk.

6   Neat people are bums and clods at heart. They have cavalier attitudes toward possessions, including family heirlooms. Everything is just another dust-catcher to them. If anything collects dust, it's got to go and that's that. Neat people will toy with the idea of throwing the children out of the house just to cut down on the clutter.

7   Neat people don't care about process. They like results. What they want to do is get the whole thing over with so they can sit down and watch the rasslin' on TV. Neat people operate on two unvarying principles: Never handle any item twice, and throw everything away.

8   The only thing messy in a neat person's house is the trash can. The minute something comes to a neat person's hand, he will look at it, try to decide if it has immediate use and, finding none, throw it in the trash.

9   Neat people are especially vicious with mail. They never go through their mail unless they are standing directly over a trash can. If the trash can is beside the mailbox, even better. All ads, catalogues, pleas for charitable contributions, church bulletins and money-saving coupons go straight into the trash can

without being opened. All letters from home, postcards from Europe, bills and paychecks are opened, immediately responded to, then dropped in the trash can. Neat people keep their receipts only for tax purposes. That's it. No sentimental salvaging of birthday cards or the last letter a dying relative ever wrote. Into the trash it goes.

10   Neat people place neatness above everything, even economics. They are incredibly wasteful. Neat people throw away several toys every time they walk through the den. I knew a neat person once who threw away a perfectly good dish drainer because it had mold on it. The drainer was too much trouble to wash. And neat people sell their furniture when they move. They will sell a La-Z-Boy recliner while you are reclining in it.

11   Neat people are no good to borrow from. Neat people buy everything in expensive little single portions. They get their flour and sugar in two-pound bags. They wouldn't consider clipping a coupon, saving a leftover, reusing plastic non-dairy whipped cream containers or rinsing off tin foil and draping it over the unmoldy dish drainer. You can never borrow a neat person's newspaper to see what's playing at the movies. Neat people have the paper all wadded up and in the trash by 7:05 A.M.

12   Neat people cut a clean swath through the organic as well as the inorganic world. People, animals, and things are all one to them. They are so insensitive. After they've finished with the pantry, the medicine cabinet, and the attic, they will throw out the red geranium (too many leaves), sell the dog (too many fleas), and send the children off to boarding school (too many scuffmarks on the hardwood floors).

Questions for Critical Thinking

1. When did you first become aware that this essay is written in a humorous vein?

2. What explanation does Suzanne Britt Jordan give for a sloppy person's behaviour? Do you agree with her?

3. In paragraph 3, what examples does the writer list as projects the sloppy person plans to do? Do these plans seem admirable?

4. Does the author use the block method or the point-by-point method to contrast sloppy people with neat people?

5. In paragraph 11, the author states: "Neat people are no good to borrow from." Discuss the examples the author gives to support her statement. What makes them humorous? Suzanne Britt Jordan's ability to provide details that the reader recognizes as true about himself or herself is what makes her writing so appreciated.

6. Do you know anyone who has done the things listed in the concluding paragraph? Which type of person do you think the author is?

Writing in Response

1. Write an essay that takes the opposite viewpoint of Suzanne Britt Jordan. Defend the neat person and criticize the sloppy person.

2. Describe two people you know who have very different approaches to being neat and organized. Explain what it is like to be with each of them.

3. How would you describe the household in which you grew up? In what ways were your parents very organized? In what areas were they disorganized? What are the problems of growing up in a household that is extreme one way or the other?

4. Write an essay in which you give advice to a young couple setting up a household. How would you advise them in being neat and organized?

5. Suzanne Britt Jordan claims that sloppy people cannot part with anything. Write an essay in which you analyze your own attitude about possessions. What are the things you have a hard time parting with? What things do you especially like to collect and save?

Paranoia Shopping

KAREN VON HAHN

The list of new products that are designed to protect us from bacteria and germs keeps getting longer. Recent outbreaks of tainted water in Walkerton, Ontario, North Battleford, Saskatchewan, and elsewhere have fuelled our fear of germs and bacteria. In the following article, *Globe and Mail* columnist Karen von Hahn explores the causes and effects of our fears of bacteria and germs.

1   It's one of the clichés of intellectual history that back in the Dark Ages, when people lived in fear of the unknown, we were saved by science. Centuries later, largely because of science, we have come to fear everything: from the water we drink and the air we breathe to the genetically modified food we eat and the antibacterial-resistant germs on the kitchen counter. This fear is alive and well at your friendly neighbourhood grocery store.

2   At my grocer, which is more like an aircraft hangar than a store, somewhere between the spray cheese and precooked bacon, there is now an extensive organic food section, with aisles of natural herbal remedies, and an expensive additive-free kosher meat and cheese department. Right next to the red peppers are bottles of Fit fruit and vegetable wash, a product I never knew I needed. All this time, I was content with mere water.

3   A short tour of the pharmacy area reveals such paranoid products as 60 SPF sunblock, immune-system-boosting homeopathic tinctures and antibacterial wipes that kill 99.9 per cent of common household germs, viruses and fungi on contact (but nonetheless moisturize with aloe vera).

4   In the household area, next to such anachronisms as hand soap, there's now the Swiffer Wet-Jet—a product geared to obsessives who want floors so clean they could eat off them, and child-friendly hand sanitizers (Caution: Flammable).

5   Along with countless new products aimed at "wellness," nearly 700 new antibacterial products hit the U.S. market from 1992 to 1998. Fear is now a multibillion-dollar industry.

6   Marketers preying on our paranoia is hardly new. Growing up in the 1960s with feminine deodorant spray commercials on television and Lo-Fat, No-Cal and Odour-Free on the shelves, my generation has been raised on anxiety advertising.

7   What is new is the scale of the fear, the consensus that, after the plastic revolution of the past century, our environment is so loaded with indestructible toxins that we are now at risk everywhere we turn, from our own fridges to the next Air Canada 747 arrival that is teeming with indomitable strains of TB, flesh-eating disease and Ebola.

8   A sure sign of how freaked out we have become is that paranoia is now chic. Fashion runways from Celine to Ralph Lauren are full of commando-styled looks

from olive drab suiting complete with ammo belts to aviator glasses and camou-flage chiffon. The status car now is the uber-paranoid gangster rapper's vehicle of choice: a stretch SUV limo with tinted windows. Fashion print campaigns convey the graininess of surveillance camera images, the models feigning a sexy, "shocked" appearance. Commes des Garçons and Prada have taken the concept one step further, packaging their signature perfumes and beauty products in chic, hyper-hygienic blister packs.

9   What makes us so afraid? After the silent, deadly arrival of AIDS in the early 1980s, our collective faith that infectious disease had been licked by science got a swift kick in the butt. Just last month, the fear quotient jumped again with the media hype over the cryptosporidium outbreak in the tap water of North Battle-ford, Sask. Less than a year after tainted drinking water killed seven people and made 2,300 others sick in Walkerton, Ont., the new outbreak has sparked a rise in the stock prices of water-filtration firms. Unsurprisingly, nearly half of Canadians now worry that their tap water is unsafe to drink, according to a recent COMPAS poll.

10   The fear of mad cow disease, which resulted in the mass destruction of the beef industry in Britain and France—even before foot-and-mouth disease turned Europe into a mass funeral pyre—has raised a whole new crop of vegetarians.

11   But what's the point? There are now more than 23,000 chemicals in commercial use in Canada, with more than 900 new substances being introduced each year. Some of the effects of these substances are neither known nor understood. Mean-while, cancers and immune-disorder illnesses such as asthma, Crohn's disease and MS are inexplicably on the rise, and more children in industrialized nations have allergies than ever before.

12   With some cause, we are running scared. But at the checkout counter, our ram-pant fear has made us irrational. Rather than drink from the tap, our handbags are heavy with $2 bottles of European mineral water. Yet many of these designer waters have actually tested poorly for purity against our own taps. Fearing contam-inants in commercially produced foods, we blow wads of dough on "organic" pre-pared foods, whose association with small-scale, old-fashioned methods of production is often dubious.

13   The Country Herb frozen organic dinner by U.S. natural-food firm Cascadian Farms, for example, lists a whopping 31 ingredients, including guar and xanthan gum, soy lecithin, carageenan and natural grill flavour. In a recent *New York Times* magazine piece by Michael Pollan on the organic-food industry, it was determined that in the making of this dinner, Cascadian trucked the broccoli to Alberta to meet up with pieces of organic chicken that had already been processed in Salem, Ore., where they were "defrosted, injected with marinade, cubed, cooked and refrozen." Cascadian Farms has recently become a subsidiary of General Mills, the continent's third-largest food conglomerate.

14   But most ironically, our obsession with sanitation may be making us sick. In the way that casual antibiotic use for common infections are credited with creating superbugs, there is a growing evidence that the scorched-earth reign of household cleansers is behind the growth of immune disorders and allergies.

15   According to the "hygiene hypothesis," our immune systems, which evolved back in the pestilential Dark Ages hut, don't develop normally without consistent childhood contact with disease and dirt.

16   "We human beings used to possess immune cells to deal with outside germs and parasites," Dr. Koichiro Fujita, a Tokyo parasitologist and author of the 1999 book *Cleanliness is a Sickness*, told *Newsweek* magazine. "But the cleanliness boom took away the job of those cells. They became unemployed. That is why they began to react to such items as pollen."

17   Sitting in our spotless kitchens, scrubbed down with antibacterial soaps, we are afraid. Afraid of everything from the water in our taps and the fumes from our

carpets to whether cellphones cause cancer. Worried about the ozone layer, toxic waste, the safety of our food and the safety of our shampoos, we are sitting ducks for the next scare tactic, the next new product targeted at our fear.

Questions for Critical Thinking

1. What is the purpose of this article? Find a sentence that best expresses the author's thesis.

2. What does the author cite as the most unexpected result of our obsession with sanitation (paragraph 14)?

3. Why does the author suggest it is pointless for people to become vegetarians out of fear of eating meat (paragraph 11)?

4. What two examples does the author use to show that some natural or organically produced items may not necessarily be as safe and chemical-free as people think?

5. Carefully reread the article and underline all the causes for our fear of germs and bacteria. What are the effects for each cause?

Writing in Response

1. The article states: "Marketers preying on our paranoia is hardly new." Do you agree that advertising and the media play a role in shaping our fears about our health? Think of some examples that support your ideas.

2. Traditional herbal remedies have become very popular alternatives to the conventional medicine practised by doctors. Research and write an essay on the reasons why somebody might choose a herbal medicine to cure an illness. Provide examples of herbal remedies and describe some of the effects they have on human physiology.

3. A common cold, while not a serious illness for most people, can certainly be unpleasant. There are many misconceptions about how people get colds. List some of these misconceptions and conduct research to find out how a cold really starts. Describe some of the symptoms of a cold you recently had. What remedies would you recommend to others suffering from a cold?

Adding Weight to an Image of Beauty

CATHERINE PIGOTT

How we feel about ourselves can often be determined by societal expectations. For Catherine Pigott, her own perceptions about her beauty changed when she moved from Canada to Africa in order to teach. When you read this essay, think about how your perceptions of beauty have been shaped.

1   The women of the household clucked disapprovingly when they saw me. It was the first time I had worn African clothes since my arrival in tiny, dusty Gambia, and evidently they were not impressed. They adjusted my head-tie and pulled my *lappa*,

the ankle-length fabric I had wrapped around myself, even tighter. "You're too thin," one of them pronounced. "It's no good." They nicknamed me "Chicken-hips."

2   I marvelled at this accolade, for I had never been called thin in my life. It was something I longed for. I would have been flattered if those ample-bosomed women hadn't looked so distressed. It was obvious I fell far short of their ideal of beauty.

3   I had dressed up for a very special occasion—the baptism of a son. The women heaped rice into tin basins the size of laundry tubs, shaping it into mounds with their hands. Five of us sat around one basin, thrusting our fingers into the scalding food. These women ate with such relish, such joy. They pressed the rice into balls in their fists, squeezing until the bright-red palm oil ran down their forearms and dripped off their elbows.

4   I tried desperately, but I could not eat enough to please them. It was hard for me to explain that I come from a culture in which it is almost unseemly for a woman to eat too heartily. It's considered unattractive. It was even harder to explain that to me thin is beautiful, and in my country we deny ourselves food in our pursuit of perfect slenderness.

5   That night, everyone danced to welcome the baby. Women swivelled their broad hips and used their hands to emphasize the roundness of their bodies. One needed to be round and wide to make the dance beautiful. There was no place for thinness here. It made people sad. I reminded them of things they wanted to forget, such as poverty, drought and starvation. You never knew when the rice was going to run out.

6   I began to believe that Africa's image of the perfect female body was far more realistic than the long-legged leanness I had been conditioned to admire. There, it is beautiful—not shameful—to carry weight on the hips and thighs, to have a round stomach and heavy, swinging breasts. Women do not battle the bulge, they celebrate it. A body is not something to be tamed and moulded.

7   The friends who had christened me Chicken-hips made it their mission to fatten me up. It wasn't long before a diet of rice and rich, oily stew twice a day began to change me. Every month, the women would take a stick and measure my backside, noting with pleasure its gradual expansion. "Oh Catherine, your buttocks are getting nice now!" they would say.

8   What was extraordinary was that I, too, believed I was becoming more beautiful. There was no sense of panic, no shame, no guilt-ridden resolves to go on the miracle grape-and-water diet. One day, I tied my *lappa* right across my hips and went to the market to buy beer for a wedding. I carried the crate of bottles home on my head, swinging my hips slowly as I walked. I felt transformed.

9   In Gambia, people don't use words such as "cheating," "naughty," or "guilty" when they talk about eating. The language of sin is not applied to food. Fat is desirable. It holds beneficial meanings of abundance, fertility and health.

10   My perception of beauty altered as my body did. The European tourists on the beach began to look strange and skeletal rather than "slim." They had no hips. They seemed devoid of shape and substance. Women I once would have envied appeared fragile and even ugly. The ideal they represented no longer made sense.

11   After a year, I came home. I preached my new way of seeing to anyone who would listen. I wanted to cling to the liberating belief that losing weight had nothing to do with self-love.

12   Family members kindly suggested that I might look and feel better if I slimmed down a little. They encouraged me to join an exercise club. I wandered around the malls in a dislocated daze. I felt uncomfortable trying on clothes that hung so elegantly on the mannequins. I began hearing old voices inside my head: "Plaid makes

you look fat ... You're too short for that style ... Vertical stripes are more slimming ... Wear black."

13   I joined the club. Just a few weeks after I had worn a *lappa* and scooped up rice with my hands, I was climbing into pink leotards and aerobics shoes. The instructor told me that I had to set fitness goals and "weigh in" after my workouts. There were mirrors on the walls and I could see women watching themselves. I sensed that even the loveliest among them felt they were somehow flawed. As the aerobics instructor barked out commands for arm lifts and leg lifts, I pictured Gambian women pounding millet and dancing in a circle with their arms raised high. I do not mean to romanticize their rock-hard lives, but we were hardly to be envied as we ran like fools between two walls to the tiresome beat of synthesized music.

14   We were a roomful of women striving to reshape ourselves into some kind of pubertal ideal. I reverted to my natural state: one of yearning to be slimmer and more fit than I was. My freedom had been temporary. I was home, where fat is feared and despised. It was time to exert control over my body and my life. I dreaded the thought of people saying, "She's let herself go."

15   If I return to Africa, I am sure the women will shake their heads in bewildered dismay. Even now, I sometimes catch my reflection in a window and their voices come back to me. "Yo! Chicken-hips!"

Questions for Critical Thinking

1. According to the author, what is the definition of beauty in Gambia? Compare this with how she defines beauty in Canada.

2. How should a person define him or herself? To what extent do people have to accept the definition other people have of them? What are some of the problems we encounter when we try to define an entire group of people?

3. Why do you think so many people are quick to judge others for having a different body size?

4. Why do you think that the author reverted to her old criticisms of herself once she returned to Canada? In our society, what would account for her perceptions?

Writing in Response

1. People define themselves in different ways such as a student, a working mother, a member of a church congregation, or an athlete. Write about the ways in which people define themselves. (You may want to survey the class, with each student writing on a slip of paper his or her own definition.) What categories have people included as central to their identities? What do you believe are the problems that arise when one tries to define oneself?

2. What do you believe are the factors that determine whether a person grows up proud or resentful of his or her appearance?

3. In the first part of the essay the author describes the culture shock she experienced when she first travelled to Africa. Write about a time that you experienced a culture shock or an identity crisis of some kind. Did you eventually solve the crisis, or is it ongoing?

4. What advice could you give to a person who feels insecure about his or her appearance?

5. Why do you think that Canadians fear being overweight? Research this topic first and then write an essay on it.

6. The writer tells us that her definition of herself changed during her travels. Write about one of your experiences when you had to change or adapt your definition of yourself.

7. Write an extended definition for one of the following terms: Canadian, freedom, power, discrimination, prejudice. Remember to give examples to illustrate your points.

Woes of a Part-Time Parent

NICK CHILES

Many North Americans have had to adapt to difficult family situations that make being a good parent an even harder task. The following observations by Nick Chiles not only show his objectivity as a reporter (he writes for the *New York Newsday*), but also reveal his personal dilemma as a parent who cannot be present at all the important moments in his child's life.

1 I often feel something is missing. A living, vital part of me that sprouted under my eyes for two years is now a part-time visitor in my life. For about ten hours during the week and every waking hour every other weekend, my son, Mazi, and I tinker with our developing relationship. We laugh a lot, and sometimes he cries a lot—often in a span of ten minutes. During those few hours I can feel my heart hum along at a peaceful clip, uncluttered, dancing atop a divine Sarah Vaughan contralto.

2 But then he is gone. He's off to brighten another corner of the world with his 3-year-old's unleavened energy and infectious glee. He's out of my sight, out of my realm of knowing, until the next time.

3 What I regret most about the dissolution of my marriage is the absence of a partner conversant in Mazi, fluent in Mazispeak. Sure, I can talk with his grandparents or my friends about his latest leap in reasoning or physical advance. But their interest doesn't compare with the undying fascination of a parent. I miss having a companion with whom I can exchange reports about Mazi's day or Mazi's behavior—or misbehavior—in day care. I miss the daily conversation about his life.

4 Being a part-time parent means being cut off from a huge portion of your child's life. It means not having any idea what he does with much of his time when you're not around. His life with Mommy is now in another place. Does that also make him another child?

5 My notions of fatherhood were formed as much by television and the mass media as my life with my own dad. For me, being a father means being the stolid protector, the rock-solid shoulder to lean on when the child gives up a homer in the last inning. It means being Mr. Brady on *The Brady Bunch*. How can you be these things when half the time you aren't there? How can you avoid missing some of the important moments when your child needs you?

6 As Mazi is carried off into the night, I can't help but wonder where he's going and if he'll be okay. If he's not, am I to blame? He seems so happy to see Mommy. Have I done something wrong? My guilt is strong. It's the gnawing ache I feel when I must go days without seeing him. The second he is in my arms, the ache disappears. The second he disappears, it resumes its burdensome place.

7 I don't foresee that ache ever leaving me. I fear it only mutates to fit new circumstances. I'm beginning to learn to live with it, however, accepting it as a

cloying companion, dressing it up as parental concern, paternal responsibility, love. Perhaps one day I'll come to respect the guilt, acknowledging its power to feed my fatherly instincts and impel me to make the extra effort on behalf of my son. But for the time being the guilt just throws me into a deep funk.

8   One day I spent time in the house Mazi shares with his mother, doing some repairs in preparation for its sale. As I stumbled upon his toys and the evidence of his life there, I was shocked by how strangely unfamiliar and distant it all seemed to me. He could now walk up and down the stairs with ease. Did he have free run of all four floors? There were new toys I had never seen him play with. Did he still use the combo climber? Had he become bored with the large number mats? What did he do here? I couldn't really get the answers to these questions, even if his mother provided daily dissertations. You have to be there.

9   Things probably won't get better as Mazi's world begins to widen and his outside interests broaden. Our visits will be even more infrequent when his mother relocates to a new job out of state. I still won't know what happens during much of his waking hours. Then when he goes to school and begins to immerse himself in the awesome possibilities beyond his home, I will merely join legions of parents the world over who agonize over the same basic question every day: I wonder what he's doing now?

Questions for Critical Thinking

1. Which one of the writer's sentences best states the thesis of the essay?

2. The essay reveals much about the author's involvement in his child's life. What examples does Nick Chiles give that tell us what kind of parent he is?

3. In paragraph 3, the author makes the point that the language, "Mazispeak," he speaks with his son is a special way of communicating with the child. What are some other examples of "a special language" that two people (or a group of people) use to communicate?

4. Make a list of the part-time parent's special problems, as the writer presents them. (Do not forget to add the problems mentioned in the last paragraph.) Are there any additional problems the author has not included?

5. The father in this essay regrets the limited time he has with his son. How important is the amount of time a parent spends with a child? Do you believe it is not the *quantity* of time but the *quality* of that time that matters when it comes to taking care of a child?

6. In paragraph 5, the writer tells us that his ideas of fatherhood "were formed as much by television and the mass media as my life with my own dad." To what extent have your own ideas and beliefs about being a parent been shaped by what you have seen on television or in the movies, by your own parents, and by personal influences outside your own immediate family?

Writing in Response

1. Write a story that focuses on the struggle of a person who is trying to be a good parent.

2. Write an essay of definition and analysis that presents the essential qualities of a good parent.

3. Write an essay that classifies the types of parents you have observed.

4. Write an essay in which you give advice to parents who are separated from their children. What can they do to maintain a close relationship?

5. Write an essay about the effects on a child of growing up in a single parent household.

6. Argue for or against the following statement: Children always need to grow up in a home that has two parents if these children are to feel safe and psychologically healthy.

Paying Attention to Snow
MARGARET VISSER

Canadians spend a great deal of their lives shovelling, sliding on, or walking through snow. In fact, some parts of the country are never really free of its grasp. Since they live with snow almost year round, the Inuit have become experts on classifying and categorizing snow. As Margaret Visser attests in the following essay, if the Inuit don't have the most to say about snow, they certainly have the most words to describe it.

1   The vocabularies of all the languages we speak differ in richness, in their insistence on making distinctions, or in their refusal to note them. English, for instance, is very poor in demonstratives: "this" for something near, and "that" for something far. The Inuit, however, and the Slave Indians of the Mackenzie River, have up to thirty different words expressing specific locations, such as "that in there," "that high up there," and "that—unseen." The theory is that words accurately pinpointing places are especially useful to people in hunting cultures.

2   Arabs use many words both denoting and describing "horse" and "camel"; Australian languages have lists of terms for different kinds of hole, and for the variations in sand. English is peculiarly interested in the forms and functions of motor vehicles: car, lorry, van, bus, streetcar, truck, jeep, taxi, tractor, and so on.

3   In Hopi, everything that flies—insects, planes, pilots, everything except birds—is denoted by one word, *masa'y-taka*. This does not mean that a Hopi speaker cannot conceive what, say, a helicopter could be. There used to be a theory that if a language has no term for something, a speaker of that language lacks the concept. The idea has been largely discredited. Languages use circumlocutions; translations, and if necessary explanations, are always possible. But it remains true that richness of vocabulary is a pointer to the importance a culture places upon certain regions of the real rather than upon others.

4   One of the most famous examples of verbal differentiation is the Eskimo panoply of designations for snow. Their number of separate terms for ice is almost as large. The Inuit need words that not only distinguish between different kinds of snow, but also words that refer to the advisability of travel, given weather conditions. The following—a selection merely—gives some idea of the sensory attentiveness and discrimination that is built into the actual components of the language. This list might help to sharpen our own awareness.

5   There is snowflake, *qannik*; recently fallen snow, *qannitaq*; snow roughened by rain and frost, *kavislaq*; melting snow, *mannguq*; a fine coat of powdered snow, *minguliq*; crystalline snow, usually found under other snow levels, that breaks down, separates, and looks like rough salt, *pulak*; the very first snowfall of autumn, *apinngaut*.

6   Snow with a hard crust that gives under one's steps is *katakartanaq* (but whenever snow or ice breaks under the weight of a person standing on it and he or she

falls from a height, a special word is called for: *katappuq*). Soft snow on the ground is *maujaq*; snow that is difficult to travel on because it is melting and therefore too soft, *aumannaq*; very hard compressed and frozen snow, *aniugaviniq*; mixed snow and water that is thawing, *aqillupiaq*; snow that has thawed and has refrozen with an iced surface, *qiasuqaq*.

7   While still in the air, snow requires a different set of terms entirely. Blowing snow is *piqtuluk*; falling wet snow, *masak*; fine snow carried by the wind, *natiruvaaq*; very light snow falling in still air, *qanniapaluk*; and so on.

8   Once snow has fallen, it becomes important to describe the landscape it has created. Snow on the ground is *aputi*, sparkling snow *pataqun*, a long large snowdrift *qimutjuk*, a small snowdrift or ripple *quyuqlak*, something with snow drifted over it so you can't see what it is *apiyaq*, a thin coat of soft snow deposited on an object *piirturiniq*, a drift of hard snow *sitilluqaaq*, and snow resting on cold water *qanisqinik*. A stick to measure the depth of snow is *havgun*. If something shows up from under snow, you say "*Hatqummiqtuq.*"

9   In Inuktitut, a snowhouse is *illu*. A place where there is the right kind of snow for cutting snowblocks is *auvvivuk*, a snowblock *saviujartuaq*, a hole made in the surface of the snow by cutting out a block *saviutsaq*, melting snow used as cement for the snowhouse *sirmiq*. If powdery snow comes into the house through a window or door, you exclaim "*Natiruvittuq.*" Frost formed inside a house, in garments, or on glasses is *ilu*, but snow on clothes or boots is *ayak*. Snow collected for melting into water is called *aniu*.

10   A snowball made by rolling snow on the ground (*atsakaaq*) is quite different from a snowball made by packing it in the hand for throwing (*milluuti*). And I shall be looking out this winter for a snowdrift that happens to be shaped by the wind so that its profile resembles a duck's head. If I find one I shall be able to designate it with Arctic precision, not to say pedantry: *qayuqhak*.

Questions for Critical Thinking

1. How many Inuit words for snow does Margaret Visser mention in the article? In your opinion, which word for snow has the most unusual definition?

2. Throughout the article, Margaret Visser organizes the different forms of snow into a particular order. Into what order does she put the different types of snow?

3. Explain the meaning of the author's statement: "... richness of vocabulary is a pointer to the importance a culture places upon certain regions of the real rather than upon others."

4. In the course of reading this article, did you come across any examples of snow that you have experienced? What were they?

5. In the essay, Margaret Visser uses two words for the people who live in the North: Eskimo and Inuit. Find the meaning of these words in a Canadian dictionary. Do these words have the same meaning? Why do you think she uses these two words?

Writing in Response

1. Classification often provides us with an opportunity to look at everyday items with a unique perspective. Write an essay that classifies common household items, such as electrical appliances or articles of clothing in your closet, in a creative and unusual way.

2. Often when we travel we are quick to pick up on basic differences between our home country and the place we are visiting. Describe a time when you travelled or moved to a new country. What were the differences and similarities between your home country and the place you were visiting?

3. Write an essay that classifies your friends or classmates. What criteria would you use to develop your system of classification?

Photo Credits

page 11 Christopher Morris

page 156 Superstock

page 206 Zefa Visual Media/Image Network

page 269 First Light

page 283 Phil Cantor/Image Network

page 301 Gary Conner/Image Network

Literary Credits

INDEX